AF695134

CLINICAL LEGAL EDUCATION IN EUROPE

Innovation and Social Justice

Edited by
Paul McKeown, Laura Bugatti,
Rachel Stalker, Aleksandra Klich,
Liubou Krasnitskaya and Jason Tucker

BRISTOL
UNIVERSITY
PRESS

First published in Great Britain in 2026 by

Bristol University Press
University of Bristol
1-9 Old Park Hill
Bristol
BS2 8BB
UK
t: +44 (0)117 374 6645
e: bup-info@bristol.ac.uk

Details of international sales and distribution partners are available at bristoluniversitypress.co.uk

© Bristol University Press 2026

DOI: 10.51952/9781529251296

British Library Cataloguing in Publication Data
A catalogue record for this book is available from the British Library

ISBN 978-1-5292-5127-2 hardcover
ISBN 978-1-5292-5128-9 ePub
ISBN 978-1-5292-5129-6 ePDF

The right of Paul McKeown, Laura Bugatti, Rachel Stalker, Aleksandra Klich, Liubou Krasnitskaya and Jason Tucker to be identified as editors of this work has been asserted by them in accordance with the Copyright, Designs and Patents Act 1988.

All rights reserved: no part of this publication may be reproduced, stored in a retrieval system, or transmitted in any form or by any means, electronic, mechanical, photocopying, recording, or otherwise without the prior permission of Bristol University Press.

Every reasonable effort has been made to obtain permission to reproduce copyrighted material. If, however, anyone knows of an oversight, please contact the publisher.

The statements and opinions contained within this publication are solely those of the editors and contributors and not of the University of Bristol or Bristol University Press. The University of Bristol and Bristol University Press disclaim responsibility for any injury to persons or property resulting from any material published in this publication.

Bristol University Press works to counter discrimination on grounds of gender, race, disability, age and sexuality.

Cover design: Liam Roberts Design
Front cover image: Stocksy/Yaroslav Danylchenko
Bristol University Press uses environmentally responsible print partners.
Printed and bound in Great Britain by CPI Group (UK) Ltd, Croydon, CR0 4YY

Bristol University Press' authorised representative in the European Union is:
Easy Access System Europe, Mustamäe tee 50, 10621 Tallinn, Estonia,
Email: gpsr.requests@easproject.com

FSC
www.fsc.org
MIX
Paper | Supporting responsible forestry
FSC® C013604

Contents

List of Figures and Tables

Figures

Tables

Notes on Contributors

Liliia Amelicheva is Professor in the Department of Civil Law and Process at Vasyl' Stus Donetsk National University and Head of the University's Legal Clinic. She holds a Doctor of Law and is a board member of the Association of Legal Clinics of Ukraine.

Ketevan Bakhtadze is Invited Lecturer and Head of Legal Clinic at Sulkhan-Saba Orbeliani University, and is currently pursuing a PhD in Law. A licensed attorney since 2014, she specializes in strategic litigation, human rights advocacy and LGBTI rights. Her research interests focus on gender-based violence, legal gender recognition, and intersectional discrimination. Her recent publications include 'The "Russian Law" in Georgia: Human Rights, Legal Certainty, and the Passions of the Georgian Lawmakers' in Review of European and Comparative Law (in *Review of European and Comparative Law,* 2025) and *Qualifying the Restriction of Survivors' Freedom of Expression as Gender-Based Violence* (2024). She works extensively with nongovernmental organizations (NGOs) and international organizations on human rights training and advocacy.

Lyndsey Bengtsson is Associate Professor at Northumbria University, where she supervises students in both the Student Law Office and the Policy Clinic. She is a qualified employment solicitor and her research focuses on equality and diversity, with a particular interest in inclusive employment practices and ageing.

Cecilia Blengino is Associate Professor of Sociology of Law and Philosophy of Law at the Department of Law of the University of Torino. She is also the Director of the Legal Clinic Prison, Rights and Social Vulnerability in the same university, and is a member of the steering committee of the Italian Law Clinic Network. Her field of research mainly deals with clinical legal education, reflective practice, justice management, human rights and access to justice. She is author of several publications in these areas and has participated as guest speaker or panellist in several international conferences and European Network for Clinical Legal Education (ENCLE) meetings, cooperating with colleagues from different countries.

Juraj Brozović is Higher Teaching Assistant in Civil Procedure at the Faculty of Law, University of Zagreb, where he earned his PhD in 2021. Engaged in clinical legal education for over a decade, he has served as mentor, trainer and co-manager in the Zagreb Law Clinic. His research interests include civil procedure, legal aid, clinical legal education, mediation and arbitration. His publications include *The Financial Challenges of Clinical Legal Education: An Example from a Zagreb Law Clinic* (2016), *Increasing Employability of Law Graduates by Introducing Live-Client Clinics: The Experience of Law Clinic Zagreb* (2023) and *Combining Simulations and Live-Client Clinics in Addressing Cross-Cutting Topics: The Best of Both Worlds* (2023). Since 2025, he has served on the ENCLE Board.

Laura Bugatti is Researcher in Comparative Private Law at the University of Brescia (Italy) and Coordinator of Legal Clinics I and II (live-client, multidisciplinary model). She holds a PhD in Comparative Law from the University of Milan. Her research interests include professional regulation (particularly legal profession), legal education, legal ethics, LGBTIQ+ inclusion and nondiscrimination, and European private law. She has published extensively on these topics and regularly presents at national and international conferences, while coordinating and participating in various research projects. She is also an ENCLE board member.

Lee-Anne Paula Doyle is a faculty member at the Migrant's Rights Clinic, International University College of Turin (IUC). She holds a Bachelor of Social Science in Political Science and Dance degree from the University of Cape Town (UCT), as well as master's degrees in international law (UCT) and comparative law in economics and finance (IUC). Her research focuses on critical legal studies, arts and law, and African economic development. She is the co-author of *The Interconnection between the Arts, Refugee and Migration Law in the Context of Clinical Legal Education as a Discourse* (2024).

Rachel Dunn is a Reader at Leeds Law School, Leeds Beckett University and specializes in animal law and legal education. She has worked in policy clinics since 2018, guiding students through various projects on animal law and domestic abuse.

Tamar Ebralidze is Associate Professor in the Law Department at the University of Georgia, Tbilisi. She holds a doctorate in Law from Tbilisi Ivane Javakhishvili State University. Her research specializes in criminal law, with particular focus on crimes against humanity, economic crime and corruption. Her publications include *Criminal Court Practice Comments: The Crime against Humanity* (2002), *Criminal Court Practice Comments: Economic Crime* (2004) and *Corruption in Georgia: Criminology Analysis and Commentary* *of Court Practice* (2011). She has taught criminal law courses at various levels since 2010, including subsumption and qualification issues in crimes against humanity and property, and regularly participates in national and international conferences on legal issues.

Andrés Gascón-Cuenca is a researcher at the Human Rights Institute, co-director of the Legal Clinic and Professor in the Department of Philosophy of Law and Politics at the University of Valencia. His research focuses on theory of recognition, human rights protection for social minorities, hate speech and clinical legal education. His recent publications include 'Ethnic Profiling as a Practice of Systemic Institutional Discrimination' (in *Derechos y Libertades*, 2025) and 'Luigi Ferrajoli's Theory of Fundamental Rights and Clinical Legal Education' in *Thinking about Clinical Legal Education: Philosophical and Theoretical Perspectives* (2022).

Jeff Giddings is Associate Dean (Experiential Education) and Professor of Law at Monash University. He has written extensively on clinical legal education and established the Griffith clinical program in 1995. In 2010, he completed his PhD on the sustainability of clinical legal education programmes. His thesis was subsequently published as a book, *Promoting Justice through Clinical Legal Education* (2013), a Mandarin-language version of which was published in 2017. He is a co-author of *Australian Clinical Legal Education* (2017) and the editor of *Global Clinical Legal Education* (2025).

Richard Grimes qualified as a solicitor in 1977 and has combined legal practice with law teaching and research throughout his career. He established pioneering clinical legal education programmes, notably at Sheffield Hallam University, and has held senior academic positions including Professor of Legal Education at the University of Derby and Director of Clinical Programmes at York Law School. He has consulted internationally on legal education reform across multiple continents. Currently a Visiting Professor at Charles University, Prague and University of Dundee, his recent publications include *Re-thinking Legal Education under the Civil and Common Law* (2018), *Public Legal Education* (2021), *How to Set up and Run a Law Clinic* (2023) and *Teaching and Learning Climate and Environmental Justice in Law Schools* (2025).

Mária Havelková is Deputy Director of the Institute of Clinical Legal Education at the Faculty of Law, Comenius University Bratislava. Her research focuses on legal aid, administrative sanctioning and gender equality in the legal profession. She manages legal clinics and teaches courses in legal aid, administrative law and lawyering skills. She is a member of the Steering Committee of the Global Alliance for Justice Education and serves on advisory bodies at the Slovak Ministry of Justice and the Slovak

Whistleblower Protection Office. As a Fulbright scholar, she completed a research stay at California Western School of Law in 2022.

Lela Aisha Jones is Assistant Professor of Dance at Bryn Mawr College. She earned degrees from the University of Florida, Florida State University and Texas Woman's University. The founder of FlyGround, her work engages Black diasporic movement traditions through performance, choreography, community-based arts practice and scholarships. She has performed internationally, including in South Africa and Nigeria, and premiered 'Plight Release and the Diasporic Body' at the African American Museum of Philadelphia (2019). Her awards and honours include a 2015 Leeway Foundation Transformation Award and a 2016 Pew Fellowship in the Arts.

Renáta Kálmán is Senior Lecturer of Constitutional Law at the University of Szeged, Hungary. Her work focuses on clinical legal education and children's rights, exploring innovative teaching methods in legal training as well as practical and theoretical aspects of child rights. Her publications include 'Legal Clinic as an Exotic Phenomenon in Hungary' (in *International Journal of Clinical Legal Education*, 2020), *The Legal Clinic Methodology: The Role of Legal Clinics in Legal Education in Hungary and the United States* (2023) and *What Is It Like to Be a Child in the V4 Countries? Lessons from the Concluding Observations of the Committee on the Rights of the Child* (2025).

Ana Kharaishvili is Director of Legal Clinics at Ivane Javakhishvili Tbilisi State University. In September 2023, she was unanimously elected Deputy Chairman of Georgia's Network of Free Legal Aid Providers, a coalition established in 2017 with support from the European Union and United Nations Development Programme (UNDP). The network unites organizations providing free legal assistance in Georgia, including government agencies, NGOs and university legal clinics. Under her leadership, TSU's Legal Clinic has become a key member of this collaborative network, which has grown from ten founding organizations to 21 members. She works closely with the Legal Aid Service to improve beneficiary referral mechanisms and coordinate free legal services across Georgia.

Diana Kirsch is Legal Advice Centre Director at LSE Law School. She practised as a criminal defence solicitor for many years and taught at BPP Law School and Hertfordshire Law School before joining LSE in 2024. She has been involved in setting up several legal clinics including BPP's Criminal Appeals Project, Hertfordshire Law Clinic and LSE Legal Advice Centre.

Tsira Komakhidze, an East European University Visiting Lecturer, invited lecturer at Batumi Shota Rustaveli State University since 2016, delivers lectures and guides practical courses in various disciplines. She served as the coordinator of the Practical Law Clinic during the 2023–2024 academic year within the framework of a USAID-funded grant project. Since 2017, she has been a member of the Association of Civil Education Lecturers and has delivered the course 'Democracy and Citizenship', under which she has supervised students' university projects. She is a certified civics education teacher and has pedagogical experience at school.

Marina Kvachadze is Head of the Bachelor's Programme and Professor at Telavi State University (TESAU), where she co-founded the Legal Clinic. For over ten years, she directed the first Legal Clinic at Tbilisi State University and has also led clinics at Georgian-American University and Caucasus International University. She co-authored the *Legal Clinic Handbook for Law Faculties* (2023) with Richard Grimes. Currently, she serves as Head of the Analytical Department at Georgia's Supreme Court. She has been a member of the Georgian Bar Association's Ethics Commission and Legal Aid Council, and has worked on international projects with UNWOMEN and UNDP.

Yuliia Matvieieva is Senior Lecturer in the Department of Legal Theory and Public Law at the National University of Kyiv-Mohyla Academy, and is Head of the Educational Laboratory Legal Clinic. She earned her PhD on the principle of legal certainty as a component of the rule of law in 2019.

Siobhan McConnell is Assistant Professor at Northumbria University. She is an experienced clinician and a qualified solicitor (nonpractising) who has taught in the Policy Clinic at Northumbria Law School since 2018. Her research focuses on legal education and the inter-relationship between law students, employability and the legal profession.

Ketevan Mchedlishvili is Guest Lecturer at the Georgian National University and a PhD candidate in Law at Tbilisi State University. She teaches the 'Practical Civic Education Course – Street Law', actively contributing to legal education through teaching and academic engagement. Her professional experience includes positions in both public administration and legal practice, with interests in civic legal education and public sector communication. She recently co-translated *The Handbook of Environmental Education* (2023), published under the US Embassy's American Author Translation Program with the support of Georgian National University.

Paul McKeown is Professor of Legal Education at Northumbria University and Principal Fellow of the Higher Education Academy. A qualified solicitor, he practises in the multi-award-winning Student Law Office and has held numerous leadership roles including Director of the Student Law

Office, Director of Education (Undergraduate) and Head of Education. He led the development of Northumbria Law School's curriculum, expanding clinical legal education throughout the law programmes. His research focuses on clinical legal education and access to justice. He is co-editor of *Social Justice and Legal Education* (2018) and was a founding board member of the ENCLE.

Sarah Morse is Assistant Professor in Law at Northumbria University and editor of the *International Journal of Clinical Legal Education*. She is a non-practising solicitor. She serves as academic tutor for the Student Law Office and leads the Street Law module. Her research interests include clinical legal education, public legal education, legal literacy and artificial intelligence within these fields. She has published on Street Law pedagogy, litigants in person and access to justice. She contributes to national and international conferences on clinical and public legal education.

Olga M Piaskowska is Professor at the Institute of Law of the SWPS University of Social Sciences and Humanities, and is also an advocate. She currently serves as the Academic Ombudsman at SWPS University. She specializes in civil proceedings and the application of the European Convention on Human Rights. She is also actively involved in research on innovative methods of legal education and is a co-author of a new law school curriculum. For more than ten years, she worked at the Supreme Court of the Republic of Poland. She also completed postgraduate pedagogical studies. Currently, she is pursuing a master's degree in psychology.

Piotr F Piesiewicz is Professor at the Institute of Law of the SWPS University of Social Sciences and Humanities, and is also an advocate. He specializes in civil, criminal and intellectual property law. His legal work has extensively covered matters related to film production, advertising and media law. Additionally, he is actively involved in research on innovative methods of legal education at SWPS University and is a co-author of a new law school curriculum. Currently, he serves as the Dean's Delegate for the Development of International Cooperation at the Faculty of Law and is the Head of the Centre for Legal Education at SWPS University.

Tamás Pongó is Senior Lecturer of Constitutional Law at the University of Szeged, Hungary. His research explores the protection of human rights in the digital environment, with a particular focus on online freedom of expression, cyberbullying and the accountability of social media platforms. He is the author of *Cyberbullying and the Students' Free Speech* (2021) and has written articles including 'The Development of Hate Speech Assessment in the Practice of the Oversight Board (in *European Review of Public Law*,

2023) and 'Anomalies in the US Cyberbullying Jurisprudence' (in *Masaryk University Journal of Law and Technology*, 2016).

Frances Ridout is Director of the Queen Mary Legal Advice Centre and is a Professor of Clinical Legal Education and Pro Bono. She is a criminal lawyer, and expert in the law around image-based sexual abuse. She is the co-author of *Street Law: Theory and Practice* (2023), the first student textbook in this field.

Liudmyla Rudenko is Board Member of the Association of Legal Clinics of Ukraine and Head of the Legal Clinic at Sumy State University. She holds a PhD in Law and is as Associate Professor at the Educational and Research Institute of Law at Sumy State University.

Nana Shonia is Professor of Finance and Dean of the Faculty of Business, Law and Social Sciences at Akaki Tsereteli State University. She holds a PhD in Economics from Tbilisi's Institute of Economic and Social Research Problems (1997). With over 30 years in academia, her research focuses on banking competition, insurance, investment management, financial education and procurement management. She serves on the Business and Administration Field Council and has been an expert with Georgia's Training and Consultation Center since 2019. Her recent projects include the USAID Rule of Law Program on legal education quality. She has published extensively on banking sector analysis, financial literacy and insurance regulation in Georgia.

Sandro Sordia holds a master's degree in law from Ivane Javakhishvili Tbilisi State University (2015) and is currently enrolled in a doctoral program at Grigol Robakidze University. He served as legal advisor at Zugdidi Municipality City Hall (2014–2017) and was twice elected to Zugdidi Municipal Council (2017–2025), chairing the Legal Affairs and Human Rights Protection Commission during his first term. He heads the Practical Law 'Street Law' Clinic at Shota Meskhia State Teaching University of Zugdidi. Since 2018, he has represented Georgian local authorities in the Conference of Regional and Local Authorities for the Eastern Partnership, and since 2021 has served as a Council of Europe expert in local self-government and local democracy.

Rachel Stalker is Clinical Legal Education Subject Leader in the School of Law at Liverpool John Moores University (LJMU). She read Jurisprudence at Christ Church, Oxford, qualifying as a solicitor in 2005. After seven years as a commercial litigator in private practice in Liverpool and Manchester, she joined LJMU in 2013, where she coordinates the School of Law's pro bono activities, establishing the award-winning Legal Advice Centre (LAC) in April 2014. Her research interests include place-based education, ethics and legal capability, and empowerment.

Ulrich Stege is Faculty Member at the International University College of Turin (IUC) and is Director of its Clinical Legal Education Programme. He has taught at the University of Pretoria (South Africa), has collaborated with the University Mohammed V Law Clinic (Morocco) and is a practicing lawyer in Italy and Germany. His research focuses on asylum and migration law and clinical legal education. His recent publications include 'The Italian Clinical Legal Education Movement – Years of Consolidation?' (in *Global Clinical Legal Education*, 2025) and *Teaching Migration and Asylum Law: Theory and Practice* (2021).

Amanda Thurston is Director of Law Clinic and Principal Lecturer at the University of Hertfordshire, and is also a solicitor. After practising family law for many years, she joined the University in 2019 and now runs their pro bono law clinic plus other experiential learning projects. She also teaches professionalism and practical skills on both undergraduate and postgraduate programmes.

Ani Topuria graduated from the Faculty of Law at Ivane Javakhishvili Tbilisi State University, earning a Master of Laws (LLM) degree with honours, and specializes in criminal justice and human rights. She gained practical experience at the National Agency for Crime Prevention, Execution of Non-custodial Sentences, and Probation, where she worked on legislative analysis and policy development. Currently, she is a lawyer at the Anti-corruption Bureau of Georgia, where she is engaged in legal research, legislative review and supporting anti-corruption initiatives. Her combined academic and professional experience has deepened her commitment to promoting the rule of law, legal reform and public sector transparency.

Judit Tóth is Associate Professor of Constitutional Law at the University of Szeged, Hungary. Her research interests include the enforcement of fundamental rights, humanitarian and migration rights in the European Union and Hungary, as well as legal ethics. She is the co-author (with K Kaponyi Erzsébet) of 'Homo Digitalis in the EU and in Hungary' (in *Journal of International and European Law*, 2024) and (with Bán-Forgács Nóra) 'Towards the Dismantling of Freedom of Information in Hungary' (in *Pravny Obzor*, 2024) and, among others, of *Migration Law in Hungary: International Encyclopaedia of Law* (2016).

Leila Tskhovrebashvili is a human rights lawyer, law lecturer and former supervisor at the Legal Clinic of Telavi State University, where she contributed to integrating Street Law methodology into clinical legal education. She was recently a Chevening Scholar (2024–2025) pursuing an LLM in International Human Rights Law and Practice at the University of York. Leila is a researcher at the York Human Rights City Network, co-authoring the report 'UK Human Rights Cities and Rights-Respecting Areas', and Research Assistant in the Beyond Compliance Consortium's project 'Building Evidence on Promoting Restraint by Armed Actors'. Previously, she provided free legal aid to women affected by violence and discrimination at Rights Georgia, combining legal practice with grassroots legal education. Her research interests include freedom of expression under authoritarian regimes, corporate accountability in surveillance technology and the application of human rights in transitional democracies.

Mariia Tsypiashchuk is Head of the Pro Bono Legal Clinic at the National University of Ostroh Academy. She serves as a Board Member of the Association of Legal Clinics of Ukraine and as Partnerships Manager of the Ukraine War Archive, which she co-founded in March 2022.

Amy Wallace is Assistant Professor of Law at New York Law School, where she directs the Street Law Program and co-directs the Advanced Legal Methods Program. She serves as Associate Editor for Book Reviews for the *Journal of Legal Education* and is Advisor for Law School Programs at Street Law, Inc. An expert in interactive teaching methodology, she works internationally assisting law schools and organizations in developing Street Law and clinical programmes. She has published and presented extensively on public legal education. In 2023, she received the NYLS Otto L. Walter Distinguished Writing Award. Since leaving private practice, she has focused on education with an emphasis on public legal education programmes in underserved communities.

Acknowledgements

We would like to express our gratitude to everyone involved in the creation of this important and timely collection. We thank the authors who worked with us, our reviewers who provided constructive feedback, and our publishers, Bristol University Press, who have supported us throughout the journey.

1

Introduction

Paul McKeown, Rachel Stalker and Laura Bugatti

Clinical legal education in Europe

Clinical legal education has emerged as a transformative force in reshaping legal education and promoting access to justice across Europe in the past 30 years, with an exponential growth during the past decade in particular. Initially rooted in common law jurisdictions, such as the US, clinical legal education has progressively expanded to other legal systems, gradually evolving into the global movement it is today.

In Europe, clinical legal education represents a relatively recent development, particularly in civil law countries. The first significant expansion occurred in Eastern European states – especially Poland – during the transitional phase following the fall of communist regimes. In this context, legal clinics played a pivotal role in fostering the rule of law and redefining the function of legal professionals in emerging democratic systems. The model later reached Western Europe, where initial resistance to clinical methodologies led to its characterization, until recently, as the 'last holdout in the worldwide acceptance of clinical legal education'.[1] Despite variations shaped by historical and legal contexts, clinical legal education in Europe has preserved its dual essence, balancing the pursuit of social justice with innovative pedagogical approaches. Understanding this evolution is particularly crucial given the unprecedented challenges facing legal education today.

The beginning of the 21st century has significantly shifted away from the world order we grew up with in the 20th century, and those of us who are lawyers and educators in Europe have had to navigate the changes. We have

[1] Richard J Wilson, 'Western Europe: Last Holdout in the Worldwide Acceptance of Clinical Legal Education' (2009) 10 German *Law Journal* 823.

experienced the revolution that digitization – and, more recently, artificial intelligence (AI) – have made across all aspects of our lives, improving it in many respects, while bringing with it new concerns about privacy, ethics, bias and wellbeing. Concerns about climate change are growing, but progress to tackle it is inconsistent. Economic fluctuations, recessions, political upheavals and of course the COVID-19 pandemic have created ever-widening wealth and health gaps across many sectors of society and waves of refugees. At the same time, university education is experiencing a range of pressures as the climates within which we operate, and our students themselves, change. Some of us have even had the misfortune to experience full-scale armed conflict. Within this maelstrom, clinical legal educators seek to adapt and sometimes transform their pedagogical practices in order to work alongside their students to address unmet needs as they arise from time to time in their own locales, to help our communities and make changes to policy and legal practice for the better wherever we can.

This edited collection presents a panoramic view of the evolution, challenges and innovative approaches that characterize the current landscape of European clinical legal education and offers a glimpse of possible future development. Through a diverse array of contributions organized around four central themes – clinical theory, clinical pedagogy in specific national contexts, social justice challenges and the global picture – this volume offers a comprehensive exploration of the multifaceted nature of clinical legal education in Europe.

Part I: Clinical theory

This part provides a theoretical underpinning for the rest of the volume.

Paul McKeown highlights how the four-level (or 4M) framework provides a lens to help us understand and analyse the factors that have influenced, or driven, the impact of clinical legal education across Europe. This chapter provides a theoretical primer for understanding the value and significance of clinical legal education for those new to the topic on the one hand, and a re-statement and re-evaluation of the foundations of our discipline for experienced clinicians on the other hand, always challenging the traditional notions of classroom-based legal education seen in continental and common law systems alike, and advocating for a more holistic and socially engaged approach.

Part II: Clinical pedagogy in the national context

Here the volume examines the practical implementation of clinical legal education across Spain and Italy (Cecilia Blengino and Andrés Gascón-Cuenca), Slovakia (Mária Havelková), Hungary (Judit Tóth, Renáta

Kálmán and Tamás Pongó), Croatia (Juraj Brozovic), the UK (Sarah Morse and Frances Ridout, and Siobhan McConnell, Lyndsey Bengtsson and Rachel Dunn) and Georgia (Ketevan Bakhtadze, Tamar Ebralidze, Richard Grimes Ana Kharaishvili, Tsira Komakhidze, Marina Kvachadze, Ketevan Mchedlishvili, Nana Shonia, Sandro Sordia, Ani Topuria, Leila Tskhovrebashvili and Amy Wallace).

Each one of the clinical and public legal education activities discussed explores how these pedagogies reflect their unique legal systems, educational traditions and sociocultural contexts. From the development of specialized clinics focused on refugee rights, public legal education and policy clinics, to the integration of clinical components within curricula that have previously been purely doctrinal, these chapters offer insights into the striking pedagogical innovations and adaptations that have taken root across Europe.

The methodologies discussed will help the reader to consider some fundamental questions which all clinical teachers must ask of themselves. How can clinical legal education guarantee the equality of the plurality of groups that make up our societies? How can we educate our students and train our future lawyers in such a way that the value of pro bono is instilled, grown and maintained alongside the professional competences they must acquire? What level of responsibility should students bear, and how much should we as their teachers shoulder? What specializations should we be introducing into our work? Should we sit inside or outside the law school curriculum? And what role can innovations such as public legal education and policy clinics have in benefiting our communities while also assuring or even increasing access to justice?

Part III: Social justice challenges

This part addresses the vital role that clinical legal education plays in advancing access to justice and promoting social equity. European clinics have the means to empower communities through public legal education initiatives, fostering legal aid consciousness, and addressing the legal needs of marginalized and vulnerable populations. They highlight the transformative potential of clinical legal education in dismantling barriers to justice, amplifying the voices of those without legal representation and seeking to effect systemic change wherever possible, as well as assistance for individuals. Some of our most pressing current issues of our time make their presence felt in this section.

The growing recognition of the importance of student mental health and wellbeing is explored in the UK context by Amanda Thurston and Diana Kirsch. Their research is aimed at supporting clinicians in developing their wellbeing and empathic lawyering frameworks for students in a way that supports student wellbeing and safeguards clients, while also allowing them to bring their authentic self – including experience of traumatic life events – into their clinical work.

The interconnection between the arts, refugee, and migration law is explored by Ulrich Stege, Lee-Anne Paula Doyle and Lela Aisha Jones, who have developed artistic approaches through clinical legal education, activism and community development initiatives. Their work not only supports refugees but also empowers them to actively participate in the discourse.

Lawyers across every area of specialty are grappling with the rapid changes being wrought by AI. Olga M. Piaskowska and Piotr F. Piesiewicz advocate for a balanced approach to the integration of AI into student legal clinics. While AI can significantly enhance clinical work and open up new possibilities for legal education, it is essential not to neglect the critical human elements, such as developing skills in critical thinking, empathy and independent decision making. Understanding both the benefits and limitations of AI, as well as fostering the appropriate competencies, will be crucial in shaping future generations of lawyers in an increasingly technologized legal profession.

This part concludes with Mariia Tsypiashchuk, Liliia Amelicheva, Yuliia Matvieieva, and Liudmyla Rudenko's exposition of clinical legal education in a time of war. The Russian invasions of Ukraine have created unprecedented conditions for legal clinicians. This chapter documents how Ukrainian clinics have dealt with: threats to the physical safety and integrity of educational facilities; the forcible displacement of people and educational institutions; the psychological conditions within which legal clinics have to operate (encompassing legal clinical supervisors, students and clients); unknown and unexplored areas of law that legal clinics have had to deal with, including international humanitarian law, international criminal and international human rights law; and, finally, sociolegal dilemmas arising from the cases clinics find themselves handling.

Part IV: The global picture

This final part situates European clinical legal education within the broader international context. Jeff Giddings explores the interconnections and cross-pollination of ideas and practices between European clinics and their global counterparts. He provides an Australian perspective on how European clinics, the *European Network for Clinical Legal Education* (ENCLE) and the *International Journal of Clinical Legal Education* (IJCLE) are connecting with colleagues across the globe, including the Global South. These connections have been strengthened by various uses of technology in order to overcome the 'tyranny of distance'.

The development of local and regional networks is important in supporting and sustaining clinical legal education. At the same time, the legacy of colonialism means that while the influence of the US on clinical legal education may be greater than that of Europe as a whole, we nonetheless see strong connections across the Francophone clinic network, the involvement of Spanish clinicians in Latin American networks, and between the UK and various former Commonwealth countries.

An important recurring theme in this collection is a critical discussion of how we can maintain student wellbeing in clinical settings, recognizing the unique emotional and psychological challenges that can arise in our pedagogy. Wherever they hail from, our authors emphasize the importance of cultivating a supportive and nurturing environment for students, ensuring that their personal growth and development – not to mention the safeguarding of client interests – are prioritized alongside their professional training and education as good citizens. Our clinic students will be helping to shape the legal profession, and society more widely, as we head into the next quarter of this century.

In light of these discussions, this volume not only maps the current landscape of clinical legal education in Europe but also looks ahead to its future evolution. The shared commitment to student wellbeing, social justice and pedagogical innovation underscores the importance of fostering resilient and reflective legal practitioners. As clinical education continues to adapt to emerging challenges, its role in shaping both the legal profession and society at large remains more crucial than ever.

PART I

Clinical Theory

2

An Analysis of Clinical Legal Education in Europe Through the Lens of the 4M Framework

Paul McKeown

Introduction

This chapter will explore the development of clinical legal education within Europe through the lens of the four-level (or 4M) framework. The 4M framework uses four levels of impact – micro (individual), meso (departmental/faculty), macro (university) and mega (national/international) – to provide a structure for understanding and analysing layers of influence within educational systems. This is the first application of the 4M framework within the field of clinical legal education. In doing so, it provides a theoretical underpinning to the later chapters in this edited collection as well as offering a helpful framework that can be used by those researching in this area in the future.

The 4M framework developed from systems theory and has been utilized within the Scholarship of Teaching and Learning (SoTL), a term initially coined by Boyer in 1990.[1] SoTL is the investigation of teaching and learning processes with the intention of improving student learning and enhancing the quality of education.[2] Shulman states that 'scholars of teaching and learning are prepared to mess with the world … they mess with their

[1] Ernest L Boyer, *Scholarship Reconsidered: Priorities of the Professoriate* (Carnegie Foundation for the Advancement of Teaching 1990).

[2] Nicola Simmons, 'The 4M Framework as Analytic Lens for SoTL's Impact: A Study of Seven Scholars' (2020) 8(1) *Teaching & Learning Inquiry* 76, https://files.eric.ed.gov/fulltext/EJ1251299.pdf

students' minds and hearts ... Scholars of teaching and learning are prepared to confront the ethical as well as the intellectual and pedagogical challenges of their work ... They insist on stopping by the scene to see what more they can do'.[3] This description is analogous with those involved in clinical legal education; people who are committed to social justice and prepared to mess with the world in order to advance that mission; people who will mess with their students' minds and hearts, often cited as the 'disorientating moment';[4] and also people confronting the ethical issues in legal practice, the law and society.[5] In light of the similarities between SoTL and clinical legal education, transposing the theoretical framework from SoTL provides a robust analysis model.

The literature on European clinical legal education suggests a mosaic of drivers, producing a complex picture of the evolution of the European clinical legal education movement. It is impossible to consider European clinical legal education, all the forms it takes, and the students and educators who are the sum of its parts as a homogeneous group due to the differing academic and practice traditions of various legal jurisdictions. Beyond the legal culture of a particular jurisdiction, other factors will influence the development of clinical legal education, such as the resources available and the needs of the community in which the clinical programme operates.

Using the lens of the 4M framework, this chapter will examine the drivers, the influences and the motivations behind the development of clinical legal education, considering the individuals involved in clinical programmes, the law departments and institutions where clinical programmes operate and the wider national, and international, factors which impact upon clinical legal education. It will also consider the impact clinical legal education has on the individuals, law departments, universities and wider society.

The analysis in this chapter adds significantly to knowledge and understanding of the drivers of clinical legal education by employing a framework that allows for data to analysed holistically, and in a different way from normal, at the micro, meso, macro and mega levels to identify common themes which emerge from a diverse range of clinical legal education programmes. Identifying these themes is intended not only to

3 Lee Shulman, 'Foreword' in Pat Hutchings (ed), *Ethics of Inquiry: Issues in the Scholarship of Teaching and Learning* (Carnegie Foundation for the Advancement of Teaching 2002) v.

4 Fran Quigley, 'Seizing the Disorienting Moment: Adult Learning Theory and the Teaching of Social Justice in Law School Clinics' (1995) 2 *Clinical Law Review* 37.

5 Anna Cody, 'Reflection and Clinical Legal Education: How Do Students Learn about Their Ethical Duty to Contribute Towards Justice' (2020) 23(1–2) *Legal Ethics* 13, https://doi.org/10.1080/1460728x.2020.1799303; Nigel Duncan, 'Ethical Practice and Clinical Legal Education' (2005) 7 *International Journal of Clinical Legal Education* 7.

aid understanding, but also to potentially help shape the development of future clinical legal education programmes in Europe and potentially beyond.

The 4M framework

The 4M framework allows for the analysis of data to be understood from a spectrum of perspectives, from the individual at the micro level through to wider society at the mega level. It is therefore a useful lens through which to analyse the development of clinical legal education. Clinical programmes are driven by committed individuals and therefore it is important to understand their motivations for establishing and running a clinical programme. However, clinical programmes run within law departments, which themselves are part of the larger university. As such, the success of any clinical programme will be dependent on the support provided by the department and institution as a whole. Beyond the university, there will also be factors influencing the work of clinical programmes and the resources available to operate those programmes. It is therefore necessary to consider these wider factors in order to understand the development of clinical legal education.

The 4M framework consists of four levels: micro, meso, macro and mega. The micro level considers the individual academic or clinician[6] as well as the students engaged in clinical legal education; the meso level considers the law department or faculty; the macro level considers the institution; and the mega level considers the wider national and international factors. The diagram in Figure 2.1 illustrates the levels within the 4M framework. Friberg suggests that the 4M framework provides an important starting point for purposeful and strategic advocacy.[7] While the 4M framework can be used to advocate for clinical legal education programmes, it can also be used to help understand the impact of factors, some of which may seem remote, on the clinical legal education programme.

This chapter will illustrate how the 4M framework can be used as a tool for the analysis of clinical legal education and will draw upon the literature to identify and explore the themes that emerge within the European clinical legal education movement, the influences and motivations for undertaking clinical legal education, the obstacles hindering development, and the impact of clinical legal education from the perspective of academics/clinicians and

6 The term 'clinician' reflects that not all individuals engaged in clinical legal education are employed on academic contracts.

7 Jennifer Friberg, 'Might the 4M Framework Support SoTL Advocacy?' (*The SoTL Advocate*, 11 July 2016), https://illinoisstateuniversitysotl.wordpress.com/2016/07/11/might-the-4m-framework-support-sotl-advocacy/

Figure 2.1: 4M framework diagram

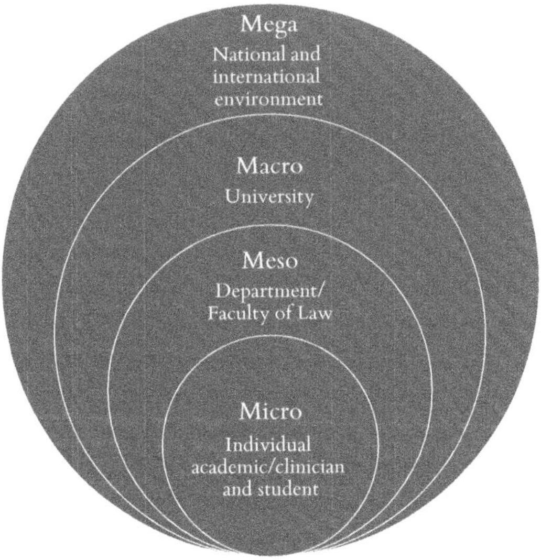

Source: Mandy Frake-Mistak, Jennifer Friberg and Melanie Hamilton, 'Reimagining the 4M Framework in Educational Development for SoTL' (2023) *Teaching & Learning Inquiry: The ISSOTL Journal* 11. doi: 10.20343/teachlearninqu.11.14 (adapted by the author).

students, law departments and faculties, universities and the national and international context in which the clinical programme occurs.

The literature on European clinical legal education has been criticized as 'a mosaic of introspective accounts with the inevitable result that authors talk past one another'.[8] The criticism is well founded, with the literature often being repetitive. Broad themes emerging from the literature are identified, but illustrative examples from across Europe will be used in applying the 4M framework analysis. This is not intended to be dismissive of the literature not cited, but merely addresses the aim of this chapter within the word limit and without repetition.

Applying the 4M framework

The development of clinical legal education in Europe can broadly be split across three regions; the UK, Central and Eastern Europe, and Western Continental Europe. The themes which emerge from the literature relate to

[8] Alberto Alemanno and Lamin Khadar, 'Introduction' in Alberto Alemanno and Lamin Khadar (eds), *Reinventing Legal Education: How Clinical Education Is Reforming the Teaching and Practice of Law in Europe* (CUP 2018) 9.

the integration of theory and practice within the curriculum, the funding and resources available to operate a clinical legal education programme, the emergence of clinical legal education networks, and the social justice mission.

Integrating theory and practice in the law school curriculum

The study of law has evolved throughout Europe in different ways. Broadly, we can categorize its development to fall into three traditions: the common law tradition of the UK; the civil law tradition of Western Europe; and the postcommunist reforms in Central and Eastern Europe.

The UK has a long history of clinical legal education, with its roots tracing back to the University of Kent in 1973, followed by a clinic at Warwick University in 1975.[9] The impetus for the law clinic at Kent came from Adrian Taylor, a faculty member who had become increasingly dissatisfied with students learning law in a vacuum.[10] Taylor therefore sought to unify theory and practice within the curriculum, including court visits, a moot court programme, a clinical programme and the law clinic.[11] At Warwick University, the clinical programme originated from the desire of four faculty members to experiment with new methods and relate teaching to the reality of law.[12] As such, the forerunners of clinical legal education in the UK emanated at the micro level, with academics seeking to innovate within the design of their respective curriculums, bringing the theory and practice of law together.

However, it was not until the 1990s when the clinical movement began to gather pace in the UK. In the mid-1990s, 13 per cent of universities were offering a live-client clinic and 38 per cent of universities offered a placement scheme as part of the curriculum.[13] Live-client and placement models of clinic were more common in the post-1992 or new universities.[14] These universities are institutions that gained university status following the elimination of the distinction between polytechnics and universities under the Further and Higher Education Act 1992. As polytechnics focused on

9 Jeff Giddings, Roger Burridge, Shelley AM Gavigan and Catherine F Klein, 'The First Wave of Modern Clinical Legal Education: The United States, Britain, Canada, and Australia' in Frank S Bloch (ed), *The Global Clinical Movement: Educating Lawyers for Social Justice* (OUP 2010).

10 Peter S Smith, 'Developments in Clinical Legal Education in England' (1979) 7 *CLEPR News* 83, 91.

11 ibid.

12 ibid 93.

13 Richard Grimes, Joel Klaff and Colleen Smith, 'Legal Skills and Clinical Legal Education: A Survey of Undergraduate Law School Practice' (1996) 30 *The Law Teacher* 44, 61–63.

14 ibid.

vocational education, it was natural that this focus would include the adoption of clinical legal education. This expansion in the 1990s of clinical legal education operated at the meso level, driven by an institutional philosophy on vocational learning.

The expansion of clinical legal education continued with the most recent survey of law school pro bono activity[15] in 2020 suggesting that at least 64 per cent of law schools in the UK are engaged in pro bono/clinical legal education activities.[16] A number of factors have contributed to the establishment of clinical legal education within what could now be regarded as the mainstream of legal education in the UK, with drivers emanating from both the legal profession and the culture of higher education, and therefore a shift to the mega-level influence.

The legal profession has sought to integrate skills and ethics training within the law school curriculum for many years.[17] Most recently, following the introduction of the Solicitors Qualifying Examination,[18] participation in a live-client clinic is recognized as being able to contribute to Qualifying Work Experience.[19] This means that time spent within a university law clinic can count towards the two-year training period that prospective solicitors must obtain, gaining experience of real-life work and having the opportunity to develop the skills and competences needed to be a solicitor.

The drive to embed legal skills within the curriculum coincided with a widening gap in access to justice. The Legal Aid, Sentencing and Punishment of Offenders Act 2012 restricted the availability of legal aid, with many areas taken out of its scope. As a consequence of the reforms to legal aid, there was a surge in the number of individuals who could not afford or access legal advice and representation, particularly in areas such as family law, where it was necessary to demonstrate you had experienced domestic violence or were involved in care proceedings to still be able to access legal aid. In addressing the demand for unmet legal need, a report from the Civil

---

15 The survey did not define the term 'pro bono activity', but it included the clinical legal education project.

16 James Sandbach and Richard Grimes, *Law School Pro Bono and Clinic Report 2020* (LawWorks 2020).

17 See ACLEC (Lord Chancellor's Advisory Committee on Legal Education and Conduct), *Annual Report for 1993–1994* (HMSO 1994); Legal Education and Training Review, *Setting Standards: The Future of Legal Services Education and Training Regulation in England and Wales* (2013), https://letr.org.United Kingdom/wp-content/uploads/LETR-Report.pdf

18 For further information, see Solicitors Regulation Authority, 'Solicitors Qualifying Examination (SQE) Route' (2025), www.sra.org.uk/become-solicitor/sqe/

19 Solicitors Regulation Authority, 'Qualifying Work Experience for Candidates' (26 January 2024), www.sra.org.United Kingdom/become-solicitor/sqe/qualifying-work-experience-candidates/

Justice Council recommended, inter alia, that law students could contribute with appropriate support and supervision.[20]

Beyond the legal profession, the general understanding in academia of the nature and purpose of a law degree has also contributed to the promotion of clinical legal education within the curriculum of the UK. There appears to be a consensus that law school is not just for learning legal theory, and that our job as educators extends to helping students to develop transferable skills for legal practice and other employment settings. For example, the Quality Assurance Agency Benchmark Statement for Law (written by law academics) explicitly cites numerous skills –including problem solving, ethical awareness and the development of professional reflective practice – that can be developed through clinical legal education and other experiential learning methodologies.[21]

Universities in the UK are also increasingly monitored and assessed in relation to external metrics that evaluate, or at least purport to evaluate, things such as the student experience and graduate outcomes. The Teaching Excellence Framework (TEF) seeks to encourage universities to improve and deliver excellence in teaching, learning and positive graduate outcomes.[22] Universities are assessed against a set of minimum requirements for quality and standards with the award of a gold, silver or bronze rating:[23] gold is awarded for a typically outstanding student experience and student outcomes; silver for a very high-quality student experience and student outcomes; and bronze for typically a high-quality student experience and student outcomes.[24] Universities may receive a lower category of 'requires improvement' if they have not provided evidence of excellence above the minimum quality requirements.[25] Universities are also included in a number of published league tables, which can be filtered by institution, subject and programme.[26] The relative weighting of ranking criteria varies by league table, but is based on a range of criteria, including research quality, entry

---

[20] Working Group on Litigants in Person, Report on Access to Justice for Litigants in Person (or self-represented litigants) (Civil Justice Council, November 2011).

[21] Quality Assurance Agency for Higher Education, *Subject Benchmark Statement: Law* (QAA 2023).

[22] Office for Students, 'About the Teaching Excellence Framework (TEF)' (Office for Students), www.officeforstudents.org.United Kingdom/for-providers/quality-and-standards/about-the-tef/

[23] ibid.

[24] ibid.

[25] ibid.

[26] For example, the Complete University Guide (www.thecompleteuniversityguide.co.uk); *The Times* UK University Rankings (www.thetimes.com/uk-university-rankings); and *The Guardian* University Guide (www.theguardian.com/education/ng-interactive/2025/sep/13/the-guardian-university-guide-2026-the-rankings).

criteria, student satisfaction, staff-student ratios, completion rates and graduate outcomes. The TEF and league tables can be very influential in attracting prospective students, but have attracted criticism and have been accused of changing the relationship between students and their institutions to a more consumer-based model.[27]

The higher education marketplace is competitive and therefore it is important for universities to demonstrate the quality of their programmes through a high ranking within the TEF exercise and league tables in order to demonstrate the quality and potential benefits of their programmes to prospective students. Clinical programmes provide students with the requisite skills they need in the graduate job market, thus boosting their employment prospects, while also enhancing their experience at university.[28] As such, the introduction of clinical legal education provides a university with the opportunity to enhance the metrics against which their TEF rating is measured and their league table position is determined.

What is interesting in the UK is that the origins of the clinical legal education movement were at the micro and macro levels; academics and institutions with a philosophy of integrating the theory with practice. However, the subsequent boom in clinical legal education coincided with mega-level influence. There are a range of factors within the legal profession and the higher education sector, as outlined earlier, which have contributed to the development of clinical legal education programmes in the UK.

In the civil law tradition of Continental Western Europe, the theoretical study of law and legal practice is kept separate. Academics are not traditionally practitioners; they are scholars who undertake research and teaching.[29] An academic's career progression is measured by their scholarship and thus there is little motivation to engage in clinical legal education, as it is often not regarded as a legitimate 'science'.[30] This cultural separation of theory and practice has meant that law schools in Western Europe have been resistant to clinical legal education, with Wilson's much-cited article referring to it as 'the last holdout in the worldwide acceptance of clinical legal education.'[31]

---

[27] Margaret Thornton, 'What Is the Law School for in a Post-pandemic World?' in Rachel Dunn, Paul Maharg and Victoria Roper (eds), *What Is Legal Education for? Re-assessing the Purpose of Early Twenty-First Century Learning and Law Schools* (Routledge 2022).

[28] Paul McKeown, 'Law Student Attitudes towards Pro Bono and Voluntary Work: The Experience at Northumbria University' (2015) 22 *International Journal of Clinical Legal Education* 1; Paul McKeown, 'Pro Bono: What's in It for Law Students? The Students' Perspective' (2017) 24 *International Journal of Clinical Legal Education* 43.

[29] Richard J Wilson, 'Western Europe: Last Holdout in the Worldwide Acceptance of Clinical Legal Education' (2009) 10 *German Law Journal* 823, 837–838.

[30] ibid 838.

[31] ibid.

However, Western Europe is starting to see a shift with clinical legal education entering many law schools throughout the region.

Historically, those engaged in clinical legal education have either not engaged in scholarship or, where they have engaged in scholarship, the account has often been a narrative of their clinical experience lacking the scientific rigour associated with theoretical research. The literature has not built upon previous scholarship, which has hindered the development of clinical legal education as a recognized 'science' within the academy.

The Bologna Process has often been cited as a catalyst for the growth of clinical legal education in Western Europe throughout the 2000s and 2010s, suggesting the influence for clinical legal education started at the mega level. The framework sought to harmonize the structures of higher education with the goals of enhancing international competitiveness and promoting mobility and employability.[32] As outlined earlier, the Western European tradition separated the theory and practice of law, and consequently, students were ill-prepared to enter the legal profession, thus impacting their mobility and employability. The Bologna Process opened up 'a space to introduce practical approaches into traditional legal education'.[33] Hovhannisian identified clinical legal education as a methodology which could be adopted within the curriculum to teach fundamental lawyering skills.[34] While the Bologna Process may have provided impetus to the spread of clinical legal education in Europe, there is little evidence that its call for a more practice-focused system of legal education has been fully realized. More than 25 years after the Bologna Declaration was signed, clinical programmes still do not enjoy full acknowledgement or acceptance in Europe.[35]

The separation of the academic study of law and the practice of law concerned some scholars, with Aurey, a French academic, noting that he was 'reproducing an extremely theoretical model of education … without having spared a thought about its purpose, its qualities, or its defects'.[36] Kjos and Nollkaemper observe that the Dutch legal education system, with its emphasis on theory, does not adequately prepare students for legal practice.[37]

---

[32] Lusine Hovhannisian, *Clinical Legal Education and the Bologna Process* (PILI Papers No 2, December 2006) 4.

[33] ibid 6.

[34] ibid 10–16.

[35] Ulrich Stege and Jeff Giddings, 'Clinical Legal Education in Western Europe' in Jeff Giddings (ed), *Global Clinical Legal Education* (Routledge 2025).

[36] Xavier Aurey, 'Law Clinics in France through the Prism of Fundamental Rights Law Cliic, University of Caen Normandy' in Alberto Alemanno and Lamin Khadar (eds), *Reinventing Legal Education: How Clinical Education Is Reforming the Teaching and Practice of Law in Europe* (CUP 2018).

[37] Hege Elisabeth Kjos and Andre Nollkaemper, 'The Amsterdam International Law Clinic' in Alemanno and Khadar (n 36).

The demand for more skills-based teaching emanated not only from a few academics, but also students themselves.[38] Clinical legal education provides an interesting and innovative teaching methodology which bridges the theory/practice gap, allowing students to be engaged in making law school 'more appealing and meaningful.'[39]

A further obstacle in the development of clinical legal education related to jurisdictional restrictions, and therefore a mega-level barrier, on who can practise law. For example, legal clinics were not permitted in Germany under the German Law (Rechtsberatungsgesetz) requiring permission from the state to provide legal advice, with permission only being granted to members of the Bar.[40] Even where clinical legal education is established, the work carried out by the legal clinic may be dictated by what is permissible within the regulatory framework. For example, in England and Wales, the Legal Services Act 2007 restricts the ability of individuals to carry out reserved legal activities,[41] unless they are authorized to do so. As such, a law clinic may be limited to the provision of advice as it is not permitted to 'conduct litigation'.

In Western Europe, the culture of legal education has been driven by law departments and faculties at the meso level, as well as universities at the macro level. This culture of separation has hindered the development of clinical legal education with resistance to the notion of integration. However, recent developments in the adoption of clinical legal education have been driven at the mega level, such as the Bologna Process, and the micro level, with an increasing call from both academics and students for a more integrated, practice-based curriculum.

Countries in Central and Eastern Europe, in contrast to Western Europe, typically have more established clinical legal education programmes, albeit with varying degrees of sustainability. Following the fall of communism in the 1990s, countries in Central and Eastern Europe set about reforming their legal systems, including the legal profession.[42] Despite the need for reform

---

[38] Cecile Kashetu Kyenge, 'Foreword' in Clelia Bartoli, *Legal Clinics in Europe: For a Commitment of Higher Education in Social Justice* (special issue, Diritto e Questioni Pubbliche, May 2016) 10.

[39] ibid.

[40] Jan-Gero Alexander Hannemann and Georg Dietlein, 'The Development of Refugee Law Clinics in Germany in View of the Refugee Crisis in Europe' (2018) 25 *International Journal of Clinical Legal Education* 160.

[41] Section 12 of the Legal Services Act 2007 defines reserved legal activities as exercising rights of audience, conducting litigation, undertaking reserved instrument activities, undertaking probate activities, undertaking notarial activities and administering oaths.

[42] Mariana Berbec-Rostas, Arkady Gutnikov and Barbara Namyslowska-Gabrysiak, 'Clinical Legal Education in Central and Eastern Europe: Selected Case Studies' in Frank S Bloch (ed) *The Global Clinical Movement: Educating Lawyers for Social Justice* (OUP 2010).

and the demand for educated lawyers, legal education did not adequately address the postcommunist reforms with a tradition of teaching law and theory, with limited focus on the knowledge, skills and values of the legal profession.[43] The response to these issues came at the mega level, with various international organizations such as the American Bar Association's Central European and Eurasian Law Initiative, the Ford Foundation, the Open Society Institute and the Soros Foundation Network-sponsored initiatives, developing clinical legal education programmes aimed at enhancing the quality of legal education through the introduction of skills-based teaching.[44] The scale of this funding saw the establishment of 27 university-based law clinics across more than 20 countries.[45] However, the funding for the law clinics was precarious, as will be explored later on in the chapter.

Poland has one of the most established and sustained network of European clinical legal education programmes which continues to thrive. The first legal clinic was established in Law Faculty of the Jagiellonian University in Kraków in 1997.[46] Following the rapid expansion of clinical legal education in Poland, the Polish Legal Clinics Foundation was established in 2001 with financial, logistical and professional assistance from the Stefan Batory Foundation.[47] The Polish Legal Clinics Foundation provided financial support to legal clinics in Poland as well as providing educational activities to strengthen the clinical movement. All state-owned law faculties now operate a clinical legal education programme in Poland.[48]

We see that throughout Europe, there has been a cultural shift to embed more skills-based teaching within the curriculum. The impetus for this shift varies, driven by professional bodies, political declarations or regime change (mega level). However, it is also evident that the shift has also been influenced by individuals with an interest in legal education, either as an academic or as a student (micro level). As a teacher, academics are seeking to enhance the learning experience through innovative teaching practices. As students, it is important to learn the skills and competencies required in professional life while also having a positive learning experience. As such, universities (macro level) and law schools (meso level) must adapt their curriculum due to the need to produce highly skilled graduates to enter the legal profession, as well

43 ibid.

44 ibid.

45 ibid.

46 Filip Czernicki, 'The History and Distinctiveness of the Polish Legal Clinics Program' in Giddings (n 35).

47 ibid.

48 ibid.

Figure 2.2: Integrating theory and practice in the curriculum

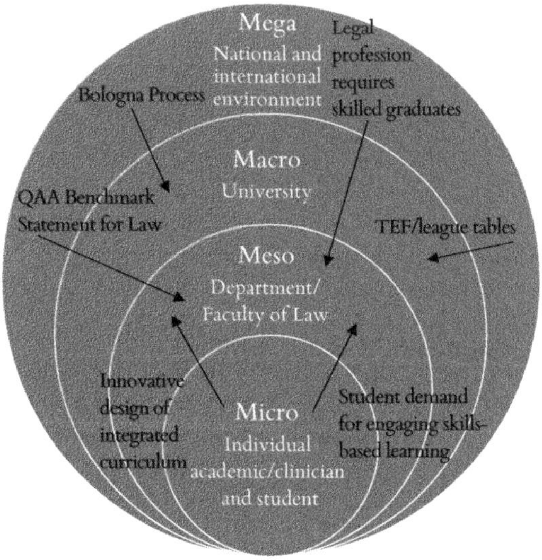

Source: Mandy Frake-Mistak, Jennifer Friberg and Melanie Hamilton, 'Reimagining the 4M Framework in Educational Development for SoTL' (2023) *Teaching & Learning Inquiry: The ISSOTL Journal* 11. doi: 10.20343/teachlearninqu.11.14 (adapted by the author).

as the need to attract students in a competitive higher education landscape. The interaction between the levels is given in Figure 2.2.

Funding and resources

While law schools are usually cost-efficient departments within the university compared to subjects requiring specialist equipment and facilities, clinical legal education programmes can require significant investment due to high staff/student ratios, physical space in which to operate the law clinic and the resources required to deliver legal casework.[49] However, it should be noted that the cost of providing a clinical legal education programme will be dependent upon the type of programme. For example, live-client programmes are typically more resource-intensive than placement models or public legal education programmes which do not require the same level of resources. In considering whether the clinical programme is embedded

[49] Lydia Bleasdale, Beverley Rizzotto, Rachel Stalker, Lucy Yeatman, Hugh McFaul, Francine Ryan, Nick Johnson and Linden Thomas, 'Law Clinics: What, Why and How?' in Linden Thomas and Nick Johnson (eds) *The Clinical Legal Education Handbook* (University of London Press 2020).

within the institution or operating separately, it is important to consider the resource implications. The existence of a clinical programme may be dependent upon institutional support to ensure appropriate resources are available.

The financial health of higher education presents a bleak picture. At the macro level, many universities are facing a financial crisis. For example, in the UK, 72 per cent of universities are facing a budget deficit in 2025–2026.[50] Universities have cited years of frozen tuition fees and government action to reduce the number of international students as reasons for their financial difficulties, suggesting that the macro-level crisis is a consequence of mega-level decision making.[51] The situation is similar across Europe, with costs, particularly for staff and operations, rising faster than growth in income sources, again highlighting the impact of mega-level factors at a macro level.[52] The financial health of universities is significant in relation to clinical legal education, with a reported 60 per cent of law clinic budgets drawn from university funds,[53] as the higher running costs expose them as an area where efficiency savings could potentially be made. Thus, in relation to funding, there is a trickle-down effect from the mega to the micro level where political decisions on the funding of higher education and immigration, as well as the overall health of the economy, potentially have an adverse impact on the development of clinical programmes.

As mentioned earlier, in Central and Eastern Europe, the initial boom in clinical legal education was significantly influenced at the mega level through funding by international sponsors. However, reliance on external funding can be precarious, with many clinical programmes failing to survive once outside funding was withdrawn.[54] The exception is Poland, where through support and coordination from the Polish Legal Clinics Foundation, clinics

---

50 Office for Students, 'Financial Sustainability of Higher Education Providers in England: November 2024 Update', www.officeforstudents.org.United Kingdom/media/nn2fnrkx/financial-sustainability-november-2024.pdf

51 Universities UK, 'Universities Grip Financial Crisis: But at What Cost to the Nation?' (27 May 2025), www.universitiesuk.ac.uk/what-we-do/creating-voice-our-members/media-releases/universities-grip-financial-crisis-what

52 Enora Bennetot Pruvot, Thomas Estermann and Nino Popkhadze, 'Financially Sustainable Universities: State of Play and Strategies for Future Resilience' (April 2025), www.eua.eu/publications/briefings/financially-sustainable-universities-state-of-play-and-strategies-for-future-resilience.html

53 Bartoli (n 38) 49.

54 Philip M Genty, 'Reflections on US Involvement in the Promotion of Clinical Legal Education in Europe' in Alberto Alemanno and Lamin Khadar (eds), *Reinventing Legal Education: How Clinical Education Is Reforming the Teaching and Practice of Law in Europe* (CUP 2018) 9.

operate in a 'very modest and efficient way' with law schools, at the meso level, financing the clinic to ensure they are not reliant on external funders.[55]

However, despite the challenges which clinical legal education can present to law school and university budgets, the question arises as to whether they present value for money. With increased marketization, and therefore competition, within the higher education sector, universities are seeking to attract students.[56] Universities in the UK will be mindful of their TEF ranking as well as their positioning within league tables as an indicator of quality. As discussed previously, the metrics which impact upon these rankings include graduate outcomes and student experience. Bartoli highlights that European universities are also experiencing a more competitive environment with private for-profit institutions entering the market, which was once exclusively the purview of public institutions.[57] While clinical legal education programmes may be more expensive to run, the experience also benefits students by enhancing their employability through the development of their legal skills, as well as providing a positive student experience.[58] As such, universities and law schools may appreciate the cost/benefit in funding a clinical legal education programme as an attractive proposition for students.

The funding and resources available for clinical programmes is dependent upon the law school (meso level) and the university (macro level). The financial health of universities is often a wider issue (mega level), including political decisions on student fees, immigration and even foreign aid, as illustrated in the examples given earlier. As seen in Central and Eastern Europe, where external investment is withdrawn and not replaced, it can have a devastating impact on the clinical programme. However, the focus should shift to the micro level, namely prospective students. If the university and law school offer an attractive programme which benefits the students, the extra investment in a fully resourced clinical programme is likely to benefit the institution as a whole through enhanced student recruitment. The trickle-down effect is illustrated in Figure 2.3, which shows the significance of the mega level in relation to funding and resources.

National and international networks

As clinical legal education has established itself in Europe, a number of national and international networks have been established to facilitate

55 Interview with Filip Czernicki in Bartoli (n 38).

56 See Thornton (n 27).

57 Bartoli (n 38).

58 McKeown, 'Law Student Attitudes towards Pro Bono and Voluntary Work' (n 28); McKeown, 'Pro Bono' (n 28).

Figure 2.3: Funding and resources

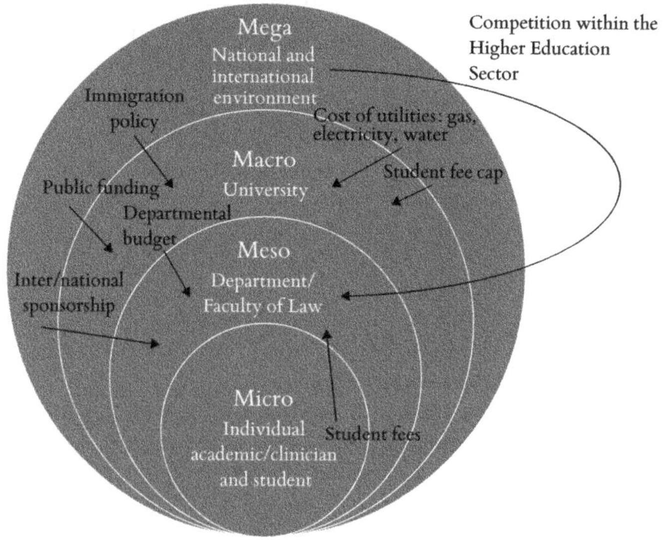

Source: Mandy Frake-Mistak, Jennifer Friberg and Melanie Hamilton, 'Reimagining the 4M Framework in Educational Development for SoTL' (2023) *Teaching & Learning Inquiry: The ISSOTL Journal* 11. doi: 10.20343/teachlearninqu.11.14 (adapted by the author).

and support the development of clinical legal education within the region. By their very nature, these networks are operating within the mega level.

The Clinical Legal Education Organisation (CLEO) is the longest-established network in Europe, initially conceived in 1994[59] as 'an umbrella group for the promotion and furtherance of clinical ideas' in the UK.[60] For many years, the activities of CLEO were somewhat sporadic, although it did produce a set of Model Standards for Clinical Legal Education (however, they are no longer publicly available).[61] In 2013, CLEO decided to formally constitute the organization to better represent its members and enable it to contribute to national debates on legal service and education.[62] CLEO

59 Richard Grimes, Rachel Dunn, Rebecca Samaras and Larry Donnelly, 'Legal Clinics in the UK and Ireland: Past, Present and Future' in Giddings (n 35).

60 Richard Grimes, 'Reflections on Clinical Legal Education' (1995) 29 *The Law Teacher* 169, 170.

61 References to the Model Standards can be found in Richard Lewis, *Clinical Legal Education Revisited* (Cardiff Law School 2000), https://orca.cardiff.ac.uk/id/eprint/27655/1/cliniced.pdf

62 Clinical Legal Education Organisation, 'About CLEO', www.cleo-uk.org/about-cleo/

is now a Charitable Incorporated Organisation, a form of legal structure designed specifically for charities, with over 250 members from over 80 institutions.[63] CLEO, through its members, has produced a range of materials seeking to facilitate clinical legal education in the UK, such as *The Clinical Legal Education Handbook*.[64] This is a free, open access resource which, in the words of Thomas (its editor), 'informs and enables your clinical practice, so that you may focus your energies where they are most valuable: delivering high quality legal education and promoting access to justice'.[65] CLEO also assists members in navigating the professional and regulatory framework associated with running a legal clinic, producing guidance on issues such as Qualifying Work Experience.[66]

As mentioned earlier, clinical legal education in Poland can be traced back to 1997,[67] leading to the establishment of the Polish Legal Clinics Foundation (FUPP)[68] with support from the Stefan Batory Foundation.[69] FUPP has produced a set of Standards for Clinical Legal Education setting out the operation of a law clinic.[70]

Significantly, across the border from Poland, Ukraine has also developed a strong clinical network, the National Association of Ukrainian Law Clinics (ALCU), which boasts a membership encompassing more than 50 legal clinics.[71] In 2014, the ALCU adopted standards for the operation of legal clinics of Ukraine which foster the development and operation of legal clinics governing the administration of the law clinic; integration within the law school curriculum; supervision of pro bono legal services; and applying a Street Law[72] approach to public legal education activities.[73] In addition, the ALCU has developed a Quality Performance Assessment Tool for Legal Clinics to monitor compliance with the standards, which seeks to

---

63 ibid.

64 Linden Thomas and Nick Johnson (eds), *The Clinical Legal Education Handbook* (University of London Press 2020), https://read.uolpress.co.uk/projects/the-clinical-legal-education-handbook

65 Linden Thomas, 'Introduction' in ibid.

66 Lucy Blackburn, 'Qualifying Work Experience Guidance for University Law Clinics' (CLEO, October 2021), www.cleo-uk.org/wp-content/uploads/2022/01/QWE-Guidance-complete427.pdf

67 Filip Czernicki, 'The History and Distinctiveness of the Polish Legal Clinics Program' in Giddings (n 35).

68 Fundacja Uniwersyteckich Poradni Prawnych.

69 Czernicki (n 67).

70 FUPP, 'Standards' (no date), www.fupp.org.pl/en/legal-clinics/standards

71 Mariia Tsypiashchuk, 'Clinics in Ukraine' in Giddings (n 35).

72 See Street Law, 'Street Law' (no date), https://streetlaw.org/

73 Tsypiashchuk (n 71).

support clinical staff and their university in the administration activities.[74] Since the Russian invasion of Ukraine, the ALCU has been instrumental in coordinating clinical activities and maintaining ties with international partners in the UK, the European Union and the US through a 'buddy scheme' enabling Ukrainian clinicians to benefit from international experience and support.[75] Other national clinical networks have emerged in Spain,[76] Italy[77] and Germany.[78]

Beyond the national networks, a number of international networks have emerged, including the Global Alliance for Justice Education (GAJE)[79] and the Network of Francophone Legal Clinics.[80] These networks promote the international exchange of information and experience, and therefore facilitate the development of legal clinics by bringing together experienced clinicians with those seeking to develop clinical programmes throughout the globe. In 2013, the European Network for Clinical Legal Education (ENCLE) was established as a not-for-profit organization. ENCLE seeks to bring together people from different countries as well as legal, educational and organizational settings to collaborate and exchange ideas in order to promote justice and enhance the quality of teaching through clinical legal education in Europe.[81] It engages in a range of activities to achieve its objectives, including, inter alia, the organization of conferences and workshops, facilitating transnational collaboration and fostering research on clinical legal education.[82] It also provides a critical role in coordinating dialogue with local, regional and international institutions supporting the sustainability of clinical legal education in Europe.[83] As seen in the UK, Poland and Ukraine, standards have been influential the development of the clinical legal education movement. ENCLE has drafted European Standards

---

74 ibid.

75 ibid.

76 See Clínicas Jurídicas, 'Quiénes somos' (no date), https://clinicas-juridicas.blogspot.com/p/quienes-somos.html

77 See 'Coordinamento Nazionale Cliniche Legagali Italiane' (*Facebook*, no date), www.facebook.com/groups/197429648218860/about

78 See Refugee Law Clinics Germany, 'Home' (no date), https://home.refugeelawclinics.de. See also Refugee Law Clinics Deutschland eV, 'Start' (no date), https://dachverband-srb.de/start

79 See Global Alliance for Justice Education, 'Home' (no date), www.gaje.org/

80 See Réseau des Cliniques Juridiques Francophones, 'Accueil' (no date), https://cliniques-juridiques.org/

81 European Network for Clinical Legal Education, 'What Is ENCLE' (no date), https://encle.org/about-us/what-is-encle

82 ibid.

83 Bartoli (n 38).

for Clinical Legal Education which begin to provide a sense of a common understanding as to clinical legal education in the European context.[84] As a consequence of these activities, Stege and Giddings state that ENCLE has 'played a pivotal role in the development of [clinical legal education] across Europe'.[85]

National and international networks, operating at the mega level, have been crucial in supporting the development of clinical legal education across Europe. Interacting with individual clinicians, at the micro level, but also providing a unified voice to influence and advocate on behalf of clinical legal education to law departments (meso), universities (macro) and other national/international institutions (mega), demonstrates how these networks interact at all levels to promote clinical methodology. However, it is important to recognize the influence of individual clinicians, at the micro level, on the networks, at the mega level. The networks have been shaped through individual contributions, through conferences, workshops and scholarship. The members of CLEO, FUPP, ALCU and ENCLE have come to a shared understanding of clinical legal education, as espoused in the standards. As such, the pivotal role of these networks is a combination of the micro/mega levels interacting with one another. Figure 2.4 illustrates how networks interact cyclically with their members at the micro level, providing support and guidance while also providing members with the opportunity to inform policy developments. Furthermore, networks exercise influence by providing a unified voice across the mega, macro and meso levels, advocating for clinical legal education at international and national levels and encouraging universities and law departments to support clinical programmes.

Social justice mission

Clinical legal education and social justice are inextricably intertwined,[86] and date back to the birth of the modern clinical legal education movement in the US during the social ferment of the 1960s.[87] This is an overarching mega-level factor within the clinical legal education movement. As discussed earlier, the US was influential in developing the global clinical legal education movement, particularly in postcommunist Central and Eastern Europe. As a consequence, the social justice mission of the US clinical movement was

[84] European Network for Clinical Legal Education, 'Quality Standards for Legal Clinics' (adopted 15 July 2022), www.encle.org/upload/lg/news/ENCLE-Standards-Final-Version-July-2022.pdf

[85] Stege and Giddings (n 35).

[86] Paul McKeown and Elaine Hall, 'If We Could Instil Social Justice Values through Clinical Legal Education, Should We?' (2018) 5(1) *Journal of International and Comparative Law* 143.

[87] Giddings et al (n 9).

Figure 2.4: National and international networks

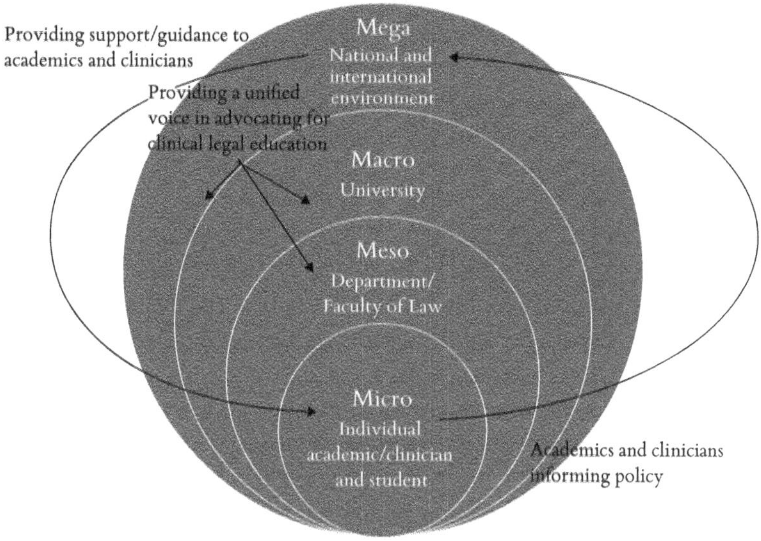

Source: Mandy Frake-Mistak, Jennifer Friberg and Melanie Hamilton, 'Reimagining the 4M Framework in Educational Development for SoTL' (2023) *Teaching & Learning Inquiry: The ISSOTL Journal* 11. doi: 10.20343/teachlearninqu.11.14 (adapted by the author).

adopted in the Central and Eastern European clinics. This can be contrasted with the development of clinical legal education in the UK, where the adoption of clinical legal education to provide legal assistance to the poor was not a significant factor in its development.[88] The social justice mission continues to be pervasive within clinical legal education, with each of the national and international networks citing the promotion of social justice as an organizational objective.[89] Again, given the influence of these networks in the development of clinical legal education throughout Europe, the social justice mission continues to imbue clinical legal education. As a consequence, many individuals establishing a clinical programme will abide by the cultural ethos of the clinical legal education movement.

While the clinical movement in Central and Eastern Europe had significant involvement from the US, the US influenced the development of other clinical programmes throughout Europe. Inspired by the movement in the

[88] McKeown and Hall (n 86).

[89] See European Network for Clinical Legal Education (n 81); Clinical Legal Education Organisation(n 62); FUPP, 'History and Mission' (2024), www.fupp.org.pl/en/foundation/history-mission; Association of Legal Clinics of Ukraine, 'Home' (2025), https://legalclinics.in.ua/

US, some individuals involved in clinical legal education emerged from the 'radical student movements of the late 1960s and early 1970s and a climate of strong social commitment'.[90] Norwegian scholars Thomas Mathiesen, Kristian 'Kikki' Andenæs and Jon T. Johnsen sought to combine scientific knowledge with a legal aid infrastructure to address unmet legal need for disadvantage groups.[91] Juss-Buss was established in 1971 at the University of Oslo, Norway, as a mobile outreach to provide legal information to those in need as accessibly as possible.[92]

The clinical movement has not solely been led by academics, and in some parts of Europe, students have taken the lead. In Germany, a relative newcomer to clinical legal education, it has primarily been a student-led initiative, with 35 of the 41 refugee law clinics being established by students rather than academics.[93] Between 2014 and 2016, Germany, and Europe as a whole, experienced a significant influx of refugees and asylum seekers rooted in war, expulsion, political and religious persecution and social poverty.[94] During this period, there were over one million asylum applications in Germany.[95] As a consequence of the refugee crisis, and recognizing the need for appropriate legal advice, students established numerous legal clinics across Germany to provide assistance.[96] The impact of migration has had a profound impact on the development of clinical legal education within continental Europe with the establishment of legal clinics in Italy,[97] Spain[98] and the Netherlands.[99]

---

90 Ole Hammerslev, Annette Olesen and Olaf Halvorsen Rønning, 'Juss-Buss [Law Bus]: A Student-Run Legal Aid Clinic' in Olaf Halvorsen Rønning and Ole Hammerslev (eds), *Outsourcing Legal Aid in the Nordic Welfare States* (Springer 2018) 147, https://library.oapen.org/bitstream/handle/20.500.12657/27884/1/1002118.pdf#page=155

91 ibid 148.

92 ibid.

93 Bian Sukrow, 'Clinical Legal Education in Germany: A Brand New Old Story' in Giddings (n 35).

94 Hannemann and Dietlein (n 40) 167.

95 ibid 168.

96 Sukrow (n 93).

97 See Ulrich Stege, 'How Clinical Legal Education Is Crossing Borders' in Cecilia Blengino and Andrés Gascón-Cuenca (eds), *Epistemic Communities at the Boundaries of Law: Clinics as a Paradigm in the Revolution of Legal Education in European Mediterranean Context* (Ledizioni 2019); Jovana Bogicevic, 'Representing the Other: A Case for Interdisciplinary Clinical Legal Education: Example of the Human Rights and Migration Law Clinic' (2019) 26 *International Journal of Clinical Legal Education* 93.

98 For example, Universitat de València, 'Migration Clinic' (no date), www.uv.es/uvweb/law/en/clinic/clinics/migration-clinic-1286076597557.html

99 For example, Vrije Universiteit Amsterdam, 'Migration Law Clinic' (Amsterdam Centre for Migration and Refugee Law, no date), https://vu.nl/en/about-vu/research-institutes/amsterdam-centre-for-migration-and-refugee-law/more-about/migration-law-clinic-acmrl

These examples illustrate how mega-level factors relating to social justice directly influence and inspire individual academics/clinicians and students at the micro level into action. Concerns around social and economic issues have influenced clinical development in Norway and Germany. No doubt, many more examples could be provided. However, questions could be raised as to whether these social and economic factors are the responsibility of universities, institutions dedicated to teaching and research rather than the provision of legal assistance. While many universities are publicly funded institutions, and therefore it could be argued that they have a public duty to serve the communities in which they are situated, there is also a political driver in the form of the Sustainable Development Goals (SDGs).

The SDGs are a set of 17 global goals adopted by all United Nations Member States in 2015 as part of the 2030 Agenda for Sustainable Development that provide 'a shared blueprint for peace and prosperity for people and the planet, now and in the future'.[100] While Member States are primarily responsible for sustainable development, effective implementation requires cooperation across all sections of society, including universities. Universities play a significant role, providing a 'unique contribution' to sustainable development through 'cutting-edge research, high quality education, and ground-breaking innovation'.[101] As a methodology, clinical legal education is well positioned to address the SDGs. Although the specific goals will be dependent on the type of programme, clinical legal education can contribute towards the achievement of goals such as: SDG 1 (No Poverty); SDG 4 (Quality Education); SDG 5 (Gender Equality), SDG 10 (Reduced Inequalities); SDG 13 (Climate Action); SDG 16 (Peace, Justice, and Strong Institutions); and SDG 17 (Partnerships for the Goals).[102] Through the provision of legal information, advice and representation, clinical legal education can address issues such as poverty, gender inequality and environmental concerns. Clinical legal education has a dual mission; education and social justice.[103] Inherently, clinical legal education is about the provision of quality education, both in relation to the students participating in a clinical programme and members of the public

[100] United Nations, *Sustainable Development Goals* (2025), https://sdgs.un.org/goals

[101] European University Association, *Universities and Sustainable Development: Towards the Global Goals* (2018), www.eua.eu/downloads/publications/universities-and-sustainable-development-towards-the-global-goals.pdf

[102] Paul McKeown, Ulrich Stege and Maxim Tomoszek, 'Clinical Legal Education in Europe and Implementation of Sustainable Development Goals' in Walter Leal Filho et al (eds), *SDGs in the European Region: Implementing the UN Sustainable Development Goals – Regional Perspectives* (Springer 2023), https://doi.org/10.1007/978-3-031-17461-2_20

[103] This dual mission can be seen in the objectives the national and international clinical networks. See n 89.

benefiting from the programme. Similarly, clinical legal education, at its core, promotes peaceful and inclusive societies, provides access to justice, and fosters accountable and inclusive institutions. Finally, clinical programmes often work in partnership with other institutions and organizations to strengthen sustainable development. Engagement in clinical legal education is therefore significant in terms of law departments, and consequently universities, contributing to sustainable development.

Clinical legal education is a product of its environment with the world around it (mega level), inspiring individuals, both academics and students (micro level), and moulding the clinical programme to address the needs of society. There is also a political influence (mega level), albeit universal and nonpartisan, for universities (macro level) and their constituent faculties and departments (meso level) to contribute to developing a peaceful and prosperous environment. However, even where the mega-level influences have failed to spur the university and law department into action, in some instances individuals have influenced their department and institution to provide the necessary resources and support, as in Germany and Norway. Figure 2.5 illustrates how social justice factors and the SDGs influence the development of clinical programmes and the subsequent contribution of these clinical programmes in terms of enhancing society.

Figure 2.5: Social justice mission

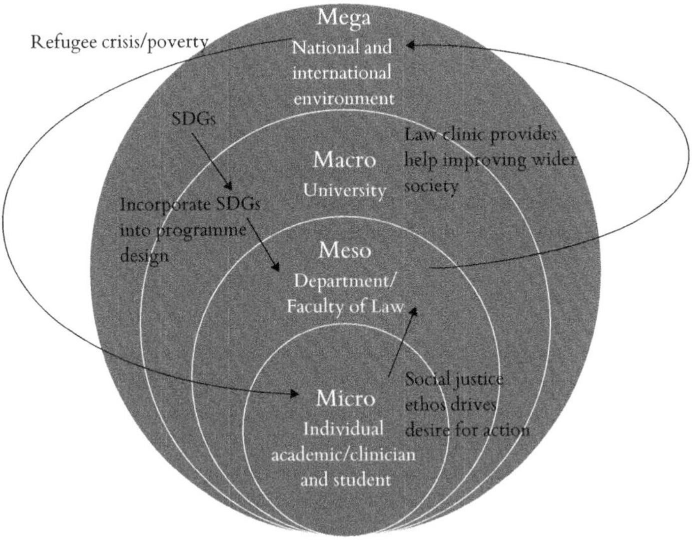

Source: Mandy Frake-Mistak, Jennifer Friberg and Melanie Hamilton, 'Reimagining the 4M Framework in Educational Development for SoTL' (2023) *Teaching & Learning Inquiry: The ISSOTL Journal* 11. doi: 10.20343/teachlearninqu.11.14 (adapted by the author).

Conclusion

As was acknowledged earlier, Europe is a diverse region within the global clinical legal education movement. It contains the different legal traditions of common law and civil law; it contains divergent national histories, including former communist countries; and the social and economic issues are broad, including poverty, migration and even armed conflict. Yet despite the differences, analysis using the 4M framework highlights that the drivers and problems associated with the development of clinical legal education in Europe are the same, regardless of where the clinical programme is located. There is a pan-European shift towards embedding practice-based skills and competencies within the law school curriculum. Clinical programmes are in a precarious position financially, being dependent on the university or an external funder for support. However, that said, clinical programmes are also in a strong negotiating position, offering the law school, and the university, a selling point to prospective students in a competitive market. Further, membership of national and international networks has galvanized the clinical legal education movement, providing not only support in the establishment of clinical programmes, but also a strong unified voice in advocating the benefits of clinical legal education within the law school curriculum. There is also a distinct social advantage to clinical legal education addressing unmet need within the community in which the university is located. As discussed previously, universities also have an obligation to embed the SDGs and contribute to sustainable development for a better world, something which is at the core of clinical legal education.

If we consider the micro-meso-macro-mega-level perspectives, it is apparent that each level is interacting with the others, influencing the development of clinical legal education. The drivers for clinical legal education typically emanate at the micro or mega levels. However, the direction of influence is not one-way; the influence not only flows from the mega level (that is, the wider national and international landscape) down through the other levels, but also from the micro level (for example, the influence of individual academics and students) up through the levels, creating a circle of influence as seen in Figures 2.4 and 2.5. The analysis highlights that support is required at all levels if a clinical programme is to be sustained.

This chapter presents findings from the first application of the 4M framework to clinical legal education. It has outlined the various and complexly interwoven influences, or drivers, that have facilitated the shift of clinical legal education from the periphery to, if not the mainstream, then a recognized and ever-evolving methodology within European legal education. While this chapter has presented an overview of the current position of clinical legal education in Europe, it is hoped that this framework will help to reframe some of the discussions and contribute to the further development the clinical legal education movement in Europe and beyond.

References

Alemanno A and Khadar L (eds), *Reinventing Legal Education: How Clinical Education Is Reforming the Teaching and Practice of Law in Europe* (CUP 2018)

Aurey X, 'Law Clinics in France through the Prism of Fundamental Rights Law Clinic, University of Caen Normandy' in A Alemanno and L Khadar (eds), *Reinventing Legal Education* (CUP 2018)

Bartoli C, *Legal Clinics in Europe: For a Commitment of Higher Education in Social Justice* (special issue, Diritto e Questioni Pubbliche 2016)

Berbec-Rostas M, Gutnikov A and Namyslowska-Gabrysiak B, 'Clinical Legal Education in Central and Eastern Europe: Selected Case Studies' in FS Bloch (ed), *The Global Clinical Movement* (Oxford University Press 2010)

Bleasdale L, Rizzotto B, Stalker R, Yeatman L, McFaul H, Ryan F, Johnson N and Thomas L, 'Law Clinics: What, Why and How?' in L Thomas and N Johnson (eds), The *Clinical Legal Education Handbook* (University of London Press 2020)

Bogicevic J, 'Representing the Other: A Case for Interdisciplinary Clinical Legal Education: Example of the Human Rights and Migration Law Clinic' (2019) 26 *International Journal of Clinical Legal Education* 93

Boyer EL, *Scholarship Reconsidered: Priorities of the Professoriate* (Carnegie Foundation for the Advancement of Teaching 1990)

Cody A, 'Reflection and Clinical Legal Education: How Do Students Learn about Their Ethical Duty to Contribute towards Justice' (2020) 23(1–2) *Legal Ethics* 13, https://doi.org/10.1080/1460728x.2020.1799303

Czernicki F, 'The History and Distinctiveness of the Polish Legal Clinics Program' in J Giddings (ed), *Global Clinical Legal Education* (Routledge 2025)

Duncan N, 'Ethical Practice and Clinical Legal Education' (2005) 7 *International Journal of Clinical Legal Education* 7

European Network for Clinical Legal Education, 'Quality Standards for Legal Clinics' (adopted 15 July 2022), https://www.encle.org/upload/lg/news/ENCLE-Standards-Final-Version-July-2022.pdf

European University Association, *Universities and Sustainable Development: Towards the Global Goals* (2018), https://www.eua.eu/downloads/publications/universities-and-sustainable-development-towards-the-global-goals.pdf

Frake-Mistak M, Friberg J and Hamilton M, 'Reimagining the 4M Framework in Educational Development for SoTL' (2023) 11 *Teaching & Learning Inquiry: The ISSOTL Journal*, https://doi.org/10.20343/teachlearninqu.11.14

Friberg J, 'Might the 4M Framework Support SoTL Advocacy?' (*The SoTL Advocate*, 11 July 2016), https://illinoisstateuniversitysotl.wordpress.com/2016/07/11/might-the-4m-framework-support-sotl-advocacy/

Genty PM, 'Reflections on US Involvement in the Promotion of Clinical Legal Education in Europe' in A Alemanno and L Khadar (eds), *Reinventing Legal Education* (CUP 2018)

Giddings J, Burridge R, Gavigan SAM and Klein CF, 'The First Wave of Modern Clinical Legal Education' in FS Bloch (ed), *The Global Clinical Movement* (Oxford University Press 2010)

Grimes R, 'Reflections on Clinical Legal Education' (1995) 29 *Law Teacher* 169, 170

Grimes R, Dunn R, Samaras R and Donnelly L, 'Legal Clinics in the UK and Ireland: Past, Present and Future' in J Giddings (ed), *Global Clinical Legal Education* (Routledge 2025)

Grimes R, Klaff J and Smith C, 'Legal Skills and Clinical Legal Education: A Survey of Undergraduate Law School Practice' (1996) 30 *The Law Teacher* 44

Hammerslev O, Olesen A and Rønning OH, 'Juss-Buss [Law Bus]: A Student-Run Legal Aid Clinic' in OH Rønning and O Hammerslev (eds), *Outsourcing Legal Aid in the Nordic Welfare States* (Springer 2018), https://library.oapen.org/bitstream/handle/20.500.12657/27884/1/1002118.pdf#page=155

Hannemann JGA and Dietlein G, 'The Development of Refugee Law Clinics in Germany in View of the Refugee Crisis in Europe' (2018) 25 *International Journal of Clinical Legal Education* 160

Hovhannisian L, *Clinical Legal Education and the Bologna Process* (PILI Papers No 2 December 2006)

Kyenge CK, 'Foreword' in C Bartoli, *Legal Clinics in Europe* (Diritto e Questioni Pubbliche, May 2016)

Lewis R, Clinical Legal Education Revisited (Cardiff Law School 2000), https://orca.cardiff.ac.uk/id/eprint/27655/1/cliniced.pdf

McKeown P, 'Law Student Attitudes towards Pro Bono and Voluntary Work: The Experience at Northumbria University' (2015) 22 *International Journal of Clinical Legal Education* 1

McKeown P, 'Pro Bono: What's in It for Law Students? The Students' Perspective' (2017) 24 *International Journal of Clinical Legal Education* 43

McKeown P and Hall E, 'If We Could Instil Social Justice Values through Clinical Legal Education, Should We?' (2018) 5(1) *Journal of International and Comparative Law* 143

McKeown P, Stege U and Tomoszek M, 'Clinical Legal Education in Europe and Implementation of Sustainable Development Goals' in Walter Leal Filho and others (eds), *SDGs in the European Region* (Springer 2023), https://doi.org/10.1007/978-3-031-17461-2_20

Office for Students, 'About the Teaching Excellence Framework (TEF)' (Office for Students), https://www.officeforstudents.org.uk/for-providers/quality-and-standards/about-the-tef/

Office for Students, 'Financial Sustainability of Higher Education Providers in England: November 2024 Update', https://www.officeforstudents.org.uk/media/nn2fnrkx/financial-sustainability-november-2024.pdf

Quality Assurance Agency for Higher Education, *Subject Benchmark Statement: Law* (QAA 2023)

Sandbach J and Grimes R, *Law School Pro Bono and Clinic Report 2020* (LawWorks 2020)

Shulman L, 'Foreword' in P Hutchings (ed), *Ethics of Inquiry* (Carnegie Foundation 2002) v

Simmons N, 'The 4M Framework as Analytic Lens for SoTL's Impact: A Study of Seven Scholars' (2020) 8(1) *Teaching & Learning Inquiry* 76, https://files.eric.ed.gov/fulltext/EJ1251299.pdf

Smith PS, 'Developments in Clinical Legal Education in England' (1979) 7 *CLEPR News* 83

Solicitors Regulation Authority, 'Qualifying Work Experience for Candidates' (26 January 2024), https://www.sra.org.uk/become-solicitor/sqe/qualifying-work-experience-candidates/

Solicitors Regulation Authority, 'Solicitors Qualifying Examination (SQE) Route' (2025), https://www.sra.org.uk/become-solicitor/sqe/, accessed 5 June 2025

Stege U and Giddings J, 'Clinical Legal Education in Western Europe' in J Giddings (ed), *Global Clinical Legal Education* (Routledge 2025)

Street Law, 'Street Law' (no date), https://streetlaw.org/

Sukrow B, 'Clinical Legal Education in Germany: A Brand New Old Story' in J Giddings (ed), *Global Clinical Legal Education* (Routledge 2025)

Thomas L and Johnson N (eds), *The Clinical Legal Education Handbook* (University of London Press 2020), https://read.uolpress.co.uk/projects/the-clinical-legal-education-handbook

Thornton M, 'What Is the Law School for in a Post-pandemic World?' in R Dunn, P Maharg and V Roper (eds), *What Is Legal Education for?* (Routledge 2022)

Tsypiashchuk M, 'Clinics in Ukraine' in J Giddings (ed), *Global Clinical Legal Education* (Routledge 2025)

United Nations, *Sustainable Development Goals* (2025), https://sdgs.un.org/goals

Universities UK, 'Universities Grip Financial Crisis: But at What Cost to the Nation?' (27 May 2025), https://www.universitiesuk.ac.uk/what-we-do/creating-voice-our-members/media-releases/universities-grip-financial-crisis-what

Wilson RJ, 'Western Europe: Last Holdout in the Worldwide Acceptance of Clinical Legal Education' (2009) 10 *German Law Journal* 823

Working Group on Litigants in Person, *Report on Access to Justice for Litigants in Person* (Civil Justice Council, November 2011)

PART II

Clinical Pedagogy in the National Context

3

The Transformative Role of Law Clinics in Spanish and Italian Legal Education

Cecilia Blengino and Andrés Gascón-Cuenca

Introduction

The legal culture of Italy and Spain share many characteristics. Both are countries whose constitutions define them as democratic welfare states developed, at least, through three ways. The first is establishing the protection of a series of civil, political, economic, social and cultural fundamental rights that guarantee a minimum standard for all citizens. Second, the constitutional texts include a set of higher values for the system, such as equality, plurality, justice and solidarity. Finally, both texts establish mechanisms for the incorporation of ratified international texts that protect human rights into the internal legal system. This set of safeguards must direct the activity of all the powers of the state, as they must take them into account in the development of their activities as a protected threshold that cannot be degraded. However, in the continuing scenario of political and economic crisis, these legal guarantees become fragile. Positive law does not always guarantee the equality of the plurality of groups that make up our societies. And it is precisely the study of these situations where clinical legal education finds its reason for being.

In this chapter we analyse and develop the theory behind legal-clinical education that adopts the human rights model and the reasons that led to its development in Italy and Spain – a theory that is based on the examination of discriminatory situations, on many occasions created by the legal system itself. This clinical work serves us to achieve two goals: on the one hand, to promote the critical study of law through projects with common objectives on immigration law; and, on the other hand, to train future legal experts committed to the protection of the rights of people who are in the borders of the law.

The second section will analyse the structural crisis of the Spanish and Italian constitutional systems. Both systems provide for the protection of a series of fundamental rights, but they nevertheless lack measures of substantial control of the legislative activity that would make it possible to evaluate the actual content of the rights protected and whether this complies with the international standards of protection to which Spain and Italy have committed themselves by ratifying international covenants on the protection of human rights. These cyclical crises have also affected access to justice and the right of education within the general framework of the erosion of the constitutional protections, and will therefore also be analysed as a crucial factor in the process of creation and development of the legal-clinical networks in both states.[1]

Legal clinics in Spain and Italy: towards a shift in the paradigm of legal education

The spread of clinical legal education should be seen as an integral part of development policy.[2] This statement is true in a double sense, referring to both the social context and legal education. This is particularly evident in countries such as Spain and Italy, which have similar legal and academic systems. The establishment of clinics in the Italian and Spanish contexts is intrinsically linked to the growth patterns exhibited by the global clinical movement.[3] The proliferation of legal education in these clinical countries is due to a cultural exchange between the clinical movement and indigenous factors.[4] In terms of pedagogy, the spread of legal clinics in these countries represents a paradigmatic leap towards a new model of legal education in the context of the prevailing crisis in legal education. In Spain and Italy, the methods of teaching law are mainly based on the assumptions of modern legal positivism. Legal science has been conceptualized as a specialized technical discipline, acquired through the understanding of legal, substantive and procedural

---

[1] This chapter is the result of shared reflections amongst the authors. Nevertheless, for organization purposes, the writing of the chapter has been divided as follows: Andrés Gascón-Cuenca wrote the Introduction and the sections entitled 'The crisis of the Spanish and Italian constitutional models' and 'Legal aid clinics and migrant exclusion: responding to state neglect'. Cecilia Blengino wrote the sections entitled 'Legal clinics in Spain and Italy: towards a shift of the paradigm of legal education' and 'How do legal clinics challenge the crisis in the legal studies in Italy and Spain?'. Conclusions have been written by both the authors.

[2] Richard J Wilson, 'Beyond Legal Imperialism: US Clinical Legal Education and the New Law and Development' in Frank S Bloch (ed), *The Global Clinical Movement: Educating Lawyers for Social Justice* (OUP 2011) 143.

[3] Bloch (n 2); Richard J Wilson, *The Global Evolution of Clinical Legal Education: More Than a Method* (CUP 2017).

[4] Cecilia Blengino and Andrés Gascón-Cuenca (eds), *Epistemic Communities at the Boundaries of Law: Clinics as a Paradigm in the Revolution of Legal Education in the European Mediterranean Context* (Ledizioni 2019).

norms. This conception of jurisprudence, deeply rooted in the mindset of civil lawyers, has given scientific legitimacy to a model of legal education for the last century, implicitly identifying the 'good lawyer' as a *servum legum*.[5]

As Paolo Grossi has observed, the cultural internalization of the model has been such that lawyers are often convinced and proud to present themselves as servants of the law, dominated by the unquestionable majesty of that supreme product of human progress, the 'code', even though they are the first victims of the legalistic paroxysm, having been deprived of their usual role as sources of law.[6] The educational model resulting from the primacy of statute law and an interpretation of the law based on logical-deductive reasoning has led to an acritical, dogmatic model of the lawyer.[7] Given the profound changes that have occurred in recent centuries through the processes of constitutionalization of rights and the configuration of legal principles,[8] the concept of legal interpretation and the role of the jurist have been radically transformed. Despite this, the concept of legal knowledge as the result of the transmission of legal content has not changed for many years, suggesting a considerable indifference on the part of law faculties to didactic strategies. In fact, in Italian and Spanish universities, a reductionist reading of this transformation tends to prevail. In essence, it does not overcome legal formalism, but considers that the crisis of legal positivism is merely its evolution due to the crisis of the state as the main source of the legal system.[9] From this point of view, the metaphor of the network would only indicate the expansion of the normative sources with respect to the legislative one, but the jurist's knowledge is still essentially conceived in his ability to interpret written texts, even if his interpretive freedom is enormously expanded by the multiplicity of normative sources upon which he can draw and by a less strong perception of the duties of obedience that jurists should have towards the legislator.

Contesting this perspective, the primacy of the study of law through codes, the use of the exegetical methodology, and the historical reluctance towards a practical dimension of education, the humanities and interdisciplinarity are precisely the premises challenged[10] by the clinical legal movements that have emerged in these countries. From this point of

---

5 Paolo Grossi, *L'Europa del diritto* (Laterza 2007) 154.

6 ibid.

7 Diego Blázquez Martín, 'The Bologna Process and the Future of Clinical Education in Europe: A View from Spain' in Bloch (n 2).

8 Robert Alexy, *Concetto e validità del diritto* (Einaudi 1997).

9 Cecilia Blengino and Claudio Sarzotti, *Quale formazione per quale giurista? Insegnare il diritto nellaprospettiva socio-giuridica* (Quaderni del Dipartimento di Giurisprudenza dell'Università di Torino 2021).

10 Cecilia Blengino, *Dentro il diritto. La clinica legale come pratica riflessiva* (Giappichelli 2023) 210.

view, the essentially spontaneous process that introduced clinics in Italy and Spain from the early 2000s should be seen as a paradigmatic shift aimed at challenging the impenetrability[11] of the traditional pedagogical models adopted by law faculties to discuss their theoretical premises, in particular the primacy of law and its apolitical nature. Indeed, the development of the clinics emerged as a largely unplanned process, stemming from a deep dissatisfaction with the cultural and political foundations[12] of legal education in universities. The aim of the clinics was to overcome the reluctance to question the assumptions and methodological corollaries of legal formalism, including the separation between law and the ends of justice. In doing so, legal clinics restore to legal knowledge the ancient character of interpretive knowledge.[13]

They also challenge one of the fundamental features of traditional legal education in civil law systems, namely the assumption that the law is a 'thing' which the jurist must comprehend in its objectivity,[14] and the legal reasoning is based on abstractions and that judicial decisions are syllogisms. In doing so, legal clinics challenge established notions of legal knowledge formed within the modern paradigm of law, as well as the Kelsenian account of law as a system endowed with its own internal coherence. Postulating that the general and abstract norm contains within itself every possible concrete case, the legal positivist perspective reduces the interpretation of law to a series of operations of pure logical deduction and consequently claims its neutrality from a political and moral point of view. This assumption reduces legal education to teaching students how to combine principles and rules in a formal and purely logical structure. On the contrary, legal clinics identify the object of legal education in the interaction between legal norms and the social and institutional environment. This conception of law as law in context[15] entails the emancipation of law from the pretence of systematic completeness, corresponding to a progressive shift in the transmission of

---

[11] Richard J Wilson, 'Western Europe: Last Holdout in the Worldwide Acceptance of Clinical Legal Education' (2009) 10(7) *German Law Journal* 823.

[12] Marzia Barbera, 'Il movimento delle cliniche legali e le sue ragioni' in Angelo Maestroni, Paola Bambrilla and Matteo Carrer, *Teorie e pratiche nelle cliniche legali* (Giappichelli 2018) xx.

[13] Grossi (n 5); Cristina Amato, 'Experiential Learning from the Continental Viewpoint: If the Cap Fits ...' in Richard Grimes (ed), *Re-thinking Legal Education under the Civil and Common Law: A Road Map for Constructive Change* (Routledge 2018); Blengino and Sarzotti (n 9); Laura Bugatti, 'L'identità del nuovo giurista e il diritto come pratica sociale' in Giacomo Viggiani (ed), *La didattica del diritto* (Ledizioni 2022); Blengino (n 10).

[14] Massimo Vogliotti, 'Per una nuova educazione giuridica' (2020) 2 *Diritto & Questioni Pubbliche* 229.

[15] Antoine Bailleux and François Ost, 'Droit, contexte et interdisciplinarité: refondation d'une démarche' (2013) 70(1) *Revue interdisciplinaire d'études juridiques* 25.

legal knowledge away from the mere transmission of normative substance.[16] By adopting a legal realist perspective, legal clinics overcome the dogmatic approach and promote the idea of increasing future lawyers' awareness of the breaks and gaps that characterize law in action.[17] It can be said that clinics go far beyond reducing law to its formal validity[18] and raise questions about both its effectiveness and its value justice.[19]

In fact, legal clinics firmly believe that it is necessary to participate in the processes of legal interpretation, reconceptualizing legal norms and institutional processes in the light of constitutional and international principles. Moreover, the active participation of legal clinics in the discursive spaces where processes of legal interpretation take shape is guided by a transformative horizon.

The crises of the Spanish and Italian constitutional models

If we look at the European reality from 2008 to the present day, we can affirm that Europe is living in a situation of permanent crisis: the economic crisis that began with the bursting of the real estate bubble, from which it has not been able to emerge, and which has made access to housing one of the main problems for European citizens at all levels, the various open wars, the climate emergency and many others. This reality has had a profound impact on European welfare systems, especially those of Spain and Italy. The crisis has exposed the vulnerability of the Mediterranean welfare model, characterized by low public spending and a reliance on family networks to provide services.[20] As austerity measures were implemented to reduce public debt and comply with the economic guidelines of the International Monetary Fund (IMF) and the European Union (EU), essential services such as health, education and legal aid were severely affected.

[16] Vogliotti (n 14).

[17] Katherine Kruse, 'Getting Real about Legal Realism, New Legal Realism and Clinical Legal Education' (2011–2012) 56 *New York Law School Law Review* 659; Jeremy Perelman, 'Penser la pratique, théoriser le droit en action: des cliniques juridiques et des nouvelles frontières épistémologiques du droit' (2014) 73 *Revue interdisciplinaire d'études juridiques* 133.

[18] Norberto Bobbio, *Teoria generale del diritto* (Giappichelli 1993).

[19] Alexy (n 8).

[20] Silvia Vogliotti and Sara Vattai, 'Modelli di Welfare state in Europa' (IPL), https://www.afi-ipl.org/wp-content/uploads/IPL2015_Welfare_1_it-1.pdf; Luis Moreno, *Ciudadanos precarios. La 'última red' de protección social* (Ariel 2000); Chiara Saraceno, Il *welfare tra vecchie e nuove disuguaglianze* (Il Mulino 2021).

The Mediterranean welfare model, as described by scholars such Moreno[21] or Guillén et al,[22] is characterized by a high degree of dualization of labour protection. Workers with regular employment contracts receive substantial benefits, while those in irregular or precarious employment have limited access to social protection. This dualization has been exacerbated by the economic crisis, which has led to a significant increase in short-term and long-term unemployment. Today, the result of these austerity policies continues to have a major impact on social protection. Both countries have very high levels of unemployment. According to Eurostat, in 2024 Spain had an unemployment rate of 11.1 per cent and Italy 6.1 per cent, which is much higher for those under 25, reaching 26.1 per cent in the case of Spain and 18.9 per cent in the case of Italy in 2024. Women are also disproportionately affected, with an unemployment rate of 12.3 per cent in Spain and 6.9 per cent in Italy in 2024. According to the World Bank, the incidence rate of poverty based on $2.15 a day is 0.6 in Spain and 0.8 in Italy (data for 2021), and if we consider the national poverty threshold, both countries stand at 20 per cent of their total population. This reality also affects the population's perception of the protection of the right to justice. Eurobarometer 540, conducted in February 2024, assesses the public's perception of the independence of national judicial systems in the EU.[23] In both Spain and Italy, the percentage of people who consider the independence of the judiciary to be bad or very bad far exceeds those who consider it to be good or very good, reaching 50 per cent in Spain and 54 per cent in Italy, with political and economic pressure on the judiciary identified as the main causes.

This reality poses a serious threat to the system of guarantees set out in the Spanish and Italian Constitutions. These are based on a catalogue of fundamental rights, with the right to personal dignity and everything essential to guarantee it at their apex. However, these rights remain vulnerable to economic circumstances, particularly the social and cultural ones. Nevertheless, economic conditions must under no circumstances limit the guarantees set out in constitutional texts or the standards identified in international covenants that have been validly ratified by both states.

The classical hierarchical structure of legal systems, which places constitutional or fundamental texts at the apex of the normative pyramid, establishing and protecting fundamental rights on the one hand, and

21 Luis Moreno, 'La "vía media" española del modelo de bienestar mediterráneo' (2003) 63/64 *Papers* 67.

22 Ana M Guillén, S González-Begega and D Luque Balbona, 'Austerity and Social Retrenchment in Southern Europe: The Fragmentation of the Mediterranean Welfare Model' (2016) 25(2) *Revista Española de Sociología* 261.

23 'Perceived Independence of the National Justice Systems in the EU among the General Public' (Eurobarometer 540, 2024), https://europa.eu/eurobarometer/api/deliverable/download/file?deliverableId=92592

recognizing structural values and principles that must influence not only the rest of the legal system but also the activities of governments and legislators on the other hand, is currently being challenged.[24] An example of this is the response of governments and international institutions to the different situations of crises that we have been experiencing. This is shaking the structural scaffolding of constitutional democracies and is one of the reasons why Luigi Ferrajoli identifies a crisis for constitutional democracies.[25] Introducing law students to Ferrajoli's ideas on the concept of legal validity can help them acquire the cognitive skills to identify, critique and challenge the normative framework that threatens to undermine constitutional democracy.

One of the main ideas introduced by Ferrajoli is the identification of the paradigm shift brought about by constitutional democracies through the recognition of legal validity within continental legal orders.[26] Traditionally, legal positivism has been seen as a nomodynamic system that contains norms that regulate the different ways in which laws are made. If legislators follow the formal procedure to pass a law, it is valid and therefore exists. This is what he defines as formal democracy or validity. Ferrajoli argues that constitutional democracies have introduced a paradigm shift, and this nomodynamic system now includes not only formal requirements to produce laws, but also substantive requirements of validity.[27]

Nevertheless, the validity of the law depends not only on formal democracy, but also on the principle of substantive legality,[28] according to which a norm is valid, in addition to being in force, only if its content does not conflict with the fundamental principles and rights established by the constitution. As a legal positivist, Ferrajoli defends the complete separation of law and morality. He claims that his definition of fundamental rights maintains ideological neutrality because each society is free to decide the content of the rights it considers fundamental, if they are recognized by all. However, when the validity of a law depends on its substantive legality, it is subject to critical evaluation by the competent authority (supreme or constitutional court, parliament and so on).

Ferrajoli argues that in order for a legal decision to be valid, it must not contradict fundamental rights and principles, which act as a limit both to the free-market economy and to possible abuses by the majority against minorities in the protection of their rights.[29] Protecting fundamental rights

[24] Massimo La Torre, *Il diritto contro se stesso. Saggio sul positivismo giuridico e la sua crisi* (Leo S Olschki 2020).

[25] Luigi Ferrajoli, *Poderes Salvajes: la crisis de la democracia constitucional* (Trotta 2011); Luigi Ferrajoli, *La democracia a través de los derechos* (Trotta 2019).

[26] Luigi Ferrajoli, *Derechos y garantías: la ley del más débil* (Trotta 2010) 65–68.

[27] Ferrajoli, *Poderes Salvajes* (n 25) 35–39; Ferrajoli, *La democracia* (n 25) 135–137.

[28] Ferrajoli, *Poderes Salvajes* (n 25) 39–42; Ferrajoli, *La democracia* (n 25) 149–156.

[29] Ferrajoli, *Derechos y garantías* (n 26) 50–55.

therefore means protecting them from the influence of the market and the majority. Therefore, laws must comply not only with formal rules in their drafting, but also with substantive rules in their content, to be considered fully valid. The rule of law is logically obliged to guarantee and protect fundamental rights and to punish those who violate them. In practice, however, this is not always the case. Moreover, state inaction sometimes prevents the guarantee of certain fundamental rights, such as the right to housing, by failing to develop them into specific norms that allow for their implementation. Nevertheless, contradictions and legal loopholes should not be used to detract from the importance of fundamental rights and the state's duty to fulfil them. Therefore, when faced with a legal gap in the implementation of a fundamental right, we must firmly reaffirm the state's obligation to provide a solution.[30]

Consequently, this theory will help us as teachers to face the challenge of the crisis of the right of access to justice and education: on the one hand, because of the proliferation of criminal and administrative sanctions that punish protest against the situations described earlier; and, on the other hand, because of the commercialization of the right to education, especially in university law degrees following the Bologna reform.

The crisis of access to justice

During the various crises that have affected Europe, both Spain and Italy have seen policies of criminalization of behaviours that were not previously classified as crimes, as well as an increase in penalties for minor offences. Examples include the Spanish Organic Law 4/2015 on the protection of the security of citizens and, in Italy, the 13 April 2017 Law and the 11 April 2025 Decree (so-called 'security decrees'). These policies, similar to the 2009 Policing and Crime Act in the UK or the 2002 Homeland Security Act in the US, reflect a trend towards the expansion of criminal and administrative sanctions in the legal systems of both countries, which not only jeopardizes fundamental civil and political rights, such as the right to demonstrate, but also affects, for example, the externalization of detention centres for foreigners or the punishment of boat rescues on the high seas. This reality poses a very broad challenge to the set of constitutional and international guarantees that protect the rights of people in these situations.

We must bear in mind that access to justice is a multidimensional right that includes the right to have rights, their effective recognition and the

[30] Andrés Gascón-Cuenca, 'Luigi Ferrajoli's Theory of Fundamental Rights and Clinical Legal Education' in Omar Madhloom and Hugh McFaul (eds), *Thinking about Clinical Legal Education: Philosophical and Theoretical Perspectives* (Routledge 2022).

individual's demand for their guarantee. This implies not only formal access to the courts, but also the ability to effectively exercise recognized rights.[31] In addition, both states have incorporated international standards for the protection of the right of access to justice, such as Article 14 of the International Covenant on Civil and Political Rights and Articles 6 and 13 of the European Convention on Human Rights.

Therefore, the mere existence of a legal provision allowing for the establishment of detention centres for migrants outside national borders does not make this a measure that guarantees human rights. Similarly, the criminalization of protests against the no-action policy in the Mediterranean or the prosecution of ships that rescue migrants at sea, even if they have legal backing at the national level, clearly violate international obligations that cannot be ignored by the captains of these ships.

The crisis in legal studies

The introduction of the Bologna model brought about a major change in curricula. Specifically in law, the transformation of the degree was provided by perplexities shown by the teaching staff in both countries,[32] as well as in other European countries, as it implied the elimination of subjects and a restructuring of the curriculum that did not always consider the comprehensive training needs of future lawyers.[33]

Looking at how this process was carried out, we can conclude that there was an overemphasis on employability, with a focus on practical skills and employability rather than on critical and reflective thinking. This resulted in training that was more technical and less oriented towards a deeper understanding of law and its social implications. By implementing Human Capital Theory (HCT) in curriculum design, it prioritized the needs of the labour market over the holistic education of students. HCT argues

---

[31] José García Añón, 'Acceder a la justicia la función de las universidades, las clínicas jurídicas y las ONG, y su impacto construyendo los límites del derecho' in C García Pascual (ed), *Acceso a la justicia y garantía de los derechos en tiempos de crisis: de los procedimientos tradicionales a los mecanismosalternativos* (Tirant lo Blanch 2018) 302–305.

[32] A Boix Palop, 'Saquemos los estudios de Derecho del proceso de Bolonia' (*No se trata de leer*, 2 June), http://www.lapaginadefinitiva.com/aboix/?p=206; Vincenzo Irelli and Orlando Roselli (eds), *La riforma degli studi giuridici* (ESI 2005).

[33] E García de Enterría, 'Saquemos los estudios de derecho del proceso de Bolonia' (2009) 6 *El Cronista del estado social y democrático de derecho*; Manuel Atienza, 'Reformatio in Peius' (*El Notario*, 30 June 2009), https://www.elnotario.es/opinion/opinion/1540-reformatio-in-peius-0-5887089749693023; Aldo Schiavello, 'La formazione del giurista contemporaneo' (2021) 1 *Diritto e questioni pubbliche* 105.

that education should focus on developing skills and competences that are economically productive.[34]

As a result, the right to education has been commercialized, with private interests intervening to determine the knowledge and skills to be acquired. This has been to the detriment of the value of education and knowledge as common and structural goods in the development of the personality. Subjects related to human rights, the philosophy of law, legal ethics[35] and other critical areas have been marginalized or eliminated. These subjects are essential for the training of lawyers with a critical vision and a commitment to social justice. However, there are some authors[36] who argue that, despite the difficulties we have just mentioned, this process has also served to explore new possibilities through the revision of the methodologies used, which have served to include clinical legal methodology in the curricula.

While it is true that the revision of teaching methods has promoted an experiential approach to legal studies, it is also true that this window of opportunity has been used to change educational objectives across the board. Thus, the reform promoted the training of lawyers as mere technicians whose task is to perform their professional function without being critical of the system or the status quo. This undermines the ability of future lawyers to challenge existing norms and protect fundamental rights, as the promotion of private interests in higher education may not be in the interests of society at large and may foster patterns of structural discrimination.

How do legal clinics challenge the crisis in the legal studies in Italy and Spain?

Clinical legal education, particularly as developed in Spain and Italy, and in Continental Europe in general, is a response to what has been discussed in the previous sections, with the aim of recovering the dimension of the university as a public and social good.[37] Within the framework of

[34] Patrick Fitzsimons, 'Human Capital Theory and Education' in Michael Peters (ed), *Encyclopedia of Educational Philosophy and Theory* (Springer 2015).

[35] José García Añón, 'Teaching and Learning Legal Ethics and Professional Responsibility under the Civil Law' in Grimes (n 13).

[36] Diego Blázquez Martín, 'La educación jurídica clínica en el contexto del proceso de Bologna' (2006) 5(10) *Opinión Jurídica-Universidad de Medellín* 161.

[37] Maria Rosaria Marella and Enrica Rigo, 'Cliniche legali, commons e giustizia sociale' (2015) 1 *Parolechiave* 181; Javier García Medina, 'La clínica jurídica como espacio de reflexión crítica sobre el derecho' in Tamara Ramiro Sánchez, María Teresa Ramiro Sánchez and Bermúdez Sánchez (ed), *Evaluación de la Calidad de laInvestigación y de la Educación Superior: libro de resúmenes XIV FECIES* (Asociación Española de Psicología Conductual 2017); Miguel Ángel Ramiro, Andrés Gascón-Cuenca and Paulina Ramírez, 'Una clínica jurídica en materia de VIH y derechos' in Tamara Ramiro Sánchez,

the anti-formalist movement, legal clinics represent a powerful tool to reconnect legal knowledge and society, exposing both scholars and students to relevant and concrete problems of justice.[38] Thus, legal clinics are now an appropriate tool to enable future legal practitioners to explore and address the contradictions between law in the books and law in action[39] in the horizon of equal access to rights.

Today, the transformative process activated by legal clinics in civil law faculties involves innovation in teaching methods and the pursuit of the so-called Third Mission of the university.

On the one hand, the process of redefining the learning outcomes expected at the end of study cycles within the European Higher Education Area has pushed education systems to replace the transmissive model of knowledge with experiential pedagogical methods aimed at developing skills and competences. The search for methods and tools capable of undermining the divide between dogmatic study and practical experience is a growing phenomenon within the academic world.[40]

On the other hand, universities are called upon to engage in activities of scientific and cultural transfer and productive transformation of knowledge with the aim of promoting the economic and social growth of the territory. However, it should be noted that in the light of the university trend described in the previous paragraph, legal clinics in both Spain and Italy run the risk of falling victim to misunderstandings.

Thus, in a reductive way, legal clinics today risk being seen by universities as a mere tool to allow students to gain practical experience[41] or to modernize law school curricula.[42] This reductionist perspective obscures the authentic transformative potential of clinics, both in terms of cultural and social impact. Evidence of this reductive view can be found in the exponential increase in recent years in the number of Spanish and Italian university courses that are called clinics by the faculties, but are in fact internships, moot courts or

---

María Teresa Ramiro Sánchez and Bermúdez Sánchez (eds), *Evaluación de la Calidad de la Investigación y de la Educación Superior: libro de resúmenes XIV FECIES* (Asociación Españolade Psicología Conductual).

38 Barbera (n 12); Blengino (n 10); Andrés Gascón-Cuenca, 'Cómo se aprende y cómo se enseña en las clínicas jurídicas: un ejercicio práctico' in Alejandro Fuentes, David Eile and José García Añón (eds), *Manual de Clínicas Jurídicas. Desarrollo de la Educación Clínica Jurídica en Cuba* (Raoul Wallenberg Institute for Humans Rights and Humanitarian Law 2024).

39 Roscoe Pound, 'Law in Books and Law in Action' (1910) 44 *American Law Review* 12.

40 Gascón-Cuenca (n 38).

41 Blengino and Sarzotti (n 9).

42 Costanza Agnella et al, 'Un'indagine quali-quantitativa sulle Cliniche legali nelle Università italiane' (2024) 1 *Rivista di Filosofia del Diritto* 63.

similar settings that differ from the vision we defend for legal clinics, as well as the training objectives associated with social justice that they must pursue.[43]

More profoundly, legal clinics are a critical reminder to universities of the role they must play in society.[44] Indeed, clinical legal education is rethinking not only the methods but also, more importantly, the goals and purposes of continental European legal education.[45]

Legal clinics represent a powerful 'antidote to the technical/positivist nature of legal education',[46] as they challenge the tendency of the legal positivist approach to obscure the ideological dimension of law while perpetuating the power structures and inequalities embedded in society.[47] At the same time, they seek to address the crisis afflicting contemporary universities by advocating a return to their original purpose of cultivating critical thinking,[48] as opposed to the prevailing emphasis on professionalization and competition.

In the face of the social contradictions that are prevalent in continental Europe, legal clinics are stimulating academic institutions to both confront the challenges posed by these tensions and to play a role in this context, with a particular focus on the question of fundamental rights and their solidity. Indeed, clinical legal education critically observes the impact of the neoliberal drift and contributes to countering both visible and invisible models of domination[49] and a Western and Eurocentric worldview.[50]

The innovative impact of the legal clinics on the traditional methods of teaching and studying law, which focus on the use of legal codes, helps to shake up the capacities of the educational system by transforming the very ideas of law and legal knowledge, so that they can play a pivotal role in the transformation of positive law.

Both Spain and Italy have an extensive network of legal clinics. In the Spanish case, their development began in 2005/2006, and in the Italian

---

43 ibid.

44 Giacomo Capuzzo, 'La Terza missione e le cliniche legali. Un ambito di applicazione delle teoriecritiche' (2024) 1 *Rivista di Filosofia del Diritto* 75.

45 Blengino (n 10).

46 Adrian Evans et al, *Australian Clinical Legal Education: Designing and Operating a Best Practice Clinical Program in an Australian Law School* (ANU Press 2017) 162.

47 Duncan Kennedy, *Legal Education and the Reproduction of Hierarchy A Polemic Against the System* (New York University Press 2024) 591; Giacomo Capuzzo, 'The Reproduction of Hierarchy in Italian Law Departments and Innovative Teaching: The Role of Law Clinics' (2023) *Roma Tre Law Review* 43.

48 Boaventura de Sousa Santos, *La Universidad en el siglo XXI. Para una reforma democratica yemancipadora de la Universidad* (Plural Editores 2007); Boaventura de Sousa Santos, 'The Universities at a Crossroads' in Ramón Grosfoguel, Roberto Hernández and Ernesto Rosen Velásquez (eds), *Decolonizing the Westernized University* (Lexington Books 2016).

49 Kennedy (n 47).

50 De Sousa Santos, 'The Universities at a Crossroads' (n 48) 298.

one in 2009. The seed that gave rise to this movement was the existence of social needs that were not covered by the state, and which mostly concerned what we have discussed in the previous paragraphs – the lack of formal guarantee of fundamental rights. The combination of this reality and the need to reintroduce the critical study of the legal system and, in general, of the actions of the public authorities has given rise to these new communities of reflective legal practice, whose aim is to address this situation.[51]

The Spanish and Italian legal clinic movements are committed to the concrete affirmation of the constitutional principles of substantive equality and access to justice at the current historical juncture, where it is by no means certain that human rights will continue to exist in the form to which we have become accustomed in recent decades.[52] Thus, the practical learning of law that legal clinics pursue by dealing with real cases proves to be, above all, an alternative way of looking at law.[53] The notion that law can function as an instrument of social change stems from the decision to position the lawyer within the socially instituted perspective of the disadvantaged, with respect to the power dynamics that traverse society and the processes of social and legal change.[54] In the case of Spain, the results of the network have been used for high-impact projects that required the mobilization of a large workforce. Examples of successful projects are the two legal guides developed for the reception of the Ukrainian population fleeing the war and for the people affected by the terrible floods that occurred in Valencia in October 2024. The aim of these works was to make accessible all the legislative changes that had been introduced because of these situations, and to explain in detail the procedures to be followed to benefit from the various aids that had been established. These two experiences, together with others, are a clear example of good practice in academic coordination aimed at ensuring the exercise of human rights through the training of students.

The social impact of clinics has also expanded in Italy thanks to networking. For instance, various initiatives have been promoted by networks of clinics to raise awareness of the rights of prisoners and asylum seekers. During the period of the COVID-19 health emergency, the clinics submitted appeals for the implementation of emergency legislation that would serve to protect the right to health of the prison population. Therefore, in 2024, Italian clinics dealing with asylum seekers publicly expressed their concern in a statement about the practices followed by many Italian police headquarters.

---

[51] Blengino and Gascón-Cuenca (n 4).

[52] Alessandra Sciurba, 'Le cliniche legali italiane e la risignificazione del diritto' (2019) 2 *Rivistadi filosofia del diritto* 257, 270.

[53] Barbera (n 12) 81.

[54] Barbera (n 12).

These practices increase the difficulty for individuals to exercise their right to asylum and, consequently, to access their fundamental rights.

The specific way in which the clinic integrates these training objectives is not an incidental aspect, but is essential to their achievement.[55]

The ascendant alchemy[56] generated by approaching the law to solve a problematic situation leads legal clinics to transform legal education by challenging the main pillars of legal education in civil law universities.

One of the most significant effects of the cross-fertilization of teaching practices fostered by the movement of legal clinics is the initiation of a hitherto unknown pedagogical reflection within the legal education systems of continental Europe. In Spain and Italy, the actual didactic dimension of clinical training still occupies a limited space in the theoretical debate, but the continuous exchange within the legal clinic movement has allowed, even in these countries, the development of methods and tools that have long been consolidated in clinical training in other legal contexts.[57]

First, legal clinics overcome the separation between the different disciplines – typical of continental legal formalism – and place the search for solutions to multidimensional problems[58] in a legal world that knows no precise boundaries.[59] In doing so, the clinics adopt a holistic[60] and interdisciplinary[61] approach to promote the effective recognition of rights.[62]

Second, not only does the bottom-up approach reverse the traditional direction of legal education from the abstract to the concrete, but even more so, the cases pursued by the clinics tend to escape the attention of the institutional system. It is possible that, from this perspective, they appear to be of negligible scientific relevance,[63] but in reality they are chosen because they turn out to be central to the exercise of fundamental rights, as well as being closely linked to the nerve centres of the social hierarchy.[64] Moreover, they are chosen not only as an opportunity for students to learn, but also

55 Blengino (n 10).

56 Perelman (n 17) 135.

57 Gascón-Cuenca (n 38).

58 Paula Galowitz, 'The Opportunities and Challenges of an Interdisciplinary Clinic' (2012) 18 *International Journal of Clinical Legal Education* 165.

59 José García Añón, 'La integración de la educación jurídica clínica en el proceso formativo delos juristas' (2014) 12(3) *Revista de Educación y Derecho* 153.

60 José García Añón, 'Access to Justice and the Impact of the European Legal Clinics in Case Law' in Blengino and Gascón-Cuenca (n 4) 66.

61 Galowitz (n 58).

62 García Añón (n 60) 63.

63 ibid.

64 Carlo Caprioglio, 'Rethinking Legal Education in Times of Crisis' (2019) *Roma Tre Law Review* 333, 176.

to direct the processes of interpreting the law.[65] In fact, the legal clinic is configured as a legal experience still to be structured,[66] whose aim is to stimulate concrete and meaningful social change, combining reflection and active transformation.[67]

Third, the legal clinic considers the teaching and learning of law in a way that can be considered revolutionary in the framework of civil law education. Considering learning as a socially situated, circular process through which knowledge is created that transforms experience,[68] the legal clinic is conceived as a reflective practice.[69] While abandoning the idea that the purpose of legal education is the transmission of normative knowledge, clinics consider that the main goal of legal education is to train reflective practitioners.[70] This perspective also averts the risk that the professionalizing objectives of competence-based didactics will lead to a technicalist drift in legal education. Reflective practice is instrumental in promoting the essential skills that define a 'good' legal practitioner.[71] It also directs students towards deep learning,[72] allowing them to experience that legal issues are not predefined, but are constructed in intermediate zones of practice[73] characterized by uncertainty, uniqueness and conflictuality.

A fourth and crucial aspect of the legal clinics in Spain and Italy is the transformation of the very idea of teaching and the role of the law teacher. Clinical legal education relies on a Socratic approach, but above all clinical teaching takes place through a close link between lecturers and

---

65 García Añón (n 60) 64.

66 Emilio Santoro, 'Guai privati e immaginazione giuridica: le cliniche legali e il ruolo dell'Università' (2019) 2 *Rivista di Filosofia del Diritto* 231.

67 Dennis Beach, 'The Problem of How Learning Should Be Socially Organized: Relations between Reflections and Transformative Action' (2005) 6(4) *Reflective Practice* 473; Paulo Freire, *Pedagogy of the Oppressed* (Penguin 2017); John Dewey, *Experience and Education* (Free Press 2007); Hugh McFaul, 'Towards a Capability Approach to Clinical Legal Education' in Madhloom and McFaul (n 30).

68 García Añón (n 59).

69 Blengino (n 10).

70 Donald A Schön, *The Reflective Practitioner* (Routledge 1992).

71 Anna Cody, 'Reflection and Clinical Legal Education: How Do Students Learn about Their Ethical Duty to Contribute towards Justice' (2020) 23(1–2) *Legal Ethics* 13; Gascón-Cuenca (n 30).

72 Rachel Spencer, 'Holding up the Mirror: A Theoretical and Practical Analysis of the Role of Reflection in Clinical Legal Education' (2012) 18 *International Journal of Clinical Legal Education* 181; Elaine Campbell, 'Transferring Power: A Reflective Exploration of Authentic Student-Centred Small Group Work in Clinical Legal Education' (2015) 2(22) *International Journal of Clinical legal Education* 1; Jodi Balsam, Susan L Brooks and Margaret Reuter, 'Assessing Law Students as Reflective Practitioners' (2017) 62 *New York Law School Law Review* 45.

73 Schön (n 70).

nongovernmental organizations (NGOs) working in the field. Legal clinics collaborate with NGOs, and it is this collaboration that develops both the learning and the transformation of law that the clinics promote.[74]

The link between the university and the territory is realized in a radically different way from the one-way transfer of knowledge from the university to external actors, but it is based on mutual enrichment. The clinics essentially support NGOs that are already embedded in social reality and respond to the needs of vulnerable groups. The immersion of law in its context is driven by the recognition that the efforts of these associations are insufficient to address the current welfare crisis. In this regard, legal clinics have the potential to apply legal knowledge and skills to address pressing and urgent needs. As a result, students and faculty members gain invaluable insights from direct engagement with actual cases and social workers, challenging the conventional notion of the academic teacher as the sole repository of legal knowledge.

Legal aid clinics and migrant exclusion: responding to state neglect

Within this complex panorama of the protection of fundamental and human rights in Spain and Italy, as we have already mentioned, there are certain groups that are completely abandoned to their fate by the state. Migrants are a clear example of this reality. Due to their geographical location, our two countries are the gateway for migratory flows to the EU and other neighbouring countries. Although part of the development of migration policy is determined by the EU, the Member States are still responsible for its legislative development. However, this is an area of law that should help us to rethink the concept of the Westphalian nation state and its crisis.[75]

If we look at the management of migratory flows, we can see the pressure that Northern European states put on Southern states to develop public policies on this issue, in the context of border security, which is far removed from the protection of migrants' human rights. Indeed, this is an area dominated by what Mbembe calls necropolitics.[76] The open-air cemetery that the Mediterranean has become[77] demonstrates Europe's inability to develop and manage migration policies that protect human

[74] Richard Owen, 'Rebellious Lawyering Theory, Sustainability and Clinical Legal Education' in Madhloom and McFaul (n 30).

[75] Ricard Zapata-Barrero, *Diversity Management in Spain: New Dimensions, New Challenges* (Manchester University Press 2013).

[76] Achille Mbembe, *Necropolítica* (Melusina 2011).

[77] Javier de Lucas, *Mediterráneo: el naufragio de Europa* (Tirant lo Blanch 2015).

rights. Although there is no official data on the number of deaths of migrants in the Mediterranean, NGOs and associations defending their rights have quantified them.

According to the NGO Caminando Fronteras, the year 2024 ended with a total of 10,547 victims trying to reach the Spanish coast, including 421 women and 1,538 children.[78] In Italy, according to the International Organization for Migration (IOM), between January 2024 and January 2025, 2,400 people, including 120 minors, died on the migratory routes to Italy.[79] These terrible figures can only be explained by the legacy of colonial terror,[80] which has served to construct an ideology that objectifies and depersonalizes migrants, excluding them from the substantial protection of rights accorded to them as human beings. They are not the only ones to be persecuted. As we have seen, the criminalization of rescue operations on the high seas has led to the detention of rescue vessels in ports and the arrest of their captains.

This reality has occurred in Italy and the Spanish Criminal Code would also allow it in Spain.[81] Faced with this policy of inaction, which leads to the deaths of thousands of people fleeing extremely complicated situations that make it impossible for them to develop their own life plan, the law schools of the Universities of Valencia and Turin have organized themselves to fight for the protection of the rights of migrants. Through small projects adapted to operational capacities and considering the actors already active in the field, the work of the legal clinics has a twofold objective. On the one hand, it is to recover and promote the critical reflection that law students should have on the legal system, taking into account the nonpeaceful relationship that exists between the legal system and the protection of democracy and its values based on human rights. On the other hand, it is to work specifically with groups that are abandoned by the law, forced underground and therefore oppressed and structurally discriminated against.

From the Social Justice Clinic of the Law Faculty of the University of Valencia, we have developed a stable collaboration project with the State Coordinator of HIV and AIDS (CESIDA), in which we provide assistance to people who want to migrate to Spain because in their countries of origin they are not guaranteed adequate access to antiretroviral treatments that prevent the development of the disease. Similarly, numerous studies have been carried

78 Caminando Fronteras, 'Monitoring the Right to Life 2024' (December 2024), https://caminandofronteras.org/en/monitoreo/monitoring-the-right-to-life-2024/

79 'Missing Migrants Project' (IOM 2024), https://missingmigrants.iom.int/

80 Mbembe (n 76).

81 Margarita Martínez Escamilla, 'The Criminalization of Solidarity' (2019) 18 *Revista Crítica Penal y Poder* 8.

out on immigration regulations, highlighting the many discriminatory situations that can be found within the systemic discrimination that exists against this group.

In Turin, the Prison, Fundamental Rights and Social Vulnerability Legal Clinic has a special focus on assisting migrants who have been victims of trafficking and exploitation. In order to provide these people with the legal assistance they need, the clinic has been working for several years with Anello Forte, the network of anti-trafficking associations in the region. The aim of this collaboration is to help people apply for international protection. Recognition of international protection is essential in order for these people to free themselves from exploitation, but the challenges posed by linguistic, cultural and institutional barriers make it almost impossible for them to access justice on their own.

Conclusion

As discussed previously, the political and economic crises in Spain and Italy have weakened the legal guarantees of fundamental rights, highlighting the need for a more robust legal education system that can address these challenges. Traditional legal education in these countries has been dominated by legal positivism, focusing on the technical interpretation of laws and ignoring the substantive protections provided by constitutional systems and all ratified international standards. In contrast, clinical legal education promotes a more critical approach, encouraging students to engage with real-world legal issues and social justice. They have emerged as a response to dissatisfaction with traditional legal education, with the aim of reconnecting legal knowledge with societal needs, addressing real justice issues and promoting a critical perspective on the law. While there is a risk that legal clinics will be seen merely as practical training tools, their true potential lies in transforming legal education and contributing to social change through a strong philosophical and theoretical development based on current debates about the protection of human and fundamental rights and the ways in which structural inequalities affect society and specific groups within it. Cooperation with NGOs and active participation in legal interpretation are crucial to their success. Legal clinics in Spain and Italy focus on protecting the rights of vulnerable groups, such as migrants, who are often neglected by the state. Through specific projects,[82] these clinics

[82] Cecilia Blengino, Andrés Gascón-Cuenca and Ulrich Stege, 'Clinical Legal Education within the European-Mediterranean Asylum and Migration Context: Inside Views from Valencia and Turin' in Richard Grimes, Vera Honuskova and Ulrich Stege (eds), *Teaching Migration and Asylum Law: Theory and Practice* (Routledge 2022).

work to ensure access to justice and human rights for these groups, as one of the essential purposes without which the mission of public universities cannot be understood.

References

Agnella C, Blengino C, Ciavarella R, de Martino C, de Robertis C and D'Onghia M, 'Un'indagine quali-quantitativa sulle Cliniche legali nelle Università italiane' (2024) 1 *Rivista di Filosofia del Diritto* 63

Alexy R, *Concetto e validità del diritto* (Einaudi 1997)

Amato C, 'Experiential Learning from the Continental Viewpoint: If the Cap Fits…' in R Grimes (ed), *Re-thinking Legal Education under the Civil and Common Law: A Road Map for Constructive Change* (Routledge 2018)

Atienza A, 'Reformatio in Peius' (*El Notario*, 30 June 2009), https://www.elnotario.es/opinion/opinion/1540-reformatio-in-peius-0-5887089749693023

Bailleux A and Ost F, 'Droit, contexte et interdisciplinarité: refondation d'une démarche' (2013) 70(1) *Revue interdisciplinaire d'études juridiques* 25

Balsam J, Brooks SL and Reuter M, 'Assessing Law Students as Reflective Practitioners' (2017) 62 *New York Law School Law Review* 45

Barbera M, 'Il movimento delle cliniche legali e le sue ragioni' in A Maestroni, P Brambilla and M Carrer (eds), *Teorie e pratiche nelle cliniche legali* (Giappichelli 2018)

Beach D, 'The Problem of How Learning Should Be Socially Organized: Relations between Reflections and Transformative Action' (2005) 6(4) *Reflective Practice* 473

Blázquez D, 'The Bologna Process and the Future of Clinical Education in Europe: A View from Spain' in F Bloch (ed), *The Global Clinical Movement: Educating Lawyers for Social Justice* (OUP 2011)

Blengino C, *Dentro il diritto. La clinica legale come pratica riflessiva* (Giappichelli 2023)

Blengino C and Gascón-Cuenca A (eds), *Epistemic Communities at the Boundaries of Law: Clinics as a Paradigm in the Revolution of Legal Education in the European Mediterranean Context* (Ledizioni 2019)

Blengino C and Sarzotti C, *Quale formazione per quale giurista? Insegnare il diritto nella prospettiva socio-giuridica* (Quaderni del Dipartimento di Giurisprudenza dell'Università di Torino 2021)

Blengino C, Gascón-Cuenca A and Stege U, 'Clinical Legal Education within the European-Mediterranean Asylum and Migration Context: Inside Views from Valencia and Turin' in R Grimes, V Honuskova and U Stege (eds), *Teaching Migration and Asylum Law: Theory and Practice* (Routledge 2022)

Bloch F (ed), *The Global Clinical Movement: Educating Lawyers to Social Justice* (OUP 2011)

Bobbio N, *Teoria generale del diritto* (Giappichelli 1993)

Boix Palop A, 'Saquemos los estudios de Derecho del proceso de Bolonia' (*No se trata de leer*, 2 June), http://www.lapaginadefinitiva.com/aboix/?p=206

Bugatti L, 'L'identità del nuovo giurista e il diritto come pratica sociale' in G Viggiani (ed), *La didattica del diritto* (Ledizioni 2022)

Caminando Fronteras, 'Monitoring the Right to Life 2024', https://caminandofronteras.org/monitoreo/monitoreo-del-derecho-a-la-vida-ano-2024/

Campbell E, 'Transferring Power: A Reflective Exploration of Authentic Student-Centred Small Group Work in Clinical Legal Education' (2015) 22(2) *International Journal of Clinical Legal Education* 1

Caprioglio C, 'Rethinking Legal Education in Times of Crisis' (2019) *Roma Tre Law Review* 333

Capuzzo G, 'The Reproduction of Hierarchy in Italian Law Departments and Innovative Teaching: The Role of Law Clinics' (2023) *Roma Tre Law Review* 43

Capuzzo G, 'La Terza missione e le cliniche legali. Un ambito di applicazione delle teorie critiche' (2024) 1 *Rivista di Filosofia del Diritto* 75

Cerulli Irelli V and Roselli O (eds), *La riforma degli studi giuridici* (ESI 2005)

Cody A, 'Reflection and Clinical Legal Education: How Do Students Learn about Their Ethical Duty to Contribute towards Justice' (2020) 23(1–2) *Legal Ethics* 13

De Lucas J, *Mediterráneo: el naufragio de Europa* (Tirant lo Blanch 2015)

De Sousa Santos B, *La Universidad en el siglo XXI. Para una reforma democratica y emancipadora de la Universidad* (Plural Editores 2007)

De Sousa Santos B, 'The Universities at a Crossroads' in R Grosfouguel, R Hernandez and RR Velasquez (eds), *Decolonizing the Westernized University* (Lexington Books 2016)

Dewey J, *Experience and Education* (Free Press 2007)

Eurobarometer 540, 'Perceived Independence of the National Justice Systems in the EU among the General Public' (2024), https://europa.eu/eurobarometer/api/deliverable/download/file?deliverableId=92592

Evans A, Cody A, Copeland A, Giddings J, Joy P, Noone MA and Rice S, *Australian Clinical Legal Education: Designing and Operating a Best Practice Clinical Program in an Australian Law School* (ANU Press 2017)

Ferrajoli L, *Derechos y garantías: la ley del más débil* (Trotta 2010)

Ferrajoli L, *Poderes Salvajes: la crisis de la democracia constitucional* (Trotta 2011)

Ferrajoli L, *La democracia a través de los derechos* (Trotta 2019)

Fitzsimons P, 'Human Capital Theory and Education' in M Peters (ed), *Encyclopedia of Educational Philosophy and Theory* (Springer 2015)

Freire P, *Pedagogy of the Oppressed* (Penguin 2017)

Galowitz P, 'The Opportunities and Challenges of an Interdisciplinary Clinic' (2012) 18 *International Journal of Clinical Legal Education* 165

García Añón J, 'La integración de la educación jurídica clínica en el proceso formativo de los juristas' (2014) 12(3) *Revista de Educación y Derecho* 153

García Añón J, 'Teaching and Learning Legal Ethics and Professional Responsibility under the Civil Law' in R Grimes (ed), *Re-thinking Legal Education under the Civil and Common Law* (Routledge 2017)

García Añón J, 'Acceder a la justicia la función de las universidades, las clínicas jurídicas y las ONG, y su impacto construyendo los límites del derecho' in C García Pascual (ed), *Acceso a la justicia y garantía de los derechos en tiempos de crisis: de los procedimientos tradicionales a los mecanismos alternativos* (Tirant lo Blanch 2018)

García Añón J, 'Access to Justice and the Impact of the European Legal Clinics in Case Law' in C Blengino and A Gascón-Cuenca (eds), *Epistemic Communities at the Boundaries of Law: Clinics as a Paradigm in the Revolution of Legal Education in the European Mediterranean Context* (Ledizioni 2019)

García de Enterría E, 'Saquemos los estudios de derecho del proceso de Bolonia' (2009) 6 *El Cronista del estado social y democrático de derecho*

García Medina J, 'La clínica jurídica como espacio de reflexión crítica sobre el derecho' in T Ramiro Sánchez, MT Ramiro Sánchez and MP Bermúdez Sánchez (eds), *Evaluación de la Calidad de la Investigación y de la Educación Superior: libro de resúmenes XIV FECIES* (Asociación Española de Psicología Conductual 2017)

Gascón-Cuenca A, 'Luigi Ferrajoli's Theory of Fundamental Rights and Clinical Legal Education' in O Madhloom and H McFaul (eds), *Thinking about Clinical Legal Education: Philosophical and Theoretical Perspectives* (Routledge 2022)

Gascón-Cuenca A, 'Cómo se aprende y cómo se enseña en las clínicas jurídicas: un ejercicio práctico' in A Fuentes, D Eile and J García Añón (eds), *Manual de Clínicas Jurídicas. Desarrollo de la Educación Clínica Jurídica en Cuba* (Raoul Wallenberg Institute for Humans Rights and Humanitarian Law 2024)

Grossi P, *L'Europa del diritto* (Laterza 2007)

Guillén AM, González-Begega S and Luque Balbona D, 'Austerity and Social Retrenchment in Southern Europe: The Fragmentation of the Mediterranean Welfare Model' (2016) 25(2) *Revista Española de Sociología* 261

IOM (International Organization for Migration), 'Missing Migrants Project' (2024), https://missingmigrants.iom.int/

Kennedy D, *Legal Education and the Reproduction of Hierarchy: A Polemic against the System* (New York University Press 2024)

Kruse K, 'Getting Real about Legal Realism, New Legal Realism and Clinical Legal Education' (2011–2012) 56 *New York Law School Law Review* 659

La Torre M, *Il diritto contro se stesso. Saggio sul positivismo giuridico e la sua crisi* (Leo S Olschki 2020)

Marella R and Rigo E, 'Cliniche legali, commons e giustizia sociale' (2015) 1 *Parolechiave* 181

Martínez Escamilla M, 'The Criminalization of Solidarity' (2019) 18 *Revista Crítica Penal y Poder* 8
Mbembe A, *Necropolítica* (Melusina 2011)
McFaul H, 'Towards a Capability Approach to Clinical Legal Education' in O Madhloom and H McFaul (eds), *Thinking about Clinical Legal Education: Philosophical and Theoretical Perspectives* (Routledge 2022)
Moreno L, *Ciudadanos precarios. La 'última red' de protección social* (Ariel 2000)
Moreno L, 'La "vía media" española del modelo de bienestar mediterráneo' (2003) 63/64 *Papers* 67
Owen R, 'Rebellious Lawyering Theory, Sustainability and Clinical Legal Education' in O Madhloom and H McFaul (eds), *Thinking about Clinical Legal Education: Philosophical and Theoretical Perspectives* (Routledge 2022)
Perelman J, 'Penser la pratique, théoriser le droit en action: des cliniques juridiques et des nouvelles frontières épistémologiques du droit' (2014) 73 *Revue interdisciplinaire d'études juridiques* 133
Pound R, 'Law in Books and Law in Action' (1910) 44 *American Law Review* 12
Ramiro MÁ, Gascón-Cuenca A and Ramírez P, 'Una clínica jurídica en materia de VIH y derechos' in T Ramiro Sánchez, MT Ramiro Sánchez and MP Bermúdez Sánchez (eds), *Evaluación de la Calidad de la Investigación y de la Educación Superior: libro de resúmenes XIV FECIES* (Asociación Española de Psicología Conductual)
Saraceno C, *Il welfare tra vecchie e nuove disuguaglianze* (Il Mulino 2021)
Santoro E, 'Guai privati e immaginazione giuridica: le cliniche legali e il ruolo dell'Università' (2019) 2 *Rivista di Filosofia del Diritto* 231
Schiavello A, 'La formazione del giurista contemporaneo' (2021) 1 *Diritto e questioni pubbliche* 105
Schön D, *The Reflective Practitioner* (Routledge 1992)
Sciurba A, 'Le cliniche legali italiane e la risignificazione del diritto' (2019) 2 *Rivista di filosofia del diritto* 257
Spencer R, 'Holding up the Mirror: A Theoretical and Practical Analysis of the Role of Reflection in Clinical Legal Education' (2012) 18 *International Journal of Clinical Legal Education* 181
Vogliotti M, 'Per una nuova educazione giuridica' (2020) 2 *Diritto & Questioni Pubbliche* 229
Vogliotti S and Vattai S, 'Modelli di Welfare state in Europa' (IPL), https://www.afi-ipl.org/wp-content/uploads/IPL2015_Welfare_1_it-1.pdf
Wilson R, 'Western Europe: Last Holdout in the Worldwide Acceptance of Clinical Legal Education' (2009) 10(7) *German Law Journal* 823
Wilson R, 'Beyond Legal Imperialism: US Clinical Legal Education and the New Law and Development' in F Bloch (ed), *The Global Clinical Movement: Educating Lawyers for Social Justice* (OUP 2011)

Wilson R, *The Global Evolution of Clinical Legal Education: More Than a Method* (CUP 2017)

Zapata-Barrero R, *Diversity Management in Spain: New Dimensions, New Challenges* (Manchester University Press 2013)

4

Educate Law Students on Legal Aid Before It Is Too Late

Mária Havelková

Introduction

Rapid societal development and technological progress have resulted in increasingly complex legislation and legal processes, making them difficult to navigate without proper legal training.[1] Many individuals are unable to afford legal services, depending instead on underfunded state-funded criminal and civil legal aid systems,[2] or, even more frequently, on pro bono activities of lawyers.[3] Accessible legal aid has become essential for protecting fundamental rights and freedoms.

The passionate debate regarding whether pro bono should be mandatory for the legal profession has persisted for over half a century. Proponents argue that pro bono work is a professional responsibility, justified by the legal profession's monopoly over legal services[4] and its reliance on the justice system.[5] Meanwhile, critics contend that the legal profession is not

---

1 Gillian K Hadfield, 'More Markets, More Justice' (2019) 148(1) *Daedalus* 37.

2 Ben CJ van Velthoven and Carolus M Klein Haarhuis, 'Legal Aid and Legal Expenses Insurance, Complements or Substitutes? The Case of the Netherlands' (2011) 8(3) *Journal of Empirical Legal Studies* 587, at 604.

3 Jonathan JB Mijs, 'The Paradox of Inequality: Income Inequality and Belief in Meritocracy Go Hand in Hand' (2021) 19(1) *Socio-Economic Review* 7, 8.

4 Thomas Eldred and Thomas Schoenherr, 'The Lawyer's Duty of Public Service: More Than Charity' (1994) 96(2) *West Virginia Law Review* 367, at 369.

5 Victoria Kennedy, 'Pro Bono Legal Work: The Disconnect between Saying You'll Do It and Doing It' (2019) 26(3) *International Journal of Clinical Legal Education* 25, at 34.

responsible for poverty[6] and that lawyers are not as wealthy as they once were.[7] Despite these opposing views, there is a widespread consensus that legal services are increasingly inaccessible to those in need.[8]

Regarding the debate on mandating pro bono, David Luban remarked in 1999 that further discussion on the matter would be a waste of time.[9] Rather than resolving the debate through regulation, many jurisdictions and scholars have since shifted their focus towards educating future lawyers on social justice values and the benefits of pro bono work for individuals, society,[10] law firms,[11] and their own personal wellbeing[12] and professional growth.[13]

Legal clinics have long played a pivotal role in advancing these goals. Traditionally, their primary focus has been on providing assistance to underprivileged and marginalized groups, as well as supporting nongovernmental organizations. Over time, however, their scope has expanded to encompass areas such as business and intellectual property law.[14] As a result of this broadened focus, live-client clinics with a social justice component now represent just one element of a diverse clinical portfolio. Moreover, these live-client clinics are typically offered at a later stage in students' education, once they have acquired the necessary knowledge and skills to provide meaningful assistance to clients.[15]

Motivations for entering law school are likely multifaceted, including professional prestige, financial stability, aspirations for a political career and

6 Robert Atkinson, 'A Social-Democratic Critique of Pro Bono Public Representation of the Poor: The Good as the Enemy of the Best' (2001) 9(1) *American University Journal of Gender, Social Policy & the Law* 129, 154.

7 Rebecca L Sandefur, 'Lawyers' Pro Bono Service and American-Style Civil Legal Assistance' (2007) 41(1) *Law & Society Review* 79, at 88.

8 Andrew M Perlman, 'The Public's Unmet Need for Legal Services & What Law Schools Can Do about It' (2019) 148(1) *Daedalus* 75.

9 David Luban, 'Faculty Pro Bono and the Question of Identity' (1999) 1750 *Georgetown Law Faculty Publications and Other Works* 58.

10 Deborah L Rhode, *Pro Bono in Principle and in Practice: Public Service and the Professions* (Stanford University Press 2005).

11 Vanessa C Burbano, John Mamer and Jason Snyder, 'Pro Bono as a Human Capital Learning and Screening Mechanism: Evidence from Law Firms' (2018) 39(11) *Strategic Management Journal* 2899.

12 Robert Granfield, 'The Meaning of Pro Bono: Institutional Variations in Professional Obligations among Lawyers' (2007) 41(1) *Law & Society Review* 113, at 125.

13 Fiona Ryan, 'Voices from the Front Line: Exploring What Pro Bono Means to Lawyers in England and Wales?' (2021) 28(3) *International Journal of the Legal Profession* 265, at 271.

14 Ian Walden and Patrick Cahill, 'Skills Swap? Advising Technology Entrepreneurs in a Student Clinical Legal Education Programme' in Christopher Denvir (ed), *Modernising Legal Education* (Cambridge University Press 2020) 59.

15 In the CEE region, where legal studies are divided into bachelor's and master's programmes, legal clinics are traditionally offered in the latter.

external expectations. A desire to help others is also a frequently stated motivation among future lawyers. However, research indicates that this altruistic motivation often diminishes as students progress through their studies.[16] Live-client clinics have the potential to sustain or even enhance altruistic motivation.[17] But as previously mentioned, these practical courses are often introduced too late in the curriculum, by which time students' initial interest may have waned due to the competitive and outcome-driven culture in classrooms[18] or early work experience.[19]

Since doctrinal courses often overlook issues related to legal aid and access to justice, in 2021, the Faculty of Law at Comenius University Bratislava (CU Bratislava) introduced a new course, Legal Aid Studies (LAS).

The Faculty of Law at CU Bratislava was established in 1919 and is the oldest and largest law school in Slovakia. In 2023, it enrolled 2,339 students, representing nearly 42 per cent of all law students in the country. In the same year, the Faculty also hosted 63 visiting students, most of whom spent one or two semesters at the institution, primarily through the Erasmus+ Mobility Programme.[20]

The LAS is an elective course, taught in English, and offered to second- and third-year law students enrolled at CU (home students) as well as international exchange students. Since its introduction in 2021, the LAS course has been successfully completed by 114 students from almost 20 different countries. To foster internationalization, the course maintains a balanced number of Slovak and international students each year. It is delivered entirely in person, and students receive two European Credit Transfer and Accumulation System (ECTS) credits upon successful completion.[21] Assessment is based

---

[16] Kennon M Sheldon and Lawrence S Krieger, 'Does Legal Education Have Undermining Effects on Law Students? Evaluating Changes in Motivation, Values, and Well-Being' (2004) 22(2) *Behavioral Sciences & the Law* 261, at 281.

[17] Paul McKeown, 'Pro Bono: What's in It for Law Students? The Students' Perspective' (2017) 24(2) *International Journal of Clinical Legal Education*, 43, at 80; Femi O Ajagunna and Ifeoluwa Byron, 'Clinical Legal Education and Social Justice: Assessing the Impact on Law Students in a Law Clinic in Nigeria' (2024) 31(1) *International Journal of Clinical Legal Education* 44, at 77.

[18] Nancy Soonpaa, 'Stress in Law Students: A Comparative Study of First-Year, Second-Year and Third-Year Students' (2004) 36 *Connecticut Law Review* 353, at 367.

[19] Amy M Flynn, Yan Li and Beatriz Sanchez, 'Law School Stress: Moving from Narratives to Measurement' (2017) 56 *Washburn Law Journal* 259, at 262.

[20] Faculty of Law, CU Bratislava, Annual Report 2023, pp 19, 123 (in Slovak), www.flaw.uniba.sk/fileadmin/praf/O_fakulte/Dokumenty/Vyrocne_spravy/VS_2023/VS2023_I_Sprava_o_cinnosti.pdf

[21] The course is part of a bachelor's programme that lasts three years and requires the completion of 180 ECTS credits for graduation.

on a combination of a reflective paper, group presentation, peer feedback and engagement of students during lectures.

The course aims to cultivate social responsibility among future lawyers by deepening their understanding of the right to legal aid as a fundamental human right. Students explore the influence of the European Union and the Council of Europe on legal aid frameworks, compare national systems, assess their shortcomings and recognize the value of pro bono work for society, the legal profession and individual lawyers.

The aim of this chapter is to examine whether students who complete a doctrinal course focused on legal aid demonstrate higher awareness of access to justice issues and a greater interest in legal clinics and pro bono work. Essentially, this study seeks to highlight the importance of early exposure to legal aid concepts in fostering a commitment to public interest law among future lawyers.

To explore this, a pre-post survey design was employed to compare students' responses before and after completing the course. Descriptive statistical analysis was complemented by qualitative insights gathered from anonymous student feedback.

The next section examines student motivations for pursuing legal education, with a particular focus on gender differences and the impact of legal education on students' understanding of social justice. The third section outlines the methodology for data collection, followed by an interpretation of the results. The implications of these findings are discussed in the subsequent section, and the chapter concludes with a summary of the key insights and recommendations.

From altruism to prestige: the impact of legal education on students' motivation

Despite the negative reputation, the legal profession holds significant power in society. No other profession is as prominently represented across all three branches of government – not only in the judiciary but also in the executive and legislative branches.[22]

Future lawyers enter this profession, which carries significant social responsibility, for a variety of reasons, and sometimes with no clear rationale at all. These motivations are influenced by both intrinsic factors, such as self-confidence, and extrinsic factors, particularly the influence of family members, educators and friends.[23] Additionally, motivations are shaped

[22] Deborah L Rhode, *The Trouble with Lawyers* (Oxford University Press 2015) 46.

[23] David Bozin, Gabrielle Mortimer and Shuling Wang, 'Why Law? Examining the Factors That Influence the Decision to Undertake a Law Degree' (2024) 34(1) *Legal Education Review* 134, at 135.

by the prestige of the legal profession in a particular country, the costs associated with legal education and the difficulty of gaining admission to law programmes.

At the Faculty of Law, CU Bratislava, admission is open to all who have completed secondary education, and Slovak students are not required to pay fees as higher education is publicly funded. Naturally, motivations may differ in contexts where education is free and widely accessible.[24] Initial classroom conversations with students during LAS and Legal Skills and Abilities – a compulsory course I also teach – often reveal a familiar mix of recurring responses: 'I want to be rich and successful', 'I like to argue', 'I watched *Suits*' or 'My parents told me to'. Many simply struggle to articulate a clear motivation, while a few express a sincere desire to fight for justice and help those in need.

Research suggests that among those few who begin with altruistic motivations, these will dissipate during their studies. Sheldon and Krieger found that students tend to shift from intrinsic values, specifically moving away from community service ideals towards appearance and image values.[25] Similarly, Larcombe, Malkin and Nicholson discovered that non-altruistic reasons were more commonly cited by experienced students.[26]

Women generally demonstrate stronger altruistic motivations for volunteering activities,[27] and pro bono work.[28] Furthermore, women are more likely than men to enter law school with a desire to serve others.[29] Interestingly, their commitment in public interest law seems to decline more sharply than men's during their legal education.[30]

Why is it that rather than fostering an interest in legal aid, legal education combined with early work experience appears to produce the opposite effect? Could law school itself be a factor driving students to pursue a

---

24 In anticipation of demographically strong cohorts, beginning in the 2025/2026 academic year, applicants who did not take the final secondary school examination in history or social sciences, and in a foreign language, will be required to pass an entrance exam.

25 Sheldon and Krieger (n 16) 281.

26 Wendy Larcombe, Ian Malkin and Penelope Nicholson, 'Law Students' Motivations, Expectations and Levels of Psychological Distress: Evidence of Connections' (2012) 22(1–2) *Legal Education Review* 71, at 90.

27 Christopher J Einolf, 'Gender Differences in the Correlates of Volunteering and Charitable Giving' (2011) 40(6) *Nonprofit and Voluntary Sector Quarterly* 1092, at 1093.

28 Granfield (n 12) 128.

29 Deborah Schleef, 'That's a Good Question! Exploring Motivations for Law and Business School Choice' (2000) 73(3) *Sociology of Education* 155, at 160.

30 Lani Guinier, Michelle Fine and Jane Balin, 'Becoming Gentlemen: Women's Experiences at one Ivy League Law School' (1994) 143(1) *University of Pennsylvania Law Review* 1, at 4.

comfortable and prestigious life instead of a purposeful one?[31] The Socratic method, inadequate mentoring, curve-based grading and peer competition are frequently identified as significant stressors in legal education.[32] When compounded by the burden of student debt and a societal emphasis on wealth and prestige, it is unsurprising that the legal profession is openly known as unhappy,[33] unhealthy[34] and alcohol-dependent.[35]

Legal clinics offer an alternative to traditional legal education, typically characterized by lecture-based teaching and occasionally interspersed with direct questioning of students. Institutions worldwide are increasingly prioritizing experiential learning and CLE. For example, in Singapore, undergraduate law students are required to perform at least 20 hours of pro bono work as part of their degree requirement.[36] Similarly, the American Bar Association mandates all accredited law schools to include an experiential learning component in their curriculum, ensuring that each student completes at least one course involving simulation, clinical practice or field placement.[37]

However, in the Central and Eastern Europe (CEE) region, where legal clinics were first introduced in the 1990s,[38] the curriculum continues to prioritize doctrinal learning. CLE remains a marginal aspect of legal education, and due to the lack of regulation, it is possible for law schools to offer wide portfolios of courses titled 'clinical' that do not significantly differ from doctrinal courses.[39] As a result, only a small proportion of graduates have the opportunity to enrol in live-client clinics.

---

31 Krista Cronin, 'The Intentional Pursuit of Purpose: Nurturing Students' Authentic Motivation for Practicing Law' (2024) 28(18) *George Washington University Law School Public Law Research Paper* 159, at 161.

32 Flynn, Li and Sanchez (n 19) 262.

33 Patrick Schiltz, 'On Being a Happy, Healthy, and Ethical Member of an Unhappy, Unhealthy, and Unethical Profession' (1999) 52(4) *Vanderbilt Law Review* 871.

34 Katherine Young, 'Understanding the Social and Cognitive Process in Law School that Creates Unhealthy Lawyers' (2021) 89(6) *Fordham Law Review* 2575, at 2576.

35 Yair Listokin and Ray Noonan, 'Measuring Lawyer Well-Being Systematically: Evidence from the National Health Interview Survey' (2021) 18(1) *Journal of Empirical Legal Studies* 4, at 32.

36 Benjamin Ong, 'Community Legal Clinics and Clinical Legal Education in Singapore' (2024) 31(2) *International Journal of Clinical Legal Education* 70, at 71.

37 Standards and Rules of Procedure for Approval of Law Schools. Standard 303. Curriculum, www.americanbar.org/content/dam/aba/administrative/legal_education_and_admissions_to_the_bar/standards/2024-2025/2024-2025-standards-chapter-3.pdf

38 Maxim Tomoszek, 'The Growth of Legal Clinics in Europe: Faith and Hope, or Evidence and Hard Work?' (2014) 21(1) *International Journal of Clinical Legal Education* 93, at 95.

39 The Faculty of Law, CU Bratislava, offers over 20 courses with 'clinic' in the title, including the Mergers and Acquisitions Legal Clinic and the Cybersecurity Legal Clinic. However, only two – Student Legal Counsel and the NGOs Clinic – qualify as true live-client clinics.

Regardless of whether legal clinics are well established or newly introduced into law school curricula, they provide students with valuable hands-on experience in legal aid. However, between introductory training, client meetings, legal analysis, drafting and communicating with client, supervisor and teammates, little to no time is left to thoroughly explore the benefits of pro bono work or the challenges posed by the inaccessibility of legal services. In doctrinal courses, these critical topics are often overlooked entirely or only briefly mentioned. As a result, many students graduate without being exposed to the significant gaps in access to legal services. Even those who take part in live-client clinics may find that the emphasis is on the day-to-day live-client work rather than wider societal access to justice issues.

Methodology

The LAS course is one of nearly 30 courses offered to law students in the English language. Its primary objective is to foster a sense of social responsibility among future lawyers[40] and to develop students' legal writing, presentation and communication skills in an internationalized environment.[41]

The LAS course was first introduced in 2021 with a modest enrolment of just six students. By 2023, participation had increased sevenfold, reaching 42 students. Over the past four years, a total of 114 students have successfully completed the course. The course has also achieved a high level of internationalization, with 49 home students from Slovakia (43 per cent) and 65 foreign students (57 per cent) from nearly 20 different countries, including Georgia, Germany, Iran, Ireland, Japan, Moldova, Poland, Slovenia and Spain.

To evaluate changes in attitudes towards social justice and pro bono work, a pre-post survey design was utilized. The survey included an open-ended question asking students to identify the benefits of legal aid, along with two 5-point Likert scales: one measured attitudes towards pro bono work, legal clinics and general volunteering, while the other gathered self-reported data on altruistic activities, such as charitable donations and volunteering. Furthermore, additional variables such as gender and country of origin were collected. The pre-course survey also asked whether legal aid had been

[40] Over the past three years, the course has benefited from the expertise of American lawyer Wendell Goddard, who has served as a guest lecturer. Drawing on over 40 years of experience in advocacy, he has shared invaluable insights, particularly on the importance of pro bono work, during one of the seminars.

[41] For further learning outcomes, evaluation and other details about the LAS course, see Mária Havelková, 'Teaching about Legal Aid in an Internationalised Course' in Gabriela Pleschová and Agnes Simon (eds), *Internationalising Teaching in Higher Education* (Delft University of Technology).

covered in the participants' previous studies. Participants were informed that the survey was completely anonymous and voluntary and were encouraged to respond honestly without searching for answers.

Data were collected over two consecutive years, 2023 and 2024, during which 81 students completed the course, including 58 per cent international students and 42 per cent Slovak students. A pre-course survey was completed by 66 students (81 per cent of the class), while 37 students (46 per cent of the class) participated in the post-course survey. The respondent sample was representative of the overall class composition in terms of gender distribution and the ratio of domestic and international students. The pre-course survey was administered during the first class after a brief discussion on the concepts of legal aid, pro bono and CLE to ensure students understood the topics. The post-course survey was conducted three months later at the beginning of the penultimate class of the semester.

In addition to the small sample size and the limited two-year data collection period, the research faced several other limitations. The survey's optional and anonymous format prevented the matching of individual pre-post survey responses, making it impossible to track changes in attitudes at the individual level. Moreover, the majority of students were ESOL speakers, which may have led to misinterpretation of some survey questions. Social desirability bias (the tendency of respondents to answer in a way they believe is socially acceptable or expected) may have further influenced the results.[42] Finally, the focus on a single course at one institution limits the generalizability of the findings to other contexts or regions.

To assess whether the LAS course encourages interest in live-client legal clinics, graduate enrolment in such courses was analysed. Despite the fact that the Faculty of Law, CU Bratislava offers over 20 'clinical' courses, only two – Student Legal Counsel and the NGO Clinic – qualify as true live-client clinics based on their descriptions. A third course, the Street Law Programme, was included in the analysis due to its focus on teaching real clients and its alignment with legal aid objectives.

From 2021 to 2023, 29 home students completed the LAS course and were eligible to enrol in these three clinical courses. Enrolment data were retrieved from the university's information system. A key limitation of this analysis is the lack of data on retention rates, particularly given the faculty's high dropout rates. For instance, of the 626 students who began the programme in 2020, only 280 reached their final year in 2024.

Quantitative data from surveys and the university's information system were supplemented by qualitative data from anonymous feedback forms

42 Patricia Snell Herzog, *The Science of Generosity: Causes, Manifestations, and Consequences* (Palgrave Macmillan 2020) 3.

(course evaluations) completed by students at the end of the course. Over three years, 52 out of 108 (48 per cent) students submitted voluntary and anonymous course evaluations.

Results

'Unfortunately, we did not', responded one of the home students when asked if they had ever learned about the right to legal aid. Out of 66 respondents, 55 (83 per cent) stated that they had not learnt about legal aid. While 11 respondents (17 per cent) answered affirmatively, one third of them qualified their responses with terms such as 'kind of', 'a little bit' or 'it was only briefly mentioned'. Five Slovak students and six visiting students from Georgia, Portugal, Slovenia and Spain noted that legal aid was mentioned in civil, constitutional and administrative law courses.

When students were asked to name as many benefits of legal aid as they could think of without searching for answers, responses in the pre-course survey were brief and relatively vague. Most students provided only one example, with terms such as equality, justice, trust in legal system and the elimination of discrimination being frequently repeated. In contrast, the post-survey responses were more detailed, with the majority of students identifying several benefits, suggesting a notable shift in their ability to articulate the value of legal aid.

In addition to the reasons mentioned at the beginning, after completing the course, students reasoned that accessible legal aid helps narrow the gap between the wealthy and the poor, raises legal awareness in society and has a positive effect on physical and mental health. Furthermore, they recognized benefits not only for recipients of legal aid, but also for society, the legal profession and individual lawyers. One female Slovak student from the 2023 class stated that legal aid 'helps create trust in society, improves the reputation of lawyers, and assists people who cannot afford legal services and do not understand the law'.

The analysis of a 5-point Likert scale (strongly agree = 5) with 11 statements on social justice and pro bono attitudes[43] revealed that post-course responses indicated stronger agreement that pro bono work is a moral obligation of every lawyer (3.33 v. 3.46) and increased interest in legal clinics (3.70 v. 4.00). Students also shifted towards a more empathetic response to the statement 'A person who does not have the means to pay a lawyer should represent him or herself' (1.95 v. 1.68). Additionally, after completing the course, students were less likely to agree that sufficient opportunities for pro bono work exist during their studies (2.52 v. 2.38).

[43] See Appendix 1.

A contradictory trend was observed in one statement, where post-survey responses showed weaker agreement with 'Volunteering to help someone is very rewarding' (4.56 v. 4.41). However, upon closer examination, the 2023 cohort showed the expected increase in scores (4.63 v. 4.80), whereas a decrease was observed only in the 2024 cohort (4.46 v. 4.26). It could be argued that this decline is due to insufficient volunteering experience among the 2024 students. This interpretation is supported by data showing that, when comparing the two cohorts, the 2023 students reported greater involvement in volunteering activities for charitable, religious or nonprofit organizations (2.53 v. 1.93 in the pre-course survey and 2.90 v. 2.00 in the post-course survey).[44]

Despite the aforementioned trends showing support for the hypothesis that completing the course enhances students' pro bono motivations, none of these differences was statistically significant. The closest to statistical significance was the increase in interest to participate in clinical course (3.61 v. 4.40) among the 2023 cohort.

Observations of the class over several years indicate that its gender distribution aligns with current trends in higher education, where women represent nearly 60 per cent of all students in tertiary education across the EU.[45] This approximate two-to-one female-to-male ratio is also reflected in the survey data: the pre-course survey was completed by 45 women and 21 men, while the post-course survey included 27 women and 10 men.[46]

As previously established in studies on general volunteering and pro bono work among practising lawyers, women demonstrate stronger altruistic motivation and greater interest in pro bono[47] and volunteering.[48] Similar patterns were observed in this study's student sample.

As shown in Appendices 1 and 2, women consistently scored higher than men in both the pre- and post-course surveys on statements supporting pro bono work and volunteering. In the pre-course survey, women tended to agree more strongly than men with the statements 'Volunteering to help someone is very rewarding' (4.76 v. 4.14) and 'I feel at peace when I help others' (4.69 v. 4.29). Furthermore, women reported higher motivation to provide pro bono services (4.00 v. 3.67) in the future. The same pattern is observed in pre-course interest in legal clinics (3.80 v. 3.48). Interestingly, after

44 See Appendix 2.

45 Tertiary Education Statistics, Eurostat, ec.europa.eu/eurostat/statistics-explained/index.php?title=Tertiary_education_statistics

46 Two responses were excluded from the sample, as the students chose not to disclose their gender. No student selected the nonbinary option.

47 Granfield (n 12) 128.

48 Einolf (n 27) 1093.

the course, men's interest in legal clinics increased more strongly, resulting in exactly the same mean of 4.00 for both women and men.

Although student evaluations may be subject to various biases, they can still provide meaningful insight into students' perceptions of a course. This study analysed feedback to assess whether students valued the course content and whether it influenced their interest in pro bono work and legal aid. Utilizing a 5-point Likert scale,[49] where a strong agreement is represented by 1 and strong disagreement by 5, all respondents either strongly agreed (n=44) or agreed (n=8) with the following statement: 'By the end of the course, I developed a better understanding into the studied matter than I had at its beginning.' This statement received the third highest level of agreement among students, with a mean score of 1.15. The two statements that achieved even higher level of agreement were 'clearly communicated assessment criteria' (1.06) and 'teachers' willingness to communicate with students, advise them and answer their questions' (1.04). Conversely, students expressed the least agreement regarding the course's ability to foster their creativity, reflected in a mean score of 1.69 out of 5.

A total of 44 students provided further reflection in response to an open-ended question regarding what they valued most about the course. The most frequently mentioned aspect, highlighted by 50 per cent of respondents, was the supportive atmosphere and stress-free environment in the classroom. The second most prevalent theme, underscored by 25 per cent of students, was the course content itself. One participant from the 2023 cohort remarked: 'The course not only enhanced my knowledge in this area but also encouraged me in many ways.' Another student expressed a shift in perspective, stating: 'The topic itself is very important and I am glad to know new information and get a different perspective on the issue and practice it in the future because it is important. I even talked about it with lawyers in the law firm I work at.' Additionally, another student commented that: 'This course gave me a different perspective on what it means to be a true lawyer and how important is free legal aid.'

In the pre- and post-course surveys, students expressed a strong interest in enrolling in legal clinics for their future studies. Of the 29 home students who completed the LAS course between 2021 and 2023 and were eligible to enrol in one of the three live-client legal clinics offered at CU Bratislava, only three did so, resulting in a participation rate of approximately 10 per cent. While the figure may appear low, it is essential to consider the extensive number of mandatory courses, the growing trend of labelling doctrinal courses as clinics despite lacking practical components, and the high dropout rates among students.

[49] See Appendix 4.

The interest in the topic was further demonstrated by three students, one from each cohort of 2022, 2023 and 2024, who proactively selected their final theses to cover various aspects of the inaccessibility of legal services and legal aid.

Discussion

Although the findings of this study are not statistically significant, data collected over the past two years from the LAS course at Slovakia's largest law school reveal several notable trends. After completing the course, students exhibited more altruistic views and demonstrated an increased interest in participating in legal clinics and engaging in pro bono work. In anonymous feedback, several students emphasized the value of gaining new perspectives and feeling encouraged to address social justice issues. One student even reported being inspired to discuss these topics with practising lawyers at their workplace.

These findings suggest that incorporating greater emphasis on legal aid and pro bono work into the doctrinal curriculum for first- and second-year law students could help counteract the decline in altruistic motivation. Exposing students to the realities of unmet legal needs and the pivotal role that lawyers play in improving access to justice is crucial for fostering their awareness and sense of social responsibility. Supported by the survey findings, integrating this knowledge early in students' education can increase the likelihood of their participation in legal clinics and enhance the appreciation of pro bono work in their future professional practice.

Moreover, such curricular innovation serves as a vital bridge between doctrinal and clinical teaching, promoting a more holistic approach to legal education. However, it is imperative that this new doctrinal course avoids replicating traditional models characterized by conventional lecturing and high-pressure questioning. Instead, the course should embody the principles and values of CLE by prioritizing active student engagement and cultivating a supportive, stress-free learning environment. Ideally, such a doctrinal course should be integrated into the clinical programme and taught by a legal clinician.

Such innovations in curriculum design are particularly relevant in regions like CEE, where law schools have traditionally prioritized doctrinal teaching over practical, socially oriented legal education. The LAS course, with its strong European and global perspectives on the right to legal aid, is highly replicable and adaptable. Its comprehensive syllabus, enriched by diverse reading materials from international authors, offers a well-developed framework for integrating access-to-justice issues into the curriculum. This makes it an ideal model for other institutions seeking to ensure that students gain a comprehensive understanding of the legal profession's role in promoting equality and social justice.

The observed gender differences in this study, while unsurprising given prior research on volunteering and pro bono work among lawyers, are nonetheless intriguing and deserving of further investigation. Do women feel a stronger compulsion to agree with altruistic statements due to socialization that encourages them to meet societal expectations[50] and assist others?[51] Or do women genuinely care more for others, thereby making them more likely to pursue public interest law?[52] Alternatively, could the higher representation of women in this field stem from men perceiving it as insufficiently lucrative?[53] While these questions have been explored in other contexts, it is essential to examine them through the lens of women's contributions to improving access to legal services.

Notably, while women more often than men enter law school with a motivation to help others, the legal education experience tends to have a more pronounced diminishing effect on this interest.[54] However, it is important to note that these findings are primarily US-centric, and motivations to study law, particularly with a focus on gender differences, remain underexplored in the CEE region. For example, at CU Bratislava, where there is virtually no admissions process, education is state-funded, and dropout rates are high, the motivations to study law may differ significantly from those observed elsewhere.

Nevertheless, the revealed gender differences underscore the need for greater focus on gender considerations within law curricula and the promotion of supportive programmes tailored for female law students. Although many law schools worldwide are integrating gender dimensions into their curricula and research, numerous institutions, including all law schools in Slovakia, have not yet adequately addressed this important issue.

Conclusion

This chapter highlights critical shortcomings in the current approach to legal education, particularly law schools' failure to adequately engage students with the principles of social responsibility and public interest law. While CLE stands out as a notable exception by providing practical experience with pro bono work, it often comes too late in students' academic journeys.

50 Lisa Brewer, 'Gender Socialization and the Cultural Construction of Elder Caregivers' (2001) 15(3) *Journal of Aging Studies* 217, at 231–232.

51 Alice H Eagly, 'The His and Hers of Prosocial Behavior: An Examination of the Social Psychology of Gender' (2009) 64(8) *American Psychologist* 644, at 651.

52 Richard Abel, 'The Paradoxes of Pro Bono' (2010) 78(5) *Fordham Law Review* 2443, at 2447.

53 Ronit Dinovitzer and John Hagan, 'Hierarchical Structure and Gender Dissimilarity in American Legal Labor Markets' (2014) 92(3) *Social Forces* 929, at 947.

54 Guinier, Fine and Balin (n 30) 4.

Introducing a doctrinal course on legal aid early in students' studies could help address these challenges. The findings of this study suggest that exposure to legal aid concepts greatly enhances students' awareness of access to justice issues.

Feedback from students emphasized their appreciation for a supportive classroom environment characterized by interactivity, discussions, teamwork and a sense of involvement. This supports the argument that such a course should be taught by a legal clinician to maximize its impact. Unlike traditional law professors, clinicians are a different breed[55] and offer a unique perspective that prioritizes practical engagement and the real-world application of legal principles. Their involvement in the early stages of legal education can help preserve students' altruistic motivations and foster a commitment to helping others throughout their academic and professional lives.

In addition, this research opens up avenues for further exploration into gender dynamics within legal education. Understanding how motivations to pursue public interest law and pro bono work differ between male and female students could provide valuable insights for law schools. Such knowledge would enable institutions to better support students in pursuing legal careers that are both personally meaningful and socially beneficial.

Appendix 1: Summary of pre- and post-course survey results on pro bono attitudes (2023–2024)

	Pre-survey M (N=66)	**Post-survey M (N=37)**
Volunteering to help someone is very rewarding.	4.56	4.41
Helping people does more harm than good because they come to rely on others and not themselves.	2.03	1.97
Pro bono activity is a moral obligation of every lawyer.	3.33	3.46
I feel at peace with myself when I have helped others.	4.56	4.59
A person who does not have the means to pay a lawyer should represent himself or herself.	1.95	1.68
Pro bono activity of lawyers should not be mandatory; doctors and other professionals are also not required to work free of charge.	2.98	3.38
I am planning to accept pro bono cases in my future career.	3.89	3.92
I had good examples in my family about the importance of volunteering and helping others when I was growing up.	4.03	3.95

55 Jane Aiken and Stephen Wizner, 'Teaching and Doing: The Role of Law School Clinics in Enhancing Access to Justice' (2004) 303 *Georgetown Law Faculty Publications and Other Works* 997, at 999.

	Pre-survey M (N=66)	Post-survey M (N=37)
I have enough opportunities to do pro bono work during my studies.	2.52	2.38
If possible, I would like to select a practical course (such as Student Legal Counsel or NGO Clinic) to help people in material needs.	3.70	4.00
It is not an obligation of a state to pay for a lawyer for people without sufficient means to afford legal services.	2.09	1.97

Appendix 2: Summary of pre- and post-course survey results on volunteering engagement by year (2023–2024)

	Pre-survey M 2023 (N=38)	Pre-survey M 2024 (N=28)	Post-survey M 2023 (N=10)	Post-survey M 2024 (N=27)
I have made financial contributions to charitable, religious or nonprofit organizations.	2.53	2.57	2.50	2.26
I have given money to a stranger who needed it or asked me.	2.97	2.93	2.80	2.37
I have donated goods or clothes to a charity, religious or other nonprofit organization.	2.79	2.89	3.40	2.85
I have done volunteer work for a charity, religious or other nonprofit organization.	2.53	1.93	2.90	2.00

Appendix 3a: Summary of pre-course survey results on pro bono attitudes by gender (2023–2024)

Pre-course surveys 2023–2024	Women M (N=45)	Men M (N=21)
Volunteering to help someone is very rewarding.	4.76	4.14
Helping people does more harm than good because they come to rely on others and not themselves.	1.93	2.24
Pro bono activity is moral obligation of every lawyer.	3.42	3.14

Pre-course surveys 2023–2024	**Women M (N=45)**	**Men M (N=21)**
I feel at peace with myself when I have helped others.	4.69	4.29
A person who does not have the means to pay a lawyer should represent him or herself.	1.89	2.10
Pro bono activity of lawyers should not be mandatory, doctors and other professionals are also not required to work free of charge.	2.80	3.38
I am planning to accept pro bono cases in my future career.	4.00	3.67
I had good examples in my family about the importance of volunteering and helping others when I was growing up.	4.09	3.90
I have enough opportunities to do pro bono work during my studies.	2.40	2.76
If possible, I would like to select a practical course (such as Student Legal Counsel or NGO clinic) to help people in material needs.	3.80	3.48
It is not an obligation of a state to pay for a lawyer for people without sufficient means to afford legal services.	2.13	2.00

Appendix 3b: Summary of post-course survey results on pro bono attitudes by gender (2023–2024)

Post-course survey 2023–2024	**Women M (N=27)**	**Men M (N=10)**
Volunteering to help someone is very rewarding.	4.41	4.40
Helping people does more harm than good because they come to rely on others and not themselves.	1.96	2.00
Pro bono activity is moral obligation of every lawyer.	3.59	3.10
I feel at peace with myself when I have helped others.	4.63	4.50
A person who does not have the means to pay a lawyer should represent him or herself.	1.59	1.90
Pro bono activity of lawyers should not be mandatory, doctors and other professionals are also not required to work free of charge.	3.22	3.80
I am planning to accept pro bono cases in my future career.	4.04	3.60
I had good examples in my family about the importance of volunteering and helping others when I was growing up.	3.93	4.00
I have enough opportunities to do pro bono work during my studies.	2.19	2.90
If possible, I would like to select a practical course (such as Student Legal Counsel or NGO clinic) to help people in material needs.	4.00	4.00
It is not an obligation of a state to pay for a lawyer for people without sufficient means to afford legal services.	1.96	2.00

Appendix 4: Summary results of feedback surveys (2022–2024)

Feedback survey 2022–2024	**M (N=52)**
The teacher was willing to communicate with students, advise them and answer their questions.	1.04
The teacher clearly communicated assessment criteria for this course.	1.06
By the end of this course, I developed a better understanding into the studied matter than I had at its beginning.	1.15
There was an atmosphere which I found encouraging for my learning.	1.19
I felt part of a learning community.	1.22
I could easily access the learning materials and literature for this course.	1.35
This course has explored the issues in depth.	1.54
During the semester, my knowledge and skills were continuously tested using various methods.	1.58
This course has developed my teamwork skills.	1.63
This course has developed my creativity, which is an ability to produce new ideas and original solutions of problems based on acquired knowledge and skill.	1.69

References

Abel R, 'The Paradoxes of Pro Bono' (2010) 78(5) *Fordham Law Review* 2443

Aiken J and Wizner S, 'Teaching and Doing: The Role of Law School Clinics in Enhancing Access to Justice' (2004) 303 *Georgetown Law Faculty Publications and Other Works* 997

Ajagunna FO and Byron I, 'Clinical Legal Education and Social Justice: Assessing the Impact on Law Students in a Law Clinic in Nigeria' (2024) 31(1) *International Journal of Clinical Legal Education* 44

Atkinson R, 'A Social-Democratic Critique of Pro Bono Public Representation of the Poor: The Good as the Enemy of the Best' (2001) 9(1) *American University Journal of Gender, Social Policy & the Law* 129

Bozin D, Mortimer G and Wang S, 'Why Law? Examining the Factors That Influence the Decision to Undertake a Law Degree' (2024) 34(1) *Legal Education Review* 134

Brewer L, 'Gender Socialization and the Cultural Construction of Elder Caregivers' (2001) 15(3) *Journal of Aging Studies* 217

Burbano VC, Mamer J and Snyder J, 'Pro Bono as a Human Capital Learning and Screening Mechanism: Evidence from Law Firms' (2018) 39(11) *Strategic Management Journal* 2899

Cronin K, 'The Intentional Pursuit of Purpose: Nurturing Students' Authentic Motivation for Practicing Law' (2024) 28(18) *George Washington University Law School Public Law Research Paper* 159

Denvir C (ed), *Modernising Legal Education* (Cambridge University Press 2020)

Dinovitzer R and Hagan J, 'Hierarchical Structure and Gender Dissimilarity in American Legal Labor Markets' (2014) 92(3) *Social Forces* 929

Eagly AH, 'The His and Hers of Prosocial Behavior: An Examination of the Social Psychology of Gender' (2009) 64(8) *American Psychologist* 644

Einolf CJ, 'Gender Differences in the Correlates of Volunteering and Charitable Giving' (2011) 40(6) *Nonprofit and Voluntary Sector Quarterly* 1092

Eldred T and Schoenherr T, 'The Lawyer's Duty of Public Service: More Than Charity' (1994) 96(2) *West Virginia Law Review* 367

Flynn AM, Li Y and Sanchez B, 'Law School Stress: Moving from Narratives to Measurement' (2017) 56 *Washburn Law Journal* 259

Granfield R, 'The Meaning of Pro Bono: Institutional Variations in Professional Obligations among Lawyers' (2007) 41(1) *Law & Society Review* 113

Guinier L, Fine M and Balin J, 'Becoming Gentlemen: Women's Experiences at One Ivy League Law School' (1994) 143(1) *University of Pennsylvania Law Review* 1

Hadfield GK, 'More Markets, More Justice' (2019) 148(1) *Daedalus* 37

Herzog PS, *The Science of Generosity: Causes, Manifestations, and Consequences* (Palgrave Macmillan 2020)

Kennedy V, 'Pro Bono Legal Work: The Disconnect between Saying You'll Do It and Doing It' (2019) 26(3) *International Journal of Clinical Legal Education* 25

Larcombe W, Malkin I and Nicholson P, 'Law Students' Motivations, Expectations and Levels of Psychological Distress: Evidence of Connections' (2012) 22(1–2) *Legal Education Review* 71

Listokin Y and Noonan R, 'Measuring Lawyer Well-Being Systematically: Evidence from the National Health Interview Survey' (2021) 18(1) *Journal of Empirical Legal Studies* 4

Luban D, 'Faculty Pro Bono and the Question of Identity' (1999) 1750 *Georgetown Law Faculty Publications and Other Works* 58

McKeown P, 'Pro Bono: What's in It for Law Students? The Students' Perspective' (2017) 24(2) *International Journal of Clinical Legal Education* 43

Mijs JJB, 'The Paradox of Inequality: Income Inequality and Belief in Meritocracy Go Hand in Hand' (2021) 19(1) *Socio-Economic Review* 7

Ong B, 'Community Legal Clinics and Clinical Legal Education in Singapore' (2024) 31(2) *International Journal of Clinical Legal Education* 70

Perlman AM, 'The Public's Unmet Need for Legal Services & What Law Schools Can Do about It' (2019) 148(1) *Daedalus* 75

Pleschová G and Simon A (eds), *Internationalising Teaching in Higher Education* (Delft University of Technology 2022)

Rhode DL, *Pro Bono in Principle and in Practice: Public Service and the Professions* (Stanford University Press 2005)

Rhode DL, *The Trouble with Lawyers* (Oxford University Press 2015)

Ryan F, 'Voices from the Front Line: Exploring What Pro Bono Means to Lawyers in England and Wales?' (2021) 28(3) *International Journal of the Legal Profession* 265

Sandefur RL, 'Lawyers' Pro Bono Service and American-Style Civil Legal Assistance' (2007) 41(1) *Law & Society Review* 79

Schiltz P, 'On Being a Happy, Healthy, and Ethical Member of an Unhappy, Unhealthy, and Unethical Profession' (1999) 52(4) *Vanderbilt Law Review* 871

Schleef D, 'That's a Good Question! Exploring Motivations for Law and Business School Choice' (2000) 73(3) *Sociology of Education* 155

Sheldon KM and Krieger LS, 'Does Legal Education Have Undermining Effects on Law Students? Evaluating Changes in Motivation, Values, and Well-Being' (2004) 22(2) *Behavioral Sciences & the Law* 261

Soonpaa N, 'Stress in Law Students: A Comparative Study of First-Year, Second-Year and Third-Year Students' (2004) 36 *Connecticut Law Review* 353

Tomoszek M, 'The Growth of Legal Clinics in Europe: Faith and Hope, or Evidence and Hard Work?' (2014) 21(1) *International Journal of Clinical Legal Education* 93

Van Velthoven BCJ and Klein Haarhuis CM, 'Legal Aid and Legal Expenses Insurance, Complements or Substitutes? The Case of the Netherlands' (2011) 8(3) *Journal of Empirical Legal Studies* 587

Young K, 'Understanding the Social and Cognitive Process in Law School That Creates Unhealthy Lawyers' (2021) 89(6) *Fordham Law Review* 2575

5

The Competence Development Impact of the Legal Clinic Methodology in Hungarian Legal Education

Judit Tóth, Renáta Kálmán and Tamás Pongó

Introduction

This chapter summarizes what has changed in legal education in the 35 years since the constitutional reform that began in 1990, using the results of a survey in a country with a democratic deficit and fragmented rule of law.[1] In the absence of a transparent and independent professional evaluation of law schools by a professional organization (for example, a bar association, a judges' training organization or an academic law committee), we can only rely on statistics and our survey data. The training and outcome requirements are set, funded and evaluated by the Ministry responsible for tertiary education and are therefore *sui generis*: 'The educational autonomy of institutions is moderately low or low by the international standard ... which makes them highly dependent on government action.'[2] In view of this, the Bloom taxonomy[3] or its updated version in 2021 is not applicable to the Hungarian legal education system and could not have been intended

1 European Commission, '2024 Rule of Law Report on Hungary' (Brussels, 24 July 2024) SWD(2024) 817 final.

2 A Derényi, 'A tanítás és tanulás minőségének javítása az elmúlt 10 évben' in G Kováts and J Temesi (eds), *A magyar felsőoktatás egy évtizede 2008–2017* (Budapesti Corvinus Egyetem Nemzetközi Felsőoktatási Kutatások Központja 2018) 145.

3 BS Bloom et al, *Taxonomy of Educational Objectives: The Classification of Educational Goals, Vol Handbook I: Cognitive Domain* (David McKay Company 1956).

by this survey. Therefore, our aim is to respond to the adaptation to various challenges of legal education in Hungary, in contrast to other countries in the region, by presenting the obstacles and modest successes of legal clinic education in Hungary. This is also important because, apart from us, no one else has reported on legal clinical training in Hungary.

In short, the changes have been an increase in the number of educational institutions and the ratio of academic degrees among lecturers, the creation of mass student training[4] and the transfer of most universities to nongovernmental organizations (NGOs)[5] (church, corporate and foundation). The emphasis on competence development has only started in recent years in a rather formal way. The following have not changed: in the continental legal tradition, the state plays a dominant role in the content of training,[6] with a very high proportion of theoretical knowledge – the aim is to train generalists rather than lawyers specializing in particular areas of law; the teaching of national legal standards dominates rather than supranational law; teaching is almost exclusively frontal and only subsidiary to interactive, small-group and student-needs-based training; and there is a strong orientation towards examination performance.

Several disciplines are concerned with the learning habits of adults. These studies show that adults learn most effectively when they are confronted with real problems, followed by an exploration of options and then feedback on solutions.[7] Therefore, the success of the introduction of legal clinical training can also be an indicator of the effectiveness of adult/tertiary education.

This chapter examines the role of legal clinical training (and its specific methodology) in Hungarian legal education. Therefore, it is essential to briefly describe how legal education is provided in Hungary. Although legal education in Hungary has a long history and has undergone many changes over the centuries, there are still many problems in legal education that have long been unresolved. The most prominent of these difficulties is the theoretical orientation of legal education, which is significantly sustained by an unstable legal system that is growing in size and complexity, requiring a solid theoretical basis for its application. At the same time, law students and employers of graduated experts have for decades been calling for the need

---

4 EURYDICE, 'Hungary: Higher Education', https://eurydice.eacea.ec.europa.eu/national-education-systems/hungary/higher-education

5 Act CCIV of 2011 on National Higher Education, § 117/C (1).

6 Z Körtvélyesi, 'A magyar jogászképzés 2015-ben – A jogi karok helyzete', https://jog.tk.hu/uploads/files/35_Kortvelyesi_Zsolt.pdf

7 K O'Leary, 'Evaluating Clinical Law Teaching: Suggestions for Law Professors Who Have Never Used the Clinical Teaching Method' (2002) 29 *Northern Kentucky Law Review* 491, at 495.

to start acquiring the skills and knowledge needed to apply the law during their university years.

Therefore, this chapter deals with: (i) the scope of Hungarian legal education, in particular, the training and outcome requirements (TOR) set by the state for legal education; (ii) clinical legal education in Hungary; and (iii) the results of a survey conducted by the lead author among students enrolled in a legal clinical course, which examined whether the clinical legal methodology can develop the legal competences defined by the TOR.

Hungarian legal education

In Hungary, the beginning of university legal training dates back to 1667, which represents a long-lasting tradition of high-level theoretical education, with special attention to the needs of the state (education of officials, judges, prosecutors and public notaries). Such an educational tradition includes the text-bound interpretation of the law and a high degree of formalism, as well as historical and analytical approaches to law.[8] The Hungarian training system follows the continental model, in which the role of the state is decisive in terms of requirements, financing and appointments at universities.[9] Legal education has traditionally meant a five-year (ten-semester) single-cycle programme; thus, the law degree is considered as an MA degree. In the course of the training, law students must complete 300 ECTS credits, of which a total of 15 credits can be allocated to optional courses such as legal clinic. Even though the Bologna system set up two cycles of education for BA and MA programmes in 2006, this approach has been formally refused in Hungary. On 17 May 2003, at the Deans' meeting, the resistance was worded as follows: 'the two-cycle structure is alien to the function and peculiarity of legal education'.

In 2019, the Minister of Education uniformly defined the general TOR for students in tertiary education as follows:[10] acquisition of professional competencies.

Due to the new TOR, the process of adapting the curricula to the requirements has started. Due to the content-bound and discipline-oriented nature of the TOR, there are only a few general skills development opportunities for teachers and institutions, although this is a prominent area of employability:[11] 'In the coming decades, it is expected that employability

[8] J Tóth and R Kálmán, 'Legal Education at the Crossroads of Social Responsibility and the Development of Individual Competencies – Experience at the University of Szeged (Hungary)' (2021) 34(2) *Acta Iuris Stetinensis* 59, at 60.

[9] Z Nagy, *A jogi oktatás fejlődése és aktuális kérdései* (Pólay Elemér Alapítvány 2007) 68–69.

[10] Ministerial Decree of Human Resources No 3 of 11 February 2019 on Tertiary Professional Education's Output Competencies, art 8.

[11] Derényi (n 2) 136.

skills will be consciously integrated into the higher education system, and a network of links with employers will be established.'[12] Changes in employment have brought with them the need for interpersonal skills.[13] Institutions committed to employability are also trying to adapt their training programmes and curricula to achieve this goal, for example, by introducing more practical subjects, volunteering and new ways of organizing learning, such as project-based learning and group work.[14] The current Hungarian qualifications framework approaches the objectives from the output side, so it focuses on the expected learning outcomes.[15]

At the end of 2021, there was a major change in the TOR for all higher education vocational education and training, BA and MA programmes. Previously, the scope of the competencies to be acquired was regulated by law, but now the competent minister defines them in a publication (the ITM publication) and there is no reference, either explicitly or implicitly, to the fact that any organization of the legal profession had a say in this, or that the standards were developed in consultation or jointly.

The Hungarian qualifications framework consists of four elements: knowledge; skills; attitudes; and autonomy and responsibility. In defining these elements, the ITM publication moves from the general to the detailed. First, it defines the general characteristics and competencies describing the levels of qualification, then the characteristics of the levels of qualification attainable at each level of education (higher vocational education, BA and MA) and, finally, the specific competencies to be acquired in the different fields of study.

The first element is *knowledge*. Knowledge in the ITM publication means theoretical or textbook knowledge, the forms of organization of which are literacy and expertise.[16] For Master's programmes, it further specifies these characteristics – for instance, the general and specific features, correlations and terminology of the field belong to the knowledge element.[17] In the case of legal training, knowledge includes theoretical and practical knowledge of the legal profession, problem-solving methods, specific vocabulary, ethical standards and dilemmas.[18]

---

[12] K Czető et al, 'Helyzetfeltárás' in I Lukács and A Derényi (eds), *Kézikönyv a képzési programok tanulási eredményeken alapuló fejlesztéséhez, felülvizsgálatához* (Oktatási Hivatal 2017) 12.

[13] ibid 13.

[14] ibid 16.

[15] ibid 22.

[16] Ministry for Innovation and Technology, 'Training and Outcome Requirements for Higher Education Vocational Education and Training, Bachelor's and Master's Degrees and Training in Theology Applicable from the Academic Year 2022/23' 6.

[17] ibid 847.

[18] ibid 1477–1478.

Skills are motoric (manual dexterity, the use of methods, materials, tools and instruments) or cognitive (the use of logical, intuitive or creative thinking) skills manifested in action.[19] For a Master's degree, skills include: (i) the ability to analyse the different concepts that make up the knowledge base of a given discipline; (ii) the ability to identify professional problems using an interdisciplinary approach and to apply innovative methods to solve them; and (iii) the ability to research information effectively and to collaborate with other disciplines.[20] Law graduates are expected to have the skills to use legal terminology with confidence, articulate complex legal issues clearly, think critically, communicate and write professionally, see the point, formulate opinions, reason, put into practice what they have learned, research and apply alternative methods of resolution, and to work in a team.[21]

Attitude means a perceptive attitude towards something abstract or factual, and applies to learning, to work and to one's own actions. It has three components: emotion, thought and behaviour.[22] Attitudes in the Master's programme include: (i) a commitment to professional identity; (ii) the contribution of professional knowledge to the common good; and (iii) continuous professional development.[23] These are to a large extent related to legal culture and legal literacy, and it is doubtful to what extent they can be determined by cognitive, knowledge-transferring methods, since we are dealing here with interrelated elements of legal socialization. As the ITM publication states, sensitivity to professional and social problems can only be developed indirectly in the legal profession, through a commitment to legal aid and pro bono legal work, and openness to mediation.[24]

The final element of the qualifications framework is *autonomy and responsibility*, which '[e]xpresses the degree of autonomy and responsibility with which a person can carry out a given activity'.[25] Specifically in the field of law, the ability to work punctually and independently, to take responsibility for one's own actions or omissions, and for work done in the public interest, to value commitment, to strive to develop the values of the legal profession, and to take the initiative in professional and public affairs is highly emphasized.[26] This reflects a democratic culture based on respect for equal rights and equal opportunities, and on self-aware legal professionals who are able to control both themselves and their power. Such a culture

[19] ibid 6.

[20] ibid 847–848.

[21] ibid 1478–1480.

[22] ibid 6.

[23] ibid 848.

[24] ibid 1480–1481.

[25] ibid 6.

[26] ibid 1481.

can only be developed indirectly if the training institution itself also takes on democratic and social responsibility.

Even though we have mentioned only a few of the professional competencies to be acquired, the results of our research, which will be presented later on, illustrate that the legal clinic methodology can be a real help in mastering these. Of course, in addition to the legal clinic, it is essential to integrate other practical, experiential and alternative teaching methods such as argumentation classes, mock trials, alternative dispute resolution courses, document drafting seminars and so on into the curriculum. Students have different skills and attitudes, so they need to be offered a wide range of options to develop the competencies they are not satisfied with or to improve those they have already developed.

Although the ITM publication itself states that the orientation of the degree is highly theory-focused, still the acquisition and development of these competencies should be ensured by the higher education institutions during the legal training. According to the results of a survey of recent graduates in 2010, lawyers are satisfied with the quality of theoretical training (rated 4.51 on a scale of 1–5), but much less satisfied with the practicality of the training (rated 3.13).[27] As a result, they are also less satisfied with the applicability of the knowledge acquired (3.86) and with the development of general skills and competencies that can be used in the workplace (3.56).[28] According to the results of the law student motivation survey conducted by Helga Feith and Attila Badó, students believe that a practising lawyer should have the following skills: a sense of justice, good communication skills, logical thinking and empathy.[29] Consistent with our research findings, other researchers have also found that[30] the current Hungarian legal education system, dominated by traditional, frontal education and theoretical lectures, are not able to meet the expectations of law students, employers and legislators.

Although the majority of those who choose the legal profession will work in practice (public administration, judiciary and law firms), the ITM publication itself still states that the orientation of the training is highly theoretical, as 70–80 per cent of the credits are acquired in theoretical courses, even though we have seen earlier that some of the competencies expected from lawyers are practical and skill-based. This results in a 'vicious circle'. The gap between training and practice could be reduced by practice-oriented

---

27 M Fónai et al, 'A joghallgatók rekrutációja és a professzió-képének néhány eleme' (2014) 2 *Pro Futuro* 33–34.

28 ibid.

29 H Feith and A Badó, 'Magyar Joghallgatók motivációs vizsgálata' (2000) 4 *Jogelméleti Szemle*, https://jesz.ajk.elte.hu/bado4.html

30 Z Nagy and JZ Tóth, 'A jogi oktatás helyzete (Felmérés a jogi oktatást befolyásoló tényezőkről)' (2002) 4 *Jogelméleti Szemle*.

education, that is, by teaching and developing practical competencies. In other words, achieving employability as an objective, which is also an institutional mission, is very far from legal education. However, the ITM publication defines the educational aim of the course as 'the training of professionals with a legal education, who, having acquired the foundations of political and legal sciences and other social sciences related to legal activities … are capable of carrying out legal activities in the public and private sectors'.[31]

Legal clinic training in Hungary

Although there are many definitions of legal clinic methodology,[32] which is beyond the scope of this chapter, all definitions have in common the dual purpose of legal clinic training: educational and social justice. Nowadays, there is no hierarchical relationship between these two purposes, but they are complementary, both being of equal importance and mutually reinforcing. In terms of the historical development of the methodology, certain periods have given priority to the social purpose, for instance, in the 1960s and 1970s in the US, based on the social and societal situation of that time, due to the activist movements, such as the protests against the Vietnam War.[33] However, this was quickly followed by an era that emphasized the broader development of legal competencies and the role of practice-based legal education.[34]

Legal clinic training includes two types of training. On the one hand, professional skills training aims to develop the legal skills needed to practise law, so that students leave university with the necessary skills to become competent lawyers.[35] On the other hand, values training, whereby students understand and commit to professional values, includes professional responsibility and ethics.[36] Professional skills training involves: (1) communication with the client, including interviewing and counselling;

[31] Ministry for Innovation and Technology (n 16).

[32] See ENCLE, 'What Is CLE?', https://encle.org/about-us/what-is-cle; JR Wilson, 'Training for Justice: The Global Reach of Clinical Legal Education' (2004) 22(3) *Penn State International Law Review* 423; E Winkler, 'Clinical Legal Education: A Report on the Concept of Law Clinics', www.academia.edu/40214205/Clinical_Legal_Education_A_report_on_the_concept_of_law_clinics, 4.

[33] JC Dublin, 'Clinical Design for Social Justice Imperatives' (1998) 51 *SMU Law Review* 1465.

[34] MJ Kotkin, 'The Violence against Women Act Project: Teaching a New Generation of Public Interest Lawyers' (1996) 4 *Journal of Law and Policy* 446.

[35] F Bloch and M Menon, 'The Global Clinical Movement' in F Bloch (ed), *The Global Clinical Movement Educating Lawyers for Social Justice* (Oxford University Press 2011) 270.

[36] ibid.

(2) fact-finding and eliciting relevant facts; (3) legal research; (4) decision making regarding alternative solutions; (5) negotiation; (6) professional responsibility, including the application of ethical rules; (7) preparation for trial and remedy; and (8) other necessary activities, such as document drafting.[37] To what extent do the curricula of traditional law schools provide opportunities to acquire and develop these skills?

Although the social justice purpose of clinical legal education is as important as the educational, but this chapter focuses only on the educational purpose of legal clinic training. From an educational point of view, the legal clinic method helps to develop the skills, attitudes, professional responsibility and ethical sense expected of lawyers by having students engage in activities typical of the legal profession in an undergraduate course, either in simulated or live-client cases.

In Hungary, there are currently eight law faculties, four of which have a live-client legal clinic programme. This is disheartening if we consider, on the one hand, the history of Hungarian legal education, which has been continuously developing and evolving over the centuries, and, on the other hand, after the political transition, the fact that the spread of the legal clinic methodology in Europe was supported by several institutions (such as the Open Society Justice Initiative or the American Bar Association), either with financial resources or even with knowhow. This is unfortunate when compared to Poland, where all law faculties have some type of legal clinic, and even the Polish Legal Clinics Foundation has been able to develop a unified system based on common standards.[38] This situation can be explained by the dominance of theoretical education, the overload of teachers, the lack of a comprehensive strategic reform of legal education, and the specific factors that hinder the introduction and spread of the legal clinic methodology as an experiential learning method (see Table 5.1).

Since the legal clinic literature in Hungary is very scant, we mapped the legal clinic programmes through informal professional meetings with colleagues and the official curricula and websites of the available legal clinics.

Hungarian law faculties can be divided into three groups in terms of legal clinic programmes:

1. The first group includes those universities where no form of legal clinic training existed and still does not exist, such as Pázmány Péter Catholic University and Széchényi István University.

[37] G Grossman, 'Clinical Legal Education: History and Diagnosis' (1974) 26(2) *Journal of Legal Education* 187–188.

[38] Polish Legal Clinics Foundation, 'Standards of the Polish Legal Clinics', www.fupp.org.pl/en/legal-clinics/standards

Table 5.1: Hindering factors of clinical legal education in Hungary

Institutional factors	Economic sustainability	Students' attitude
Lack of proper implementation of the legal clinic methodology in the curriculum[a]	Lack of financial support	Passivity of students' participation in education
University lecturers must learn a whole new methodology	The desired split of funding: more than 60 per cent of clinics' budget draws on university funds; 26 per cent is sponsored by foundations and private entities[b]	Lack of a tradition of pro bono activities in Hungary
Teaching load of a nonclinical lecturer is the same as that of a legal clinic lecturer. To resolve this, there are two solutions: (i) an hourly allowance for legal clinic lecturers, as their workload is more significant than for traditional courses; and (ii) an income supplement[c]	Legal clinics with a strong track record have been forced to close due to financial difficulties – for example, the legal clinic of Maastricht University in the Netherlands[d]	
lack of recognition of the clinicians' work[e]		
Lack of liability and professional insurance[f]		
Lack of Hungarian-language materials (textbooks, casebooks, etc.) dealing with the methodology of the legal clinic[g]		

[a] R Uitz and E Polgári, 'Clinical Legal Education at Central European University, Budapest: A Small Project with Big Ambitions in a Supportive Institution' in A Alemanno and L Khadar (eds), *Reinventing Legal Education: How Clinical Education is Reforming the Teaching and Practice of Law in Europe* (Cambridge University Press 2018) 242.

[b] C Bartoli, *Legal Clinics in Europe: For a Commitment of Higher Education in Social Justice*' (Diritto & Questioni Pubbliche 2016) 49.

[c] A Asbóth et al, 'Jogklinika kézikönyv – ELTE ÁJK', https://jogaszkepzes.kormany.hu/admin/download/6/54/32000/Jogklinika%20kezikonyv.pdf, 66.

[d] Bartoli (n 40) 95.

[e] R Dunn and P McKeown, 'The European Network of Clinical Legal Education: The Spring Workshop 2015' (2015) 22(3) *International Journal of Clinical Legal Education* 17.

[f] Tóth (n 40).

[g] ibid.

2. The second group consists of universities where a legal clinic, including street law activities, has been or is in operation periodically. The University of Debrecen and Károli Gáspár University of the Reformed Church in Hungary belong to this group.[39]
3. The third and final category includes those where a live-client legal clinic is part of the legal education as an optional course for ECTS credits, such as the University of Pécs (PTE), Eötvös Loránd University (ELTE, Budapest), the University of Miskolc (ME) and the University of Szeged (SZTE).[40]

The legal clinic programmes of Hungarian universities are a good example of the fact that no one has adopted a uniform method of operation, so the legal clinics that are currently operating, and are dealing with the real cases of real clients, have many features in common, although they differ in many elements.

ELTE has a longer history of legal clinic training, being the first law school in Hungary to establish a legal clinic programme in the late 1990s. Since then, many university initiatives have died out, for all the reasons we have already mentioned. However, one particularly successful programme is the legal clinic programme with the BAGázs Public Benefit Association, which has been operating since 2014, through which students actively contribute to solving the legal difficulties of people living in Roma settlements. So far, around 100 law students have participated in the programme, solving 80–100 cases a year with the help of their mentors.[41] In addition to providing legal advice, the students are helping to break the debt trap and promote the social integration of Roma. As an example of the usefulness of the programme, the legal clinic project was awarded the SozialMarie Prize in 2016.[42]

Another successful programme of the ELTE Faculty of Law is the Streetlawyer Legal Clinic, established in cooperation with the Streetlawyer Association. This optional course has been available since 2016. The Association's streetlawyers, and since 2016 also ELTE law students, are involved in helping people who are homeless or living in housing poverty and enforcing their rights. Both programmes aim to get more students involved in social rights and to give them an insight into how segregated groups in society live and what legal and nonlegal (housing, health, social

---

39 The reasons for the closure of law clinics are mainly lack of financial resources and legal clinic lecturers leaving academia.

40 J Tóth, 'Legal Clinic as a Promising Alternative Instrument in Hungary' (2017) 4 *Jogelméleti Szemle* 150, at 153.

41 BAGázs, 'Jogklinika', https://bagazs.org/jogklinika/

42 ELTE ÁJK, 'SozialMarie díjat kapott a BAGázs jogklinika projektje', www.ajk.elte.hu/content/sozialmarie-dijat-kapott-a-bagazs-jogklinika-projektje.t.2564

and so on) problems they face in their daily lives. This provides students with a complex picture of the structure of society, which they would not be able to understand in a primarily theoretical university course.

Over the years, the ME Law School[43] has hosted a legal clinic in several different formations. Initially, it took the form of street law, and in 2016 a separate unit, the Legal Advice and Legal Clinic Centre, was established, which manages the administration of the legal clinic programme. In addition to its administrative tasks, the Centre also supervises and evaluates student work. Clients can access the Legal Clinic by post or online via the Centre's website. In the latter case, in addition to the contact details, the client must also provide a brief description of the case or legal problem. The admissibility of cases is decided by the President and the Secretary of the Centre. Cases where legal representation is mandatory or where there are tight deadlines are not taken on by the Legal Clinic; except for these, a wide range of cases are brought to the programme, from the fields of labour law, family law or neighbour disputes.

PTE (University of Pécs) has been offering legal clinic as an optional course since 2013. The course consists of an introductory semester (Legal Clinic I), during which students will expand their theoretical knowledge and receive skills development. During the course, students will learn about the characteristics of legal clinic activities, participate in case simulations, draft documents and study ethical rules. In addition, they will meet external mentors (judges, attorneys, legal advisors and so on) who will advise them on how to solve a case professionally and in their future careers. If the students like the course, they can apply to Legal Clinic II, which is more practice-oriented. Law students can choose to join the Campus Legal Aid Clinic programme, which has been operating in Pécs since 2015, or to learn about the operations of the partner institutions of the Faculty of Law of the University of Pécs. The latter offers the opportunity to participate in hearings at the organizations cooperating with the legal clinic, such as the Pécs Regional Court or the Pécs Regional Court of Appeal, to work on a case together, or to participate in the prosecution complaint days of the Baranya County Chief Prosecution Office or the Pécs District Prosecution Office, and to learn about the tasks performed by prosecutors. They can see the daily work of a legal professional in practice. In addition to gaining professional experience, this is also a good way for students to find out which legal professions they should follow or avoid. Students who choose to participate in the Campus Legal Aid Clinic (CLAC) will advise Hungarian

[43] Authors have information about the University of Miskolc's legal clinic programme from an interview with Dr Edina Vinnai (former head of the legal clinic programme). The authors would like to thank Edina Vinnai for her help.

and foreign students on real cases, while their work is supervised by a mentor (a lecturer, attorney or judge). The students work in groups of three to solve the cases and send their expert opinion to the client in writing, after consultation with the mentor. CLAC is unique in the country in the sense that no other organization deals with the legal problems of foreign students. According to their annual report published in 2022,[44] they resolved 312 cases between 2016 and 2021. Their cases cover many areas of law, such as criminal law, civil law and labour law. By providing legal advice to foreign students, they also develop students' professional foreign language skills, which are nowadays almost indispensable for recent law graduates.

The legal clinic at the University of Szeged is the only programme that has been operating without interruption since its establishment in 2005. Students can choose the course over three semesters,[45] which build on each other (Legal Clinics I, II and III). The difference between the three courses is that the first one (Legal Clinic I) requires students to attend a three-day training to learn 'the methods, communication and ethical framework of legal advice'.[46] Introductory training is no longer provided in Legal Clinics II and III, as those who continue their work in the legal clinic already have the necessary theoretical background. After the theoretical training, the students spend 30 hours of legal consultation at organizations that have a cooperation agreement with the legal clinic, such as the Csongrád County Association of the Blind and Visually Impaired, the Fatima House Foundation and the National Autism Association. A special feature of the training in Szeged is that the students visit the partners in person, so clients can talk about their problems and ask questions in a safe and familiar environment. After meeting with the clients, the students work out a solution for the case in question, which is discussed with a tutor teacher and, after his or her approval, they meet the client again to present the outcome.

The latest available statistics of the programme concerning the number and type of cases, the nature of the legal assistance provided and so on date back to 2017. According to the data, between 2005 and 2017, 750 clients received legal assistance, and 700 cases were dealt with, most of which were social, discrimination and housing cases.[47] In 20 years, at least 1,000 clients (including NGOs and individuals) have received pro bono legal assistance in 1,200 cases.[48] In the majority of cases, students provided legal advice and

44 Campus Legal Aid Clinic, 'Annual Report', https://international.pte.hu/annual-report-campus-legal-aid-clinic

45 University of Szeged, 'Introduction and Aims of the Legal Clinic', http://www.juris.u-szeged.hu/oktatas/jogklinika-bemutatasa/jogklinika-bemutatasa

46 J Tóth, *Kézikönyv a jogklinikai képzéshez* (Iurisperitus Kiadó 2017) 25.

47 Tóth and Kálmán (n 8) 68–69.

48 The authors' own calculations based on the LC Statistical Register.

wrote appeals and official letters. A few years ago, the legal clinic in Szeged also started a legal awareness-raising activity and organized roundtable discussions for partner organizations on various legal topics, including copyright, data protection and public interest work. Students also deliver presentations to members of partner organizations on requested topics such as consumer protection and equal treatment. In addition to providing legal assistance to clients, the legal clinic's awareness-raising activities also contribute to the 'dissemination' of legal knowledge.

The aforementioned legal clinics have different clientele and profiles, as PTE mainly provides legal assistance to Hungarian and foreign students at the university, ELTE to people living in housing poverty and the Roma minority, while SZTE mainly provides legal advice to NGOs and their members, who are mostly disabled. The structure of the courses is similar in that each faculty has a theoretical, introductory course followed by practical training, but the content and length of these courses differ. Overall, however, all programmes aim to test students' theoretical knowledge in real cases, to strengthen solidarity with people in need of advice, and to provide theoretical and practical training in ethical rules.

In recent years, there has also been a tendency in Hungary to try to bring together legal clinic programmes, for example, by organizing meetings for coordinators and producing newsletters, so stakeholders are trying to institutionalize the legal clinic network. The legal clinic in Szeged has created the Legal Clinic Newsletter, in which it publishes online short articles on issues relating to methodology and legal clinic models abroad. We can see that Hungary is trying to catch up with the American and Polish models, but there is still a long way to go before the legal clinic as an educational methodology receives the same wide recognition as in those countries.[49]

Research results

The research was based on the hypothesis that legal clinic training is suitable for the development of specific legal skills. Among the authors, Renáta Kálmán surveyed the impact of the legal clinic on legal competencies. The survey was sent to the heads of the live-client legal clinic programmes currently operating in the country (ELTE, ME, PTE and SZTE) to forward to their current and former legal clinic students. Completion of the survey was done on the Google Drive platform. Approximately two months[50] were allowed to complete the survey, and it was completed on a voluntary,

[49] R Kálmán, *A jogklinikai módszertan – A jogklinika szerepe Magyarország és az Egyesült Államok jogászképzésében* (Iurisperitus Kiadó 2023) 108.

[50] The survey was completed between 15 November 2019 and 20 January 2020.

anonymous, self-reporting basis. A total of 78 students from the four law faculties completed the form. Through this, it is possible to get an idea of the opinions of students who have completed a live-client legal clinic course in the country. Given that the legal clinics of the aforementioned law faculties have had an unpredictable presence because the project money runs out, and some of the legal clinic teachers have even left academia over the years, we have no data on how many students have completed the course in the four law schools in recent years or even decades.

The survey included simple closed, open-ended, free-choice closed and demographic questions. It addressed three major themes: (a) student motivation; (b) the range of legal competencies that could be acquired through the course concerning the educational objective of the legal clinic (some of which will be analysed in detail) and the achievement of the social objective; and (c) collected general demographic data on the respondents. For some questions, the respondent could self-report whether he or she had a particular skill (for example, problem-solving skills) prior to the legal clinic course or whether the skill had improved as a result of the legal clinic experience.

Although there is no intention to analyse issues related to student motivation, it is worth briefly mentioning the reasons that led students to enrol on the course. The survey's first question was a free-choice closed question exploring students' motives for motivation. The nature of the question allowed respondents to tick more than one answer. Almost 80 per cent (63 students) of the students enrolled in the course in order to test their theoretical legal knowledge in practice, while 73 per cent (57 students) enrolled to acquire the skills needed for a career in law (for example, communication with clients). In third place, the social purpose of the legal clinic training also appeared as a motivating factor, as nearly 49 per cent (38 persons) of the respondents enrolled (also) to assist the needy members of society (for example, people living in poverty). The responses make it clear that the primary motivation of students was to acquire and develop the legal competencies required by the state rules, as the theoretical nature of the education that dominates legal training makes it difficult to meet these needs.

The survey, within the range of legal competencies that can be acquired by a legal clinic, focused first on the basics of legal ethics. The issue of ethical standards has been undergoing significant changes in recent times. As a result of the explosion in innovation that is still taking place – for example, the spread of artificial intelligence – new ethical problems are emerging alongside classical ethical rules. Hence, today's law students must also be prepared for the ethical challenges of the times, as the development of various algorithms and artificial intelligence will affect law and therefore social relations. In this context, the survey included two closed questions: first, whether the respondent was aware of the rules of legal ethics prior to the legal clinic

Figure 5.1: Prior to the legal clinic course, were you familiar with the basics of legal ethics?

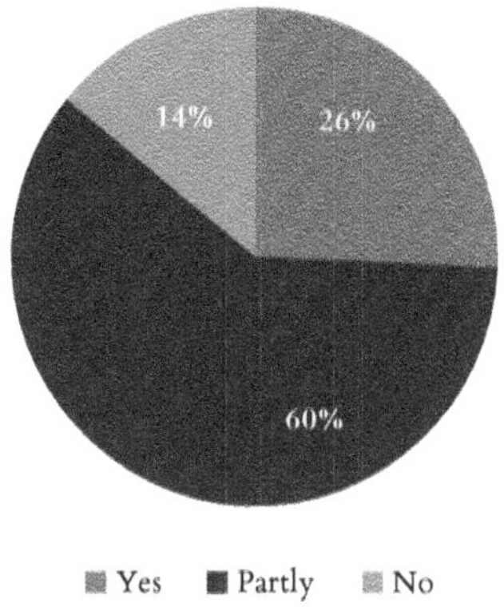

course; and, second, whether this knowledge had been developed through the legal clinic experience.

The questionnaire was originally completed in Hungarian, so Figures 5.1 to 5.4 are the authors' translations of the research results, which are identical to the original.

Nearly 14 per cent of respondents (11 students) did not know all of the rules of legal ethics before the legal clinic, while nearly 90 per cent said that their knowledge had improved or partially improved as a result of their legal clinic experience (see Figures 5.1 and 5.2). This may be because knowledge of the rules themselves often proves insufficient when faced with an ethical dilemma. There is often a very thin line between ethical and unethical behaviour – just think of confidentiality. There may also be a case where the legal clinic is approached by the opposing party as well, in which case students need to know how to deal with the conflict of interest between the parties.

Regarding problem-solving skills, respondents had to answer a similar set of questions. First, it was explored whether the students had good problem-solving skills before the legal clinic. Second, the extent to which these had improved after their participation in the legal clinic programme. In response to the first question, almost 63 per cent of students (49 students) said that they had developed these skills before the course, while 34.6 per cent (27 students) said they had partially developed them, and only 2.6 per cent (2 students) said they had no such skills. Concerning the second question, nearly 68 per cent (53 students) said they had developed this skill, while 24.4 per cent (19 students) partially developed it and only the remaining 7.7 per cent (6 students) said they had not developed this skill at all. Overall, we can see that nearly 92 per cent of the respondents reported

Figure 5.2: Did the course strengthen your legal ethics?

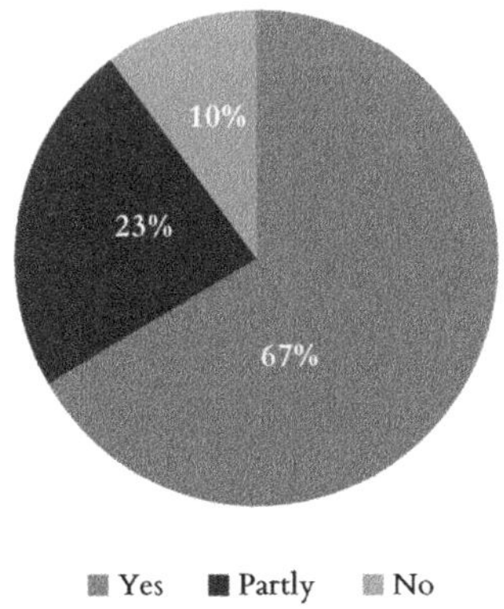

some improvement in their problem-solving skills. The following question may be asked: if nearly 63 per cent of the students already had advanced problem-solving skills before the legal clinic course, why did 68 per cent of the students believe that their legal clinic experience had taken their problem-solving skills to a higher level? One explanation is that problem-solving skills consist of several factors, namely identifying and analysing the problem, developing alternative solution strategies, developing and implementing a 'plan of action', and being ready to amend the 'plan of action' if new information or ideas arise.[51] Thus, some of the preceding factors may have occurred in the course of working with their clients, and students may have experienced what it is like when a new, previously unknown fact arises during the procedure, which changes their previous plans in a major way, requiring them to adapt quickly. In the reasoning accompanying the question, some explained that they had learned to look at a problem from different angles so that they could develop several alternative solutions for their client. Others pointed out that although they thought they had developed problem-solving skills, it was during their legal clinic cases when they realized that legal problems required a completely different approach and they needed to be more precise and targeted. In addition, clients' problems are rarely exclusively legal in nature; they often have more complex, multidisciplinary problems, such as housing issues, difficulties in accessing social assistance and mental health problems. Providing assistance in such cases is particularly difficult for law students, as it is not common

[51] F Zoll and B Namyslowska-Gabrysiak, 'The Methodology of Clinical Teaching of Law' in D Lomowski (ed), *The Legal Clinic, The Idea, Organization, Methodology* (CH Beck 2005) 192.

for students to get to know professionals from other fields, such as social workers and mental health professionals.

Several questions addressed professional communication skills; however, due to space constraints, this chapter only analyses one. A total of 92 per cent (72 students) of respondents felt that they had developed or partially developed this skill. The question shown in Figure 5.3 was accompanied by an open-ended question where students reasoned their answers. The reasons given included the need to use legal terminology, the need to explain legal terms clearly and understandably to laypeople, and the development of confidence, as respondents felt that since participating in the legal clinic programme they were able to communicate more easily with both professionals and lay people. Finally, the reasons highlighted the improvement of written communication due to the preparation of submissions and correspondence with the different authorities. As for professional communication, most legal clinic courses already include situational exercises in their introductory theoretical training, where students can practise how to communicate with clients without anything being at stake while being instructed by legal clinic lecturers. Professional communication includes oral and written communication with lawyers, public institutions and nonlaw-educated people. In all cases, students must be able to tailor their communication to their partner, so that when advising a nonlawyer client, they must explain everything clearly and understandably, avoiding legal jargon.

In the area of insight and fact finding, nearly 86 per cent (67 students) of students considered that they had improved as a result of their experience at the legal clinic. Clients often do not give the full details of the case or even provide unnecessary information that is irrelevant to the case. The students' task is to fill in the gaps by finding relevant facts. The question was accompanied by an open-ended question so that the respondents could

Figure 5.3: Has the course improved your professional communication skills?

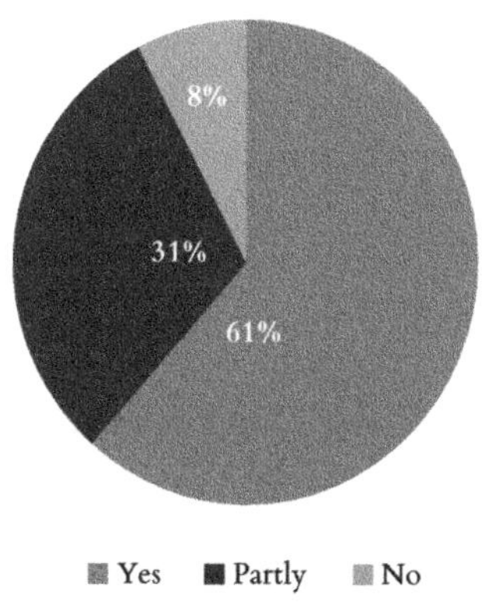

reason their answers. Many respondents highlighted that they had learned to outline facts so that they could 'filter the useful facts from the complaints' and guide the discussion to get relevant answers that might be useful later in developing a solution. Fact finding is a complex process that involves the investigation, organization and evaluation of facts. A casebook study or an analysis of a judicial decision can be a great help in developing this skill, but they lack the human element, which, according to the respondents, is often a complicating factor.

This leads to the *legal mindset*, which is a divisive issue among lawyers. Some see law as a science and, as such, consider it inconceivable to incorporate practical knowledge into legal education. Others argue that law is a practical profession and that if education focuses only on doctrines, lawyers who are ill-adapted to the demands of the profession will graduate from university. A longstanding concern of the profession is the issue of integrated education, where theory and practice are combined, while interchangeability between subjects is ensured. According to Zsolt Nagy, 'siloed' subjects give the impression that there is no link between the disciplines, whereas practice shows the opposite.[52] Because of the diversity of professional views, the research also sought to find out whether students believed that their theoretical knowledge had improved their legal mindset by applying it in their counselling sessions. More than 92 per cent of respondents (72 students) thought that it had improved, as they often had to advise on complex cases, covering several areas of law, while also testing a number of their legal skills. Legal mindset as a competence is not mentioned in the ITM publication as a standalone competence, but it is essential for all professional competencies in the legal profession.

As regards professional responsibility, the question asked whether the respondents felt that their ability to bear professional responsibility had improved (see Figure 5.4).

Only 9 per cent of students (seven students) considered that they had not developed this skill at all. In terms of professional responsibility, the majority of respondents stressed that they were now really comforted with the trust their clients place in them and their advice, and the impact this has on the lives of others. With the legal clinic being the only or even the last place for most clients to turn to, students felt that they had to be the best they could be in cases, making up for years or decades of experience of lawyers. Others emphasized the importance of pro bono work, and some even responded that, as practising lawyers, they would definitely include free legal assistance in their professional work.

These figures and statistics confirm the authors' hypothesis that the legal clinic course clearly supports the acquisition and development of specific

[52] Z Nagy, cited in Kálmán (n 49) 151.

Figure 5.4: Has your professional responsibility developed as a result of your work at the legal clinic?

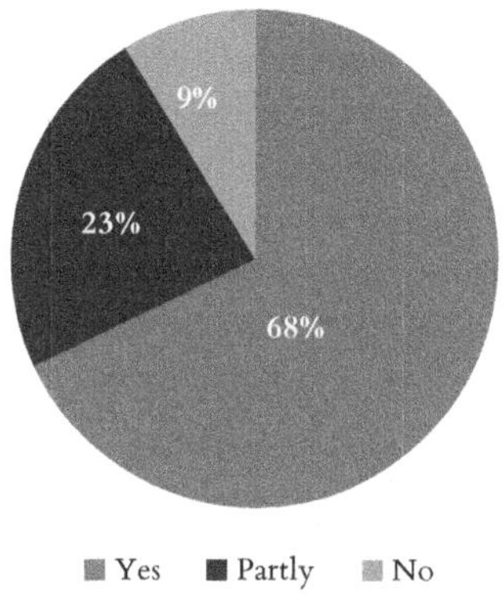

legal competencies. There are some competencies that respondents self-reported to have developed before their legal clinic experience, such as problem solving, yet in a real-life legal setting, these skills have been further improved. In terms of professional responsibility, 91 per cent of students thought that working in a legal clinic had a big impact on this competence. Although the ITM publication groups competencies into four separate sets, the responses suggest that these sets often intersect. The importance of commitment to pro bono work was also mentioned by many in the context of professional responsibility, even though the legislators mention voluntary legal aid as one of their attitudes. This illustrates that it is not possible to rigidly separate competencies and, therefore, it is difficult to assess each skill, knowledge and attitude independently. By assisting live clients with real cases, students need to have the communication and insight skills to identify the legal problem and the relevant facts of the case when meeting the client. In order to apply their problem-solving skills in practice, they need to have a level of knowledge of the facts and details of the case that allows them to develop alternative solutions and to work out a 'plan of action'. Furthermore, students are expected to be empathetic yet confident. For instance, they should not rush the client while telling their story just because they have an agenda, but at the same time, they should occasionally guide the conversation because clients may tell stories that are irrelevant to the case. These competencies are therefore complementary and mutually reinforcing of each other in practice. The role of case solving in a seminar or a moot court course in legal education is indisputable, but the simulated cases lack spontaneity, stakes and the human element. In many cases, the respondents explained that they had to be flexible, the client might not show up for the second appointment or they might bring documents that had 'destroyed' the students' previous work.

Conclusion

The predominance of theoretical, doctrinal training in legal education in Hungary is still emphasized today, and this is reinforced by the legislative background itself. The ITM publication on TOR defines legal training as a highly theoretical degree programme, where 70–80 per cent of the credits earned must be from theoretical courses. This is highly ambivalent in a helping profession where employers have been demanding for decades that law students be better prepared for practice. It may be contended that the demand represented by future employers does not adequately correspond with the supply represented by law students.

The survey on student motivation confirmed that students choose the legal clinic course primarily to test their theoretical knowledge in practice and to acquire the skills necessary for a career in law. However, the transition to practice-based education is hampered by several factors, such as the attitude of the trainers, the content of the courses, and the applied teaching methods.[53] Nevertheless, it is welcomed that there are efforts in all Hungarian law faculties to introduce practice-oriented courses such as the legal clinic. A total of 95 per cent of the respondents of the survey recommend participation in legal clinics to their fellow students. The reasons included not only learning and developing certain legal skills, but also exploring social problems, stepping out of their comfort zone, building relationships, experiencing real legal work and handling complex cases. Professional training integrated into the legal clinic courses includes, for example, communication with clients, fact finding, problem solving and professional responsibility. The results of the survey confirmed the hypothesis that the legal clinic methodology can develop specific legal skills and attitudes. Given the fact that students are providing assistance in live cases, they use a range of skills such as communication, problem solving, professional responsibility and legal ethics in a complex way. The human factor and spontaneity, in turn, force students to be flexible, but at the same time decisive and empathetic.

Not only are students and clients the beneficiaries of the legal clinic programme, but so are the attorneys, because students are reducing their pro bono legal workload. Moreover, legal clinics also strengthen the social and societal role of universities by helping local communities and marginalized groups access justice.

A number of changes are needed for the widespread use of legal clinics in Hungary. First and foremost, the hindering factors described in this

[53] R. Kálmán, 'A jogklinika, mint alternatív oktatási módszertan?!' (2019) 14 *Miskolci Jogi Szemle* 68–93.

chapter need to be overcome. Second, it is important to implement international legal clinic best practices. Also, further research on domestic legal clinic experience should be conducted and law schools should consider adopting the Hungarian legal clinic model developed by the lead author.[54]

At the same time, the research also indicates that without the feedback, and financial and professional support of market, advocacy, employer and civil society organizations, legal clinical training alone cannot achieve the necessary turnaround to adapt legal education to the new global legal challenges. Even battleships are slow to turn, even if the wind or the direction of the waves has changed. True, Hungary has no seaside.

References

Asbóth A et al, 'Jogklinika kézikönyv – ELTE ÁJK', https://jogaszkepzes.kormany.hu/admin/download/6/54/32000/Jogklinika%20kezikonyv.pdf

Bagázs Legal Clinic, https://bagazs.org/jogklinika/

Bartoli C, *Legal Clinics in Europe: For a Commitment of Higher Education in Social Justice*' (Diritto & Questioni Pubbliche 2016)

Bloch F and Menon NRM, 'The Global Clinical Movement' in F Bloch (ed), *The Global Clinical Movement Educating Lawyers for Social Justice* (Oxford University Press)

Bloom BS, Engelhart MD, Furst EJ, Hill WH and Krathwohl DR, *Taxonomy of Educational Objectives: The Classification of Educational Goals. Vol. Handbook I: Cognitive Domain* (David McKay Company 1956)

Campus Legal Aid Clinic, 'Annual Report', https://international.pte.hu/annual-report-campus-legal-aid-clinic

Czető K, Lénárd S, Lukács I and Tókos K, 'Helyzetfeltárás' in I Lukács and A Derényi (eds), *Kézikönyv a képzési programmeok tanulási eredményeken alapuló fejlesztéséhez, felülvizsgálatához* (Oktatási Hivatal 2017)

Derényi A, 'A tanítás és tanulás minőségének javítása az elmúlt 10 évben' in G Kováts and J Temesi (eds), *A magyar felsőoktatás egy évtizede 2008–2017* (Budapesti Corvinus Egyetem Nemzetközi Felsőoktatási Kutatások Központja 2018)

Dublin JC, 'Clinical Design for Social Justice Imperatives' (1998) 51 *SMU Law Review* 1461

Dunn R and McKeown P, 'The European Network of Clinical Legal Education: The Spring Workshop 2015' (2015) 22(3) *International Journal of Clinical Legal Education* 312

ENCLE (European Network for Clinical Legal Education), 'What Is CLE', https://encle.org/about-us/what-is-cle

[54] Kálmán (n 49).

European Commission, 2024 *Rule of Law Report on Hungary* (Brussels, 24 July 2024) SWD(2024) 817 final, https://commission.europa.eu/document/download/e90ed74c-7ae1-4bfb-8b6e-829008bd2cc6_en?filename=40_1_58071_coun_chap_hungary_en.pdf

EURYDICE, 'National Education Systems: Hungary – Higher Education', https://eurydice.eacea.ec.europa.eu/national-education-systems/hungary/higher-education

Feith H and Badó A, 'Magyar Joghallgatók motivációs vizsgálata' (2000) 4 *Jogelméleti Szemle*, https://jesz.ajk.elte.hu/bado4.html

Fónai M, Barta A, Gyüre A and Csilla-Pénzes F, 'A joghallgatók rekrutációja és a professzió-képének néhány eleme' (2014) 2 *Pro Futuro* 11

Grossman G, 'Clinical Legal Education: History and Diagnosis' (1974) 26(2) *Journal of Legal Education* 162

ITM, 'Training and Outcome Requirements for Higher Education Vocational Education and Training, Bachelor's and Master's Degrees and Training in Theology Applicable from the Academic Year 2022/23', https://cdn.kormany.hu/uploads/document/4/4b/4bf/4bf9f81a4c9fce6f09222294d1f6e2aedb010ad4.pdf

Kálmán R, 'A jogklinika, mint alternatív oktatási módszertan?!' (2019) 14 *Miskolci Jogi Szemle* 68

Kálmán R, *A jogklinikai módszertan – A jogklinika szerepe Magyarország és az Egyesült Államok jogászképzésében* (Iurisperitus Kiadó 2023)

Körtvélyesi Z, 'A magyar jogászképzés 2015-ben – A jogi karok helyzete', https://jog.tk.hu/uploads/files/35_Kortvelyesi_Zsolt.pdf

Kotkin MJ, 'The Violence against Women Act Project: Teaching A New Generation of Public Interest Lawyers' (1996) 4 *Journal of Law and Policy* 435

Ministerial Decree of Human Resources No 3 of 11 February 2019 on Tertiary Professional Education's Output Competencies

Nagy Z, *A jogi oktatás fejlődése és aktuális kérdései* (Pólay Elemér Alapítvány 2007)

Nagy Z and Tóth JZ, 'A jogi oktatás helyzete (Felmérés a jogi oktatást befolyásoló tényezőkről)' (2002) 4 *Jogelméleti Szemle*

O'Leary K, 'Evaluating Clinical Law Teaching: Suggestions for Law Professors Who Have Never Used the Clinical Teaching Method' (2002) 29 *Northern Kentucky Law Review* 491

Polish Legal Clinics Foundation, 'Standards of the Polish Legal Clinics', www.fupp.org.pl/en/legal-clinics/standards

SozialMarie Award for the BAGázs Legal Clinic Project, www.ajk.elte.hu/content/sozialmarie-dijat-kapott-a-bagazs-jogklinika-projektje.t.2564

Tóth J, *Kézikönyv a jogklinikai képzéshez* (Iurisperitus Kiadó 2017)

Tóth J, 'Legal Clinic as a Promising Alternative Instrument in Hungary' (2017) 4 *Jogelméleti Szemle* 143

Tóth J and Kálmán R, 'Legal Education at the Crossroads of Social Responsibility and the Development of Individual Competencies: Experience at the University of Szeged (Hungary)' (2021) 34(2) *Acta Iuris Stetinensis* 59

Uitz R and Polgári E, 'Clinical Legal Education at Central European University, Budapest: A Small Project with Big Ambitions in a Supportive Institution' in A Alemanno and L Khadar (eds), *Reinventing Legal Education: How Clinical Education is Reforming the Teaching and Practice of Law in Europe* (Cambridge University Press 2018)

University of Pécs Faculty of Law, 'Legal Clinic', https://ajk.pte.hu/hu/hallgatoknak/jogklinika/hallgatoknak

University of Szeged, 'Introduction and Aims of the Legal Clinic', http://www.juris.u-szeged.hu/oktatas/jogklinika-bemutatasa/jogklinika-bemutatasa

Wilson RJ, 'Training for Justice: The Global Reach of Clinical Legal Education' (2004) 22(3) *Penn State International Law Review* 421

Winkler E, 'Clinical Legal Education: A Report on the Concept of Law Clinic', www.academia.edu/40214205/Clinical_Legal_Education_A_report_on_the_concept_of_law_clinics

Zoll F and Namyslowska-Gabrysiak B, 'Chapter Five: The Methodology of Clinical Teaching of Law' in D Lomowski (ed), *The Legal Clinic, The Idea, Organisation, Methodology* (CH Beck 2005)

6

Student Zeal as the Pillar of Sustainable Clinical Programmes in Croatia

Juraj Brozović

Introduction

I vividly remember my third year of law studies when the assistant of the Department of Criminal Law (now its Head) invited me to join our newly established clinical programme. Since we had collaborated academically in the field of medical law a year earlier, as a newly appointed academic mentor and supervisor, she invited me to lead a new specialized group of students offering free legal advice to patients. Excited by the opportunity of getting a chance to apply the law to real-life cases and engage in pro bono work, I accepted the offer without realizing how this would affect my career. Later that year, I became one of two student administrators responsible for everyday management of the Law Clinic. I believe the main reason why I got 'chronically infected' with the clinical idea is the specific organization of the Law Clinic which – dramatically unlike everything I had faced up to that point in my studies – strongly encouraged independent work and student initiative. The lack of a strict hierarchy made us co-creators of the clinical programme.[1] When I later became an academic supervisor and assistant

[1] There have been some recent changes in the clinical programme at my university. I have no intention of criticizing the current reform, as it has already been done elsewhere (see A Uzelac, 'The Peculiar Case of Zagreb Law Clinic' in J Giddens (ed), *Global Clinical Legal Education* (Routledge 2025), 156–182, at 164–165). Instead, I intend to focus on why I believe the initial model turned out to be successful. The programmes change, but the results and the ideas stay, as long as there is someone to remember.

managing director and saw that same fire in my students' eyes, I realized how truly transformative clinical experience had been for everyone involved.

Now with over a decade of clinical experience behind me, I have found a second family in the global clinical community, particularly the European Network for Clinical Legal Education (ENCLE). By exchanging ideas and experience at its conferences, I learn and grow both personally and professionally. Celebrating its anniversary, I decided to share with the clinical community the Croatian experience with live-client programmes where student enthusiasm fuelled their success and sustainability. This chapter starts by presenting a brief history of the development of clinical legal education in Croatia. Afterwards, based on a special questionnaire I sent out to partner law clinics,[2] I compare the basic characteristics of Norwegian student-driven legal aid clinics that were used as a role model in Croatia, while highlighting and comparing the level of student involvement in their organization. Finally, I pinpoint three distinctive features of student-driven models and, after that, address common challenges, as well as criticisms and doubts surrounding this model.

'Can I speak to the doctor, please?': introducing the clinical concept to Croatian law faculties

The development of clinical legal education (CLE) in Croatia could be best described as a 'Big Bang' event. When you read about CLE in Croatia, you usually focus on the era from 2009 to 2010 onwards, as though nothing existed before then. The traditional law faculty curricula seem to have overshadowed the individual implementation of ideas of experiential learning. However, even before an official introduction of the clinical concept at Croatian law faculties, one could find traces of clinical methods.

For instance, the University of Zagreb had for decades run externship programmes which would send students to observe court hearings and analyse court files within seminars, without ever calling it a 'clinical' course.[3] Furthermore, as early as the 1990s, the University of Rijeka had students

[2] I am thankful to Jacob Anker Eide (Juss-Buss); Oda Bernett Lilleskare Lu (Jussformidlingen); Åsne Solberg (JURK); Lucia Radić, Karla Pavlović and their colleagues (Split); Zvonimir Jelinić (Osijek); Dejan Bodul (Rijeka); and Elena (Shaghayegh) Deliran (Amsterdam) for answering my questionnaire. I could not have written this chapter without their focused answers and inspiring work.

[3] A Uzelac and J Brozović, Increasing Employability of Law Graduates by Introducing Live-Client Clinics: The Experience of Law Clinic in Zagreb' in B Djuričin, M Kostić Mandić and A Uzelac (eds), *A Guidebook on Best Practices in Running Live Client Clinics for the Academic and Non-academic Community* (Pravni fakultet Univerziteta Crne Gore 2023), 11–24, at 6–7.

analysing and discussing hypothetical cases in the presence of practitioners, naming such practical courses 'law clinics'. Some of these students in the early 2000s informally started assisting authorized nongovernmental organizations (NGOs) in legal aid provision, but it has not remained a permanent feature of the programme.[4] Simultaneously, at the University of Osijek, there were more concrete attempts to establish live-client clinical initiatives. Unfortunately, such early project-based clinical programmes ended up being a mere drop in the bucket. Having been based on the external funding and the enthusiasm of several young scholars, they could not really offer the continuity which is needed to sustain such projects in the long run. Unfortunately, once external project funds ran out, the interest in developing and maintaining live-client clinical programmes faded.[5]

The strongest push into that direction was actually given years later by the first Legal Aid Act of 2008, which introduced live-client law clinics as providers of so-called primary legal aid within the newly established legal aid scheme.[6] If they registered with the Ministry of Justice, legal aid clinics were authorized to provide simple information and legal advice to citizens, whereas representation in court proceedings was reserved for attorneys only. This kind of legislative push coincided with the need to implement the Bologna system at the final year of master's level studies in Croatian law faculties. Consequently, several universities started establishing live-client legal aid clinics as a semi-mandatory part of the curriculum of the fifth year.[7] Effectively, however, only the Law Clinic Zagreb started its live-client work in 2010, while others engaged more actively a couple of years later.

The path to success was rocky at the beginning. Although some forms of clinical legal education had already existed, the notion of a 'clinic' was simply too exotic for most citizens. The best illustration of peculiarity of the clinical concept is the situation at the Law Clinic Zagreb in 2011 when one client asked the Group for the Protection of Patients' Rights where she could leave her mucus for tuberculosis inspection. Confused by her request,

---

4 D Akšamović and P Genty, An Examination of the Challenges, Successes and Setbacks for Clinical Legal Education and Eastern Europe' (2014) 20(1) *International Journal of Clinical Legal Education* 427, at 431–432.

5 B Preložnjak, 'Clinical Legal Education in Croatia: From Providing Legal Assistance to the Poor to Practical Education of Students' (2013) 19 *International Journal of Clinical Legal Education* 373, at 374.

6 Z Jelinić and A Koch, 'Elucidation of the Concept of a Law Clinic as a Prerequisite for Developing the Standards for Law Clinics in Europe' (2020) 7(2) *Asian Journal of Legal Education* 127.

7 Preložnjak (n 5) 373–374; A Uzelac, The Peculiar Case of Zagreb Law Clinic' in Giddings (n 1) 156–182, at 158. It is semi-mandatory, because students can opt for externship practice or moot courts instead; see Uzelac and Brozović (n 3) 11.

we explained that we provided legal and not medical advice, which only resulted in her response: 'OK, you are lawyers. Can I talk to the doctor now?' It indeed took a while until the clinical concept was accepted by the general public.

The efforts to be present in the media eventually paid off and clients started to realize the great value of students' clinical work. The timing could not have been better, because the effects of the financial crisis of 2008 went on much longer in Croatia than in the rest of the Europe (or the world), which increased the need for legal assistance. Simultaneously, the first legal aid framework failed to adequately respond to the needs of the citizens. Despite these malfunctions – or perhaps exactly because of them – law clinics managed to fill the void in legal aid system caused by insufficient funding.[8] Instead of relying on state funding like NGOs did, they relied on student and academic volunteering. This made the issue of insufficient funding less relevant, although it did not remove it entirely.[9]

For the Law Clinic Zagreb, such a void materialized in the considerable influx of new cases. After having only one case in the first semester and about 60 in the second, the numbers started rising dramatically. In the years when the outreach projects began, the numbers rose to 2,500 new cases per year, later stabilizing at an annual rate of around 1,500 cases. Recent statistics have shown that the Law Clinic Zagreb assisted more than 15,000 clients in the 13 years of its work.[10] The annual influx of cases at other universities is approximately three or four times lower, which can primarily be interpreted as a consequence of the smaller size of these programmes and the challenging regional disparities.[11] Today, legal aid clinics cover about 10 per cent of all cases of primary legal aid, and in recent years their numbers have been growing, which is the opposite trend compared to the NGOs.[12] Overall, they seem to be a success story. To everyone involved, this is not a surprise, but a consequence of a careful consideration of clinical role models which were the source of inspiration.

---

[8] Z Jelinić and K Knol Radoja, 'Analiza hrvatskoga sustava besplatne pravne pomoći u građanskim stvarima u svjetlu dosadašnje prakse europskoga suda za ljudska prava' (2014) 30(2) *Pravni vjesnik* 185, at 206–207; J Brozović, 'Transformation of the Croatian Legal Aid System: From Normative to Functional Insufficiency' in A Uzelac and CH van Rhee (eds), *Transformation of Civil Justice: Unity and Diversity* (Springer 2019), 274–276.

[9] For Zagreb, see B Preložnjak and J Brozović, 'The Financial Challenges of Clinical Legal Education: An Example from a Zagreb Law Clinic' (2016) 23(4) *International Journal of Clinical Legal Education* 136, at 156–160.

[10] Uzelac (n 7) 161.

[11] Akšamović and Genty (n 4) 431–432.

[12] Ministry of Justice, *Report on Legal Aid in 2023* [*Izvješće o ostvarivanju prava na besplatnu pravnu pomoć i utrošku sredstava u 2023*] (2024), https://sabor.hr/sites/default/files/uploads/sabor/2024-11-29/093802/IZVJ_BESPLATNA_PRAVNA_POMOC_2023.pdf, 10.

Sources of inspiration and student involvement in Croatian clinical legal education

The northern (Norwegian) inspiration

The first functioning live-client legal aid clinic at the University of Zagreb was founded in line with the Norwegian law clinic Juss-Buss as a source of inspiration, attracted by 'the idea that students need to enjoy broad autonomy, participate in all strategic and organisational decisions and be independent in their work as much as possible'.[13] Juss-Buss was the oldest and most active clinic that had started its work in 1971, as a student movement in the 1970s, which was later followed by other universities in other major cities.[14] The answers to my questionnaire revealed interesting key features of such student-driven clinical programmes.[15]

Juss-Buss provides legal aid in the areas which are not covered by the official legal aid scheme, thus specializing in the areas of prison and debt law, labour and social law, tenancy and fraud law, and immigration law. It also engages in policy work and street law. Juss-Buss describes its organization as a 'flat structure', meaning that all student workers have an equal vote in all matters regarding the operation of the clinic – from everyday management to supervision, case work, budget and other important questions. A student managing director (*leder*) and students, specifically chosen in the plenary session, carry out interviews to enrol new students each semester. When enrolled, the training of new students is carried out by last year's students, thus allowing the transfer of knowhow through the generations. New students do not work on the case alone straight away, but are supervised by senior students first three weeks of their work. Each case is distributed

13 Uzelac (n 7) 159.

14 O Halvorsen Rønning, 'Legal Aid in Norway' in O Halvorsen Rønning and O Hammerslev (eds), *Outsourcing Legal Aid in the Nordic Welfare States* (Springer International Publishing 2018) 15–42, at 32.

15 Not all law clinics from Norway responded to my questionnaire. There are more programmes in Norway and neighbouring Sweden which employ similar methods (I Schoultz, 'Legal Aid in Sweden' in Halvorsen Rønning and Hammerslev (n 14) 43–76, at 68), so the list provided in this chapter is not exhaustive. Many of them have been shortly described in recent edited publications (see M Langford, D Uehara and TL Waerstad, 'Clinical Legal Education in Norway' in Giddings (n 1). It seems that nowadays, there are new programmes in Northwestern Europe that also try to give students a more prominent role. The most notable is the new CLE programme of University of Amsterdam, where students get to team up and to deal with systemic issues and policy work, with broader social influence. However, when compared to the Norwegian programmes described earlier, students do not enjoy the same degree of autonomy, as they are enrolled, managed and supervised by professors, postdoctoral researchers and practitioners. This is why they are not more extensively described in this chapter.

to the specialized group that is formally in charge of the case and shares responsibility for the provided advice. While there is a space for individual work – as individual students contact or interview the client – each case is thoroughly discussed and evaluated during weekly meetings by all students. The meeting is directed by the student managing director who is chosen on an annual basis during a plenary session. Students perform their work completely independently. Only one professor is available to assist students when they encounter difficult questions, but without influencing the final result.

Throughout the years, we learned and came across similar programmes in Norway. Juss-Buss is by no means the only student-driven legal aid clinic. In fact, in Norway, student law clinics provide legal aid in 17,000 cases, constituting a good use of public money.[16]

Jussformidlingen, founded at the University of Bergen, is another student-driven legal aid initiative with a 'flat structure'. The organization is comparable to Juss-Buss, with a similar case focus and specialization, but with a slightly more complex structure. It too has weekly general meetings where students jointly discuss which cases to take on and how to resolve them, with equal voting rights for each student. However, they have a special steering board (*faggruppe*) that consists of a union representative, student leader (*leder*) and four former experienced clinical students who continue their work in the clinic for an extra semester to pass knowledge to new generations and to guide their everyday work. They are elected to these positions by other students. Some of these steering board members are in charge of coordinating public relations (PR) activities, legal aid and policy work.

While individual students prepare the first draft, everything is first supervised by two other students and then discussed in a meeting with seven other students and a lawyer employed by the University, all of whom share responsibility for the final outcome. More simple general advice can be given on the spot, but students are encouraged to consult others before providing any assistance to clients. Students elect a student committee that oversees interviewing and enrolling new students. After new students start their clinical work, they have an intense one-week training, carried out by former clinicians, and they are also assigned to a supervisor who helps them during their first weeks. Although a qualified lawyer, paid and hired by the University, serves as a daily leader, this position has an advisory rather than decisive role. Lawyers are especially important in advising the students on their caseloads, which are generally monitored and controlled by students.

JURK – Legal Counselling for Women (*Juridisk rådgivning for kvinner*) – is a specialized independent organization that is mostly run by students who

[16] Halvorsen Rønning (n 14) 33.

deal with different areas of law, such as tenancy law, immigration, labour and social security law, anti-discrimination law, debt collection law, privacy and family law. It also focuses on street law and policy work. It consists of 24 students, managed and coordinated by the managing director and legal advisor, who are qualified lawyers. While there are similarities in task division and casework, especially in terms of weekly general meetings, there is a stronger influence from the qualified lawyers when compared to the previous two clinics. In JURK, the qualified lawyers not only provide guidance to students but also help them to manage their everyday work and take care of financial management. Still, student groups decide on their own whether to take on a specific case or not, and how to distribute cases among different case workers. Other activities are also shared between the qualified lawyers and students. The appointed students and managing director enrol new students and take care of their training.

The southern (Croatian) implementation

When the Law Clinic Zagreb was starting in 2010, it was obvious that the transplantation of the Norwegian concept may turn into an irritation, which could jeopardize the successful integration of law clinics in the legal aid system. The structure of the clinical programme thus had to balance quality experiential learning goals with expectations of clients and other legal professionals that provide legal services.[17] The idea of students providing legal aid on their own seemed too ambitious, so some form of soft (horizontal) hierarchy had to be implemented. A balance was found in a well-thought-out concept pursuant to which students and teaching staff share the responsibilities for strategic and everyday management of the clinic.[18]

Students are organized into groups, focusing on different types of vulnerable clients (asylums seekers and aliens, victims of discrimination, victims and witnesses of crime, workers, patients, children and overindebted citizens). Students interview the clients individually and make a group decision on whether to accept a new case or not, taking into consideration not only the case type and specialization, but also the social relevance and educational value for students.[19] Although individual case workers do the research and prepare first drafts, the group discusses each case and shares the responsibility for the information and advice provided.

---

17 There were intense pressures from the Bar, later even (unsuccessfully) challenging the constitutionality of the new legal aid legislation. See Jelinić and Koch (n 6).

18 Uzelac (n 7) 158–159.

19 ibid 161.

To ensure consistency and quality, each group has one or more student mentors who are experienced students managing the activities of the group, taking responsibility for the training of new students and ensuring the preliminary supervision of the advice provided. The most experienced students are elected as student administrators who coordinate the work of groups and monitor the case flow at the everyday level, distribute the cases to groups and individual case workers, and also take part in general training of the new generation and communicate with managing teaching staff. There are special independent student groups which are in charge of PR activities and editing the official clinical bulletin. Student mentors and student administrators carry out interviews to enrol new students twice a year, with only minimal guidance from the managing teaching staff.[20]

Generally speaking, the role of managing teaching staff is modest. They carry out general training for each successive generation of students and provide guidance (how to distribute cases, when to reject the case, ethical duties and so on), but they do not directly influence the legal aid provided.[21]

The final level of supervision, after student mentors and the group have prepared the draft, is carried out by individual (assistant) professors and practitioners serving as academic and external mentors. Student mentors and administrators join the managing teaching staff and academic and external mentors in the special management board (*Malo vijeće*), which makes the most important strategic decisions in the clinic and also monitors the case flow on general meetings once or twice per semester. Additional management tasks, such as management of different projects and reporting, are divided between the managing directors and student administrators. This division of tasks is carried out in dialogue, instead of just enforcing a simple hierarchy.[22] A similar approach was later implemented by other Croatian universities,[23] albeit with their own unique features reflected in the answers to my questionnaire.

The Law Clinic at the University of Split followed the Zagreb example quite closely and gave students a decisive role in basically all everyday operations, only occasionally supported by teaching staff as and when the need arose. Students specialize in four areas of law (civil law, labour law, administrative law and enforcement law) and each group has a student

20 ibid 158–159; Uzelac and Brozović (n 3) 12–13.

21 Uzelac and Brozović (n 3) 25–26.

22 ibid 12–13; Uzelac (n 7) 160–161.

23 S Aras Kramar and B Preložnjak, 'Clinical Legal Education and Importance of Cooperation with Non-governmental Sector, State Bodies and Entities' in Djuričin, Kostić Mandić and Uzelac (n 3) 268–269.

mentor, an experienced clinical student. After an interview with the client, which is jointly conducted by all students in the group, usually one student takes charge of the case, whereas more complex cases are resolved in teams. These cases are thoroughly discussed in groups and supervised first by a student mentor and student administrator, and then by managing directors, who are law professors. There are two student administrators who coordinate the work of the groups, decide on the intake of new cases, help student mentors to distribute the cases to individual case workers and monitor the case flow. Student administrators and student mentors also jointly interview new students wishing to enrol in the clinical course. The training of new students is provided by the managing directors, who organize a general training programme, while knowhow regarding individual work is presented by student administrators and student mentors. External mentors and practitioners are sometimes employed to do specialized training.

A similar structure, but with slightly more involvement from the teaching staff, exists at the University of Osijek. In their law clinic, students also work in groups, but they are not specialized, as they mostly work on different cases in the field of civil law. Students interview clients, sometimes in the presence of external mentors (practitioners). Students draft general legal information and legal opinions. All types of legal advice are first supervised by student mentors, then by experienced clinical students, and later by the managing director (professor) or external mentors. There is one student coordinator who takes care of the equal distribution of cases and monitors the case flow. In the event of any doubts as to whether to accept a case, the managing director plays a decisive role. Training is conducted by the managing director, who also decides who will be enrolled in the work of the clinic. The relatively smaller size of the programme makes the law clinic in Osijek resemble a smaller law office.

The University of Rijeka restarted its live-client clinical programme in 2021. While its law clinic has followed the examples of other Croatian universities, it has given the managing director an even more prominent role. In terms of similarities, there are four nonspecialized student groups, and each has an experienced student mentor, while they are all coordinated by two student administrators. They distribute the cases to individual case workers. Unlike some previous examples, new students are enrolled after the client interview, which is carried out by the managing director and student administrators. The managing director also actively participates in some client interviews, while other interviews are carried out by individual students or student administrators. The managing director supervises all legal advice drafted by students and even provides legal advice during the interview. They also help student mentors and student administrators to monitor the case flow.

Table 6.1: Overview of student involvement

	Juss-Buss	Jussformidlingen	JURK	Zagreb	Split	Osijek	Rijeka
			Strategic decision making				
Projects and initiatives	S	S	JR	JR	T	T	T
Budget planning	S	S	T	JR	T	T	T
PR and visibility	S	S	S	S	S	JR	JR
			Core clinical activities				
Client interviews	S	S	S	S	S	S	JR
Legal assistance	S	S	S	S	S	S	JR
Supervision	S	S	JR	JR	JR	JR	JR
			Everyday management				
Enrolling students	S	S	JR	S	S	T	JR
Training	S	S	JR	JR	JR	T	JR
Intake of cases	S	S	S	S	S	JR	JR
Case distribution	S	S	S	S	S	S	S
Case flow monitoring	S	S	S	JR	JR	JR	JR

Three levels of student involvement

Despite described more or less subtle differences, there is a clear connection between Croatian and Norwegian student-driven live-client clinical programmes. Students enjoy different levels of autonomy, but their involvement may be systematized in three different levels: involvement in strategic decision making; core clinical activities; and everyday management. These activities may be carried out by students independently (S), shared by teaching staff as a joint responsibility (JR) or done by teaching staff exclusively (T) (see Table 6.1).

What makes these programmes work? What are the common denominators and key features of all these clinical programmes? In my view, there are three crucial elements which explain the success story: giving priority to social instead of educational goals, encouraging peer-reviewing instead of teacher-instructed learning, and entrusting students with management roles.

Key features of student-driven live-client law clinics

The supremacy and importance of the social component

Analysis of global clinical movement points out several distinctive features of CLE: its curricular goal is to provide skills training while promoting public responsibility and social justice, by carefully employing experiential learning methodology.[24] Despite different focuses of clinical programmes, orientation towards social justice seems to be its essential element.[25] The recent European Standards for Clinical Legal Education also stress its importance and make social justice orientation a defining feature of CLE (Article 2, paragraph 1 of the European Standards for Clinical Legal Education [ESCLE]).[26] While there are many educational methods which can achieve this goal, the fact remains that: 'Empowering our own students, giving them the capacity to shape, influence and make change is perhaps the best and only way forward that we can continue to debate and (re)frame social justice and legal education.'[27]

It is not unusual that external factors such as government policies affect the emergence of clinical programmes.[28] In Norway, where law clinics are an important substitute for legal aid which is otherwise (either due to type of cases or financial threshold) unavailable to many clients, the social mission of CLE is evident.[29] Similarly, the Croatian legislative framework which made law clinics part of the legal aid system in a way preset the direction of clinical programmes by putting social justice and equality at the very core of their mission. Without directly influencing the university programmes and instead by directing them to unprofitable areas of law which do not inspire the interest of many practising attorneys, such as asylum law or social security, the legal aid system exposed students to practical experience, which is otherwise hardly available, even to experienced practitioners.[30]

---

24 FS Bloch and NR Madhava Menon, 'The Global Clinical Movement' in FS Bloch (ed), *The Global Clinical Movement: Educating Lawyers for Social Justice* (Oxford University Press 2011) 267–278, at 268–269.

25 ibid 275; J Giddings, 'Clinical Legal Education across the Globe' in Giddings (n 1) 11.

26 In the US, the focus is more on educational goals, most likely due to the market orientation of law schools. See Jelinić and Koch (n 6).

27 C Ashford and P McKeown, 'Introduction: Social Justice and Legal Education' in C Ashford and P McKeown (eds), *Social Justice & Legal Education* (Cambridge Scholars Publishing 2018) 1–6, at 5.

28 J Giddings, 'Common Threads and Strengths in Diversity' in Giddings (n 1) 321.

29 Halvorsen Rønning (n 14) 33.

30 In some areas, the clinics can even 'exceed the expertise of competent state bodies': Uzelac (n 7) 161.

The benefits of such a choice are numerous. In terms of learning outcomes, the obvious benefit is that students come to understand their future social role rather than focusing solely on the business aspects of their future careers.[31] Simultaneously, while facing real-life situations, students are encouraged to understand the socioeconomic and emotional context, as well as the underlying issues of their clients.[32]

A social focus also fosters the employment of different activities, thus expanding the learning opportunities for students. For instance, just like their Norwegian role models, students of the Law Clinic Zagreb have occasionally engaged in policy work and lobbying activities, thus encouraging legislative changes where legislative flaws have been identified.[33] Furthermore, to obtain academic credits, students are also required to volunteer in partner NGOs.[34] Students only get the academic credits, without being closely assessed and graded, which also reduces the usual academic stress involved with evaluation.[35] All of this contributes not only to the self-satisfaction of students, but also to their understanding of rules and practices.[36] In other words, focusing on the social goals actually enhances their learning experience and makes their learning more comprehensive, without making the clinical programme 'service driven'.[37]

There are also institutional benefits for social justice orientation in terms of the continuity and sustainability of the clinical programme. None of the described clinical programmes are mandatory, nor are students required to enrol in them. In the Law Clinic Zagreb, for instance, the number of students who usually apply to engage in clinical programme exceeds the number of available spots, so priority is given to the students who persuasively demonstrate their willingness to assist underprivileged clients, especially if they plan to do so for more than one semester (which is usually sufficient to obtain credits).[38] Encouraging students to stay longer in the clinic opens

31 K Kerrigan, 'What Is Clinical Legal Education and Pro Bono?' in K Kerrigan and V Murray (eds), *A Student Guide to Clinical Legal Education and Pro Bono* (Palgrave Macmillan 2011) 1–20, at 16.

32 J Giddings, 'It's More Than the Site: Supporting Social Justice through Student Supervision Practices' in Ashford and McKeown (eds) (n 27) 43–64, at 45.

33 Aras Kramar and Preložnjak (n 23) 268–269.

34 ibid.

35 V Murray, 'Assessment' in Kerrigan and Murray (n 31) 250–268; D Nicholson, J Newman and R Grimes, *How to Set up and Run a Law Clinic: Principles and Practice* (Edward Elgar 2023) 251.

36 Supported by survey among former clinical students. See Uzelac and Brozović (n 3) 17–20.

37 H Brayne, N Duncan and R Grimes, *Clinical Legal Education: Active Learning in Your Law School* (Blackstone Press 1998) 19.

38 J Brozović, 'Combining Simulations and Live-Client Clinics in Addressing Cross-Cutting Topics: The Best of Both Worlds' in OJ Gstrein, M Fröhlich, C van den Berg and T Giegerich (eds), *Modernising European Legal Education (MELE)* (Springer 2023) 129.

up wider opportunities for peer learning and generational exchange of knowledge, which reduces the need for costly engagement of teaching personnel. It also encourages students to take on more responsible managerial roles, which helps to alleviate some of the institutional pressures but also enriches the clinical experience.

Peer learning: building intergenerational and intragenerational knowledge

Peer learning is supported by substantial empirical evidence, demonstrating benefits for students' psychological wellbeing and learning engagement.[39] Of course, the stakes are much higher if students are entrusted with mentoring roles. If they become a part of the supervision processes, they may perpetuate or even amplify the common pitfalls of poor supervision, such as the inability of students to learn from experience, reflect on their work or build professional confidence.[40] The threshold, however, is by no means unreachable. To achieve the learning goals by way of peer learning effectively, a proper structure and clear division of roles are crucial, and they must also be clearly communicated to students.[41]

It would seem that in basically all student-driven clinical programmes in Norway and Croatia, the passing on of knowledge through generations is a key ingredient to achieve continuity, sustainability and quality assurance. Peer-to-peer learning is essential both within initial clinical training and afterwards when performing core clinical activities.

While in some Norwegian law clinics, students learn the basic work processes and practical skills almost exclusively from their peers, in Croatia student training is provided jointly by managing teaching staff and experienced students. Students get to share their experience with the new generation of clinicians and also explain the basic work processes, while teaching staff can focus on connecting their examples to key ethical principles and values, which effectively achieves the educational goals. Such a general

---

39 L Hewitt and L Yeatman, 'Feeding up and Feeding Back: Exploring the Value of Peer Learning through a Law Clinic Setting' (2023) 30 *International Journal of Clinical Legal Education* 102, at 108–109; AM Lluch, C Lluch, M Arregui, E Jiménez and L Giner, 'Peer Mentoring as a Tool for Developing Soft Skills in Clinical Practice: A 3-Year Study' (2021) 9(5) *Dentistry Journal* 57, 7–8.

40 Giddings (n 32) 48.

41 Hewitt and Yeatman (n 39) 114–115; PA Husband and PA Jacobs, 'Peer Mentoring in Higher Education: A Review of the Current Literature and Recommendations for Implementation of Mentoring Schemes' (2009) 2(1) *Plymouth Student Scientist* 228, at 233; TA Ntho, AJ Pienaar and LA Sehularo, 'Peer-Mentees' Challenges in an Undergraduate Peer-Group Clinical Mentoring Programme in a Nursing Education Institution' (2020) 25(0) *Health SA Gesondheid* 1, 4.

training is supported by learning materials, such as student manuals.[42] They are also helpful and important to the experienced students who now undertake the more responsible roles.[43] External mentors, especially from specialized NGOs, also sometimes provide additional training concerning specific aspects of law for groups.[44]

The importance of these experienced students cannot be stressed enough. In many of the clinical programmes in Norway and Croatia, peers actively mentor the students, first letting them observe the work and then slowly allowing them to assume the individual responsibility which is required from full-fledged clinicians. This can be a valuable experience for student mentors as well, since they get to apply the knowledge and skills they acquired when they were the mentees, thus creating the 'tiered' mentoring structure.[45] For students, this type of 'collaborative tutoring'[46] can indeed be less invasive and more effective, also minimizing the fear of underperformance.[47] Additional support in their work can be provided by consulting previous cases which are closely documented in the electronic database, thus serving as a source of inspiration.[48] Of course, limited access to these cases is needed to preserve the privacy of clients, which in an important ethical consideration.[49] In the Law Clinic Zagreb, for instance, this is achieved by giving access to the closed cases in the database only to student administrators and group members.

Group specialization has both psychological and educational value.[50] In terms of psychological benefits, group cohesion develops student identity and a sense of belonging.[51] In terms of educational goals, group activities can multiply the knowledge of everyone involved if students engage in reflective practice.[52]

---

42 Also in Norway. See Langford, Uehara and Waerstad (n 15) 205.

43 Student mentors need to be properly trained, both before and during their mentoring activities, in order to be able to assume their role of supervisor. See Husband and Jacobs (n 41) 235.

44 J Brozović and A Uzelac, 'Guide on Legal Clinics' (2023), https://mele-erasmus.eu/wp-content/uploads/2023/10/Manual-of-CLE-all-final_inklDeckblat.pdf, 24–25.

45 J Fowler and T Muckert, 'Tiered Mentoring: Benefits for First Year Students, Upper Level Students, and Professionals' (2004), www.researchgate.net/publication/29453733_Tiered_mentoring_Benefits_for_first_year_students_upper_level_students_and_professionals, 156.

46 N Falchikov, *Learning Together: Peer Tutoring in Higher Education* (Routledge 2001) 4.

47 Brayne, Duncan and Grimes (n 37) 69.

48 Brozović (n 38) 133.

49 AC Budzinski, 'Clinics, the Cloud, and Protecting Client Data in the Age of Remote Lawyering' (2023) 19 *Clinical Law Review* 201, at 238–239.

50 Nicholson, Newman and Grimes (n 35) 69.

51 E Ball and C Hennessy, 'De-mystifying the Concept of Peer Mentoring in Higher Education: Establishing Models for Learning' in C Woolhouse and LJ Nicholson (eds), *Mentoring in Higher Education* (Palgrave Macmillan 2020) 22.

52 G Bolton, *Reflective Practice: Writing and Professional Development* (Paul Chapman Publication Company 2001) 83.

In all the described clinical programmes, both experienced and new students discuss each case in a group, deepening their understanding of rules and practices. More importantly, it engages more students, even those to whom the case has not initially been assigned, thus encouraging their critical thinking, teaching them how to manage different opinions when working in teams, creating an additional layer of quality control and giving the feeling of joint responsibility for the final result.[53] For students who assume mentoring roles, their self-esteem and self-satisfaction is also affected, while giving them the opportunity to enhance their own learning.[54] It truly seems that '[s]tudents relate better to a regime in which they are more involved, in which they have some ownership in what is going on'.[55] There are also institutional benefits in opting for such a model. Supervision ratios have been identified in the literature as one of the crucial supervision challenges, both in terms of the organization and in terms of funding.[56] In student-driven law clinics, there is less or even no such pressure.[57]

Students as (co-)managers: transforming the traditional hierarchy model

A recent global study has shown that in many countries, the value of student management in a clinical setting is well recognized.[58] This kind of organization actually dictates a completely different academic and management setting where there is either no hierarchy within a clinical programme or only a (soft) horizontal one.[59] These two approaches cannot be more different. While vertical structures maintain a clear hierarchy where decisions flow from faculty supervisors to students, horizontal structures in clinics are 'flatter' and less centralized, encouraging more collaborative decision making in all important aspects of their work.[60]

In Norway and Croatia, all clinical programmes seem to have a 'leader' or 'administrator', a devoted student who undertakes many important

---

53 Hewitt and Yeatman (n 39) 115.

54 AR Stein, 'The Need for Peer Mentoring Programs Linked to the Legal Writing Class: An Analysis and Proposed Model' (2019) 27(1) *Perspectives: Teaching Legal Research and Writing* 32–37, at 33.

55 Brayne, Duncan and Grimes (n 37) 259.

56 A Evans et al, *Australian Clinical Legal Education: Designing and Operating a Best Practice Clinical Program in an Australian Law School* (ANU Press 2016) 137–138.

57 Nicholson, Newman and Grimes (n 35) 152.

58 Giddings (n 25) 330.

59 Uzelac (n 7) 162.

60 For the differences between vertical and horizontal management arrangements, see RT Dauphin, Analytical Perspective on the Importance of Coordination in Implementing Vertical and Horizontal Organizational Designs' (2019) 9(12) *International Journal of Humanities and Social Science* 77, at 77.

managerial responsibilities and is specifically hired for that purpose.[61] They enter the data about the case in the electronic database and distribute the cases to groups and individual case workers. In common with their Norwegian colleagues, they are specifically instructed to filter the cases which they will accept, first by choosing the type of assistance the clients are requesting (simple legal information or legal advice) and then by giving priority to cases where the clients are faced with statutory deadlines, pending court hearings or life-threatening situations. They also ensure deadlines are complied with.

The managerial activities of students can also influence strategic planning and the organization of the clinical programme. In the Law Clinic Zagreb, student administrators and student mentors jointly decide the number of students that is required in each group, and also interview students interested in enrolling in their work. They also decide whether the Law Clinic should change focus, thus responding to big social challenges. In 2012, the necessity of fighting the overindebtedness of citizens after long-lasting financial crises resulted in the establishment of a special group assisting clients in enforcement proceedings. Similarly, students initiated the establishment of several special ad hoc groups dealing with major social events, like the migrant crisis in 2015 or massive earthquakes in 2020.[62] In Juss-Buss, students decide on their own how to distribute their finances, which effectively allowed them to focus their energy where their clients needed it the most.[63]

In clinical settings, giving students a more prominent managerial role builds their confidence and gives them the opportunity to develop their leadership skills in a supportive environment.[64] Having such devoted peers around is also helpful to other students, as they have the reliable and approachable person to turn to.[65] In my view, the most significant outcome of entrusting students with management roles is that it motivates their peers to engage in clinical activities and eventually assume leadership positions themselves. This

---

[61] In the Law Clinic Zagreb, the student administrators are the only students who are not pure volunteers, but are paid for their services; see Uzelac and Brozović (n 3) 13. Conversely, in Juss-Buss, all students get student credits and small remuneration. See O Hammerslev, A Olesen and O Halvorsen Rønning, 'Juss-Buss [Law Bus]: A Student-Run Legal Aid Clinic' in Halvorsen Rønning and Hammerslev (n 14) 147–168, at 150.

[62] Uzelac (n 7) 161.

[63] Langford, Uehara and Waerstad (n 42) 205.

[64] S Mokshagundam, J Pitkin, M Dekhtyar, S Santen, M Hammoud and SE Skochelak, 'Engaging Medical Students in Leadership Development' (2019) 29 *Medical Science Educator* 849, at 851.

[65] J Gowland and P McKeown, 'Working with Your Supervisor and Others' in K Kerrigan and V Murray (eds), *A Student Guide to Clinical Legal Education and Pro Bono* (Palgrave Macmillan 2011) 88–106, at 103.

approach not only eases the institutional burden in maintaining programme continuity but also facilitates a seamless transition between cohorts.

The challenges of the student-driven model: the (un)justified scepticism?

The most pressing concern relating to a student-driven clinical model is the potential for malpractice and consequent damages claims by clients. Naturally, law schools are committed to maintaining high standards of client service and are understandably cautious of potential lawsuits that could arise from student or staff involvement in live-client work. In challenging the student-driven model, some authors have gone so far as to argue that unsupervised student involvement could itself constitute unethical conduct.[66] Although such scepticism reflects legitimate caution, these concerns can be appropriately managed, especially where proper safeguards are built into clinical programmes.

First of all, liability insurance can alleviate some of the financial burdens of such potential detrimental consequences. For Croatia, there is no doubt that each clinic should have that kind of insurance, because it is a statutory obligation.[67] In the 15 years of the existence of the Law Clinic Zagreb, however, there has not been a single liability claim.[68] On the contrary, the data show that one third of clients requested assistance multiple times, proving their satisfaction with the provided assistance.[69]

Furthermore, the careful structuring of clinical work processes can serve as an effective means of managing potential risks and quality assurance. In both Norway and Croatia, clinical programmes stress the selection of motivated students and provide thorough training in professional ethics. Student managers make sure that the cases are dealt with in a timely manner. The programmes also ensure that all major decisions are made in teams, and that no advice is given immediately. This allows (either student or academic) supervisors to jump in and prevent detrimental errors. For instance, in Zagreb, if students fail to gather all the necessary information during client interviews, they are encouraged to consult other students and, if necessary, the clients.[70] While this cannot fully eliminate all potential issues in client

66 Nicholson, Newman and Grimes (n 35) 155.

67 Z Jelinić, 'Legal Clinics and Access to Justice in Croatia: Perspectives and Challenges' (2017) 5(1) *Asian Journal of Legal Education* 99, at 105.

68 Uzelac (n 7) 162. To my knowledge, this is also the case for three other law clinics in Croatia.

69 Uzelac and Brozović (n 3) 13.

70 B Bilić, T Čupić and J Havaš, 'Hrvatska pravnoklinička iskustva u svjetlu dobrih europskih praksi' (2019) 53(1) *Pravnik* 101, at 117.

interactions (rude or inappropriate behaviour, client repetition fatigue and so on), a more directive approach where the supervisor does all the work alone reduces the experiential learning opportunity, which is the whole purpose of these programmes.

In my view, the idea that leaving students on their own to deal with most of their clinical work is unethical seems generalized and potentially misleading when taken out of context. As noted by Critchlow, 'it is difficult to prescribe specific standards to govern teacher intervention' and 'core values relevant to the question can be gleaned from professional conduct rules'.[71] Much therefore depends on the type of the assistance that is provided to clients, but also on the applicable codes of conduct. In this regard, all of the clinical programmes discussed in this chapter limit their activities to legal advice and do not involve representation in court proceedings. While the general standard of care applies to all types of legal assistance, representation in court proceedings is a much more formal activity that requires a more complex set of specific skills. This is not to suggest that advice alone cannot result in serious errors and harm. However, professional codes of conduct usually mandate that lawyers avoid overpromising and refrain from advising on matters beyond their competence.[72] If law students are instructed to follow the same ethical guidelines, as they certainly are in all of the clinical programmes described in this chapter, the risk of unethical or negligent behaviour is no greater than that posed by practising lawyers. I fully support the statement that too directive supervisors 'should consider whether their intervention is driven by an unrealistically high standard of client service'.[73]

Finally, another concern surrounding student-driven clinical models is the educational value of such models. Do students really learn without prompt and comprehensive reflection, followed by detailed evaluation by the supervisor? Even if peers assume the role of the reviewer, do students really get the best possible learning experience? Admittedly, education-oriented clinical programmes seem to offer more effective guidance than social justice-oriented programmes, by encouraging early reflection, offering evaluation, and delivering constructive and structured teacher feedback.[74] However, it may be the case that even the closely supervised clinical environment does not necessarily meet its learning outcomes.[75] Besides, not

---

[71] G Critchlow, 'Professional Responsibility, Student Practice, and the Clinical Teacher's Duty to Intervene' (1990) 26(2) *Gonzaga Law Review* 415, at 441.

[72] As an international standard, see, for example, art 3.1.2 of the Code of Conduct for European Lawyers. See also art 10 ESCLE.

[73] JH Stark, J Bauer and J Papillo, 'Directiveness in Clinical Supervision' (1993) 3 *Public Interest Law Journal* 35, at 67.

[74] Nicholson, Newman and Grimes (n 35) 67, 153–154, 157–158.

[75] Giddings (n 32) 60.

all knowledge and practical skills have to be obtained in the same place.[76] In Norway and Croatia, much of the reflection is carried out by peers within the team, and students are always welcome to request additional feedback from their academic supervisors. In clinical programmes where supervisory tasks are shared between students and teachers, teacher feedback is naturally embedded in the review process. Additionally, simulation courses can be used as a supplement to offer more teacher guidance, structured reflection and evaluation in a safe environment, while maintaining the benefits of student-driven clinical model.[77]

Conclusion

In my first contact with a new clinical generation during general training, I always emphasize two important features of our clinical programme. First, I stress that this course was not just preparing them for legal practice; instead, it *was* actually giving them the chance to practise law as full-fledged professionals. Second, I always emphasize how crucial this is for clients who have no one else to turn to. In clinical programmes at my university, as well as in numerous other universities across Croatia and Norway, dedicated volunteer work helps thousands of clients who otherwise would be unable to access justice. These programmes are structured to empower students and to utilize their enthusiasm, allowing them to take full ownership of their learning experience in every possible aspect. At the same time, from an institutional perspective, this model ensures a level of sustainability which would otherwise be difficult to achieve through traditional models. Especially when combined with other available experiential learning opportunities, this kind of approach cultivates not only the legal expertise of students but also their sense of social responsibility, creating a domino effect that benefits their peers, teachers, clients and, ultimately, the broader community – a transformative educational outcome that resonates far beyond the classroom.

References

Akšamović D and Genty P, 'An Examination of the Challenges, Successes and Setbacks for Clinical Legal Education and Eastern Europe' (2014) 20(1) *International Journal of Clinical Legal Education* 427

[76] Nicholson, Newman and Grimes (n 35) 150–151.

[77] J Brozović, 'Combining Simulations and Live-Client Clinics in Addressing Cross-Cutting Topics: The Best of Both Worlds' in OJ Gstrein, M Fröhlich, C van den Berg and T Giegerich (eds) *Modernising European Legal Education* (Springer 2023) 125–137, at 134.

Aras Kramar S and Preložnjak B, 'Clinical Legal Education and Importance of Cooperation with Non-governmental Sector, State Bodies and Entities' in B Djuričin, M Kostić Mandić and A Uzelac (eds), *A Guidebook on Best Practices in Running Live Client Clinics for the Academic and Non-academic Community* (Pravni fakultet Univerziteta Crne Gore 2023)

Ashford C and McKeown P, 'Introduction: Social Justice and Legal Education' in C Ashford and P McKeown (eds), *Social Justice & Legal Education* (Cambridge Scholars Publishing 2018)

Ball E and Hennessy C, 'De-mystifying the Concept of Peer Mentoring in Higher Education: Establishing Models for Learning' in C Woolhouse, LJ Nicholson (eds), *Mentoring in Higher Education* (Palgrave Macmillan 2020)

Barić S, 'Pravna pomoć i neprofitne organizacije u Republici Hrvatskoj' (2004) 25(2) *Zbornik Pravnog fakulteta Sveučilišta u Rijeci* 935

Bilić B, Čupić T and Havaš J, 'Hrvatska pravnoklinička iskustva u svjetlu dobrih europskih praksi' (2019) 53(1) *Pravnik* 101

Bloch FS and Madhava Menon NR, 'The Global Clinical Movement' in FS Bloch (ed), *The Global Clinical Movement: Educating Lawyers for Social Justice* (Oxford University Press 2011)

Bolton G, *Reflective Practice: Writing and Professional Development* (Paul Chapman Publication Company 2001)

Brayne H, Duncan N and Grimes R, *Clinical Legal Education: Active Learning in Your Law School* (Blackstone Press 1998)

Brozović J, 'Combining Simulations and Live-Client Clinics in Addressing Cross-Cutting Topics: The Best of Both Worlds' in OJ Gstrein, M Fröhlich, C van den Berg and T Giegerich (eds), *Modernising European Legal Education (MELE)* (Springer 2023)

Brozović J, 'Transformation of the Croatian Legal Aid System: From Normative to Functional Insufficiency' in A Uzelac and CH van Rhee (eds), *Transformation of Civil Justice: Unity and Diversity* (Springer 2019)

Brozović J and Uzelac A, 'Guide on Legal Clinics' (2023), https://mele-erasmus.eu/wp-content/uploads/2023/10/Manual-of-CLE-all-final_inklDeckblat.pdf

Budzinski AC, 'Clinics, the Cloud, and Protecting Client Data in the Age of Remote Lawyering' (2023) 19 *Clinical Law Review* 201

Critchlow G, 'Professional Responsibility, Student Practice, and the Clinical Teacher's Duty to Intervene' (1990) 26(2) *Gonzaga Law Review* 415

Dauphin RT, 'Analytical Perspective on the Importance of Coordination in Implementing Vertical and Horizontal Organizational Designs' (2019) 9(12) *International Journal of Humanities and Social Science* 77

Evans A, Cody A, Copeland A, Giddings J, Joy P, Noone MA and Rice S, *Australian Clinical Legal Education: Designing and Operating a Best Practice Clinical Program in an Australian Law School* (ANU Press 2016)

Falchikov N, *Learning Together: Peer Tutoring in Higher Education* (Routledge 2001)

Fowler J and Muckert T, 'Tiered Mentoring: Benefits for First Year Students, Upper Level Students, and Professionals' (2004), www.researchgate.net/publication/29453733_Tiered_mentoring_Benefits_for_first_year_students_upper_level_students_and_professionals

Giddings J, 'It's More Than the Site: Supporting Social Justice through Student Supervision Practices' in C Ashford and P McKeown (eds), *Social Justice & Legal Education* (Cambridge Scholars Publishing 2018)

Giddings J, 'Clinical Legal Education across the Globe' in J Giddings (ed), *Global Clinical Legal Education* (Routledge 2025)

Giddings J, 'Common Threads and Strengths in Diversity' in J Giddings (ed), *Global Clinical Legal Education* (Routledge 2025)

Gowland J and McKeown P, 'Working with Your Supervisor and Others' in K Kerrigan and V Murray (eds), *A Student Guide to Clinical Legal Education and Pro Bono* (Palgrave Macmillan 2011)

Halvorsen Rønning O, 'Legal Aid in Norway' in O Halvorsen Rønning and O Hammerslev (eds), *Outsourcing Legal Aid in the Nordic Welfare States* (Springer International Publishing 2018)

Hammerslev O, Olesen A and Halvorsen Rønning O, 'Juss-Buss [Law Bus]: A Student-Run Legal Aid Clinic' in O Halvorsen Rønning and O Hammerslev (eds), *Outsourcing Legal Aid in the Nordic Welfare States* (Springer International Publishing 2018)

Hewitt L and Yeatman L, 'Feeding up and Feeding Back: Exploring the Value of Peer Learning through a Law Clinic Setting' (2023) 30 *International Journal of Clinical Legal Education* 102

Husband PA and Jacobs PA, 'Peer Mentoring in Higher Education: A Review of the Current Literature and Recommendations for Implementation of Mentoring Schemes' (2009) 2(1) *Plymouth Student Scientist* 228

Jelinić Z, 'Legal Clinics and Access to Justice in Croatia: Perspectives and Challenges' (2017) 5(1) *Asian Journal of Legal Education* 99

Jelinić Z and Koch A, 'Elucidation of the Concept of a Law Clinic as a Prerequisite for Developing the Standards for Law Clinics in Europe' (2020) 7(2) *Asian Journal of Legal Education* 127

Jelinić Z and Knol Radoja K, 'Analiza hrvatskoga sustava besplatne pravne pomoći u građanskim stvarima u svjetlu dosadašnje prakse europskoga suda za ljudska prava' (2014) 30(2) *Pravni vjesnik* 185

Kerrigan K, 'What Is Clinical Legal Education and Pro Bono?' in K Kerrigan and V Murray (eds), *A Student Guide to Clinical Legal Education and Pro Bono* (Palgrave Macmillan 2011)

Langford M, Uehara D and Waerstad TL, 'Clinical Legal Education in Norway' in J Giddings (ed), *Global Clinical Legal Education* (Routledge 2025)

Lluch AM, Lluch C, Arregui M, Jiménez E and Giner L, 'Peer Mentoring as a Tool for Developing Soft Skills in Clinical Practice: A 3-Year Study' (2021) 9(5) *Dentistry Journal* 57

Ministry of Justice, *Report on Legal Aid in 2023* [*Izvješće o ostvarivanju prava na besplatnu pravnu pomoć i utrošku sredstava u 2023*] (2024), https://sabor.hr/sites/default/files/uploads/sabor/2024-11-29/093802/IZVJ_BESPLATNA_PRAVNA_POMOC_2023.pdf

Mokshagundam S, Pitkin J, Dekhtyar M, Santen S, Hammoud M and Skochelak SE, 'Engaging Medical Students in Leadership Development' (2019) 29 *Medical Science Educator* 849

Murray V, 'Assessment' in K Kerrigan and V Murray (eds), *A Student Guide to Clinical Legal Education and Pro Bono* (Palgrave Macmillan 2011)

Nicholson D, Newman J and Grimes R, *How to Set up and Run a Law Clinic: Principles and Practice* (Edward Elgar 2023)

Ntho TA, Pienaar AJ and Sehularo LA, 'Peer-Mentees' Challenges in an Undergraduate Peer-Group Clinical Mentoring Programme in a Nursing Education Institution' (2020) 25(0) *Health SA Gesondheid* a1435

Preložnjak B, 'Clinical Legal Education in Croatia: From Providing Legal Assistance to the Poor to Practical Education of Students' (2013) 19 *International Journal of Clinical Legal Education* 373

Preložnjak B and Brozović J, 'The Financial Challenges of Clinical Legal Education: An Example from a Zagreb Law Clinic' (2016) 23(4) *International Journal of Clinical Legal Education* 136

Schoultz I, 'Legal Aid in Sweden' in O Halvorsen Rønning and O Hammerslev (eds), *Outsourcing Legal Aid in the Nordic Welfare States* (Springer International Publishing 2018)

Stark JH, Bauer J and Papillo J, 'Directiveness in Clinical Supervision' (1993) 3 *Public Interest Law Journal* 35

Stein AR, 'The Need for Peer Mentoring Programs Linked to the Legal Writing Class: An Analysis and Proposed Model' (2019) 27(1) *Perspectives: Teaching Legal Research and Writing* 32

Uzelac A, 'The Peculiar Case of Zagreb Law Clinic' in J Giddings (ed), *Global Clinical Legal Education* (Routledge 2025)

Uzelac A and Brozović J, 'Increasing Employability of Law Graduates by Introducing Live-Client Clinics: The Experience of Law Clinic in Zagreb' in B Djuričin, M Kostić Mandić and A Uzelac (eds), *A Guidebook on Best Practices in Running Live Client Clinics for the Academic and Non-academic Community* (Pravni fakultet Univerziteta Crne Gore 2023)

Zografou A and McDermott L, 'Mentorship in Higher Education: The Keys to Unlocking Meaningful Mentoring Relationships' (2022) 2 *GiLE Journal of Skills Development* 71

7

The Case for Public Legal Education Within the Expansion of Clinical Legal Education

Sarah Morse and Frances Ridout

Public legal education (PLE) is a widely used and recognized term internationally to describe activities which seek to educate and empower individuals regarding their legal rights and responsibilities. However, this term is not universally adopted and, in other jurisdictions, activities fulfilling this aim may be categorized differently, 'such as law related education and legal literacy in the United States and community legal education in Australia'.[1] Regardless of the term adopted, there is a broad commonality in the aims and objectives, and a strong association with legal literacy and the concept of legal capability – all allied with the promotion of democracy and the rule of law.

PLE is not a new initiative, with the first examples having been seen thousands of years ago.[2] However, it was in the 1950s that it rose to greater prominence and visibility in a time of civil unrest and drive for social reform, civil rights and access to justice.[3] In the US, a law-related movement aimed at improving civil learning contributed to the development of arguably the most significant PLE programme, Street Law, in 1972,[4] when a group of students at Georgetown University Law

1 Lisa Wintersteiger, Sarah Morse, Michael Olatokun and Christopher Morris *Effectiveness of Public Legal Education Initiatives: A Literature Review* (Legal Services Board 2021) 9.

2 ibid.

3 Margaret Fisher, 'So What Is Street Law Anyway: A US Perspective' (2017) 1(1) *International Journal of Public Legal Education* 87, 89.

4 ibid. 90

Center developed an innovative programme which involved them going out into the District of Columbia to teach high school students about the law and legal system. This programme was highly practical and interactive in nature – a learner-centred, constructivist methodology which is a key feature of all modern-day Street Law programmes.[5] This Street Law programme thrived in the US and extended its reach internationally in 1986 with the development of a programme in South Africa. Over the next decade in South Africa, the importance of education relating to human rights, civic rights and democracy was highlighted.[6] Additionally, it served as a tool to break down racial barriers enabling young people to debate societal issues together.[7]

Many such programmes focus on these areas of education, believing that active, informed citizens are empowered to influence change, challenge and hold public bodies or leaders to account,[8] and to gain access to justice, leading to a fairer and more just society.[9] Street Law flourished in South Africa and in 2003 Street Law South Africa was established as a nonprofit organization.[10] Throughout the 1990s, Street Law also expanded into other areas across the globe. In the UK, the first Street Law programme was introduced at the University of Derby in 1997,[11] while in 2008 the Ministry of Justice funded the Public Legal Education Network (PLENET) and then there was the development of the charity Law for Life: The Foundation for Public Legal Education (now known as Advicenow).[12]

In 1996, the original Street Law initiative was incorporated as Street Law Inc., with its mission of 'Education. Empowerment. Justice'.[13] It is estimated

5 Lee Arbetman, 'Street Law, Inc.: Context, History and Future' (2018) 2(1), *International Journal of Public Legal Education* 3.

6 David Jan McQuoid-Mason, 'The Genesis of Street Law in South Africa' (2017) 1(1) *International Journal of Public Legal Education* 93, 96.

7 Richard Grimes, David McQuoid-Mason, Ed O'Brien and Judy Zimmer, 'Street Law and Social Justice Education' in Frank S Bloch (ed), *The Global Clinical Movement: Educating Lawyers for Social Justice* (Oxford University Press 2011).

8 Lisa Wintersteiger, 'Legal Education beyond the Academy: The Neoliberal Reorientation of Public Legal Education' (2019) 30(2) *Law and Critique* 123, 124.

9 The key texts – Edward L O'Brien, Eleanor Greene and David McQuoid-Mason, *Human Rights for All* (West Publishing Co 1996) and David McQuoid-Mason, Mandla Mchunu, Karthy Govender, Edward L O'Brien and Mary Curd Larkin, *Democracy for all Education Towards a Democratic Culture* (Juta & Co Ltd 1994) – have been translated into many languages for use as a resource for Street Law programmes.

10 McQuoid-Mason (n 6) 96.

11 Grimes et al (n 7); Richard Grimes, 'Legal Literacy, Community Empowerment and Law Schools: Some Lessons from a Working Model in the UK' (2003) 37 *The Law Teacher* 273.

12 Advicenow, www.advicenow.org.uk

13 For a full history of Street Law Inc., see www.streetlaw.org/who-we-are/history

that Street Law programmes based on this model involving teachers, law students, law enforcement and the judiciary are found in every American State and more than 40 countries worldwide.[14]

PLE also gathered pace in Canada – for example, the Alberta Law Foundation was formed in 1973[15] and later partnered with the Centre for Public Legal Education Alberta,[16] providing PLE services.[17] Over the next two decades, PLE, with a primary focus on Street Law, spread throughout the world, often responding to pressing political and social issues of the time. In 1996, the Global Alliance for Justice Education (GAJE), a nonprofit organization, was established, which aims to promote justice through education with a particular focus on accessibility and affordability for individuals in developing countries.[18] Street Law is perhaps the most prominent and widespread form of PLE activity undertaken, but there are many other examples falling within a wider definition of PLE. We have also seen a positioning of PLE alongside, and arguably within (although this is a point of debate), the remit of Clinical Legal Education (CLE), with CLE organizations, such as the European Network for Clinical Legal Education[19] and the *International Journal of Clinical Legal Education*[20] showing support for the work notably through inclusion in international conferences and publications.

There is no universal definition for PLE. In 2006 in the UK, an independent Public Legal Education and Support (PLEAS) Task Force was set up with a view to considering a national strategy for PLE. In doing so, it developed a well-adopted, working definition of PLE as follows:

> PLE provides people with awareness, knowledge and understanding of rights and legal issues, together with the confidence and skills they need to deal with disputes and gain access to justice. Equally important, it helps people recognise when they may need support, what sort of advice is available, and how to go about getting it.

[14] Arbetman (n 5).

[15] Alberta Law Foundation, https://albertalawfoundation.org/who-we-are/our-vision-mission-values

[16] Centre for Public Legal Education Alberta, www.cplea.ca

[17] For a fuller history of the development of PLE in Canada, see Lois Elaine Gander, 'The Radical Promise of Public Legal Education in Canada' (Master's thesis, Alberta, Edmonton, 1999).

[18] Global Alliance of Justice Education, www.gaje.org/

[19] European Network of Clinical Legal Education, www.encle.eu/

[20] International Journal of Clinical Legal Education, www.northumbriajournals.co.uk/index.php/ijcle

> PLE has a further key role in helping citizens to better understand everyday life issues, making better decisions and anticipating and avoiding problems.[21]

There has been a focus on three core elements, notably the development of 'knowledge', 'skills' and 'attitudes',[22] although the latter are sometimes referred to instead as 'attributes'[23] or simply 'confidence'. It is beyond the scope of this chapter to explore the need for PLE beyond a recognition that in many jurisdictions, there are individuals without the means to access legal help to resolve their issues.[24] This is felt most by the vulnerable in society – by age, health, disability, education and income.[25] This results in individual hardship and injustice, but also a cost to society and the economy. The meeting of two All-Party Parliamentary Groups in 2018 noted 'a high economic cost of low legal capability with over 1 million civil justice problems unresolved annually as a result of poor legal capability, at a cost of £13 billion over the course of a three and-a-half year period'.[26]

Within their formative report, the PLEAS Task Force concluded that PLE was a vital tool for combating injustice and achieving legal capability leading to better outcomes and social justice. Furthermore, it noted that PLE supported social inclusion and the promotion of human rights, as well as potentially contributing to a more responsible society 'by helping people avoid problems that may lead them into offending behaviour'.[27]

A wide and varied range of activities are undertaken within the remit of PLE. A significant number involve face-to-face interactions, particularly those initiatives and programmes which are based on the original Street Law model that hails interactivity as its hallmark feature – Street Law being

---

21 PLEAS Task Force, *Developing Capable Citizens: The Role of Public Legal Education* (2007), www.plecanada.org/wp-content/uploads/2018/10/Developing-Capable-citizens-the-role-of-public-legal-education-2007.pdf, 9.

22 For definitions, see Wintersteiger et al (n 1) 13.

23 Rachel Dunn, 'The Knowledge, Skills and Attributes Considered Necessary to Start Day 1 Training Competently and Whether Live Client Clinics Develop Them' (PhD thesis, Northumbria University 2017).

24 Leader describes the laws 'exclusionary complexity' and the 'profound undermining of trust and faith in legal processes that can result from negative experiences of going to law'. See Kate Leader, *Litigants in Person in the Civil Justice System: In Their Own Words* (Bloomsbury Publishing 2024) 2.

25 PLEAS Task Force (n 21) 8.

26 'A Vision for Public Legal Education and the Rule of Law: A Joint Meeting of the All-Party Parliamentary Groups of the Rule of Law and Public Legal Education & Pro Bono', 31 October 2018, www.lawworks.org.uk/sites/default/files/files/APPG-BriefingPaper-A-10y-Vision-forPLE-.pdf

27 PLEAS Task Force (n 21) 10.

a subsection of PLE.[28] Of these, much work takes place in school settings, with facilitated workshops which are designed to introduce and explore legal concepts, and develop awareness and understanding of morality, ethics and the rule of law. Historically, PLE provision has focussed predominantly on high schools; however, more recently there has been a move towards considering 'child-focused PLE' for younger members of society.[29]

Other face-to-face PLE activities involve the provision of training courses or workshops, presentations, mock-trials or even plays and dedicated radio shows.[30] Examples can be seen in many different settings, such as prisons,[31] young offenders' institutions, Employment Tribunals[32] and courts or other community groups outside education,[33] to name but a few. Alternative methods of delivering PLE can include paper-based or online provision of information for example factsheets, self-help guides or videos,[34] applications or blogs.[35] Notably, PLE is a form of information rather than being legal advice. This has impacted on its wide and varied delivery and form, with some programmes being more bespoke and tailored, and others having a more generalized focus on civic engagement.[36]

There are many providers of PLE, with varying offerings in terms of the scale and type of activities undertaken. Charitable organizations and nonprofit organizations play a significant role. There are providers that operate on an international scale and with cross-jurisdictional relevance, such as Street Law Inc., others which operate actively country wide such as the Alberta Law Foundation (Alberta, Canada) and online, such as Advicenow (England and Wales), and other providers at a regional level (albeit perhaps as part of a national or state-wide network), for example, by law centres or community legal centres. PLE can be less accessible for those with less confidence, societal

---

28 See Frances Ridout and Linden Thomas, *Street Law: Theory and Practice* (Bloomsbury Publishing 2023) 21, Figure 1.5.

29 Dawn Watkins, Effie Lai-Chong Law, Joanna Barwick and Elee Kirk, 'Exploring Children's Understanding of Law in Their Everyday Lives' (2018) 38(1) *Legal Studies* 59.

30 Keren Lloyd Bright and Maria McNicholl, 'The Open University Law School's Public Legal Education in Prisons: Contributing to Rehabilitative Prison Culture' (2021) 5(1) *International Journal of Public Legal Education* 94.

31 ibid.

32 Sarah Saunders, 'Street Law Assisting Access to Justice in the Employment Tribunal: A Practice Report' (2019) 3(1) *International Journal of Public Legal Education* 50.

33 See the resources produced by Young Citizens, www.youngcitizens.org/

34 Such as those provided by Advicenow, www.advicenow.org.uk/

35 Victoria Roper, 'Blogs as a Teaching Tool and Method of Public Legal Education: A Case Study' (2018) 2(1) *International Journal of Public Legal Education* 46.

36 For a general discussion on PLE and Street Law, see the podcast 'ReImagine Law, Public Legal Education and Street Law', 23 January 2025, https://open.spotify.com/episode/2QLQZF9jbY1XmJ3cz8dS6G

engagement or digital literacy. This means that it is vital to maintain a varied and diverse offering of PLE and undertake impact evaluation of programmes.

Other notable providers of PLE are those who are involved, in a wide sense, in legal practice or provision. This includes judges, lawyers, law students, law enforcement[37] and others. Indeed, a significant contribution to PLE is that made by law schools, with law students and academics undertaking this work on an intracurricular and/or extracurricular basis. In the UK, the LawWorks and Clinical Legal Education Organisation (CLEO) Law School Pro Bono and Clinic Report 2020 notes that out of the 78 law school respondents to an online survey regarding pro bono activity, 68 per cent ran Street Law/PLE projects.[38] This picture is not unique to the UK.

Across Europe we are seeing a growing trend towards popularism, individualistic ideologies and a questioning of democracy. In the UK, the think tank Onward noted a 'destructive form of disconnection among younger generations that is undermining support for democracy and storing up social problems for the future'.[39] It is against this backdrop, and drawing on its rich history, that we consider the opportunities for PLE through the lens of three particular themes; the student perspective, design and resources, and university value.

The student perspective

Legal education throughout Europe is considered a prestigious, challenging and enriching education; flourishing in an environment where many other (less vocational) subjects are experiencing slowed recruitment.[40] CLE (and within that, to an ever-increasing extent, PLE) is firmly established as a 'norm' of the law school. While the marketization of education is an uncomfortable feeling for many clinicians, there can be no doubt that PLE is well placed in modern education settings.[41]

---

[37] An example can be seen with Street Law Inc.'s Police and Teens programme at www.streetlaw.org/programs/police-and-teens

[38] A total of 120 institutions were identified for the survey, although two of these had multiple sites in different regions and were allowed to provide a separate response from each key site. See www.lawworks.org.uk/sites/default/files/files/LawWorks%20Law%20Schools%20Report%202020_0.pdf

[39] Onward, 'The Kids Aren't Alright', www.ukonward.com/wp-content/uploads/2022/09/kids-arent-alright-democracy.pdf

[40] In 2022, the most frequently awarded degrees in the EU were in the field of business, administration and law. See https://ec.europa.eu/eurostat/statistics-explained/index.php?title=Tertiary_education_statistics

[41] By this we mean how students view, acknowledge and participate in their education and experience of higher education.

Employability

Throughout Europe, the vocational[42] nature of legal studies leads to an expectation that courses will increase the employability prospects of students. This is simultaneously echoed in the expectation that employers have of graduates.[43] PLE and in particular its highly interactive subform, Street Law, directly support many employability skills; teamwork, communication, independent work, critical thinking and creativity, to name but a few.[44]

The European University Association sought to emphasize the education mission of universities outlining Ten Principles for the Enhancement of Learning and Teaching, the first of which promotes many of the employability benefits that PLE develops:

> The higher education learning experience nurtures and enables the development of learners as active and responsible citizens, critical thinkers, problem solvers, equipped for life-long learning. Higher education equips people with the confidence and skills to live and learn in a changing world, able to proactively address their own and the world's grand challenges.[45]

These are all nurtured through varying PLE projects.

However, there can often be a disconnect in the rich (and sometimes subtle) experience PLE offers to the development of employability skills and the fact that its plentiful benefits are not always realized initially by students and employers. Thomas notes there can often be a misalignment, with many employers not knowing what CLE means, but seeking all the skills participating students gain from it.[46] Equally, many students do not select PLE or Street Law programmes because of confusion about what they actually are.[47] Research from Charles University in Prague examined

---

42 We appreciate that whether law is a vocational subject is a matter of debate.

43 QS Global Employer Survey 2022, 'What do Employers Want from Todays Graduates', https://insights.qs.com/hubfs/Reports/What%20do%20employers%20want%20from%20todays%20graduates%20%20(1).pdf?utm_medium=email&_hsmi=65742003&utm_co.

44 Ridout and Thomas (n 28) ch 12.

45 European University Association, 'Enhancing the Education Mission of European Universities: A Proactive Response To Change', www.eua.eu/downloads/content/ten%20european%20principles%20for%20the%20enhancement%20of%20learning%20and%20teaching16102017.pdf

46 Linden Thomas, '"It Puts the Law They've Learnt in Theory into Practice": Exploring Employer Understandings of Clinical Legal Education' in L Thomas, S Vaughan, B Malkani and T Lynch (eds) (Hart Publishing 2018).

47 Care is often needed when naming Street Law courses. Use of the terms 'public legal education', 'community' and 'access to justice' alongside Street Law in a title can all be helpful for clarity.

students' own views of the knowledge and skills that they learnt, and their perceived development. Their overall experiences of Street Law were very positive and they recognized improvement in their ability to communicate law to nonlawyers, but surprisingly they did not recognize the value in research skills development or extending their legal knowledge which came from this work:

> The research proved that Street Law graduates feel that Street Law helps to develop key skills for lawyers, among which communication of legal information to a non-lawyer proved to be one of the most important, followed by presentation skills. The important realisation is that those benefits make it suitable for every regular law student, not only those who are interested in teaching in future.[48]

Perdue and Wallace examined 63 student responses (from six different countries) to 'conclude that Street Law provides significant and often unique benefits for law students including developing vital cultural competency skills, practicing legal communication with non-lawyers, and cementing content knowledge in a non-academic environment'.[49] We can highlight the benefit that PLE provides to student employability by properly articulating what it is, and both the obvious skills (mentioned earlier) and subtle skills and attributes it develops in students. Those subtle skills include: coping when things go wrong; commercial awareness in how the law actively works for (or against) different groups in society; and emotional intelligence. When discussing CLE more broadly, Thomas notes that 'we must not just tell students that participation in clinical legal education is good for their employability: we must also create a space in which they come to understand and accept how this applies to them as individuals'.[50] The same is true of PLE.

There is a tension that exists in CLE between it being viewed as a training ground for employability skills (often initially sought by students and promoted by faculties) and experiential learning modules. Such CLE and PLE modules typically seek to be tools for social justice meant in its widest sense – in other words, not just the actual delivery, but also shaping the career paths of graduates entering the legal profession. There are various intrinsic

48 Hana Draslarová, 'Street Law as a Unique Learning Method: What Do Students Themselves Actually Find to Be Its Benefits? Answers from the Czech Republic' (2019) 3(1) *International Journal of Public Legal Education* 123.

49 Amy Wallace and Ben Perdue, 'Preparing Lawyers for Practice: Developing Cultural Competency, Communication Skills, and Content Knowledge through Street Law Programs' (2020) 70(2) *Journal of Legal Education* 95.

50 Draslarová (n 48) 150.

and extrinsic motivations that students start programmes with,[51] which often morph and change as the experience of PLE brings about a wider enlightenment. To what extent should a PLE clinician place emphasis on the development of employability skills, risking a surface learning approach to courses? Such strategic learning can be used by students to follow the pathway of a corporate agenda, which can, at face value, be contrary to the ethos of PLE. There are numerous anecdotal accounts of students whose whole perspective on law and the legal system changes through the undertaking of PLE courses. This of course could be due to the temperament of the types of students who choose these courses, but this is to a large extent creditable to the movement and methods that PLE embodies. McKeown explores the motivations for law students within the context of CLE as 'practical, tactical and ethical'.[52] He reflects that 'there has been little empirical research reporting the reasons students cite as motivating them to carry out pro bono work'.[53] However, in a study on the student perspective, it was noted that students cited employability as one of the draws to pro bono work. Other reasons include, public service, skills, networking, experience and satisfaction.[54] These are equally likely to apply to PLE.

In higher education, 'success' of students is often measured by graduate income, type of work, the size of the employer and the speed with which students move into graduate roles. Do we have an ethical duty to equally value the outcomes of those who work in the nonprofit or charitable sector? Is success a student deciding not to pursue private practice and instead going into teaching or civic engagement roles? Given the financial pressures of higher education and lure of large commercial salaries, is success perhaps a measurement of graduate happiness, role fulfilment or positive social impact? As universities and clinicians, we need to re-align our measurement of successful employability and ensure that suitable recognition is given to the themes promoted by PLE. Overall, there can be no doubt that PLE improves the employability prospects of students; ensuring this is recognized by our students should be our next priority.

The student experience

Even in jurisdictions where there are no or limited fees for education, universities are rightly placing an increasing emphasis on students enjoying, benefiting and thriving from their education. The implementation of PLE provides an important opportunity for law schools to enhance this.

---

51 Paul McKeown, 'Pro Bono: What's in It for Law Students? The Students' Perspective' (2017) 24(2) *International Journal of Clinical Legal Education* 43.

52 ibid.

53 ibid.

54 ibid.

It is well documented that student mental health is declining and there has been a significant rise in the stress levels of law students. The American Survey of Law Student Well-Being 2021 showed that those needing help for an emotional or mental health problem in the year before the survey was nearly 70 per cent.[55] The EUROSTUDENT 8 data (collected from 25 European countries between 2020 and 2023, which look at comparable data on students within Europe) gathered data from students from European countries, showing that approximately one fifth of students had a disability, with the prevailing disability type being mental health. Against this backdrop, PLE can be an important tool to improve friendships and connections between law student peers.[56] This is partly the constructivist nature of the teaching style, and partly the emphasis given to independent group learning. At Queen Mary University of London, the simple act of introducing name badges during PLE and Street Law lessons helps to foster friendship and develop peer-to-peer bonds. The Student Well-Being Report 2024 (produced by Eurostudent.eu) stated that 'well-being of students in Europe is a cause of concern' and acknowledged an association with better wellbeing when students have 'a better personal fit within higher education' and 'more contact with other students about their study subjects'.[57]

Part of the concern around student wellbeing stems from students finding the content on a traditional law degree as hard.[58] It is well documented that CLE provides welcome relief through a different method of teaching and different content, often being one of the few subjects on a law degree taught in a constructivist way. PLE provides another opportunity outside of the typical client centric clinic to vary this pedagogical approach as welcome relief from often 'thick' legal content (particularly for students who are more practically rather than intellectually minded). Many PLE courses and projects directly connect with local communities, providing a tangible and meaningful example of place-based education within a curriculum.[59]

---

[55] David Jaffe, Katherine Bender and Jerome Organ, '"It Is Okay to Not Be Okay": The 2021 Survey of Law Student Well-Being' (2021) 60 *University of Louisville Law Review* 441.

[56] Wallace and Perdue (n 49) 16, with comments from students at New York Law School and Charles University, Prague.

[57] Ardita Muja et al, 'Student Well-Being: The Role of Socio-demographic Background, Contextual Conditions, and Study Demands and Resources on the Well-being of Students in the European Higher Education Area' (2024), *Eurostudent.eu*, www.eurostudent.eu/download_files/documents/EUROSTUDENT_2024_student_well_being.pdf

[58] One in three students would like to study less – see the Eurostudent Survey Viii, Report on the social and living conditions of higher education students in Ireland 2022 (April 2023), Stephen Erskine, David Harmon, https://hea.ie/assets/uploads/2023/04/Eurostudent-8-Final-Report.pdf

[59] Place-based education is 'concerned with the context and the value of learning from and nurturing specific places, communities and regions' Sarah Buhler and Rachel Stalker,

Learning how to 'teach' or communicate with nonlegal communities can often prompt students to question why more traditional lecture-style teaching is still predominantly used on degrees.

PLE is an important conduit for improving widening participation and access to universities in two ways. The community groups who interact with the universities are having greater exposure and having positive interactions with otherwise distant institutions, which breaks down barriers. Also, those who attend universities as students from backgrounds that are less represented in the legal profession are often attracted to take part in pro bono opportunities, and once on such projects are often very successful at them. Whether due to their prior experiences and interactions or the different style of teaching and learning, this helps to boost the student perspective of their course and institution. Throughout the years we have been teaching PLE, students often give us feedback that they would have benefited at school from seeing students like them from a university – a comment probably heard by many other clinicians.

PLE has many key ingredients to improve the student experience via teaching methods, friendships and different legal content, to name but a few. Through PLE, students often have a higher quantity and quality of interactions with staff, enhancing their learning, their bond with the institution and their satisfaction.[60] The real challenge is how to organically embed PLE into the life of a law school in order to improve the student experience rather than it being a small unique selling point that is only available to relatively few students.[61] There can be no greater satisfaction for students who can undertake a whole PLE project from start to finish, and a project which is specific rather than generic in nature. Research has shown that 'shorter interventions can be just as effective as longer-term interventions' and 'tailored interventions potentially achieve their goals more effectively than generic approaches',[62] meaning that projects can be designed to be desirable to education and beneficial for communities.

'Place-Based Education: Clinical Legal Education and Ethics' in *Thinking about Clinical Legal Education* (Routledge 2021) 27.

[60] Alex Nicholson, 'The Value of a Law Degree' (2020) 54(2) *The Law Teacher* 194, 202.

[61] The University of Birmingham's compulsory module entitled 'Legal Solutions' uses PLE methods to help students working in teams to solve real-life problems. See https://program-and-modules-handbook.bham.ac.uk/webhandbooks/WebHandbooks-control-servlet;JSESSIONID_PMH=FWwUpxD9ph1Qjrsm0G43z14AiNKjg9o1DW33z6x81qVYTcPpQcwg!-936296336?Action=getModuleDetailsList&pgSubj=08&pgCrse=33567&searchTerm=002025

[62] Wintersteiger et al (n 1).

Marketization

Aside from the potential educational benefit for student providers of PLE, there is also a potential commercial motivation for law schools and universities themselves to offer these types of programmes because: 'In a competitive market, it is important that universities offer courses and extra-curricular activities which are appealing and relevant to prospective students.'[63] With an increasing need to modernize law degrees and teach to the expectations of often fee-paying students, CLE and PLE can helpfully and unhelpfully find themselves commoditized. Indeed, Nicholson proposes a Value Slices Model to 'encourage and equip providers to evaluate, create and articulate a unique value focus'[64] in a 'changeable and increasingly competitive market'. Two of the six 'slices' are experiential and community. If students (and prospective students) are fully aware of the plentiful benefits of this resource-heavy method of learning, this increases the pressure on universities to spend the money on CLE. Playing to this advantage leaves an uncomfortable feeling, devaluing the academic discipline and its values and ethics, as well as the value of the social justice mission.[65]

Within Europe and globally, PLE is less developed and less practised than traditional advisory clinic models of CLE. While an area of growth, it is not equal in terms of the quantity of programmes, academic research and the level of understanding that students have. This is interesting given the potential of PLE to impact significantly more community individuals and involve more law students. Furthermore, its methods are more amenable to interdisciplinarity and in many jurisdictions it can be practised without the need for regulatory restrictions. Recent changes to solicitor qualifications in England and Wales further devalue PLE. It is generally considered by most clinicians that the majority of PLE projects cannot count towards the requisite two years of work experience that need to be obtained by applicants[66] (although we note that it supports the development of skills which need to be demonstrated in SQE 2 – the practical component of the qualification assessment). This reduction in commoditization devalues its worth from the student perspective, which inevitably reduces the opportunities for PLE expansion. Despite this depreciation, this does not detract from the transferable skills which are developed and the inevitable positive impact this has on employability generally.

---

[63] Paul McKeown and Sarah Morse 'Litigants in Person: Is There a Role for Higher Education?' (2015) 49(1) *The Law Teacher* 122, 128.

[64] Nicholson (n 60) 206 and 196.

[65] Stephen Wizner, 'Beyond Skills Training' (2000) 7 *Clinical Law Review* 327.

[66] As they do not count as 'advice or assistance' under s 12(3)(b)(i) of the Legal Services Act 2007.

Design and resources

One of the many attractions of PLE is its flexibility and sustainability in terms of design and resources. Unlike its clinical counterpart, PLE activities are often less constrained by regulatory or professional body requirements, which, depending on the jurisdiction, can limit the work which law students or universities are permitted to undertake or which, justifiably, imposes more onerous obligations – for example, regarding insurance, oversight and compliance procedures. However, this is not to say that PLE courses should not be mindful of the nature of the activities undertaken, standards, the need for supervision and resources, to name but a few. In the following section of this chapter, we seek to highlight a number of points to enable you to consider how you could develop a PLE course (or expand an existing provision) which best meets your own needs. We recognize that there will undoubtedly be other considerations and opportunities to which we are not able to do justice here.

Intracurricular or extracurricular public legal education

A PLE offering can be standalone (within or outside your existing curriculum) or it can be aligned to other courses as part of a scaffolded, incremental approach to learning and skills development within a range of experiential environments (such as CLE). We have chosen to consider further the former, in particular the advantages and disadvantages of a standalone, intracurricular versus extracurricular PLE course.

Student engagement

Within the context of the student experience, we have previously explored the value of PLE as a tool for widening participation. This is also potentially relevant when considering whether PLE is more suitable within your institution as an intracurricular or extracurricular activity. There is evidence to suggest that students from particular economic and social backgrounds are less inclined or have fewer opportunities to undertake extracurricular activities.[67] This may be due to a student's lack of confidence or belief in their ability to participate or their available time (or resources)[68] to do so,

[67] Jeanette Ashton, 'Law at Sussex One Year on: Where Did We Come from, How Far Did We Get and Where Are We Going?' (2024) 31(2) *International Journal of Clinical Legal Education* 36, 48.

[68] A situation which impacts upon many opportunities such as internships. See www.suttontrust.com/our-research/unpaid-and-underpaid-internships/

taking into account commitments they may have alongside their studies (for example, family or employment). An intracurricular PLE course may be better placed to address a time disadvantage as it will sit alongside, rather than in addition to, their other studies. An extracurricular course could result in some recognition for the student involved (for example, a certificate of participation), but academic credit is less likely. Although it is arguable that receiving credit for such a module might detract from more altruistic motivations for taking part, nonetheless this could be an important factor for a student who would like to take part, but is constrained by external factors. There are two further observations to make here. First, a 'truism in education theory is that "we value what we measure" and "we measure what we value"'.[69] If this is the case, does this make the case for a credit-bearing, intracurricular PLE course more or less attractive for those involved? Second, a question that is often posed is whether PLE (like CLE) qualifies as pro bono work if students receive credit for engaging.[70] The answers to these questions are beyond the scope of this chapter; however, it is worth noting that across Europe and elsewhere, you will find many different examples of the type of credit awarded (such as credit for attendance, a record of pass/fail or the award of a mark), the type of work required to gain this credit and the nature of any form of assessment – a further example of PLE's flexibility.

In terms of addressing any confidence gap from a widening participation perspective, there will likely be greater opportunity for providing structured academic support and teaching on a PLE course which sits within the curriculum, which may go some way towards building self-assurance and capability in students who find such activities challenging. Furthermore, as discussed earlier, PLE as a subject has the ability to build this confidence through the use of teamwork and development of oral communication skills. Thought can also be given to where in a degree course PLE is best placed to achieve this.

Conversely, we recognize that some students may prefer to undertake PLE on an extracurricular basis. They may have an interest in the work and appreciate its value, but may wish to choose how much time they dedicate to it. Alternatively, they may prefer to opt for a credit-bearing course which

---

69 Karen Barton, Clark D Cunningham, Gregory Todd Jones and Paul Maharg 'Valuing What Clients Think: Standardized Clients and the Assessment of Communicative Competence' (2006) 13(1) *Clinical Law Review* 1, 2.

70 Although it is noted that in some jurisdictions there is a requirement to complete a prescribed number of pro bono hours in order to qualify into the profession. An example of this is the Singapore Institute of Legal Education, which stipulates that students need to undertake 20 hours of pro bono work at the Law School. See, www.sile.edu.sg/pro-bono-programme

more readily aligns to their career aspirations rather than those, like PLE, whose value may seem less obvious or less traditional.

This discussion presupposes that PLE will be an elective rather than compulsory course, which is overwhelmingly the case. This is not to say that PLE could not be compulsory or that PLE activities, as they are so often grounded in inquiry or problem-based learning, could not form part of a compulsory module.[71] Ultimately the motivations and requirements of your students, the culture of your law school and the design of CLE provision may influence your decision here.

Staffing and resources

It is widely recognized that clinical courses are an expensive offering for universities. They require a high degree of academic input and supervision (to maintain professional and regulatory standards), they do not readily conform to a standard workload model which many universities rely on (with small staff/student ratios and less large group-style teaching) and they often demand additional resources (whether that is bespoke physical spaces to maintain a confidential workspace, facilities for storage of casework, electronically or otherwise, or a budget for insurance or to maintain staff membership of professional bodies).[72] These points are certainly true when comparing CLE to traditional law courses, but are potentially less marked in relation to PLE.

Due to the nature of work undertaken on PLE courses (which is to provide legal information but not legal advice), there are some reduced costs. As PLE is not subject to the same standards (professional or regulatory) as CLE, the level of supervision required for the work produced by students is also arguably lower. Despite this, it is nonetheless vital (reputationally and ethically) that the PLE activities undertaken are of the highest quality.[73] This is to ensure that the needs of the third parties involved are met, as well as to deliver rich learning experiences for students which are inherent to the design of experiential courses. As such, some level of supervision will be required which likely exceeds what might be required for a more traditional law course, and the teaching style will differ.

Clinical modules, including PLE, often do not conform to a standard delivery design, in that they are not usually lecture-driven, but instead focus on a more workshop or seminar style as well as regular, often micro,

71 The University of Birmingham's compulsory module entitled 'Legal Solutions' (n 61).

72 Richard Grimes, *Public Legal Education: The Role of Law Schools in Building a More Legally Literate Society* (Routledge 2021) 96.

73 For further discussion of supervision considerations, see ibid.

interactions between students and tutors as an experience unfolds and with a built-in process of feedback or drafting to develop skills and achieve a high-quality end product. They often involve rehearsals of practical workshops, multiple drafts of lesson/session plans and help required to purchase stationery or other resources needed for an interactive workshop. They are student-centred, allowing students to discover solutions and solve problems in an organic and evolved way which needs to be inherently flexible and incorporate time and space for reflection as well as being facilitated by tutors. There is also a higher degree of administration involved in the work – for example, arranging transport, managing a budget or liaising with community groups. This presents challenges at a university level in terms of cost and practicality. We would suggest that a stronger case can be made for PLE, as it sits between client advice work and more traditional teaching while still offering significant benefits. This unique positioning of PLE opens up opportunities for a university to balance out the challenges and benefits.

In relation to PLE, these points are also relevant when considering the viability of an intracurricular or extracurricular course. An intracurricular model will ensure that staff time can be allocated. Sessions can be timetabled, building in time for student attendance and supervision as well as allocated teaching space. This dedicated time may allow for more work to be done (in pursuit of the public good), more structured learning through a programme of teaching and experience (contributing towards skills development and employability aims) as well as potentially providing inbuilt mechanisms to evaluate impact (against varying metrics). A budget (for materials and travelling expenses, for example) may also be easier to secure. However, an extracurricular programme may be more reliant on volunteers and goodwill.

Conversely, for some, an extracurricular project may afford a greater level of flexibility and further cost savings. For example, professional services staff may take responsibility for managing and supervising the work. Alternatively, across Europe there are examples of student-led PLE projects[74] with varying degrees of university input (in terms of funds and staffing).

There are further implications in relation to resources. In many jurisdictions, insurance will not be required for PLE work, staff involved may not need to maintain a legal practising status and nor will there be a need for bespoke spaces specifically to accommodate client casework. However, there are some points to consider in relation to teaching spaces. As reflected upon earlier, the nature of PLE work is more suited to the workshop or seminar style. Yet, beyond that, the methodology employed when teaching PLE is typically highly collaborative and interactive, so thought may need to be

[74] An example can be found at the University of Leicester: https://le.ac.uk/engagement/case-studies/street-law

given to teaching spaces which allow for this – whether that is larger rooms, the flexibility to move furniture (which may accommodate fewer students) or equipment such as large screens or multiple whiteboards for group work. Interactive sessions with community groups are routinely enhanced through the use of hardcopy printed resources or props, which again can add to the cost associated with PLE.

Enhancing public legal education through technology

To a greater or lesser extent, technology is rightly, and organically, interwoven into many aspects of CLE, whether this is to facilitate teaching students or in the tools used to deliver advice or information to the public. This is also the case with PLE. As we know, technology and artificial intelligence (AI) have the potential to widen reach, increase accessibility and engage all learners (whether that is those delivering or receiving PLE) in new and engaging ways. However, there are also challenges, such as cost, sustainability and the need to ensure appropriate checks and balances. Given its currency and relevance in the current climate, it is important to explore these further and in particular to look at the potential of technology and AI more broadly to enhance the teaching of PLE modules and increase public benefit.

For many readers, technology will already be a regular feature within the university student educational setting, from using AI designer tools to prepare slides, to checking emails in Large Language Models (LLMs). Videos, no-code apps and the use of virtual reality can all be incorporated into student PLE projects. Everyday tasks within a PLE project can be improved in terms of content and efficiency with AI. AI can also support PLE to create resources such as leaflets and videos, or even to prepare a session plan for a community group. Embracing this has significant value when scaling up projects for output and teaching ability. In addition, technology, including AI, will undoubtedly be an integral feature of future roles in the workplace, so, bearing in mind our observations regarding employability, harnessing and embracing, this arguably helps prepare students to enter the job market. It is vital that those leading PLE projects know what many students might already be using and ensure they support these activities being done ethically – for example, not entering confidential information into a public LLM like ChatGPT. Care needs to be taken by students to understand how to draft prompts and refine results – something which could form part of their professional ethics obligations. Those leading PLE projects will need to support students to view results produced by LLMs as starting points, not end products, be mindful of hallucinations and be particularly careful of jurisdiction inaccuracies when conducting legal research. These same points are also relevant for any PLE project which encourages members of the public to use AI to help them with their legal issues.

In this regard, technology and AI also have huge potential to be used to produce PLE outputs and tools for use by members of the public. These can range in terms of complexity and cost, and operate on a micro- or macro-scale.

Non-exhaustive examples include the following:

- *Social media:* a cost-effective and relatively easy form of disseminating information on a large scale. It has the potential to forge links between communities and provide accessible information via posts, blogs or forums, but can be unchecked in terms of content, accuracy and bias.
- *Podcasts:* these can have greater or lesser production costs to suit your needs (video podcasts often costing more) and can often be released on multiple podcast player platforms quite easily. Once produced and released, the static nature of podcasts could mean that any black letter law in them dates. The Kids Law podcast[75] and the ReImagine Law podcast[76] are two such examples of audio podcasts.
- *Virtual experiences:* these can be used in a number of ways, including as a means to deliver legal information and destigmatize legal environments such as the Open University virtual courtroom.[77]
- *Apps:* undoubtedly these require a great deal of expertise and cost to produce and maintain (to ensure legal and technical accuracy over time). However, they do reflect how many individuals currently and regularly engage with technology, including on their mobile devices. Apps have unlimited potential in terms of creative design, including gameplay, and can provide invaluable functions such as generating forms or letters for public use – for example, Project FORTITUDE[78] led by the University of Sheffield, which has overseen the development of the Law Yeah! digital game for use by children and young people. A further example includes ongoing work by one of the author's and colleagues at Northumbria University (in conjunction with a technology company and funded by Innovate UK) to develop a digital app designed to support individuals with legal information (using decision trees for a more tailored approach) and document generation to resolve disputes.

There will be many more examples and uses. Technology and AI are moving fast, which creates its own challenges and opportunities in the advancement of PLE.

---

75 www.kidslaw.info/

76 ReImagine Law, https://open.spotify.com/show/1miCa4ypgkaJFYdMf7F2Q8

77 https://university.open.ac.uk/open-justice/virtual-courtroom

78 https://sheffield.ac.uk/law/research/fortitude

In summary, PLE can be seen as less costly and resource-intensive than advice-based CLE, but more so than more traditional forms of teaching. Also, although there is certainly time associated with developing and maintaining external partnerships, these relationships are potentially easier to source and manage than the volume of clients that might be required for other forms of clinic work. PLE work can also involve a one-off interaction with an external organization or a series of interactions depending on your need and capacity. PLE presents valuable clinical opportunities for students on either an intracurricular or extracurricular basis. The points we have considered in relation to both design and resources support the idea that there is real potential for PLE to present a scalable means of offering clinical work to students beyond that which might be possible for advice-based work,[79] particularly through embracing technological advances.

University value

To make the case for the expansion of PLE within universities, there needs to be a positive impact in multiple ways. It is no longer sufficient to just demonstrate change for the community group engaging with the PLE project (worthy as this of course is). In any event, it is well-trodden ground that evaluating 'the causal link between PLE interventions and improved outcomes' for community participants (as opposed to measuring outputs)[80] is hard – although, we note, not impossible. It is difficult to assess the level of knowledge that participants have before a PLE initiative and then again afterwards. This is particularly the case for what is known as Just in Case PLE,[81] where participants might not be 'using' their newfound knowledge, skills or confidence for some time. Furthermore, it is difficult to measure the long-term changes that PLE projects can have on participants – for example, how do we know that a civics class attended by a 12-year-old student made them more likely to vote when they turned 18? It is even harder to measure interventions which result in individuals not taking a particular action, such as committing a crime. For many law schools, evaluating the benefit of PLE to the recipients will be limited due to timescales and resources (it is resource-heavy to track down the 12-year-old student after he has cast his first vote). To make the case for the expansion of PLE within a university,

79 Grimes (n 72) 96.

80 Wintersteiger et al (n 1).

81 'Helping to increase people's … general understanding, skills and confidence of legal issues, so that when they face problems in the future they are better equipped to know what to do.' 'A Ten Year Vision for Public Legal Education, Prepared by the Solicitor General's Committee on Public Legal Education', www.lawworks.org.uk/sites/default/files/files/10YearVisionForPLE-web.pdf

demonstrating impact beyond the community benefit will likely be more achievable and realistic, and will attract more tangible outcomes for growth. This includes the impact on law students (discussed earlier), the university, any third-party organizations and the local area. In short, there are often multiple overlapping instruments of value which law schools should build into a strategic approach.

The benefits to a university of a law school undertaking PLE are plentiful, but need to be articulated to be valued. Not only is PLE (in particular, Street Law) first-class pedagogy, it is also a blueprint which is translatable outside of law to other departments that have a desire to undertake public engagement and student knowledge exchange – for example, financial literacy courses, which are, for want of a better phrase, 'street economics', particularly in light of the European Commission's 2023 Financial Competence Framework for Children and Youth in the EU.[82] PLE projects are often held up as 'best practice' initiatives at universities, with staff and students sharing the project design, pedagogical approach and logistics. Furthermore, PLE can be the perfect conduit for interdisciplinarity, with students from multiple schools and faculties working together, reflecting this shift in the workplace.[83]

It goes without saying that universities can enhance their reputation, standing, recruitment (including widening participation in attracting students who are less represented within universities and the profession) and channels for external funding with properly engaged PLE projects. Such projects help a law school connect to local communities, not-for-profit organizations and sometimes with the legal profession. If universities want to create ethically engaged lawyers who have practical experience and a reflective mindset, then a PLE project can achieve all this, with a similar model being used in our disciplines across a university.

Universities have an important public engagement branch to their work. In many countries they are state-funded public institutions and there is a desire (or perhaps even duty) to 'be a good neighbour' within local communities. The National Coordinating Centre for Public Engagement in the UK aims to 'build an inclusive higher education sector where communities can contribute to, and benefit from, knowledge, teaching and research'.[84] In 2020

---

[82] European Commission, 'Financial Competence Framework for Children and Youth in the European Union', https://finance.ec.europa.eu/document/download/7540153e-7d3b-4d81-8bed-0cf8a80be53b_en?filename=230927-financial-competence-framework-children-youth_en.pdf

[83] Smith and Spencer advocate for 'poly technic' professionals from the Greek, meaning many-skilled. See Alexander Smith and Nigel Spencer, 'Do Lawyers Need to Learn Code?' in *Modernising Legal Practice* (Cambridge University Press 2020).

[84] The National Coordinating Centre for Public Engagement, www.publicengagement.ac.uk/, accessed 7 February 2024.

the European Commission published an Overview of Public Engagement in Research and Innovation,[85] which noted; 'Europe is investing major resources in producing research-based knowledge, but for this knowledge to become usable, accessible, transferable and valuable to citizens and society at large, investments in PE are also necessary.' PLE is the ideal forum to advance this aim of universities.

Universities play an important role within their communities and PLE programmes can potentially support and contribute to community wellbeing either directly or through working alongside nonprofit organizations. In Italy, public universities are bound by a 'third mission', which is a responsibility to use their teaching and research for the wider benefit of society, culture and the economy.[86] It is arguable that PLE can play a role in this by contributing to activities for community benefit and which demonstrate a commitment to lifelong learning in society. The University of Turin states: 'Departments carry out Third Mission activities and projects to strengthen dialogue and interaction among University, industry and society.'[87] In the UK, this is demonstrated by the growing importance of not just the Research Excellence Framework and the Teaching Excellence Framework, but since 2017 the Knowledge Exchange Framework directly valuing university outputs that use knowledge for societal good.[88]

Conclusion

With ever-growing financial pressures on universities across Europe, it might feel like the wrong time to expand this resource-demanding form of CLE. In fact, the opposite is true. There has never been a more important time for us to vibrantly and articulately make the case for increased PLE provision for law students and embrace technology to support this drive. PLE addresses many areas of increasing importance within higher education, employability and teaching, while delivering very impressive 'value for money' credentials when compared to client-focused CLE. The social justice mission of clinic is

[85] European Commission, 'Overview of Public Engagement in Research and Innovation', https://op.europa.eu/en/publication-detail/-/publication/6f3a03af-f2fb-11ee-8e14-01aa75ed71a1/language-en

[86] https://giurisprudenza.unimc.it/en/research/third-mission

[87] https://en.unito.it/research/third-mission

[88] Defined by the Knowledge Exchange Concordat as 'Knowledge Exchange (KE) is the two-way exchange of knowledge, expertise, and capabilities between higher education institutions (HEIs) and external partners (businesses, government bodies, non-profits, and communities). The goal is to create social, cultural, and economic benefits. KE includes activities like research commercialization, consultancy, public engagement, collaborative research, policy advising, and community outreach. The focus is on co-creation and mutual benefit for both academic institutions and their external partners.' See https://ke.org.uk/what-is-knowledge-exchange/

just as impressively instilled in our future lawyers through this medium and should be considered a core part of legal education, as clinic-based work is now becoming. In this chapter we have sought to make the case for more PLE investment, provision and discussion within law schools and the options to do so, highlighting these key themes:

1. A student focus: all good PLE is student-focused and led by the highest pedagogical standards.
2. A university focus: where there are multiple benefits for the university as a business and an institution.
3. Inclusion-centred: embracing the social justice mission of clinic, improving public legal capability, improving students' connectedness to the legal profession and their education, as well as promoting team work and democratic practices.

It has been shown globally that PLE has the flexibility and possibility to achieve great things. However, in some parts of the world, it is in its infancy in terms of its reach and scale. We hope the creative and responsive nature of PLE programmes (particularly as standalone courses) allows them to continue to flourish.

References

Advicenow, https://www.advicenow.org.uk/

Alberta Law Foundation, https://albertalawfoundation.org/who-we-are/our-vision-mission-values/

Arbetman L, 'Street Law, Inc.: Context, History and Future' (2018) 2(1) *International Journal of Public Legal Education* 3

Ashton J, 'Street Law at Sussex One Year on: Where Did We Come from, How Far Did We Get and Where Are We Going?' (2024) 31(2) *International Journal of Clinical Legal Education* 36

A Ten Year Vision for Public Legal Education, Prepared by the Solicitor General's Committee on Public Legal Education, www.lawworks.org.uk/sites/default/files/files/10YearVisionForPLE-web.pdf

A Vision for Public Legal Education and The Rule of Law: A Joint Meeting of the All-Party Parliamentary Groups of the Rule of Law and Public Legal Education & Pro Bono, 31 October 2018, www.lawworks.org.uk/sites/default/files/files/APPG-BriefingPaper-A-10y-Vision-forPLE-.pdf

Barton K, Cunningham CD, Jones GT and Maharg P, 'Valuing What Clients Think: Standardized Clients and the Assessment of Communicative Competence' (2006) 13(1) *Clinical Law Review* 1

Barwick J, Kirk E, Lai-Chong Law E and Watkins D, 'Exploring Children's Understanding of Law in Their Everyday Lives' (2018) 38(1) *Legal Studies* 59

Bright KL and McNicholl M, 'The Open University Law School's Public Legal Education in Prisons: Contributing to Rehabilitative Prison Culture' (2021) 5(1) *International Journal of Public Legal Education* 94

Buhler S and Stalker R, 'Place-Based Education: Clinical Legal Education and Ethics' in O Madhloom and H McFaul (eds), *Thinking about Clinical Legal Education* (Routledge, 2021)

Centre for Public Legal Education Alberta, https://www.cplea.ca/

Draslarová H, 'Street Law as a Unique Learning Method: What Do Students Themselves Actually Find to Be Its Benefits? Answers from the Czech Republic' (2019) 3(1) *International Journal of Public Legal Education* 123

Dunn R, 'The Knowledge, Skills and Attributes Considered Necessary to Start Day 1 Training Competently and Whether Live Client Clinics Develop Them' (PhD thesis, Northumbria University, 2017)

European Commission, 'Financial Competence Framework for Children and Youth in the European Union', https://finance.ec.europa.eu/document/download/7540153e-7d3b-4d81-8bed-0cf8a80be53b_en?filename=230927-financial-competence-framework-children-youth_en.pdf

European Commission, 'Overview of Public Engagement in Research and Innovation', https://op.europa.eu/en/publication-detail/-/publication/6f3a03af-f2fb-11ee-8e14-01aa75ed71a1/language-en

European Network of Clinical Legal Education, www.encle.eu/

European University Association, 'Enhancing the Education Mission of European Universities: A Proactive Response to Change', www.eua.eu/downloads/content/ten%20european%20principles%20for%20the%20enhancement%20of%20learning%20and%20teaching16102017.pdf

Fisher M, 'So What Is Street Law Anyway: A US Perspective' (2017) 1(1) *International Journal of Public Legal Education* 87

Gander LE, 'The Radical Promise of Public Legal Education in Canada' (Master's thesis, University of Alberta, 1999)

Global Alliance of Justice Education, www.gaje.org/

Grimes R, 'Legal Literacy, Community Empowerment and Law Schools: Some Lessons from a Working Model in the UK' (2003) 37 *The Law Teacher* 273

Grimes R, *Public Legal Education: The Role of Law Schools in Building a More Legally Literate Society* (Routledge, 2021)

Grimes R, McQuoid-Mason D, O'Brien E and Zimmer J, 'Street Law and Social Justice Education' in F Bloch (ed), *The Global Clinical Movement: Educating Lawyers for Social Justice* (Oxford University Press, 2011)

International Journal of Clinical Legal Education, www.northumbriajournals.co.uk/index.php/ijcle

Jaffe D, Bender KM and Organ J, '"It Is Okay to Not Be Okay": The 2021 Survey of Law Student Well-Being' (2021) 60 *University of Louisville Law Review* 441

Kidslaw, www.kidslaw.info/

Knowledge Exchange UK, https://ke.org.uk/what-is-knowledge-exchange/

LawWorks, www.lawworks.org.uk/sites/default/files/files/LawWorks%20Law%20Schools%20Report%202020_0.pdf

Leader K, *Litigants in Person in the Civil Justice System: In Their Own Words* (Bloomsbury Publishing, 2024)

McKeown P, 'Pro Bono: What's in It for Law Students? The Students' Perspective' (2017) 24(2) *International Journal of Clinical Legal Education* 43

McKeown P and Morse S, 'Litigants in Person: Is There a Role for Higher Education?' (2015) 49(1) *The Law Teacher* 122

McQuoid-Mason D, Mchunu M, Govender K, O'Brien EL and Curd Larkin M, *Democracy for All: Education towards a Democratic Culture* (Juta, 1994)

McQuoid-Mason DJ, 'The Genesis of Street Law in South Africa' (2017) 1(1) *International Journal of Public Legal Education* 93

Muja A, Menz C, Danaii D, Hauschildt K, van Mensvoort C and Cuppe J, 'Student Well-Being: The Role of Socio-demographic Background, Contextual Conditions, and Study Demands and Resources on the Well-being of Students in the European Higher Education Area' (2024), *Eurostudent.eu*, www.eurostudent.eu/download_files/documents/EUROSTUDENT_2024_student_well_being.pdf

Nicholson A, 'The Value of a Law Degree' (2020) 54(2) *The Law Teacher* 194

O'Brien EL, Greene E and McQuoid-Mason D, *Human Rights for All* (West Publishing Co, 1996)

Onward, 'The Kids Aren't Alright', www.ukonward.com/wp-content/uploads/2022/09/kids-arent-alright-democracy.pdf

PLEAS Task Force, *Developing Capable Citizens: The Role of Public Legal Education* (2007), www.plecanada.org/wp-content/uploads/2018/10/Developing-Capable-citizens-the-role-of-public-legal-education-2007.pdf

QS Global Employer Survey 2022, 'What do Employers Want from Todays Graduates', https://insights.qs.com/hubfs/Reports/What%20do%20employers%20want%20from%20todays%20graduates%20%20(1).pdf?utm_medium=email&_hsmi=65742003&utm_co

ReImagine Law, https://open.spotify.com/show/1miCa4ypgkaJFYdMf7F2Q8

ReImagine Law, Public Legal Education and Street Law, 23 January 2025, https://open.spotify.com/episode/2QLQZF9jbY1XmJ3cz8dS6G

Ridout F and Thomas L, *Street Law: Theory and Practice* (Bloomsbury Publishing, 2023)

Roper V, 'Blogs as a Teaching Tool and Method of Public Legal Education: A Case Study' (2018) 2(1) *International Journal of Public Legal Education* 46

Saunders S, 'Street Law Assisting Access to Justice in the Employment Tribunal: A Practice Report' (2019) 3(1) *International Journal of Public Legal Education* 50

Singapore Institute of Legal Education, www.sile.edu.sg/pro-bono-programme

Smith A and Spencer N, 'Do Lawyers Need to Learn Code?' in C Denvir (ed), *Modernising Legal Practice* (Cambridge University Press, 2020)

Street Law Inc., www.streetlaw.org

The National Coordinating Centre for Public Engagement, www.publicengagement.ac.uk/

The Open University, https://university.open.ac.uk/open-justice/virtual-courtroom

The Sutton Trust, www.suttontrust.com/our-research/unpaid-and-underpaid-internships/

Thomas L, '"It Puts the Law They've Learnt in Theory into Practice": Exploring Employer Understandings of Clinical Legal Education' in L Thomas, S Vaughan, B Malkani and T Lynch (eds), *Clinical Legal Education* (Hart Publishing, 2018)

University of Birmingham, https://program-and-modules-handbook.bham.ac.uk/webhandbooks/WebHandbooks-control-servlet;JSESSIONID_PMH=FWwUpxD9ph1Qjrsm0G43z14AiNKjg9o1DW33z6x81qVYTcPpQcwg!-936296336?Action=getModuleDetailsList&pgSubj=08&pgCrse=33567&searchTerm=002025

University of Leicester, https://le.ac.uk/engagement/case-studies/street-law

University of Macerata, https://giurisprudenza.unimc.it/en/research/third-mission

University of Sheffield, https://sheffield.ac.uk/law/research/fortitude

University of Turin, https://en.unito.it/research/third-mission

Wallace A and Perdue B, 'Preparing Lawyers for Practice: Developing Cultural Competency, Communication Skills, and Content Knowledge through Street Law Programs' (2020) 70(2) *Journal of Legal Education* 95

Wintersteiger L, 'Legal Education beyond the Academy: The Neoliberal Reorientation of Public Legal Education' (2019) 30(2) *Law and Critique* 123

Wintersteiger L, Morse S, Olatokun M and Morris C, *Effectiveness of Public Legal Education Initiatives: A Literature Review* (Legal Services Board 2021)

Wizner S, 'Beyond Skills Training' (2000) 7 *Clinical Law Review* 327

Young Citizens, www.youngcitizens.org/

8

Clinical Legal Education in Georgia and the Street Law Experience

Ketevan Bakhtadze, Tamar Ebralidze, Richard Grimes, Ana Kharaishvili, Tsira Komakhidze, Marina Kvachadze, Ketevan Mchedlishvili, Nana Shonia, Sandro Sordia, Ani Topuria, Leila Tskhovrebashvili and Amy Wallace

Introduction

Legal clinics based in and/or organized by law schools are an increasingly prominent feature across the civil, common, Shari'a and customary law worlds. They have existed in the Republic of Georgia for at least the last 20 years.[1] In common with many countries, these clinics take a variety of forms in order to reflect existing need and available expertise and resources. The models include in-house advice and representation services, law reform and campaign initiatives, partnerships with nongovernmental organizations (NGOs), placements with local government and other law-related offices, and public legal education (PLE) programmes.

While much of the existing Georgian clinical legal education (CLE) provision owes its presence to the determination and commitment of particular individuals in universities and lawyers in legal practice, government too has played an important historical role at a city and a national level. In particular, in 2011, the accreditation of the Georgian regulatory process introduced a stipulation that all law schools in Georgia should offer modules/courses in 'Practical Law'.[2] Some interpret this as meaning an opportunity

1 S Rosenbaum et al, 'Clinical Legal Education in Central Asia and the Middle East' in J Giddings (ed), *Global Clinical Legal Education* (Routledge 2025) 222.

2 N Bogverdaze et al, *Study on Legal Clinics in Higher Education of Georgia* (SIFA, EU4Justice, UNDP 2018) 4.

for students to practise law in a university clinic, while others have used externships with other legal service providers. One increasingly popular Practical Law activity has been various forms of PLE, through which law schools and their staff and selected students (often at master's level) engage with the community – both urban and rural – to raise awareness of fundamental legal rights and responsibilities. This version of 'clinic' is particularly attractive as it addresses identified needs – improving legal literacy among the public and addressing the development of knowledge, skills and values among law students.

One iteration of PLE that is now well established across Georgia is termed 'Street Law', following the model that was developed at Georgetown University, Washington DC in the early 1970s. This PLE format is intended to be both beneficial to communities and students, and is a relatively straightforward way of providing legal assistance and enhancing a student's education. It is also likely to be significantly less resource-intensive than an in-house legal clinic offering services to individual clients. This is largely because Street Law can be delivered to significant numbers with there usually being no ongoing supervisory demands beyond preparation for and delivery of the relevant Street Law sessions.

This chapter looks briefly at CLE in Georgia in general and then focuses specifically on PLE/Street Law developments in the country. The chapter is the result of a collaborative effort by key actors in the Georgian clinical scene supported by two Street Law practitioners from outside of the jurisdiction, both with substantial international PLE and clinic development experience. Specific examples of clinical initiatives at named universities across Georgia are provided.

Legal education and legal clinics in Georgia

Legal education understandably plays a pivotal role in shaping the future of the legal profession and upholding the rule of law in society.[3] The importance of this is perhaps even more significant in a country such as Georgia that has experienced relatively recent and major political and constitutional change.

A critical component of effective legal education is the opportunity for students to apply theory to practice and reflect on that application. In live-client work, such as in a law school legal clinic, this also requires effective supervision to ensure that services offered meet requisite professional standards. CLE also requires appropriate assessment methods.[4] Known as

---

[3] DL Rhode, 'Legal Education: Rethinking the Problem, Reimagining the Reforms' (2013) 40 *Pepperdine Law Review* 437, 438–39.

[4] RT Stuckey, *Best Practices for Legal Education: A Vision and a Road Map* (Clinical Legal Education Association 2007) 165–67.

'experiential learning', the clinical approach has gained significant traction in legal education globally over the past few decades.[5]

In Georgia, universities have increasingly, if sometimes unevenly, integrated practical legal education programmes, such as legal clinics and Street Law courses, into their curricula. As mentioned earlier, the requirement for a Practical Law component has added to the experiential momentum. The overall aim is to bridge the gap between doctrinal knowledge and practical skills through the actual application of both while, in many instances, simultaneously serving the community through various legal service initiatives.

Some in Georgia contend that the country's legal education system is facing a deep crisis. They argue that undergraduate and graduate law programmes are often similar, with overlapping faculty membership (due to salary levels, it is common for academic staff to work at more than one institution) and with most curricula lacking individuality and originality.[6] There are significant gaps in practical legal education and training. In one study, of the 11 universities surveyed, only three offered mandatory courses on the practice of law at bachelor's level, with two more providing elective options. It is said that this lack of consistent practical training in educational programmes fails to adequately prepare students with the necessary practical and professional skills for legal practice and (other) subsequent employment.[7]

Where CLE programmes do exist in Georgian universities, they share some similarities with international 'best practice', but also exhibit notable differences particularly where assessment and supervision are concerned. While some Georgian programmes aim to provide practical legal skills training along with elements of community service, the methods employed for assessing student performance and ensuring quality vary considerably across institutions.

Georgian universities typically employ a combination of interim and final assessments for their clinical programmes. This aligns with international recommendations for using both formative and summative assessments to evaluate students' progress and achievement.[8] However, the specific components and weightings of these assessments differ across Georgian

5 MM Barry, JC Dubin and PA Joy, 'Clinical Education for This Millennium: The Third Wave' (2000) 7 *Clinical Law Review* 1, 13–14.

6 D Gegenava, 'Law as It Is, Law as It Ought to Be: Darkness at the End of the Curriculum' in D Gegenava (ed), *Lado Chanturia 60* (Davit Batonishvili Law Institute at Sulkhan-Saba Orbeliani University 2023) 454.

7 N Khantadze, *Legal Practice Programmes in Georgia: Assessment and Recommendations* (2019) 54, https://library.iliauni.edu.ge/ebooks/iuridiuli-praqtikis-programmeebi-saqarthvelo shi-shephaseba-da-rekomendatsiebi/

8 Stuckey (n 4).

institutions. The extent of integration of clinical programmes within the broader law school curriculum is another area where Georgian practices may differ from internationally accepted standards. The Carnegie Report stresses the importance of connecting clinical experiences with doctrinal learning throughout the law school experience.[9] While some Georgian universities, such as Batumi Shota Rustaveli State University, integrate their Street Law programme into their overall legal clinic programme, the extent of integration across the full curriculum is not evidenced, judging by the available data.

The regulatory requirement to have Practical Law courses means these are largely integrated into existing legal clinics, which are broadly aimed at enhancing students' theoretical knowledge, developing lawyering and related skills, and introducing concepts of professional responsibility and wider ethical considerations.

The development of 'Practical Law' in Georgian legal education

As seen in the preceding sections, all accredited law schools in Georgia are required to have a Practical Law component. This is left to universities to define and implement, and has been interpreted and applied in varying ways. Some use live-client clinic models (providing advice and/or representation), while others rely on externships/partnerships with existing legal service providers, such as those in private legal practice, NGOs and/or governmental bodies. An increasing number use the Street Law model of PLE.

As noted earlier, Street Law started in the US and originated in 1972. The programme was initially launched as an initiative of Georgetown University students, but soon became a formal clinic of the Georgetown University Law Center (GULC). Over time, this clinical programme has been introduced in over 100 law schools across the US, extending its reach from schools and community groups to juvenile correctional facilities and the wider penitentiary system. A key feature of these programmes is the emphasis on the law affecting everyday life (hence the term 'Street Law') and developing such skills as problem solving and conflict resolution, benefiting both the student Street Law trainers and community participants, fostering the principles and values of a democratic society.

The implementation of PLE, Street Law-style in Georgia began with the involvement of the American Bar Association's and its Rule of Law Initiative (ABA/ROLI). The first Georgian Street Law programme was

[9] WM Sullivan et al, *Educating Lawyers: Preparation for the Profession of Law* (John Wiley 2007) 191–192.

designed and sessions were delivered in early 2005, in a private school in Tbilisi, where six law students from Ivane Javakhishvili Tbilisi State University (TSU) prepared and presented material on basic rights and responsibilities to high school pupils. This pilot phase proved successful in terms of feedback from all concerned, and by September 2005, Street Law was up and running in ten secondary schools, seven located in Tbilisi and the rest in other Georgian cities – Telavi, Kutaisi and Batumi – spreading across much of the country from east to west. Twenty master's-level law students were trained by the ABA, under the guidance of GULC Professor Richard Roe, and in 2006, nine of these students were selected to attend a 'training of trainers' programme at GULC's Street Law Clinic.

The TSU initiative, which was renamed the Institute of Practical Law Clinic (a term later adopted by the regulatory authority for legal education, but covering a wider remit than PLE), was rapidly replicated across Georgia. It was introduced in both public and private schools in Tbilisi, Batumi, Kutaisi, Telavi, Gori and Akhaltsikhe.

The aim of the entire project was to inform schoolchildren about fundamental legal issues, supporting their civic self-awareness. Furthermore, the law students who take part were able to develop and then share their legal knowledge with the schoolchildren, contributing significantly to the education of the next generation and promoting a practical understanding of the rule of law.

The GULC model was invaluable for piloting the project at TSU, which was the first Georgian higher education institution to introduce such a Practical Law Clinic as a credit-bearing elective for master's students. By 2007, 20 graduate students from the Faculty of Law at TSU were involved in Street Law. Over time, this programme has evolved, now a mandatory component for all students in the three areas of master's-level study (Criminal Law, Civil Law and Public Law). Working with children in schools and providing them with basic legal knowledge through Street Law sessions has become an integral part of the graduate students' educational experience. In common with other forms of experiential learning, the Street Law initiative aligns with the 'Practical Law' curricula requirements of the Ministry of Education and Science of Georgia.

Master's students at TSU currently conduct 12 sessions for schoolchildren each academic semester. Class sessions last between 75 and 90 minutes. Participation in the Practical Law or Street Law Clinic is a mandatory part of the 30-credit system of so-called 'practical education', providing students with 12 credits upon successful completion. Students typically lead Street Law sessions in pairs, ideally consisting of individuals from different legal disciplines (for example, a Civil Law master's student paired with a Criminal Law student). It is also encouraged that pairs include both male and female students to enhance academic quality and diversity while boosting the confidence of the trainers.

Initially, in 2007, the training module's topics were predetermined, covering law and legal systems, human rights, the constitution and democracy, crime and conflict resolution. Today, the first eight lessons that the law students teach are mandatory and four may be chosen by the teaching pairs. Before commencing clinical activities, the students undergo three days of induction and training, including on ground rules, research techniques, and effective teaching and learning methods.

In the Practical Law Clinic, students start their activities by introducing law and legal systems, helping schoolchildren understand basic legal concepts, distinguishing between violations of law and simply socially undesirable behaviour, and grasping the basic functions of the legal system including legal procedures and the concept of a fair trial. They explore the difference between civil and criminal law as well as particular aspects of law that may affect their everyday lives. Following this, trainers cover the constitution and democracy over two training sessions, informing students about basic human rights and freedoms, thereby highlighting the importance of protecting these rights and utilizing appropriate mechanisms in case of infringement.

Mandatory training topics also include the rights of minors and crimes against the person, as well as property issues, the importance of contracts and possible forms of dispute resolution. Of the optional subjects, the law students often cover family and inheritance law, marriage prerequisites, spousal entitlements and duties, and employment rights.

Master's students conduct a mock trial as the twelfth and final session, where the schoolchildren take an active part. This activity inevitably receives very positive feedback from all concerned. Clinic staff provide organizational support throughout the process, including providing a specially equipped room for the mock trial, complete with items such as judge's robes, stationery and projectors. Preparation for the mock trial includes individual consultations with each participant, and an external person, often a real judge, may be invited to enhance the feeling of reality and impartiality.

Moreover, if students wish to deepen their experience after completing the mandatory portion of the clinic, they can volunteer to conduct an additional nine Street Law sessions in the following semester, earning them a further nine credits. During this extended period, the student selects topics and explores legal issues not covered in the initial 12 sessions. Importantly, during this extended programme, the student conducts eight sessions with their own study group and one with schoolchildren of other trainers, allowing for a broader assessment of their skills and adaptability in the context of a new audience.

Despite TSU being located in the capital Tbilisi, master's students are encouraged to conduct sessions in other cities (for example, Gori and Mtskheta).

The head of the clinic may visit any training session unannounced, keeping students 'on their toes' and reinforcing the need for graduate students to maintain high standards in their teaching. Master's students are also required to attend weekly seminars, where they present reports on each Street Law session and discuss challenges faced in the teaching process. Individual counselling is provided by the head of the clinic to support students who experience difficulties.

At the end of the Street Law sessions, participants receive certificates confirming their participation in Street Law, which appears to boost motivation. Additionally, students can request certificates that validate their academic achievements in this aspect of clinic. In recent semesters, it has also become possible to receive this documentation in English, which students say they find useful, especially when seeking employment.

Over time, the methodological approach used has improved, moving away from over-reliance on lecture-style delivery and engaging the schoolchildren more through group work, practical exercises, mock trials and other interactive learning and teaching approaches, all of which enhance student and target audience involvement and interest in the learning process. In particular, starting sessions with mind-mapping exercises – where students record and discuss initial ideas that are raised – has proven to be a particularly effective way of encouraging engagement.

Since the 2004–2005 academic year, the Practical Law Clinic at TSU has grown and developed as an integral part of the master's programme under the current leadership of Ana Kharaishvili and is a major and much-publicized feature of the whole university. This matches the experience in other places globally, where law schools often give significant publicity to their CLE work, as it addresses both a social mission to help the public as well as serving educational aims for its own students.[10]

The educational benefits of law clinics and Street Law

The educational benefits of CLE in general and Street Law in particular are wide-ranging, varied and potentially profound. Admittedly, empirical evidence for this is hard to find, but there is ample (albeit largely anecdotal) evidence that all participants – students, clients, law professors, university managers and wider stakeholders such as the legal profession, other employers and government – are frequently fulsome in their praise of legal clinics.

At Telavi State University, for example, the institution is committed to enhancing and advancing the pedagogical content of its legal clinics as both

[10] Although it must be said that institutional enthusiasm for CLE may not be met by adequate resourcing – a problem that is not limited to Georgia!

an academic and practical course of study, recognizing the necessity for its modernization in line with contemporary demands and international 'best practice'. In Georgia, this represents a significant shift away from more traditional 'top-down' approaches to learning and teaching.

Judged by feedback received, the development of the Street Law programme as part of Telavi State University's legal clinic has had significant educational benefits for university students. The Bachelor Programme in Law at Iakob Gogebashvili Telavi State University was established in 2016 and currently offers a live-client clinic dealing with general legal issues, as well as a clinic specializing in small business matters. Both initiatives are designed to enhance learning and teaching, and improve legal education more generally, as well as serving wider community interests.

While the educational benefits may manifest themselves in the form of enhanced knowledge, skills and values development (particularly evidenced by student academic and practical performance), there are a range of factors that influence the extent of progress made in this respect. These include the following:

- *Faculty support*: experienced faculty members are essential for guiding students through their clinical experiences. Faculty can provide mentorship, ensure the quality of legal work and help students reflect on their experiences to maximize attainment of learning outcomes.
- *Partnerships and resources*: universities can establish partnerships with schools, legal aid organizations, not-for-profit groups and community-based organizations to enable and expand clinical work. Universities are also well placed to contribute towards meeting local needs and complementing (and not duplicating) services provided by others. In this way, students can be provided with a wide range of clinical opportunities. Pooling resources such as legal databases, office space and administrative support can also enhance the effectiveness of clinical programmes.
- *Evaluation and improvement*: regular and ongoing evaluation of clinical programmes is crucial for ensuring the effective monitoring of performance and impact, and supporting development and sustainability. Universities can gather feedback from students, clients, communities and legal practitioners to refine and improve their clinical offerings, ensuring they meet educational and community needs.

The students involved in the Telavi State University's Legal Clinic participate in the clinic in the seventh and eighth semesters of their four-year undergraduate Law degree. In addition, ten students from the undergraduate programme in Business Studies participate in the Business Clinic. Students perform a variety of services that broadly fall into three categories:

1. In the live-client clinic, students, under the supervision of suitably qualified staff, act on behalf of clients in a wide range of legal matters. This clinic variously involves interviewing clients, conducting legal research, drafting legal documents and appearing in court or other legal proceedings under the supervision of a licensed attorney and a mentor lecturer. The legal clinic concentrates on civil and administrative law. If required and if resources permit, the clinic provides assistance to clients in dealing with administrative bodies including: representation in tribunals; requesting and searching for public information; drafting of various agreements and legal documents; the registration application of an entrepreneurial entity; and issuing permits and licences.

   Students either work individually or in groups of two to three as determined by the relevant case supervisor. Approximately five to seven clients get free legal assistance each month during the semester. The beneficiaries include academic and administrative staff and students at the university, pupils and teachers in public and private schools, young entrepreneurs, ethnic minorities (people living in the Pankisi and Karadjala regions), women suffering discrimination or abuse, people with disabilities, and NGOs from the Kakheti region. Effective communication with clients is essential. Students meet with them, explain legal matters in plain language and keep clients informed about the progress of their cases. These activities are all carried out under the supervision of an academic staff member and/or a practising lawyer. An important aspect of clinical work is legal research, and students must analyse legal issues, identify relevant rules and precedents, and draft well-reasoned legal documents and arguments.
2. The Business Clinic for young entrepreneurs involves fourth-year Business students, who have undertaken a preparation programme. In their induction, students have to carry out a range of simulated exercises – for example, drafting a business plan – to prepare them for taking part in the Business Clinic. Under the supervision of business education degree lecturers, they then assist clients in the preparation of actual business plans for their entrepreneurial ideas.

   Legal clinic students also assist the entrepreneurs alongside the Business students. Together they offer guidance to individuals seeking to establish small businesses, including forming business entities, drafting relevant contracts and other documentation, and advising on legal and business matters more generally. They also assist with administrative matters, such as registration of businesses, taxation issues, permit issuance and licensing.
3. The Street Law clinic represents a significant development in experiential learning. Although in its very early stages of development at Telavi State University, the clinic is anticipated to be a major and significant addition to the overall experiential offerings, giving many more students the chance to be involved.

To summarize, such developments are suggested as having tangible benefits for both students and the community, whether in the form of educational advancement for Law students (and possibly others as in the Telavi example) and/or legal service provision for members of the public.

As mentioned earlier in this chapter, the developments at Telavi are very much part of the growing trend in legal education to secure more effective and engaged learning and teaching in Georgia. To this end, Telavi State University cooperates with other universities in Georgia and further afield in promoting, supporting and sustaining experiential learning. CLE offers invaluable benefits to law students by bridging the gap between theory and practice, enhancing their professional skills, and preparing them for diverse legal and other careers. Universities play a pivotal role in developing and supporting robust clinical programmes, ensuring that students gain meaningful experiences that contribute to their educational and professional development. The Street Law programme at Telavi State University in particular illustrates both the potential and the impact of experiential learning by extending legal education to local communities and enriching students' educational journeys. As legal education continues to evolve globally, and in Georgia, the integration of practical, community-focused programmes will remain essential for preparing the next generation of legal professionals and equipping all for purposeful futures.

Supervising and assessing students undertaking Practical Law

In this section we examine approaches to student supervision and assessment in Georgian university legal clinics generally, but with specific reference to Street Law programmes, measuring them against accepted international 'best practice' and providing recommendations for improvement going forward. Imperative among these is the need to have clear learning outcomes that are aligned with assessment methods and criteria to ensure that such outcomes are achieved.[11] Recognition of this need has been a relatively recent development in Georgia and is now firmly enshrined in the Benchmark Standards for Law adopted by the Ministry of Education and applicable to all Georgian law schools.[12]

As noted earlier in this chapter, assessment methods across Georgian universities vary considerably, but in Street Law clinics these now typically

[11] D Gegenava and P Javakhishvili, 'Constitutional Proceedings: A New Challenge for Georgian Legal Education' (2022) *Journal of the Constitutional Court of Georgia* 15, https://constcourt.ge/files/4/2)%20Gegenava,%20Javakhishvili%20ENG%202022.pdf

[12] National Centre for Educational Quality Enhancement, *Sector Benchmark for Law; VI and VII Level(s)* (Ministry of Education 2019).

include evaluation of training plans, demonstration of presentations and materials, and observations of training sessions conducted with community groups. Some institutions, like Batumi State University and Georgian National University, require post-Street Law delivery presentations summarizing students' achievements, reflections and recommendations. Assessment may also take the form of a final exam or be part of an interim evaluation. Course supervisors commonly provide intensive induction sessions and weekly seminars to prepare students for community engagement. Additionally, some universities require students to present on current legal issues to improve their presentation skills and deepen theoretical knowledge.

Sulkhan-Saba Orbeliani University's Practical Law course, for example, employs an assessment regime, utilizing a 100-point system with 80 points allocated to interim evaluations and 20 points to the final assessment. The interim assessment components include evaluations of legal documents relating to court proceedings such as commencing actions, appeals, complaints, constitutional claims and European Court of Human Rights applications. This approach emphasizes practical skills development across various legal domains. The university's assessment strategy also incorporates practical assignments and case analyses, reflecting a focus on real-world application of legal knowledge. The final assessment involves a clinical learning report and presentation made to the class, where the students are asked to demonstrate their ability to synthesize and communicate the nature and value of their practical experiences.[13] This multifaceted assessment method aims to comprehensively evaluate students' theoretical understanding, practical skills and ability to navigate complex legal scenarios. It is designed to prepare them for the diverse challenges of legal practice. One significant difference that distinguishes Sulkhan-Saba Orbeliani University from other universities is the final evaluation of clinical reports by a panel. This approach allows not only the course leader but also other specialists to participate in the assessment of clinical education.[14]

---

[13] As part of the final assessment, the student delivers a public presentation of their clinical teaching report. The public presentation of the clinical teaching report takes place during the 14th and 15th academic weeks. The student can earn a maximum of 20 points for the public presentation of the clinical teaching report. The clinical teaching report must include a description of the clinic, a description/analysis of activities carried out during the clinical teaching process, and a summary of clinical teaching outcomes. The clinical teaching report should provide a clear understanding of the Practical Law Clinic and the implementation process of clinical teaching. The clinical teaching report must be accompanied by model lesson presentations prepared in PowerPoint.

[14] The public presentation of the clinical teaching report is evaluated by a committee established by the Dean of the Faculty. The final score is determined by calculating the arithmetic mean of the received points (the sum of points divided by the number of evaluators). The assessment criteria for the clinical teaching report and its public

International best practice, as outlined by Stuckey, emphasizes the importance of multiple assessment methods to capture the full range of student learning and skills development.[15] While Georgian programmes may incorporate various assessment tools such as practical assignments, mock trials and presentations, there appears to be less emphasis on structured self-reflection and peer assessment compared to that recommended internationally. The level of supervision and feedback provided in Georgian clinical programmes is not, as yet, clearly defined. International standards, as discussed for example by Foxhoven, stress the importance of regular, detailed feedback from supervisors and opportunities for student self-reflection.[16] The Carnegie Report also highlights the value of expert feedback in developing professional skills.[17] There is still much to be done in the Georgian context in this respect.

Georgian law schools do now (particularly since the introduction of the Practical Law regulatory requirement) emphasize learning across a range of doctrinal knowledge and legal skills, including application of theoretical principles, the value of teamwork, the development of effective communication, and a set of professional and ethical considerations. While reflective practice may not yet be fully developed in Georgia, this broad focus does, however, align with international recommendations for developing core competencies necessary for legal practice.[18] Yet, the extent to which these competencies are systematically assessed and tracked throughout the clinical experience may vary between Georgian (and other) institutions. One notable difference between Georgian practices and international recommendations is the apparent lack of standardization across institutions. This may gradually improve in light of the relatively recent adoption of the Benchmark Standards referred to earlier. While diversity in programme design can allow for innovation and adaptation to local needs, it may also lead to inconsistencies in the quality and depth of clinical legal education development, including Street Law. International best practices, as outlined in Stuckey's work, emphasize the importance of clear, consistent

presentation are: the visual aspects of presentation materials, a description of the clinic, a description/analysis of activities conducted during the clinical teaching process, and a summary of clinical teaching outcomes.

15 Stuckey (n 4) 239–240.

16 JR Foxhoven, 'Beyond Grading: Assessing Student Readiness to Practice Law' (2009) 16 *Clinical Law Review* 335, 346–348.

17 Sullivan et al (n 9) 145.

18 American Bar Association, *Legal Education and Professional Development – An Educational Continuum*, Report of the Task Force on Law Schools and the Profession: Narrowing the Gap (ABA 1992) 138–141.

standards for clinical education to ensure all students receive high-quality practical training.[19]

While Georgian legal clinical education programmes share some commonalities with international best practices, there are areas where alignment could be improved. Enhancing standardization, increasing the emphasis on structured reflection and feedback, and ensuring closer integration with the broader curriculum could help strengthen the effectiveness of these programmes in preparing students for the careers ahead of them.

A structural analysis of Georgian CLE, particularly within the Street Law component, reveals a systematized pedagogical framework that emphasizes both individual and collaborative learning methodologies. Students participate both individually and in pairs, ensuring multidimensional development of professional competencies. This approach is particularly significant in strengthening the social dimension of legal education.

The institutional supervision mechanism at Sulkhan-Saba Orbeliani University represents a multilayered system that integrates direct classroom instruction (14 hours) with structured practical components (38 hours). The assessment criteria for assignments (ranging from 6 to 8 points) emphasize not only technical competence but also collaborative working abilities, which are essential for the successful implementation of the Street Law programme. Of particular note is the paired work component, which facilitates the development of professional communication and cooperation skills, which are critical in contemporary legal practice. The structured supervisory framework demonstrates a thoughtful integration of pedagogical methodology with practical skills development, though opportunities exist for enhanced standardization in assessment practices.

Public legal education needs in Georgia

Improving PLE and raising legal awareness in society remains a significant challenge for Georgia's democratic development. Despite the increasing number of law graduates in recent years, there is still a deficit of legal knowledge among the broader population.[20] This problem is caused by several

[19] Stuckey (n 4) 167–168.

[20] Georgian Young Lawyers' Association, *Legal Awareness Study in Georgia* (GYLA 2018), https://gyla.ge/files/news/%E1%83%A4%E1%83%9D%E1%83%9C%E1%83%93%E1%83%98/Annual%20Report%202018.pdf

factors, including the lack of access to basic legal education for nonlawyers and paternalistic attitudes inherited from the Soviet era.

Street Law programmes, as the iteration of one model of PLE and one component of the responses to the Ministry's Practical Law requirement, aim to empower citizens with the provision of practical legal knowledge. This enables them to recognize and better understand their rights and responsibilities, and to identify ways in which legal issues can be addressed and possibly resolved.[21]

Evidenced by the many (admittedly anecdotal) reports from participating law students, supervisors, academic colleagues and members of the public who are involved, the introduction of Street Law programmes in Georgia is proving to be a particularly popular and effective way to address legal literacy, public empowerment and access to justice more generally.

The continuing and developing need for Street Law-style education in Georgia is driven by several important factors:

- *Raising legal awareness*: similar to the situation in many countries globally, a large portion of Georgia's population lacks sufficient knowledge about their rights and responsibilities.[22] Street Law programmes can help to increase public awareness and encourage people to recognize and actively protect their rights. This is particularly important for vulnerable groups such as ethnic minorities, socially disadvantaged individuals and people with disabilities.[23]
- *Promoting active citizenship*: active citizen participation is an essential component for strengthening democratic processes in Georgia.[24] Street Law programmes provide knowledge about rules, mechanisms and tools that allow citizens to engage more fully in society, including decision-making processes – for example, participating in public hearings, submitting petitions and collaborating with local governmental and community-based bodies.

---

[21] Street Law, Inc., 'What Is Street Law?' (2021), www.streetlaw.org/who-we-are/what-is-street-law

[22] *Human Rights at Local Level in Georgia: Assessment Report*, https://rm.coe.int/assessment-report-human-rights-at-local-level-in-georgia-eng/1680a524e0

[23] Public Defender of Georgia, 'On the Situation of Protection of Human Rights and Freedoms in Georgia' (2020), www.ombudsman.ge/res/docs/2021070814020446986.pdf

[24] T Sultanishvili, 'Shortfalls of deliberate democracy in Georgia: the analysis of the General Assembly of a settlement' (2023) 25(2) *European Societies* 326. This study examines the reasons behind citizens' refusal to participate in public deliberation through the General Assembly of a Settlement (GAofS) in remote communities of Georgia. It highlights how ineffective deliberation processes can lead to public disenchantment with civic engagement mechanisms.

- *Strengthening democratic processes*: we suggest that a legally literate society is better prepared to demand transparency and accountability from government. This, in turn, contributes to strengthening democratic institutions and being a counterbalance to corruption.[25] In Georgia, where the Corruption Perception Index score was said to be 56 out of 100 in 2020,[26] it is particularly important to empower citizens to identify and respond to such issues.
- *Crime prevention*: low levels of legal education often contribute to the formation of subcultures where reporting crimes to law enforcement agencies is considered unacceptable.[27] Street Law programmes can help change this mentality and can have a positive impact on crime. For example, strengthening legal education among young people could reduce juvenile delinquency, which has been identified as a major problem in Georgia.[28]
- *Promoting social justice*: Street Law education promotes the spread of social justice ideas, which are particularly important in a developing democracy like Georgia. This includes raising awareness about issues such as equality, prohibition of discrimination, labour rights and environmental protection.

The implementation of Street Law programmes in Georgia may not only raise general legal awareness but may also play a significant role in addressing specific social and legal concerns, including combating domestic violence, protection of labour rights, promoting environmental issues, and drawing attention to digital rights and e-related security.

Domestic violence and other forms of abuse remains a serious problem in Georgia.[29] Street Law approaches can be used to provide the public with information about forms of domestic abuse, victim protection mechanisms and assistance services. This is likely to contribute to early detection and possible prevention.

While labour legislation in Georgia has significantly improved in recent years, studies show that a large number of employees lack adequate

---

25 Transparency International Georgia, 'Corruption Perception Index 2020' (2021), www.transparency.org/en/cpi/2020/index/geo

26 ibid.

27 See the following statistics: *Criminal Justice Statistics*, www.geostat.ge/en/modules/categories/132/criminal-justice-statistics; https://police.ge/en/2023-tsels-registrirebuli-danashaulis-statistikuri-monatsemebi/16115; https://info.police.ge/uploads/606d8dcae5641.pdf

28 *Georgia's Three Year Plan for Juvenile Justice 2015–2017*, at 105, https://dlg.galileo.usg.edu/data/dlg/ggpd/pdfs/dlg_ggpd_s-ga-bg630-pc73-bm1-b2016-bj8-belec-p-btext.pdf

29 UN Women, *National Study on Violence against Women in Georgia* (2023), https://eca.unwomen.org/sites/default/files/2023-12/georgia_vaw_survey_report_eng.pdf

information about their rights.[30] Street Law can be used to provide citizens with practical information about employment contracts, job security, nondiscrimination, working hours, overtime pay and other important issues.

Environmental issues are becoming increasingly relevant in Georgia as elsewhere.[31] Street Law initiatives can be used to provide citizens with information about environmental protection legislation, their rights, and relevant responsibilities and accountability. This in turn may promote active citizen involvement in environmental and related issues.

With the rapid development of e-technology, it is important for citizens to have information about their digital rights and security. Street Law can be used to provide the public with information about personal data protection, internet security and cybercrime prevention.

As examined elsewhere in this chapter, there are a range of existing and potential ways to implement Street Law programmes in Georgia. Street Law courses can be integrated into school curricula and as an elective subject in law school. This will help introduce young people to practical legal issues at an early stage. Law students are generally involved in Street Law programmes as teachers (albeit under the supervision of professionally qualified supervisors). Teaching Street Law improves students' legal knowledge and practical skills, and helps spread knowledge in wider society, depending on the audience involved. The NGO sector can play a significant role in implementing Street Law programmes, especially when working with vulnerable groups. Finally, television, radio and social media can be used to deliver PLE materials and can be linked with existing or planned Street Law initiatives.

The introduction of Street Law in Georgia is already serving as a catalyst for broader social and legal reforms. By empowering citizens with practical legal knowledge, these programmes help bridge the gap between the law as it is written and how it is experienced in everyday life. This, in turn, can lead to more informed civic participation, improved access to justice and a stronger society.

Moreover, Street Law programmes can be tailored to address Georgia's specific legal and social challenges. For instance, they could focus on issues such as property rights, which remain contentious in some regions, or on explaining recent legal reforms to ensure that citizens understand and can benefit from, and, as necessary, comply with these changes.

---

30 See *Research Report 2021, July: Labour Rights in Georgia* (2021), at 31–44, https://georgia.peopleinneed.net/media/publications/1653/file/labour-rights-in-georgia_people-in-need.pdf; Georgian Trade Unions Confederation, 'Employee Rights Survey' (2021), https://gtuc.ge/wp-content/uploads/2024/06/eng-vers.pdf

31 *Sector Review: Environment Statistics – Georgia 2024*, www.geostat.ge/media/69495/Sector-Review-Environment-Statistics-Georgia-2024_Ed.pdf; *Natural Resources of Georgia and Environmental Protection* (2017), www.geostat.ge/media/21022/Environment_2017.pdf

Ultimately, the success of Street Law in Georgia will depend on sustained commitment from various stakeholders and the ability to adapt programmes to local needs and context. However, given the potential benefits, investing in Street Law education could be a crucial step in Georgia's ongoing journey towards a more just, equitable and democratic society.

Developing Street Law in and with the community

As already seen in this chapter, legal clinics and Street Law in Georgia have been implemented at a limited number of institutions, often operating in diverse ways. However, in recent years, helped by considerable international donor input, Street Law programmes have been directly promoted and supported with resources being allocated to ensure broader involvement. As a result, more universities, academic staff, students and other stakeholders are engaging in and will undoubtedly continue to benefit from this valuable initiative.

Typically, the target audience for Street Law sessions consists of schoolchildren, particularly between the ages of 14 and 18. This is reflected in the support from high school educators, and approval of programmes by government ministry officials.

In the main, it is university master's students that prepare and deliver Street Law sessions and they do so in a variety of settings, including in schools themselves, at university premises, in community venues and, in some cases, remotely through online platforms. These methods are tailored to suit both students and the particular target audience, with the primary objective of involving as many interested parties as possible while covering the widest geographical area. Much of Georgia is remote and rural, so flexibility in terms of means of coverage is important.

The approach to preparation and delivery varies depending on venue and audience. This can be summarized as follows:

- *Street Law in schools*: when sessions are held at schools, the university's Street Law coordinator obtains permission from the relevant department of the Ministry of Education, Science and Youth of Georgia. This permission is presented to the school, which, in turn, signs a memorandum of understanding with the university. Subsequently, the Law students begin holding Street Law sessions at times scheduled and with pupils selected by the school. Such collaboration is a clear indication of the value the state appears to put into this form of legal education.
- *Street Law at universities*: when meetings are held within the university, the university provides information in advance regarding the programme's content, target audience and schedule. Interested individuals can then register to participate. A key challenge with this method is the issue of

pre-registered participants failing to attend, making it difficult to predict the exact number of participants in individual groups.

- *Street Law in community venues*: in some instances, students who live in different parts of the country organize meetings for schoolchildren in their area, potentially involving students from various villages and schools. Communication is established through educational resource centres and, with their support and collaboration with local schools, interested pupils can attend. While schools have been the main focus of Street Law in Georgia, increasingly other community groups are being served in particular members of ethnic minorities and displaced people.
- *Street Law online*: during the pandemic, when face-to-face meetings were not possible, an alternative online methodology was developed. This enabled the Street Law programme to continue despite obvious restrictions. Universities disseminate information about programme content, target audience and schedules, allowing participants to register and attend remotely. This method is particularly advantageous as it enables the programme to reach a broader geographical area. However, a challenge similar to the in-person methods remains, namely, the non-attendance of pre-registered individuals. Street Law and legal clinics still have to establish full awareness and credibility in the public eye.

Regardless of the method employed, the key focus remains the quality and reliability of the programme, both of which are essential for the success of Street Law and its contribution to legal awareness raising. A crucial determinant of quality is the effective sharing of information and best practices. Communication and collaboration between universities offering Street Law programmes are essential. Through cooperation, the pooling of resources and joint initiatives such as workshops and projects, a unified approach can be developed, which in turn fosters public trust and engagement.

Motivation plays a critical role in the success of any clinical programme, especially in the initial stages of development. While careful planning and effective management of expectations are necessary, the award and presentation of certificates of participation – for Law students and Street Law audiences – has proven an important motivator. These certificates not only acknowledge the active participation of individuals but also serve as a means of promoting the programme.

Effective dissemination of information, active engagement with interested parties and the sharing of practices between universities will help create a robust and vibrant community of beneficiaries of Georgia's Street Law programmes.

Conclusion

The experience of CLE in Georgia may not be as longstanding as in some other parts of the world,[32] but it is now both widespread and seemingly enduring. It is perhaps worth pondering for a few moments as to why that seems to be the case.

First, the move in Georgia to align with internationally accepted 'best practice' in legal (and other areas of) education is very much part of a worldwide phenomenon. This is driven in part by changing educational theory and practice, but also by the demands of the market – students, employers and wider society – for graduates and employees who have the knowledge but also the skills and values required in the world outside of universities and colleges. In other words, they are expected to be able to 'hit the ground running' and make an immediate impact in their chosen careers.

Second, and particularly in relation to developments over the past decade or so in Georgia, partnerships have been formed between a range of social justice and rule of law stakeholders dating back perhaps to the early 2000s and the involvement of the American Bar Association. This has, in part, been discussed earlier in relation to the growth of legal clinics at TSU. As part of the ABA/ROLI programme one NGO, the East West Management Institute (EWMI), in conjunction with invited international experts and backed by USAID funding, established a range of initiatives targeted at access to justice in a number of different settings including legal education. With a project dating back to 2012 (and upon which subsequent funding rounds were approved), the most recent iteration of this project has seen Street Law take centre stage. The concept of the funder and EWMI was not only to promote and support PLE developments across Georgia (in particular in the regions, out of the capital Tbilisi) but also to introduce a strategy that would aid sustainability.

Street Law Inc. – the eventual institutional product emerging from the work of the Georgetown University Street Law team – was contracted to lead on the project with the support of international Street Law and clinic experts. The idea, which began in 2022, was to create a network of university Street Law practitioners. Termed the Georgian Street Law Academy, work was done initially with those universities that had Street Law programmes or that planned to have such offerings. A series of workshops were held between 2022 and 2024 to provide training in Street Law methods. The

[32] For a sense of the CLE picture worldwide, see F Bloch (ed), *The Global Clinical Movement: Educating Lawyers for Social Justice* (OUP 2011); J Giddings (ed), *Global Clinical Legal Education* (Routledge 2025).

academy was thereby incrementally created by encouraging those involved to share experiences and resources. Indeed, such was the enthusiasm for this development that when it came to suggesting this book chapter, volunteers were readily recruited and such collaboration is strong evidence of the power of such a movement.

One very important factor hinted at but not (for reasons of lack of space) explored in detail is the geography and demography of Georgia. With a relatively small population (under four million) and with almost 40 per cent living in rural areas, the need for legal services outside of the main urban areas is significant. Georgian law schools have made considerable efforts to spread their limited resources to serve some of the population that live outside of the main centres. This comes with financial and logistical challenges, but Street Law has proven to be a very adaptable vehicle for serving at least some of the identified need.

Despite major efforts by many of Georgia's law schools to develop and expand their CLE provision, at the time of drafting this chapter, there has been a hiatus in proceedings, with political challenges being experienced across Georgia. In addition, the current USAID funding restrictions for project development have impacted, among other things, rule of law projects in general and, in this context, Street Law in particular. It is very much hoped that the Street Law Academy project, which still has a year or so to run, will be able to revive itself and complete its work.

So often, progress can be stagnated by key individuals leaving initiatives for a variety of reasons. Unless there is a nucleus of actors and a structure to support sustainable growth, projects can be permanently or temporarily derailed. Thankfully, in the Georgian context, such a core of dedicated and able clinicians and enlightened supporters remain in place, even if resourcing is a significant challenge.

Experience elsewhere in the legal education world shows us that there is an irresistible move towards experiential learning. What was once seen as peripheral to the curriculum now often appears to be mainstream, and legal clinics along with Street Law developments are central to this progress. As contributors to this chapter, we all feel confident that such incremental growth of clinical legal education in Georgia will continue, despite the occasional bump in the road.

References

American Bar Association, *Legal Education and Professional Development: An Educational Continuum, Report of the Task Force on Law Schools and the Profession: Narrowing the Gap* (ABA 1992)

Barry MM, Dubin JC and Joy PA, 'Clinical Education for This Millennium: The Third Wave' (2000) 7 *Clinical Law Review* 1

Bloch F (ed), *The Global Clinical Movement: Educating Lawyers for Social Justice* (OUP 2011)

Bogveradze N, Beriashvili L, Gvenetadze G, Laliashvili T and Kvantaliani M, *Study on Legal Clinics in Higher Education of Georgia* (SIFA, EU4Justice, UNDP 2018)

Council of Europe, *Human Rights at Local Level in Georgia: Assessment Report*, https://rm.coe.int/assessment-report-human-rights-at-local-level-in-georgia-eng/1680a524e0

Foxhoven JR, 'Beyond Grading: Assessing Student Readiness to Practice Law' (2009) 16 *Clinical Law Review* 335

Gegenava D, 'Law as It Is, Law as It Ought to Be: Darkness at the End of the Curriculum' in D Gegenava (ed), *Lado Chanturia 60* (Davit Batonishvili Law Institute at Sulkhan-Saba Orbeliani University 2023)

Gegenava D and Javakhishvili P, 'Constitutional Proceedings: A New Challenge for Georgian Legal Education' (2022) *Journal of the Constitutional Court of Georgia, Grigol Robakidze University* 15, https://constcourt.ge/files/4/2)%20Gegenava,%20Javakhishvili%20ENG%202022.pdf

Georgian Trade Unions Confederation, 'Employee Rights Survey' (2021), https://gtuc.ge/wp-content/uploads/2024/06/eng-vers.pdf

Georgian Young Lawyers' Association, *Legal Awareness Study in Georgia* (GYLA 2018), https://gyla.ge/files/news/%E1%83%A4%E1%83%9D%E1%83%9C%E1%83%93%E1%83%98/Annual%20Report%202018.pdf

Georgia's Three Year Plan for Juvenile Justice 2015–2017, https://dlg.galileo.usg.edu/data/dlg/ggpd/pdfs/dlg_ggpd_s-ga-bg630-pc73-bm1-b2016-bj8-belec-p-btext.pdf

Geostat, *Criminal Justice Statistics* (2024), https://www.geostat.ge/en/modules/categories/132/criminal-justice-statistics

Geostat, *Natural Resources of Georgia and Environmental Protection* (2017), https://www.geostat.ge/media/21022/Environment_2017.pdf

Geostat, *Sector Review: Environment Statistics – Georgia 2024*, https://www.geostat.ge/media/69495/Sector-Review-Environment-Statistics-Georgia-2024_Ed.pdf

Giddings J (ed), *Global Clinical Legal Education* (Routledge 2025)

Khantadze N, 'Legal Practice Programmes in Georgia: Assessment and Recommendations' (2019), https://library.iliauni.edu.ge/ebooks/iuridiuli-praqtikis-programmeebi-saqarthveloshi-shephaseba-da-rekomendatsiebi/

Ministry of Education, *Sector Benchmark for Law; VI and VII Level(s)* (National Centre for Educational Quality Enhancement 2019)

Ministry of Internal Affairs, 'Criminal Justice Statistics 2023', https://police.ge/en/2023-tsels-registrirebuli-danashaulis-statistikuri-monatsemebi/16115

Ministry of Internal Affairs, 'Statistical Data on Registered Crime', https://info.police.ge/uploads/606d8dcae5641.pdf

People in Need, *Research Report 2021, July: Labour Rights in Georgia* (2021), https://georgia.peopleinneed.net/media/publications/1653/file/labour-rights-in-georgia_people-in-need.pdf

Public Defender of Georgia, 'On the Situation of Protection of Human Rights and Freedoms in Georgia' (2020), https://www.ombudsman.ge/res/docs/2021070814020446986.pdf

Rhode DL, 'Legal Education: Rethinking the Problem, Reimagining the Reforms' (2013) 40 *Pepperdine Law Review* 437

Rosenbaum SA, Newman FC, Chachava S, Tsertsvadze T, Grimes R, Noori SM, Mattar MY, AlMalki D, Dmitriachev S, Gutnikov A, Aydin U and Narziev O, 'Clinical Legal Education in Central Asia and the Middle East' in J Giddings (ed), *Global Clinical Legal Education* (Routledge 2025)

Street Law Inc., 'What Is Street Law?', www.streetlaw.org/who-we-are/what-is-street-law

Stuckey R, *Best Practices for Legal Education: A Vision and a Road Map* (Clinical Legal Education Association 2007)

Sullivan WM, Colby A, Welch Wegner J, Bond L and Shulman LS, *Educating Lawyers: Preparation for the Profession of Law* (John Wiley 2007)

Sultanishvili T, 'Shortfalls of deliberate democracy in Georgia: the analysis of the General Assembly of a settlement' (2023) 25(2) *European Societies* 326

Transparency International Georgia, 'Corruption Perception Index 2020' (2021), https://www.transparency.org/en/cpi/2020/index/geo

UN Women, *National Study on Violence against Women in Georgia* (2023), https://eca.unwomen.org/sites/default/files/2023-12/georgia_vaw_survey_report_eng.pdf

9

Advancing Clinical Legal Education and Facilitating Access to Justice Through Policy Clinics

Siobhan McConnell, Lyndsey Bengtsson and Rachel Dunn

Introduction

This chapter examines the development and role of policy clinics within clinical legal education (CLE) across Europe, with a particular focus on how policy clinics contribute to access to justice. Policy clinics provide law students with an opportunity to engage in a distinctive form of CLE, where they conduct research for individuals and organizations with specific research needs. While policy clinics have gained prominence in recent years, there remains a significant gap in the literature regarding their role and scope in European CLE, particularly in comparison to live-client clinics. Given the increasing prominence of policy clinics in legal education, the lack of scholarly attention to their impact on law reform and social justice leaves a critical gap in our understanding of how CLE can evolve to meet contemporary legal challenges and foster a more socially responsible legal profession. This chapter addresses this gap by exploring how policy clinics advance a social justice mission, enhance access to justice and prepare students to address contemporary legal challenges, while simultaneously developing their professional skills and commitment to societal change. What this chapter does not do is provide a guide for those wanting to establish a policy clinic at their own institution. We have written about our reflective experience and best practice for policy clinics elsewhere and do not have the capacity to examine this further in this chapter.[1]

[1] Siobhan McConnell, Lyndsey Bengtsson and Rachel Dunn, 'The Benefits and Challenges

This chapter begins by providing an overview of policy clinics before considering their role in promoting access to justice as part of a wider social justice aim. It then considers the development of policy clinics across Europe, using data from key databases to examine the current reach and focus of policy clinics. The work of some established policy clinics in the UK, Spain and the Czech Republic is then explored before the benefits and challenges of policy clinics and policy work are considered. This chapter highlights the distinctive contribution of policy clinics to social justice and to policy and law reform.

What policy clinics are and why they matter

There is no universally accepted definition of policy clinics, but they can generally be understood as initiatives within legal education that focus on policy and/or law reform. One interpretation of policy clinic work is that it encompasses 'any pedagogical methods which incorporate or fully embrace the contribution to policy and/or law reform as an end result'.[2] These clinics can take various forms, including operating as fully credited policy clinic modules, policy work being integrated into existing courses, or featuring as extracurricular activities. However, defining what exactly constitutes a policy clinic can be complex, as many institutions use different terms, such as law reform clinics, project-based work or research clinics, to describe similar types of initiatives. Some clinics may even avoid using the term 'policy' due to concerns that it might attract fewer students.[3]

A key feature of policy clinics is that students collaborate with a diverse range of clients, such as charities, nongovernmental organizations (NGOs), government bodies and academics, to identify areas where laws may require reform or policies require change.[4] The overarching goal of policy clinic work is to influence law and policy changes in ways that benefit society, while also providing students with hands-on experience in legal research, policy drafting and law reform. By engaging with real-world issues, students develop

of the Policy Clinic Model of Clinical Legal Education' (2024) 5(1) *European Journal of Legal Education* 89; Rachel Dunn et al, 'Policy Clinic as a Method to Engage Students with Law Reform and Social Justice: Experiences from Northumbria Law School's Student Law Office' in Ben Livings and Michael Atkinson (eds), *Contemporary Challenges in Clinical Legal Education: Role, Function and Future Directions* (Taylor & Francis 2023).

2 Rachel Dunn, Lyndsey Bengtsson and Siobhan McConnell, 'Building a Policy Clinic Network – CLEO Workshop 13th May 2021' (2021) 28(1) *International Journal of Clinical Legal Education* 244.

3 Tabea Wilkes et al, 'Not a Blueprint: Reflections on the Cardiff Environmental Law and Policy Clinic' (2024) *International Journal of Clinical Legal Education: Special Edition* 34.

4 Dunn et al (n 2).

practical skills that enhance their academic and professional capabilities, while gaining a deeper understanding of how legal change happens in practice.[5]

The nature of the work undertaken in policy clinics is diverse, but typically involves tasks such as conducting literature reviews, designing research methodologies, drafting surveys or interview questions, and making freedom of information requests. Students may also manage ethical approval processes, recruit research participants and carry out data collection. After gathering data, students may analyse it using techniques like thematic analysis and visual grounded theory methodology.[6] Students then present their findings to their clients using creative formats, such as reports and graphs, and making policy and/or law reform recommendations.[7] Ultimately, the work conducted in policy clinics allows students to contribute to meaningful legal reforms and policy changes, which can have a direct impact on society.

Policy clinics within the broader discourse on social justice

The discussion of CLE and social justice within the wider literature is extensive and has been developed over many years, but it mainly considers live-client clinics and other CLE activities, such as Street Law. Generally speaking, 'social justice means that able members of society should challenge political, economic, societal, legal and other structures that oppress the less advantaged'.[8] CLE achieves social justice by allowing underprivileged groups to access legal assistance where they would otherwise face barriers.

The methods of CLE, and how they provide access to justice to those who could not otherwise access it and instil a social justice ethos in future lawyers, are well documented in the literature.[9] How social justice is achieved through policy clinics is nascent in the literature, but is gaining more attention.[10]

---

[5] McConnell, Bengtsson and Dunn (n 1).

[6] See, for example, the work of Northumbria University policy clinic students in Alison Struthers and Siobhan McConnell, 'Improve Children's Legal Knowledge and Skills through School Tasking: Your Time Starts Now' (2024) 58 *The Law Teacher* 1.

[7] Dunn et al (n 1).

[8] Jacqueline Weinberg, 'Preparing Students for 21st Century Practice: Enhancing Social Justice Teaching in Clinical Legal Education' (2021) 28(1) *International Journal of Clinical Legal Education* 5, 12–13.

[9] Donald Nicholson, '"Our Roots Began in South Africa": Modelling Law Clinics to Maximise Social Justice Ends' (2016) 23(3) *International Journal of Clinical Legal Education* 87; Praveen Kosuri, 'Losing My Religion: The Place of Social Justice in Clinical Legal Education' (2012) 32(2) *Boston College Journal of Law and Social Justice* 336; Richard J Wilson, 'Western Europe: Last Holdout in the Worldwide Acceptance of Clinical Legal Education' (2009) 10(6–7) *German Law Journal* 835.

[10] McConnell, Bengtsson and Dunn (n 1). See also Kris Gledhill and Robin Palmer, 'Law Reform Clinical Programmes Should Be Promoted in Law Schools: An Explanation'

Aiding individuals through the legal process is a necessary social justice aim, but policy clinics can provide an alternative social justice result by changing the law for the masses. This is something that has been introduced in live-client clinics across the world to familiarize students with law reform, but full policy clinics are less common. The benefit of full policy clinics is that they can explore needed and realistic law reform in a way that there is not always the space and time for in live-client clinics.[11] Gledhill notes that 'the pressure to create practice-ready law graduates may mean that not all clinical activities are true to its social justice tradition',[12] whereas policy clinics can meet the criterion of benefiting society on a larger scale. This is not to say that individual casework is not important, and it can highlight legal injustices that require reform and provide communities with much-needed legal representation. However, policy clinics go beyond this and methodologically uncover the issues within our legal systems and make recommendations for positive reform. Academics such as McCrimmon highlight that the identification and application of the law is important for students, but that it should not be 'the sum total of their skill set'.[13] Further, for those students wanting to go into practice, policy clinic and law reform-based work can help them to understand the law in more depth, as well as the various social and economic factors that can help shape it. It allows students to take 'the law out of a contextual vacuum by seeing the law in its broader political and social framework'.[14] Understanding this framework can help law graduates be more confident in speaking out when they witness an injustice,[15] and evidence suggests that students feel more power to influence change after engaging in a policy clinic than they would have simply through live-client work.[16] For students not wanting to go into legal practice, it demonstrates how to still be involved in the legal system and advance it in order to create a more just society.[17] As Curran highlights, students 'have more choices about the areas of law they may wish to practice in and if

(2024) *International Journal of Clinical Legal Education: Special Edition – Policy Clinics across the Globe: Development, Impact and Collaboration* 6, 24.

11 McConnell, Bengtsson and Dunn (n 1).

12 Gledhill and Palmer (n 10).

13 Les McCrimmon and Edward Santow, 'Justice Education, Law Reform and the Clinical Method' in Frank S Bloch (ed), *The Global Clinical Movement: Educating Lawyers for Social Justice* (Oxford University Press 2010) 212.

14 ibid.

15 Liz Curran, 'Innovations in an Australian Clinical Legal Education Program: Students Making a Difference in Generating Positive Change' (2004) 6 *International Journal of Clinical Legal Education* 162.

16 McConnell, Bengtsson and Dunn (n 1).

17 ibid; Anna Carpenter, 'Principle for the Project Model: Eight Principles to Maximise Student Learning and Social Justice Impact' (2013) 20 *Clinical Law Review* 39.

they decide not to practise they realise there is a whole realm of activities that a law degree will give them opportunities in'.[18] Ultimately, policy clinic work can instil a social justice ethos that can follow law graduates into their career.

The development of policy clinics across Europe

Europe as a whole

The European Network for Clinical Legal Education (ENCLE) connects university clinics and clinicians across Europe. The network seeks to 'support the growth and quality of CLE programmes in Europe'[19] and to enable members to collaborate with each other. One of ENCLE's key objectives is to promote social justice as a 'core value' of the legal profession.

Institutions can register their clinic in an online ENCLE directory,[20] selecting their clinic's activities from a list of CLE activities – that is, live-client clinic, externships, street law, strategic litigation clinic and policy/advocacy clinic. Registrants can select more than one type of activity. Seventy-five clinics[21] from 13 countries (including Russia) have so far registered, with clinics selecting various areas of clinical activity. As such, the ENCLE directory provides a valuable overview of the current reach of policy clinics in Europe. However, the directory data are presented with some caveats. Although the directory provides a useful guide to the clinics and countries undertaking CLE and policy work, it may be that other clinics within the countries noted, and indeed other European countries, are also conducting CLE and/or policy work and may not have yet registered with ENCLE.[22] It is also unclear how a registrant may interpret 'policy/advocacy' work when self-selecting the type of work undertaken in their clinic. As noted earlier, there may be differences in how policy clinics are described and difficulties in understanding what policy work means. Further, the use of the term 'advocacy' may lead registrants to interpret this as advocacy in court and so representation of

[18] Curran (n 15) 174.

[19] https://encle.org/about-us/what-is-encle

[20] https://encle.org/cle-directory

[21] Please note that the number of clinics on the register is more than 75, but some clinic information has been duplicated, suggesting that some clinics may have registered twice.

[22] For example, only six UK-based law school clinics are registered with ENCLE. In reality, many law schools in the UK now provide CLE; see James Sandbach and Richard Grimes, *The LawWorks Law School Pro Bono and Clinic Report 2014* (LawWorks 2014), www.lawworks.org.uk/solicitors-and-volunteers/resources/lawworks-law-school-pro-bono-and-clinics-report-2014; see also the following discussion.

Figure 9.1: ENCLE data (2024): number of countries registered with ENCLE and types of clinic activity offered

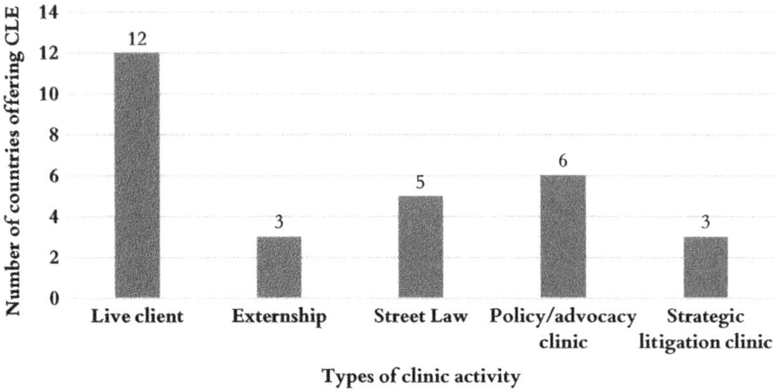

a client in formal legal proceedings. It may be that registrants interpret this in a more policy-focused way – that is, advocating for social justice and for the rights of communities.

If the directory data is taken at face value, it is possible to observe how policy/advocacy activity compares to other types of clinical activity across Europe. Figure 9.1 presents the number of countries that have registered with ENCLE and the types of work undertaken. As might be expected, live-client work is the predominant clinic offering (12 countries), but the second highest number of countries (six) have clinics that have registered as conducting policy/advocacy work: the Czech Republic, Germany, Ireland, Italy, Spain and the UK.

Further analysis reveals how many clinics undertake policy work compared to other types of clinical activities (see Figure 9.2).

Again, the data confirms the dominance of the live-client model of CLE with policy/advocacy work being the joint second most popular type of clinical activity – 23 per cent of the 75 clinics registered offered this type of work. Of the 17 clinics registered as undertaking policy/advocacy work, Spain has nine, the UK four and each of the remaining four countries has one clinic each. In addition, most of the clinics (14) registering policy work did so alongside other clinical activity such as live-client work. It is difficult to assess how long policy work has been a feature of CLE within the ENCLE membership (and Europe more generally) because the ENCLE directory provides a current overview of clinic activity. However, in the context of the UK, further insight can be gained on how policy work has become more prevalent over time from data published by LawWorks, a charity that aims to develop pro bono activity across England and Wales.

Figure 9.2: ENCLE data (2024): number of clinics and types of clinic activity

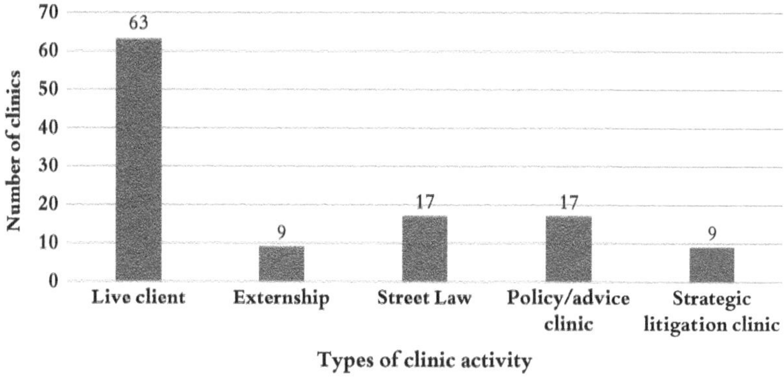

The UK

LawWorks provides advice and support to solicitors undertaking pro bono work and monitors pro bono activity in the UK. As part of this work, LawWorks has conducted surveys of law schools to understand the reach of pro bono activity across the university sector.[23] Its work therefore provides a useful overview of the development and extent of policy work activity in UK law schools.[24] In 2014 LawWorks surveyed 109 law schools, receiving 80 responses (a 73 per cent response rate).[25] Law schools were asked what type of clinics they operated and were provided with a list of 11 activities. This list included generalist advice, Street Law and court/tribunal representation. There was no reference to policy/law reform and so no responses fell into this category, although arguably policy work could have been encapsulated in the category 'other pro bono'.[26] The most popular categories were generalist advice, external placements and Street Law.[27] There was some indication that policy work was becoming an area of interest for law schools carrying out pro bono work. Although none of the respondents mentioned policy or law reform work as the model used

[23] Earlier surveys in 2000, 2003, 2006 and 2010 are referenced in the surveys, but are unavailable online.

[24] The LawWorks' surveys are sent to law schools around the UK.

[25] Damian Carney et al, 'The LawWorks Law School Pro Bono and Clinic Report 2014', www.lawworks.org.uk/solicitors-and-volunteers/resources/lawworks-law-school-pro-bono-and-clinics-report-201, 4.

[26] ibid 17 and 21, where four law schools indicated they conducted 'research (although the clientele differed)'. It is unclear what type of research this was and whether it would fall within the parameters of policy/law reform work.

[27] ibid 17.

when their clinic was first established,[28] in responses to a question asking if the type of work undertaken had increased (and what additional activities had been added), two law schools mentioned that they now undertook law reform projects.[29] However, there appeared to be little appetite more generally to increase such activities. While 64 law schools stated they planned to extend their pro bono activities, none specifically mentioned that they would be undertaking policy work.[30] That said, there was one further sign that undertaking policy work might be gaining momentum in law schools. When asked whether staff required training or support, some responses stated that staff wanted support on 'data collection to inform research and policy'.[31] Overall, in 2014 there was clearly very little recorded policy work activity in law schools and minimal interest in expanding this area of clinical practice.

The 2020 survey presented a different picture. The survey was sent to over 120 law schools and 78 responded.[32] This time, the 11 categories of activity that respondents could choose from included 'law reform projects'. As with the 2014 survey, the most popular activities were Street Law, external student placements (both over 60 per cent of respondents) and generalist advice (54 per cent of respondents). However, the category 'law reform and research projects' was selected by 30 per cent of respondents. Although this category was one of the least popular of the 11 activities, it ranked above 'generalist with casework – excluding 'Court/Tribunal representation' (casework excluding court representation) and 'Court/ Tribunal representation' (actual court representation). The qualitative comments provided further information on the type of law reform projects in which clinics were involved. These were wide-ranging and deemed to have an 'international reach (through NGO and non-UK university partnerships)' with examples including work with the Inter-American Court of Human Rights and the African Prisons Project.[33] This significant increase in policy work activity within law schools could have been due to its inclusion as a category in the survey – as noted earlier, for the 2014 survey respondents, it may have fallen within 'other pro bono' category. Another more likely interpretation is that by 2020, policy clinics had become much more established in law schools. Supporting this view is the fact that

28 ibid 12.

29 ibid 13.

30 Sandbach and Grimes (n 22) 14.

31 ibid 40.

32 The exact number of law schools contacted and the response rate are unclear.

33 Sandbach and Grimes (n 22) 13.

policy clinics were established at Northumbria Law School in 2018 and at the Open University (OU) in 2019.[34]

The data discussed earlier indicate that the concept of policy clinics and policy work is well established in both the UK and Spain. This chapter will now examine some of the policy clinics in these countries which featured in the ENCLE directory. Policy clinic activity in the Czech Republic is also explored later on – this country has been selected because of the international collaborative work undertaken by one of its policy clinics and its inclusion in the ENCLE directory.

Examples of policy clinics in the UK

The policy clinic at Northumbria Law School opened in 2018 and offers third-year undergraduate law students the opportunity to conduct policy work as part of a year-long, credit-bearing module. The students work in 'firms' of up to ten students and are supervised by experienced researchers. The policy clinic has two modes of delivery – 'pure' policy firms that only conduct policy work and 'hybrid' policy/live-client firms that undertake both policy work and legal advice to clients. The Northumbria policy clinic has undertaken a variety of doctrinal and empirical research projects. Some of this research has taken place over several years, allowing the clinic to develop longstanding relationships with its clients. For example, over three consecutive years, three separate sets of students conducted research around child-friendly justice and the Mental Health Act 1983.[35] Two groups sent freedom of information[36] requests to 50 NHS hospitals to find out what information is provided to children detained under the Act and analysed the results. Another group assessed the readability and accessibility of information provided to children in various legal settings. This involved reviewing a range of legal and nonlegal sources. The student research here has impacted on the research team in various ways, for example, informing grant applications,

[34] For further examples of policy clinic activity in the UK, see: Liz Hardie, '"Training Is Everything": How to Prepare Students for Policy Clinic Projects'; Wilkes et al (n 3); Emma Curryer and Carol Edwards, 'The Impact of Policy Work on Employability Skills in the Policy Project Connected to the Criminal Appeals Clinic at the Open University'; and Lucy Blackburn, Sadie Whittam and Kathryn Saban, 'Teamwork Makes the Dream Work: The Value of Cross Institutional Policy Law Clinic Collaboration in the Fight against Climate Change', all in (2024) *International Journal of Clinical Legal Education: Special Edition – Policy Clinics across the Globe: Development, Impact and Collaboration.*

[35] This is the legislation in England and Wales that documents the rights and treatment of mentally ill patients.

[36] The ability to require public authorities to provide information using freedom of information requests is set out in the Freedom of Information Act 2000.

publications and subsequent stages of the research project. It is likely that this work will contribute to an institutional impact case study.[37] Another project involved analysing data collected from a schools outreach project led by an academic at Warwick University. Students analysed both visual data (posters drawn by Year 5 schoolchildren) and survey data. A detailed report was produced that the client has used at conferences and in a publication.[38]

The OU opened its online policy clinic in 2019 and conducts research for charities and other organizations.[39] Like the Northumbria University policy clinic, the OU clinic takes the form of an assessed module that is open to undergraduates. Recent OU policy clinic projects include empirical research exploring how the mental health of offenders impacts on sentencing and how changes to the legislation on the registration of blind and partially sighted people is working in practice. The OU has developed longstanding research relationships with organizations. For example, it has worked with the Environmental Law Foundation in exploring the likelihood of local authorities meeting net-zero targets. It has collaborated with the Northumbria University policy clinic on projects involving the rights of tenants to keep pets in rental properties, and how the COVID-19 pandemic and the use of online court hearings affected public access to court hearings. The OU website advertises the clinic, its clients and the reports, showcasing how the clinic is making a real impact on policy and law reform.[40]

Examples of policy clinics in Spain

Nine Spanish clinics (out of 25 Spanish registrants)[41] are registered in the ENCLE directory as undertaking policy/advocacy work. A distinctive feature of some of the Spanish registrants is the clearly well-established nature of the policy clinics, as evidenced by their websites. For example, the clinic at IE University in Madrid (established in 2014) is registered solely as a policy/advocacy clinic. Students work with a range of NGOs and a variety of projects are documented on the clinic website.[42] For example,

---

[37] Impact case studies are submitted to the Research Excellence Framework, the UK framework for measuring research excellence in UK universities; see www.ref.ac.uk/about/what-is-the-ref/. The studies usually explain the social, economic and public policy benefits and impact of particular research projects to the UK and beyond. See www.ukri.org/who-we-are/research-england/research-excellence/ref-impact/

[38] Struthers and McConnell (n 6).

[39] For more on this, see Hardie (n 34).

[40] www5.open.ac.uk/open-justice/public-understanding-law/policy-clinic

[41] There are actually ten clinics registered, but two registrants represent the same human rights clinic.

[42] www.ie.edu/law-school/knowledge-exchange/legal-clinic/

students produced a comparative law report exploring how health systems are regulated in seven European countries in relation to a particular medical condition. The report recommended improvements to the Spanish healthcare system.[43] Another project involved a comparative analysis of data protection law across six countries. Both projects were conducted in conjunction with a law firm and an NGO.[44] A distinctive feature of this clinic's website is its clear promotion of its activities using the branding of both the NGOs and the law firms with which it collaborates, all of which serves to highlight the impact of its work. The Clinica Juridic de Derechos Humanos in Madrid is a multi-activity clinic and advertises policy projects it will undertake (one emphasizing how it will train students in reform and research methodology)[45] and publicizes the reports and recommendations of other projects.[46] The Clinica Juridica Dret al Dret in Barcelona has a range of legal clinics. Its Infancia (protection of children and adolescents) Clinic works with various collaborators including charities and law firms. One example of policy work provided involves students conducting studies involving children in order to make recommendations aimed at guiding children's policies in Catalonia.[47]

Example of a policy clinic in the Czech Republic

Palacký University in Olomouc, Czech Republic, has a longstanding CLE programme. Within this programme, it has offered policy clinic work that has had far reaching impact and has since established the Human Rights and Policy Legal Clinic.[48] It has conducted impactful research projects, such as exploring physical education activities for schoolchildren with disabilities. It found that they were often excluded from these educational activities and produced research to argue why this contravened the European Convention on Human Rights. Schools have since changed their policies and this has created a better educational system for young people.

Staff from the Northumbria University policy clinic also worked with Palacký University and the Catholic University of America (CUA) on a project concerning sexual abuse and harassment on campus. At the time of the project, Palacký University did not have a policy relating to sexual abuse/harassment. Northumbria University did have one, which was in further development at the time, and CUA had an extremely developed policy under the national legal requirements of Title IX. Students did in-depth research

43 ibid.

44 ibid.

45 https://clinicajuridicaidhbc.com/convovatorias/

46 https://clinicajuridicaidhbc.com/estudios/

47 www.ub.edu/portal/web/dret/clinica-proteccio-infancia-adolescencia

48 www.upol.cz/en/short-programmes/human-rights-policy-legal-clinic/

into their respective university's policy and/or experience of dealing with sexual abuse/harassment on campus, and they came together online to discuss their findings. They co-wrote a final report, which was used by Palacký University to develop and implement a reporting system for survivors.

The benefits and challenges of policy clinics and policy work

The literature on policy clinics underscores their transformative potential in linking legal education with societal impact, benefiting students, law schools and communities. As the examples of policy clinic activity given earlier demonstrate, policy clinics serve as a powerful tool for law schools to engage with real-world issues while enhancing their reputation as institutions committed to social justice, policy reform and community engagement. For students, they offer an invaluable opportunity to develop critical skills and broaden career horizons, while for law schools, they provide a platform to strengthen research-led teaching and deepen community ties through assisting with legal reform. For communities, policy clinics contribute directly to meaningful policy change, improving access to justice and addressing social inequalities.

Benefits to communities

A recurring theme in the literature is that policy clinics directly benefit communities by facilitating legal reform and enhancing access to justice.[49] As Gledhill and Palmer argue, law reform activities – which form a central component of many policy clinics – are designed to improve the regulation of legal areas, ultimately promoting fairness and social justice.[50] By working on policy clinic projects, students may actively help shape laws and policies that can have tangible benefits for communities, particularly those that are marginalized or underserved. For instance, as Wilkes et al suggest, engaging with law drafting and proposing alternative legal solutions empowers students to generate innovative ideas that have far-reaching benefits for both local and broader communities.[51] The collaborative nature of policy clinics, which often involves engaging with external partners such as NGOs, think tanks

---

[49] See, for example, Rachel Dunn, Lyndsey Bengtsson and Siobhan McConnell, 'The Policy Clinic at Northumbria University: Influencing Policy/Law Reform as an Effective Educational Tool for Students' (2020) 27(1) *International Journal of Clinical Legal Education* 68; Dunn et al (n 1); Gledhill and Palmer (n 10); Wilkes et al (n 3); McConnell, Bengtsson and Dunn (n 1).

[50] Gledhill and Palmer (n 10).

[51] Wilkes et al (n 3).

and government agencies, ensures that community needs are reflected in the policy-making process, making legal reforms more responsive, inclusive and impactful. For example, students in the Northumbria policy clinic engaged in a project concerning the legal issues preventing domestic abuse victims from obtaining court orders for protection against future abuse. Their work involved collecting data from the police and legal practitioners. Their report contributed to a new police disclosure request protocol for use in family law proceedings. Given the nature of policy and law reform development, inevitably the impact of policy work may take time to feed through and for its impact on communities to be measurable. Policy work is not a 'quick win', as may be the case with live-client work. Policy work requires persistence and patience as it may take several years for its impact to be fully realized. However, the potential of policy work to impact beyond the individual or group that usually directly benefits from the live-client model of CLE is clear.

Benefits to students

Policy clinics equip students with a wide range of practical skills, including research design, data analysis, project management and policy drafting. While these skills are also taught in other CLE models, such as live-client or simulated clinics, the focus of policy clinics is on research, policy analysis and drafting recommendations for legal reform.[52] Students gain experience in communicating with clients, research participants and broader audiences (such as at conferences) refining their ability to present findings clearly and effectively. This process enhances both their written and oral communication skills, fostering interdisciplinary research and helping them view law through a broader social and political lens.

Unlike other clinical settings, where students focus on client representation, policy clinics offer a distinct experience by concentrating on policy work and law reform. Students actively participate in the law-making process, deepening their understanding of how laws are shaped, implemented and revised. As Dunn et al and McConnell et al note, students in policy clinics use a diverse range of research methods, which are often unavailable in traditional clinical settings, allowing them to approach legal challenges from different perspectives.[53] Furthermore, as Wilkes et al observe, the opportunity to draft laws and explore alternative legal solutions broadens students' skillsets and encourages creative, innovative thinking.[54]

52 Dunn, Bengtsson and McConnell (n 49).

53 ibid; McConnell, Bengtsson and Dunn (n 1).

54 Wilkes et al (n 3).

In addition to academic skills, students also develop key project management skills, which may enhance their employability in a competitive job market. Analytical skills are honed as they synthesize case law, literature and data to make informed recommendations for reform. Students learn to use tools such as Excel to manage deadlines and collaborate effectively with supervisors, peers and clients, enhancing both their teamwork and time management skills. These experiences enhance student employability profiles while also contributing to their professional and ethical development, preparing them to advocate for legal reform and contribute to social justice.[55] Recent literature highlights the transformative nature of policy clinic work. As students engage in law reform, they begin to see their involvement not only as an opportunity to develop individual skills but also as a way to contribute to meaningful societal change.[56] As Curran observes, students come to recognize that their work can have a positive impact and contribute to improving the legal system.[57] This shift – from passive recipients of legal knowledge to active contributors to shaping the law – is a key educational benefit of policy clinics. However, as Hardie emphasizes, effective participation requires adequate training, particularly in research methods and law drafting.[58]

Finally, participation in policy clinics broadens students' career perspectives. Many students value the transferable skills gained, which extend beyond legal practice and open doors to careers in policy, advocacy and social justice.[59] As Curran suggests, exposure to diverse clients and legal issues also gives students more flexibility in choosing their legal career paths. The policy clinic experience makes students aware of the many career opportunities a law degree offers outside of conventional legal roles.[60] For instance, a student from Northumbria University policy clinic, inspired by their work involving interviews with police officers, chose to pursue a career in policing, highlighting how policy clinics can broaden students' professional horizons.[61] For students, the overall collective experience of engaging in policy work – their development of knowledge and transferable skills, their burgeoning appreciation of their potential to impact beyond their own self-interests and the realization there are careers outside professional legal practice – serves to enhance their employability. This is critical given

[55] Dunn et al (n 1); Gledhill and Palmer (n 10).

[56] McConnell, Bengtsson and Dunn (n 1).

[57] Curran (n 15).

[58] Hardie (n 34).

[59] Curran (n 15).

[60] ibid; see also McConnell, Bengtsson and Dunn (n 1).

[61] Dunn et al (n 3).

the highly competitive recruitment market into which law students are graduating.[62]

Benefits to law schools

Policy clinics also bring substantial benefits to law schools by enhancing teaching and research integration. Unlike other clinical models, policy clinics do not require supervisors to have legal qualifications or practising certificates, which enables more academic staff, including nonpractising academics, to participate. This helps bridge the traditional divide between doctrinal and clinical work in law schools, fostering collaboration between research-active faculty and clinic-based staff.[63] Supervisors can integrate their research interests into the clinic supervision process, aligning teaching with research and contributing to institutional goals such as the UK's Research Excellence Framework.

This synergy between teaching and research allows law schools to expand the range of research opportunities, including comparative, sociolegal and interdisciplinary studies. These research areas enhance academic rigour and encourage critical engagement with contemporary legal challenges. Furthermore, by addressing pressing social issues, such as inequality, access to justice and legal reform, policy clinics enable law schools to align with the social justice ethos that underpins CLE.

In fulfilling their societal role as the 'critic and conscience' of the community, law schools contribute to public debates on law reform, offering thought leadership on pressing legal challenges.[64] This broader engagement strengthens law school influence within the legal and academic spheres, enhances its reputation as a socially responsible institution, and attracts students and partners who share these values. This helps solidify the position of the law school as a leader in socially responsive legal education.

Challenges in policy clinic work

Despite its many benefits, policy clinic work presents several challenges. One of the primary difficulties is the initial hesitation that students often

[62] For example, in England and Wales, 19,913 students graduated from a first degree in law from universities in 2022, an increase of 24.6 per cent since 2017. See the Law Society, 'Trends in the Solicitor Profession: Annual Statistics Report 2022' (November 2023), www.lawsociety.org.uk/Topics/Research/Annual-statistics-report-2022

[63] Paul McKeown and Rachel Dunn, 'The European Network of Clinical Legal Education: The Spring Workshop 2015' (2015) 22(3) *International Journal of Clinical Legal Education* 312.

[64] Gledhill and Palmer (n 10).

experience, particularly when considering whether to select the option of doing policy work[65] and then when working collaboratively in teams. Studies in this area suggest that students can struggle with the complexity of policy work, as they may not fully understand its value or the specific skills required.[66] This is compounded by the fact that law students often lack prior knowledge of essential research methods and skills, such as undertaking empirical research and data analysis, necessitating their need to commit additional time and effort to learning them.[67] Without this foundational knowledge, students may find it difficult to fully grasp how their work contributes to real-world policy reforms and social justice outcomes.

Moreover, the demands of policy clinic work can exceed initial expectations, particularly in terms of time commitments from both students and supervisors.[68] Supervisors may underestimate the time needed to mentor and support students, as well as the time required for tasks such as obtaining ethical approval, conducting data analysis and reviewing student work before it is submitted to clients. These time demands are particularly challenging when work is undertaken in hybrid clinics, where supervisors need to balance policy work with live-client or simulated work.[69] In these contexts, careful planning is essential to ensure that the research project is achievable within the academic year and is not overly complex. Supervisors must also ensure that the workload is distributed effectively to avoid overwhelming students. Inadequate balancing of these demands can hinder the students' ability to take ownership of their projects and fully engage as research collaborators. Supervisors need to ensure that students are not merely performing tasks, but are actively engaging with the project as research collaborators; this is essential for both student learning and for the success of the policy clinic project.[70]

Another difficulty encountered with policy clinics is helping students conceptualize the role of the client in policy work.[71] Unlike traditional legal clinics, where clients are often individuals with immediate legal needs, the clients in policy clinic work are typically more abstract, such as communities, government agencies or advocacy groups. This can make it difficult for students to understand the broader implications of their work, particularly at the outset of a project, in terms of how their research can influence policy and create social justice outcomes. Without a clear understanding of the

65 McConnell, Bengtsson and Dunn (n 1).
66 ibid; Hardie (n 34).
67 ibid.
68 Dunn et al (n 1).
69 Dunn, Bengtsson and McConnell (n 49).
70 ibid.
71 McConnell, Bengtsson and Dunn (n 1).

social justice impact of their work, students may fail to fully appreciate the transformative potential of the policy clinic. Supervisors must provide clear guidance to help students understand the impact (or potential impact) of their work on communities and the legal system, ensuring that students recognize their role in contributing to meaningful legal and policy reform. Reflecting on these social justice impacts throughout the project is essential for keeping students engaged and motivated, ensuring that they not only develop legal skills but also cultivate a sense of social responsibility and commitment to addressing societal injustices.

Conclusion

This chapter has examined the growing significance of policy clinics to CLE across Europe. The data from both ENCLE and LawWorks demonstrates how this alternative form of CLE is gaining traction, adding a new dimension to law schools and their clinic offerings. As Giddings notes, this kind of work, which was 'previously understood as a student group research project is now being characterised as a clinic'.[72] The practical examples of policy work from established policy clinics in the UK, Spain, and the Czech Republic illustrate the diversity of policy work and its impact, often extending beyond the traditional model of live-client work. This chapter has also highlighted the numerous benefits that policy clinics and policy work offer to communities, law students and law schools, while acknowledging the inherent challenges involved.

The discussion here has presented compelling evidence that CLE can continue to evolve and contribute to broader societal goals, such as law and policy reforms. By placing law students and legal education at the heart of such reforms, policy clinics may offer law schools a renewed sense of purpose. In an era of an increasingly marketized higher education system, where law schools often face critical scrutiny,[73] policy clinics provide an alternative approach to achieving educational goals while also benefiting clients, communities and stakeholders. However, law schools must be cognizant of the long-term nature of policy work – unlike live-client work, any measurable impact on society may take years to become observable. What is clear is that policy clinics present a wealth of opportunities for law students. They gain additional skills, a deeper understanding of policy and

[72] Jeff Giddings, 'Common Threads and Strength in Diversity' in Jeff Giddings (ed), *Global Clinical Legal Education* (Routledge 2024) 327.

[73] Margaret Thornton, 'What Is the Law School for in a Post-pandemic World?' in Rachel Dunn, Paul Maharg and Victoria Roper (eds), *What Is Legal Education for? Reassessing the Purposes of Early Twenty-First Century Learning and Law Schools* (Routledge 2023).

law reform, and an enhanced employability profile. Research suggests that students involved in policy clinics come to appreciate the broader societal benefits of their work, beyond its role in their own personal skills and knowledge development.[74] This is important given that law schools are producing the next generations of lawyers, policy makers and professionals. For law schools, policy clinics assist in allaying perceptions that clinics are 'inattentive to the importance of theory and policy'.[75]

Given the long-term nature of policy and law reform projects, longitudinal research is needed to fully understand and assess the impact of policy clinics on social justice across Europe. Likewise, further research is required on the reach and focus of policy clinics within Europe. Such research is vital as the policy clinic model of CLE is likely to become more popular, given the evidence noted here of its increasing prevalence in law schools. By enabling nonpractitioners to engage in CLE, policy clinics intertwine research and education in a practical, student-focused way that provides broader benefits to society.

References

Cantrell DJ, 'Are Clinics a Magic Bullet?' (2014) 51(4) *Alberta Law Review* 831

Carney D, Dignan F, Grimes R, Kelly G and Parker R, *The LawWorks Law School Pro Bono and Clinic Report 2014* (LawWorks 2014), www.lawworks.org.uk/solicitors-and-volunteers/resources/lawworks-law-school-pro-bono-and-clinics-report-2014

Clínica Jurídica IDHBC, 'Programas clínicos', https://clinicajuridicaidhbc.com/convovatorias/

Clínica Jurídica IDHBC, 'Informes y recomendaciones', https://clinicajuridicaidhbc.com/estudios/

Curran L, 'Innovations in an Australian Clinical Legal Education Program: Students Making a Difference in Generating Positive Change' (2004) 6 *International Journal of Clinical Legal Education* 162

Dunn R, Bengtsson L and McConnell S, 'Building a Policy Clinic Network – CLEO Workshop 13th May 2021' (2021) 28(1) *International Journal of Clinical Legal Education* 244

Dunn R, Bengtsson L, Nelson T and Rutherford H, 'Policy Clinic as a Method to Engage Students with Law Reform and Social Justice: Experiences from Northumbria Law School's Student Law Office' in B Livings and M Atkinson (eds), *Contemporary Challenges in Clinical Legal Education: Role, Function and Future Directions* (Taylor & Francis 2023)

---

[74] McConnell, Bengtsson and Dunn (n 1); Dunn, Bengtsson and McConnell (n 49).

[75] Deborah J Cantrell, 'Are Clinics a Magic Bullet?' (2014) 51(4) *Alberta Law Review* 831, 838.

ENCLE (European Network of Clinical Legal Education), 'What Is ENCLE', https://encle.org/about-us/what-is-encle

ENCLE, 'The CLE Directory', https://encle.org/cle-directory

Giddings J, 'Common Threads and Strength in Diversity' in J Giddings (ed), *Global Clinical Legal Education* (Routledge 2024)

Gledhill K and Palmer R, 'Law Reform Clinical Programmes Should be Promoted in Law Schools: An Explanation' (2024) *International Journal of Clinical Legal Education: Special Edition – Policy Clinics across the Globe: Development, Impact and Collaboration* 6

Hardie L, '"Training Is Everything": How to Prepare Students for Policy Clinic Projects' (2024) *International Journal of Clinical Legal Education: Special Edition – Policy Clinics across the Globe: Development, Impact and Collaboration*

IE University, 'IE Law School Legal Clinic', www.ie.edu/law-school/knowledge-exchange/legal-clinic/

The Law Society, 'Trends in the Solicitor Profession: Annual Statistics Report 2022' (November 2023), www.lawsociety.org.uk/Topics/Research/Annual-statistics-report-2022

McConnell S, Bengtsson L and Dunn R, 'The Benefits and Challenges of the Policy Clinic Model of Clinical Legal Education' (2024) 5(1) *European Journal of Legal Education* 89

McCrimmon L and Santow E, 'Justice Education, Law Reform and the Clinical Method' in FS Bloch (ed), *The Global Clinical Movement: Educating Lawyers for Social Justice* (Oxford University Press 2010)

McKeown P and Dunn R, 'The European Network of Clinical Legal Education: The Spring Workshop 2015' (2015) 22(3) *International Journal of Clinical Legal Education* 312

Nicholson D, '"Our Roots Began in South Africa": Modelling Law Clinics to Maximise Social Justice Ends' (2016) 23(3) *International Journal of Clinical Legal Education* 87

Open University, 'Policy Clinic', www5.open.ac.uk/open-justice/public-understanding-law/policy-clinic

Research Excellence Framework, 'What Is the REF?', www.ref.ac.uk/about/what-is-the-ref/

Sandbach J and Grimes R, *The LawWorks Law School Pro Bono and Clinic Report 2020* (LawWorks and CLEO 2020), www.lawworks.org.uk/solicitors-and-volunteers/resources/lawworks-law-school-pro-bono-and-clinics-report-2020

Struthers A and McConnell S, 'Improve Children's Legal Knowledge and Skills through School Tasking: Your Time Starts Now' (2024) 58 *The Law Teacher* 1

Thornton M, 'What Is the Law School for in a Post-pandemic World?', in R Dunn, P Maharg and V Roper (eds), *What Is Legal Education for? Reassessing the Purposes of Early Twenty-First Century Learning and Law Schools* (Routledge 2023)

UK Research and Innovation, 'How Research England Supports Research Excellence', www.ukri.org/who-we-are/research-england/research-excellence/ref-impact/

Universitat de Barcelona, 'Us donem la benvinguda a la Facultat de Dret', www.ub.edu/portal/web/dret/clinica-proteccio-infancia-adolescencia

University of Palacký, 'Human Rights Policy Legal Clinic', www.upol.cz/en/short-programmes/human-rights-policy-legal-clinic/

Weinberg J, 'Preparing Students for 21st Century Practice: Enhancing Social Justice Teaching in Clinical Legal Education' (2021) 28(1) *International Journal of Clinical Legal Education* 5

Wilkes T, Pontin B, Linley-Adams G and Price J, 'Not a Blueprint: Reflections on the Cardiff Environmental Law and Policy Clinic' (2024) *International Journal of Clinical Legal Education: Special Edition* 34

PART III

Social Justice Challenges

10

Protecting Student Wellbeing in Legal Clinical Settings

Amanda Thurston and Diana Kirsch

Introduction

Student wellbeing has become a focal point in higher education, as academic institutions recognize the importance of creating learning environments that support the mental health and emotional wellbeing of students. In law schools, this focus on wellbeing has become particularly significant, given the intense competition and pressures felt by students in achieving success in their legal education and a legal career.

The definition of 'good mental health' adopted by the International Bar Association (IBA) mirrors the World Health Organization's description of a state where 'every individual realises his or her own potential, can cope with the normal stresses of life, can work productively and fruitfully, and is able to make a contribution to her or his community'.[1]

Law clinics have become a prominent pedagogical feature within universities as a means to providing practical experiential learning opportunities for students, giving them unique chances to work with real clients and real lawyers. Nonetheless, these valuable experiences may obscure critical concerns of how this real-world learning can negatively impact student wellbeing. Clinics (and other similar pro bono projects involving real clients and live cases) can expose students to the stresses and strains of professional legal work, often working within tight deadlines, and at the

[1] World Health Organization, 'WHO Urges More Investment, Services for Mental Health' (12 August 2010), www.who.int/news/item/12-08-2010-who-urges-more-investme nts-services-for-mental-health

same time introducing sensitive subjects, which some can find challenging and potentially triggering.

Law schools need to ensure they do enough to prepare students for working in clinical settings and teach them to consider and protect not only their client's wellbeing, but also their own. There is enough research[2] now to understand that higher education environments alone can impact students' mental health, without the extra pressure of clinical work. Gibson posits that 'the demographics of GenZ, the issues they have had to confront as a generational cohort, along with the anxiety, insecurity, and loneliness they feel are key producers of trauma'.[3] Law students in particular are impacted even more[4] – probably due to the extra pressure of their professional development and overall educational success.[5]

Weinstein reminds us that representing clients with real problems helps students develop their moral and emotional habits: 'Clinic work is not just about winning a case, or doing well in a class; it is about responsibility to and for another human being … a very powerful moral and emotional experience.'[6] As such, few would seek to remove law clinics from being the integral part of modern legal education they have become. They allow students to apply theoretical knowledge gained in the classroom to real clients and cases, and often their supervisors are practitioners from external law firms. Therefore, the experience not only helps meet pedagogical goals by learning relevant practical skills, such as client interviewing, legal research, case management and drafting, but is also essential for gaining a path into legal professional practice. The real-world experiences can be added to a

---

2 Further reading includes Office for Students, 'Meeting the Mental Health Needs of Students' (9 October 2023), www.officeforstudents.org.uk/publications/meeting-the-mental-health-needs-of-students/; Student Minds, 'The University Mental Health Charter' (2019), https://universitymentalhealthcharter.org.uk/; Emma Jones, 'Navigating the Landscape of Wellness in Legal Education: Obstacles and Opportunities on the Path Ahead' in Judith Marychurch, Kate Fischer Doherty and Jacqueline Weinberg (eds), *Wellness for Law: Reflecting on the Past, Shaping the Future* (LexisNexis Butterworths 2024) ch 3.

3 Brenda D Gibson, 'Lawyers, Trauma, and Professional Wellbeing: How the Legal Community Takes Back Its Mental Health' (2024) Wake Forest University Legal Papers No 5026587, https://papers.ssrn.com/sol3/papers.cfm?abstract_id=5026587

4 Research initially came from the US; see Stephen B Shanfield and Andrew H Benjamin, 'Psychiatric Distress in Law Students' (1985) 35 *Journal of Legal Education* 65. UK studies then followed; see L Elisa Lewis and Jacqueline M Cardwell, 'A Comparative Study of Mental Health and Wellbeing among UK Students on Professional Degree Programmes' (2019) 43 *Journal of Further and Higher Education* 1226.

5 See, for example, International Bar Association, *Mental Wellbeing in the Legal Profession: A Global Study* (October 2021), www.ibanet.org/document?id=IBA-report-Mental-Wellbeing-in-the-Legal-Profession-A-Global-Study

6 Ian Weinstein, 'Teaching Reflective Lawyering in a Small Case Litigation Clinic: A Love Letter to My Clinic Papers' (2006–2007) 13 *Clinical Law Review* 573.

student's CV and they gain the possibility of networking with potential future employers – 'work readiness', as Cantatore describes it.[7]

However, these invaluable learning experiences need to be balanced against the pressures inherent in legal practice. Clinic students are tasked with a unique combination of maintaining academic and professional standards, while at the same time dealing with emotional clients. This involvement in highly emotional situations and cases can be upsetting and potentially triggering for students since 'they have to deal with it in a twofold way, as a human being, and as a future lawyer'.[8] The impact can be even more profound if the student's wellbeing was already fragile and/or they had experienced an Adverse Childhood Experience (ACE), defined by Young Minds as 'highly stressful and potentially traumatic events or situations that occur during childhood and/or adolescence'.[9]

Even the profession has, over recent years, recognized the pressure on practising lawyers[10] and has started to find ways to deal with the previously hidden issues of emotional trauma. Both UK and international representative organizations have set out steps they expect firms to take to protect their practitioners,[11] and it makes sense for that to start with legal education. It then becomes an open topic for students to discuss and acknowledge well before they reach professional legal qualification.

Student wellbeing and mental health issues

Participation in higher education can be a positive and transformative experience for many students, offering opportunities for personal growth and future success. However, studies show that a growing number of students

7 Francina Cantatore, 'The Impact of Pro Bono Law Clinics on Employability and Work Readiness in Law Students' (2018) 25(1) *International Journal of Clinical Legal Education.*

8 Andrés Gascon-Cuenca, Carla Ghitti and Francesca Malzani, 'Acknowledging the Relevance of Empathy in Clinical Legal Education: Some Proposals from the Experience of the University of Brescia (IT) and Valencia (ESP)' (2018) 25(2) *International Journal of Clinical Legal Education*; Laurel E Fletcher and Harvey M Weinstein, 'When Students Lose Perspective: Clinical Supervision and the Management of Empathy' (2002) 9 *Clinical Law Review* 147.

9 Young Minds, 'Understanding Trauma and Adversity', www.youngminds.org.uk/professional/resources/understanding-trauma-and-adversity/

10 See later section on 'Mental health and wellbeing in the legal profession'.

11 See later section on 'Mental health and wellbeing in the legal profession'; and Bar Standards Board, 'Commitment to Wellbeing Statement', www.barstandardsboard.org.uk/static/2a1fb3c3-5b5e-47ae-9b260f7931146d10/78600755-390f-43f8-b366bcd96a56087a/BSB-commitment-to-wellbeing.pdf; and Solicitors Regulation Authority, 'Workplace Environment' (7 February 2022, updated 4 May 2023), www.sra.org.uk/solicitors/guidance/workplace-environment/

struggle with their mental health while at university, which can significantly impact their ability to fully participate in and complete their studies.[12] There is evidence that student mental health worsened during the COVID-19 lockdowns and has yet to recover.[13]

This is a real and pressing issue, particularly for students from low socioeconomic backgrounds, who face increased risks to their mental health and wellbeing.[14]

A report by the Office for Students (OfS)[15] reveals that the proportion of full-time undergraduate entrants disclosing the most serious type of mental health condition (defined in the Equality Act 2010 as having a substantial impact on their ability to carry out day-to-day activities and lasting at least 12 months)[16] rose from 0.7 per cent in 2010–11 to 4.5 per cent in 2021–22, equating to approximately 24,700 students. This upward trend is corroborated by research from King's College London and the Centre for Transforming Access and Student Outcomes in Higher Education (TASO),[17] which found that the share of undergraduate students experiencing mental health challenges increased over recent years, meaning around one in six undergraduates now report such issues. The TASO study showed almost a trebling of students reporting mental health challenges, from 6 per cent of students in 2016 to 2017 to 16 per cent in 2022 to 2023. While some of the recent increases occurred during the pandemic, there was a 32 per cent increase during 2022 and 2023, coinciding with the cost-of-living crisis. It was also noted that the upward trend started well before this.

Students from some groups are disproportionately affected by mental health challenges. These include women, students from low socioeconomic backgrounds, LGBTQ+ students, and students who are working alongside their studies.[18]

---

12 Office for Students, 'Meeting the Mental Health Needs of Students' (9 October 2023), www.officeforstudents.org.uk/publications/meeting-the-mental-health-needs-of-students/; and Student Minds, 'The University Mental Health Charter' (2019), https://universitymentalhealthcharter.org.uk/

13 Office for National Statistics, 'Coronavirus and Higher Education Students: 25 February to 7 March 2022' (2022), www.ons.gov.uk/peoplepopulationandcommunity/healthandsocialcare/healthandwellbeing/bulletins/coronavirusandhighereducationstudents/25februaryto7march2022

14 ibid.

15 ibid.

16 Equality Act 2010, s 6.

17 Michael Sanders, *Student Mental Health in 2023: Who Is Struggling and How the Situation Is Changing* (King's College London Policy Institute 2023), www.kcl.ac.uk/policy-institute/assets/student-mental-health-in-2023.pdf

18 ibid.

The OfS report states that since 2016–17, entrants to full-time courses who were eligible for free school meals have been more likely to report having a mental health condition than those who were not eligible (5.7 per cent compared with 4.8 per cent in 2021–22),[19] demonstrating that poor mental health disproportionately affects students from lower socioeconomic backgrounds.

There is a clear link between poor mental health and student outcomes. The TASO report found that among students considering dropping out of university, the overwhelming majority gave poor mental health as the main reason, and this was significantly higher (25 per cent) than any of the other 18 explanations.

The OfS has developed an Equality of Opportunity Risk Register,[20] identifying mental health as a significant risk to student success. This initiative aims to provide higher education providers with a framework to identify and mitigate risks that could impede students from disadvantaged backgrounds.

The tragic case of Natasha Abrahart, a second-year physics student at the University of Bristol who died by suicide in 2018 shortly before she was due to take an oral assessment in front of her peers, has also underlined the importance of universities taking action to support vulnerable students. In May 2022, a court ruled that the university had discriminated against Abrahart by failing to make reasonable adjustments for her social anxiety disorder, which contributed to her death.[21] This ruling confirmed that the university was required to take reasonable steps to avoid a disabled person suffering disadvantage, and that the duty to make reasonable adjustments might be owed to people whose disability was not known to the educational institution before the issue arose. Education providers are not expected to anticipate the needs of every student, but they must think about, and take, reasonable steps to overcome barriers which might impede people with different kinds of disability.

In response to the worrying data, the UK government has also taken action and established a taskforce[22] to look into the issue further. While the statistics and cases highlighted earlier relate to students experiencing serious mental health issues rather than 'low wellbeing' issues, they highlight worrying trends which anyone working in higher education should be mindful of. In the UK (compared to the US and Australia) 'wellness literature is still overall niche,

[19] Office for Students (n 12) 8.

[20] Office for Students, 'Equality of Opportunity Risk Register', www.officeforstudents.org.uk/for-providers/equality-of-opportunity/equality-of-opportunity-risk-register/

[21] *University of Bristol v Abrahart* [2024] EWHC 299 (KB).

[22] UK Government, 'Higher Education Mental Health Implementation Taskforce' (2023), www.gov.uk/government/groups/higher-education-mental-health-implementation-taskforce

and wellness initiatives which are identifiable within law schools – in terms of curriculum design and delivery and learning and pastoral support – have some way to go to become mainstream and normalized, even if a current spotlight on wellness is moving them in this broad direction.'[23]

Wellbeing of students in clinical settings

Students engaging in clinical settings with real clients and complex issues are required to cope with the pressures faced by all students highlighted earlier, but with the additional pressure of working in a challenging environment, often helping to support vulnerable people who have experienced trauma. Before we explore the issue of students working in law clinics, it is useful to consider research undertaken in the context of other disciplines such as nursing and social work.

A report by Health Education England provides evidence that clinical placements can have a profound impact on students' mental health and wellbeing.[24] Nursing and medical students experience high levels of stress due to the demanding nature of their clinical placements and exposure to distressing situations. The report discusses how working and learning in the healthcare sector is like no other employment environment, with staff frequently exposed to the most traumatic situations, such as the aftermath of a road traffic accident or suicide and helping people in distress or dying. The report states that there are dangers of taking for granted the 'emotional labour' required by National Health Service (NHS) staff and for those learning in the NHS, and it makes a number of recommendations on supporting the wellbeing of NHS staff and students.

Another study in the *Journal of Advanced Nursing*[25] explored the relationship between sources of stress and psychological wellbeing among nursing students. It found that nursing students experience considerable stress from academic pressure, clinical workload and the emotional demands from patient care. The study also showed that the experiential learning and patient care opportunities provided by nursing placements are not always negative. Students taking part in the study described positive stress leading to beneficial outcomes such as motivation and challenge. The study also noted that support from other students and supportive tutors, self-efficacy and coping

---

23 Sarah Wilson, 'Identifying and Responding to a "Wellness Imperative" in the UK Legal Education: Exploring the Wellness Potential of Law and History Study, through the Significance Attached to "Lives Lived" in the 21st Century' in Marychurch et al (n 2).

24 Health Education England, *NHS Staff and Learners Mental Wellbeing Commission* (2019), https://tinyurl.com/y4nwxzlv

25 Chris Gibbons, Martin Dempster and Marianne Moutray, 'Stress and Eustress in Nursing Students' (2008) 61(3) *Journal of Advanced Nursing* 282.

styles play crucial roles in moderating and mediating the effects of stress on wellbeing. We will see later on that the benefits of clinical placements are mirrored in student law clinic settings.

There is evidence that some students taking clinical placements could also experience secondary trauma, a term first used by Figley[26] to describe a phenomenon where individuals experience trauma symptoms due to indirect exposure to traumatic events through their work with affected clients. This condition shares features with post-traumatic stress disorder (PTSD), such as intrusive thoughts, avoidance behaviours and emotional arousal, but it arises from empathetic engagement rather than direct exposure.

Social work students are particularly vulnerable to secondary trauma during their placements. They often work with clients who have experienced abuse, neglect and other traumatic events. The emotional toll of hearing these stories and witnessing clients' distress can lead to secondary trauma. Research indicates that social work students may experience symptoms such as poor sleep, nightmares, flashbacks and emotional exhaustion.[27]

A study of social work students explored the prevalence of secondary trauma among students during their placements.[28] The study found that while no students in the sample appeared to suffer from secondary trauma, the potential for such trauma exists, and adequate support mechanisms are crucial. The study highlighted the importance of preparing students for the emotional challenges of their work and providing robust support systems to mitigate the risk of secondary trauma.

Proposed support mechanisms included trauma-informed organizational cultures, comprehensive training on self-care practices and regular supervision, as well as fostering a supportive environment where students can discuss their experiences and seek help when needed.

In the 2010s, Monash University's Faculty of Medicine, Nursing and Health Sciences implemented a strategy to enhance student wellbeing by teaching mindfulness-based stress management to all first-year students. A survey of these students indicated a decrease in symptoms of depression and hostility over the survey period.[29]

---

[26] Charles R Figley, 'Compassion Fatigue: Toward a New Understanding of the Costs of Caring' in B Hudnall Stamm (ed), *Secondary Traumatic Stress: Self-Care Issues for Clinicians, Researchers, and Educators* (The Sidran Press 1995).

[27] Diana Conroy, Tonimarie Benaton, Ivana Babicova and Elizabeth Eate, 'Investigating Secondary Trauma in Student Placements: An Exploratory Study' (2022) 52(7) *British Journal of Social Work* 4280.

[28] ibid.

[29] Craig S Hassed, Steven de Lisle, Gavin Brent Sullivan and Ciaran Pier, 'Enhancing the Health of Medical Students: Outcomes of an Integrated Mindfulness and Lifestyle Program' (2009) 14 *Advances in Health Sciences Education: Theory and Practice* 1.

Appleby et al cite this study and recommend incorporating similar mental health literacy programmes into law school curricula in Australia.[30]

Wellbeing and legal advice clinics: risk and remedy

There is considerable evidence from studies in Australia[31] and the UK[32] that[33] law students face significant pressures, including rigorous academic demands, competitive job markets and the emotionally charged nature of legal practice.[34] These factors can negatively impact students' ability to participate fully in their education and achieve their potential.

Research by Appleby et al in Australia found that law students are disproportionately affected by mental health issues compared to their peers in other disciplines, and highlighted the stress factors unique to law school, such as perfectionism and fear of failure, which are often exacerbated by a hypercompetitive environment.[35]

Studies show similar findings in the UK. In a 2019 study, Duffy et al found that 35.2 per cent of law students experienced high levels of psychological distress, significantly higher than for medical students (17.8 per cent) and the general population (13.3 per cent).[36]

---

30 Michael Appleby and Judy Bourke, 'Promoting Law Student Mental Health Literacy and Wellbeing: A Case Study from the College of Law, Australia' (2014) 20(1) *International Journal of Clinical Legal Education* 494.

31 Rachel Field, James Duffy and Colin James (eds), *Promoting Law Student and Lawyer Well-Being in Australia and beyond* (Routledge 2016); Lawrence S Krieger, 'Institutional Denial about the Dark Side of Law School, and Fresh Empirical Guidance for Constructively Breaking the Silence' (2002) 52 *Journal of Legal Education* 112; Norm Kelk, Sharon Medlow and Ian Hickie, 'Distress and Depression among Australian Law Students: Incidence, Attitudes and the Role of Universities' (2010) 32(1) *Sydney Law Review* 113; Norm Kelk, Georgina Luscombe, Sharon Medlow and Ian Hickie, *Courting the Blues: Attitudes towards Depression in Australian Law Students and Lawyers* (Brain & Mind Research Institute 2009) 7.

32 Caroline Strevens and Emma Jones, 'Legal Education for Wellbeing: Design, Delivery and Evaluation' (2022) 56(1) *The Law Teacher* 1.

33 Molly Townes O'Brien, Stephen Tang and Kath Hall, 'Changing Our Thinking: Empirical Research on Law Student Wellbeing, Thinking Styles and the Law Curriculum' (2011) 21(2) *International Journal of the First Year in Higher Education* 49.

34 Appleby and Bourke (n 30).

35 ibid.

36 Anne Duffy, Kate EA Saunders, Gin S Malhi, Scott Patten, Andrea Cipriani, Stephen H McNevin, Ellie MacDonald and John Geddes, 'Mental Health Care for University Students: A Way Forward?' (2019) 6 *The Lancet Psychiatry* 885.

Skipper[37] points out that the competitive and adversarial law school environment, with in-class debates, mooting and fierce competition for top grades and postgraduate jobs, can have a negative impact on wellbeing. In a study conducted with law and psychology undergraduate students in England, law students reported having a lower sense of belonging and poorer wellbeing than psychology students (although stress levels were similar). Skipper proposed targeted wellbeing interventions focusing on increasing a sense of belonging as a potential means of improving the mental wellbeing of all students.

There is also a risk that law clinic students, particularly those working with vulnerable clients, are at risk of secondary trauma in the same way as nursing and social work students. They frequently deal with clients who have experienced significant trauma, such as domestic abuse, homelessness or wrongful convictions. The emotional burden of hearing these stories and advocating for clients can lead to secondary traumatic stress and emotional exhaustion.[38]

Law clinic students may experience symptoms such as intrusive thoughts, avoidance behaviours and emotional arousal. The pressure to achieve positive outcomes for their clients can exacerbate these symptoms, leading to anxiety and burnout.

Universities have long implemented support structures for medical and nursing students,[39] and it is important that law schools also recognize the high-risk nature of clinical legal work and adopt comparable wellbeing strategies. There is already good practice developing in this area. Curryer and Mawdsley[40] describe the steps they took in their distance-learning criminal appeals clinic at the Open University to mitigate the risk of secondary trauma among their students. These included providing training on self-care practices, offering regular supervision and fostering a trauma-informed organizational culture.

Castles and Boothby highlight strategies adopted at their respective clinics in Adelaide and Northumbria Universities to support wellbeing,[41] with

37 Yvonne Skipper and Michael Fay, 'The Relationship between the Sense of Belonging, Mental Wellbeing and Stress in Students of Law and Psychology in an English University' (2023) 4(1) *European Journal of Legal Education* 5.

38 Emma Curryer and Gillian Mawdsley, 'Navigating Vicarious Trauma: The Importance of Planning, Teaching, and Delivering Vicarious Trauma Training to Support Law Students and the Legal Profession' (2024) 31(1) *International Journal of Clinical Legal Education* 126.

39 Hassed et al (n 29) 3; Cameron Johnston, 'Medical Students Talk Openly about Their Mental Health Challenges' (2015) 18 *Canadian Medical Association Journal* 1348.

40 ibid.

41 Margaret Castles and Carol Boothby, 'Which Hat Shall I Wear Today? Exploring the Professional and Ethical Implications of Law Clinic Supervision', in Caroline Strevens and Rachel Field (eds), *Educating for Well-Being in Law* (Taylor & Francis 2019) 128.

the Adelaide CLE programme expressly incorporating wellbeing into the curriculum from day one, 'emphasising the imperative of self-monitoring and supporting others, with reference to psychological resources, reflective exercises and student discussion'. There is a focus on reflection, working cooperatively and creating a sense of 'belonging' at Northumbria, so that students start to feel part of a community of practice, and the writers usefully summarize the way in which three aspects of wellbeing converge: course content that acknowledges wellbeing beyond the traditional paradigm of legal problem solving; curriculum delivery that encourages creativity, autonomy and confidence; and an environment of connectedness that engenders positive interrelationships with others.[42]

Strevens and Wilson made a compelling case for reform of the UK law curriculum to include programme learning outcomes to help students develop resilience and management of wellbeing, underpinned by principles of positive psychology including self-determination theory (SDT).[43] SDT focuses on fulfilling the psychological needs of autonomy, competence and relatedness. The Quality Assurance Agency (QAA) 'Subject Benchmark Statement: Law'[44] has been updated to incorporate wellbeing, with the Benchmark standards now requiring law students to demonstrate generic skills that include an understanding of 'the importance of well-being, mental health and emotions and their relationship with learning'.

It is submitted that law clinics offer a natural context in which SDT principles can be effectively applied. By working on real legal problems under supervision, students gain a sense of competence as they begin to apply theoretical knowledge to practical scenarios, enhancing their confidence and perceived ability. Autonomy is fostered as students often have responsibility for aspects of their casework, allowing them to make decisions, manage time and develop personal initiative within a structured but flexible learning environment. Finally, relatedness is nurtured through collaboration with peers, clients and supervising solicitors, helping students feel connected to others and to the broader social purpose of the legal profession.

Appleby and Bourke[45] suggest that experiential learning through real-world legal practice can help students develop resilience, self-awareness and coping

---

[42] ibid.

[43] Caroline Strevens and Clare Wilson, 'Law Student Wellbeing in the UK: A Call for Curriculum Intervention' (2016) 11(1) *Journal of Commonwealth Law and Legal Education* 44; Paul P Baard, Edward L Deci and Richard M Ryan, 'Intrinsic Need Satisfaction: A Motivational Basis of Performance and Well-Being in Two Work Settings' (2004) 34(10) *Journal of Applied Social Psychology* 2045.

[44] Quality Assurance Agency, 'Subject Benchmark Statement: Law' (2023), www.qaa.ac.uk/docs/qaa/sbs/sbs-law-23.pdf?sfvrsn=c271a881_6

[45] Appleby and Bourke (n 30).

strategies. By engaging with emotionally challenging cases and reflecting on their experiences, students learn to navigate the psychological aspects of legal work, thus enhancing their professional readiness.

Wapples[46] highlights the ways in which participation in a law clinic can build community and enhance student wellbeing. She discusses the steps taken by Queen Mary University of London's qLegal project introduced from 2019 to 2020 to support student wellbeing by embedding mental health training into the curriculum, which included a focus on building community by encouraging students to see qLegal as a big family, where everyone has something to contribute.

Gibby[47] writes that clinics can also develop sustainable practices which address issues such as wellbeing and provides students with 'a potentially richer learning experience not only in relation to emotional intelligence but in terms of connecting with professional values in an immersive way'.

Duncan describes focusing on developing the skill of empathy among his Bar students in order both to help students understand their client's position better, and to improve job satisfaction and protect against burnout.[48]

Mental health and wellbeing in the legal profession

When Jones et al suggested in the introduction to their book on this topic in 2020 that 'in short, practising law can make people sick',[49] they weren't being flippant. It is an unfortunate truth that the profession has taken its time to acknowledge. Despite these issues being discussed openly in many other professions and areas of our lives, within legal firms, it was until very recently still being 'swept under the carpet'.

Those of us who act as lawyers for people at extreme moments in their lives – facing eviction, conviction, loss of liberty, deportation, loss of their children, the end of a marriage, sexual or domestic violence, or detention in mental facilities – have a great burden placed on our shoulders.[50] The US and Australia were both ahead of many countries in recognizing the hazards

---

[46] Emily Wapples, 'Promoting Positive Mental Health in International Postgraduate Law Students at a Time of Global Uncertainty: A Case Study from qLegal at Queen Mary, University of London' (2020) 4 *International Journal of Clinical Legal Education* 1467.

[47] Caroline Gibby, 'Clinical Legal Education and the Hidden Curriculum in the Neoliberal University in England and Wales' in Strevens and Field (n 41) 136.

[48] Nigel Duncan, 'Resilience, Positive Motivation and Professional Identity: The Experience of Law Clinic Students Working with Real Clients' in Strevens and Field (n 41) 155.

[49] Emma Jones, Neil Graffin, Rajvinder Samra and Mathijs Lucassen, *Mental Health and Wellbeing in the Legal Profession* (Bristol University Press 2020).

[50] Helena Kennedy QC, 'Foreword' in Joanna Fleck and Rachel Francis, *Vicarious Trauma in the Legal Profession* (Legal Action Group 2021).

of working in the legal profession which Maclean describes as 'psychosocial hazards in the workplace'.[51] These can include burnout, vicarious trauma, the negative impact of dealing with so much conflict, bullying, plus the practical pressures from time-recording and billing practices. Maclean suggests that a trauma-informed approach is needed, matching a recent call from UK lawyers to create a safe feedback culture.[52]

There was a tranche of research undertaken in the UK between 2019 and 2021,[53] perhaps encouraged by the unique problems encountered during the COVID-19 pandemic. Even before this, writers in the subject such as Spearing and Field were highlighting earlier research findings (particularly in the US and Australia) that law was 'a profession in distress'.[54] In 2021 the Junior Lawyers Division of the Law Society of England & Wales and LawCare (a charity dedicated to supporting solicitors' mental health issues in the UK), published the results of surveys carried out in 2017, 2018 and 2019 into the wellbeing of legal practitioners.[55] LawCare's report highlighted an average score of participants of 42.2 on the Oldenburg Burnout Inventory, corresponding to a 'high risk of burnout', being 'the response to excessive and prolonged stress at work, although paid employment is not the only environment in which we can experience burnout … It occurs when that short-term stress response that we have is repeatedly triggered over a prolonged period, without enough chance to rest and restore in between'.[56]

A total of 69 per cent of participants had experienced mental ill-health in the 12 months before completing the survey and over half of those did not disclose it at work, with the explanations of fear of stigma, adverse career implications, and financial and reputational consequences.[57]

---

51 Claudia Maclean, 'Adopting Trauma-Informed Approaches to Manage Psychosocial Hazards in Legal Practice' in Marychurch et al (n 2).

52 Natalie Sutherland and Hannah Budd, 'Trauma Training Should Be Mandatory' (*Law Gazette*, 2024), www.lawgazette.co.uk/practice-points/trauma-training-should-be-mandatory/5121402.article

53 Including the Law Society of England and Wales – Junior Lawyers Division, 'Resilience and Wellbeing Surveys', https://communities.lawsociety.org.uk/Uploads/g/x/g/jld-resilience-and-wellbeing-survey-report-2017.pdf (2017), https://communities.lawsociety.org.uk/Uploads/p/d/i/jld-resilience-and-wellbeing-survey-report-2018.pdf (2018) and https://communities.lawsociety.org.uk/Uploads/b/y/k/resilience-wellbeing-survey-report-2019.pdf (2019) ; International Bar Association (n 5).

54 Rachel Spearing and Rachel Field, 'Well-Being and a Positive Professional Identity in the Legal Profession: A Snapshot of the UK Bar' in Strevens and Field (n 41).

55 The Law Society of England and Wales – Junior Lawyers Division (n 53).

56 Julie Smith, *Why Has Nobody Told Me This Before?* (Penguin/Random House UK 2022).

57 LawCare, 'Life in the Law 2020/21' (2021), www.lawcare.org.uk/life-in-the-law/#:~:text=2020%2F21%20report,Life%20in%20the%20Law%202020%2F21,and%20the%20Isle%20of%20Man

The Bar Standards Board (BSB) also surveyed barristers in the UK in 2021,[58] highlighting similar concerns for its practitioners' mental health and wellbeing.

It should perhaps not be surprising that the profession has taken so long to appreciate the suffering of its members, given the time it took to consider the trauma being suffered by its clients. Lawyers have traditionally maintained a professional distance from their client and would not have been prepared for considering how the client was coping with their situation, and whether they should be referred to other, appropriate support.

Family law helped to develop some good practice in the profession's dealings with clients, with the introduction of the Collaborative Process from the US,[59] which required opposing family lawyers to work harmoniously to help their clients resolve matters amicably at round table meetings. The specialist training was designed to ensure that competing professionals could work in a noncombative way and required each lawyer to assess their client's suitability for the collaborative process. Issues like domestic abuse, deep mistrust and power imbalances could all be reasons to avoid using the process for negotiating, as well as the client not being in the 'right frame of mind'.

When the process first arrived in the UK some 20 years ago, it was a leap of faith for many lawyers to start considering (and assessing) a client's state of mind and wellbeing. It could be argued that this went beyond a lawyer's professional duty and competence, but the collaborative training was not intending to make family lawyers into counsellors or therapists, but merely to make them more open and aware of the emotional struggles and trauma their clients were going through. It is now more widely known as the trauma-informed practice or approach (mentioned earlier as being proposed as a necessity by Maclean) and family practitioners in the UK have most recently called on all lawyers to receive this type of vital training to help their clients (and their cases).[60]

It is acknowledged that while the lawyer's main responsibility is to provide legal advice, this must be delivered in a way that considers the client's vulnerabilities and emotional needs – an approach that requires explicit instruction. Fletcher and Weinstein are concerned that legal education 'devotes insufficient attention to developing the attendant skills and mechanisms lawyers need to negotiate successfully the emotional demands of the profession'.[61] By being aware of historic trauma and/or current wellbeing

58 Bar Council (n 53).

59 A history of collaborative law is provided by Lawrence Maxwell Jr, 'The Development of Collaborative Law' (2007) 16(3–4) *Alternative Resolutions* 22.

60 Sutherland and Budd (n 52).

61 Fletcher and Weinstein (n 8) 135.

issues, lawyers are being good practitioners and meeting their professional obligation to do their best for the client. The case management and timeline, for example, may need to be adapted for the client and/or referrals made for other forms of professional help and support.

Awareness of client wellbeing issues eventually transformed into the recognition of such considerations for legal practitioners, both in the UK and internationally. The Solicitors Regulation Authority (SRA) now acknowledges that: 'The legal profession can be a highly pressurised and stressful working environment. If that becomes acute, it can have a serious impact on your personal health and wellbeing and your ability to work effectively.'[62] This followed a consultation in 2022 after the publication of the LawCare report mentioned earlier which resulted in SRA guidance requiring all law firms to take responsibility for the mental health and wellbeing of their staff.[63]

LawCare has continued to maintain its focus on this topic and has continued to survey practitioners in the UK. Its latest report published in October 2025 highlighted that nearly 60 per cent of those surveyed reported poor mental wellbeing and called on the whole sector to step up and take action. As well as recommending evidence-based steps that can improve working practices in legal workplaces, it promises a programme of engagement starting in 2026 to develop training and resources to support those workplaces putting them in to practice.[64]

The BSB mirrored the actions of the SRA, issuing a Commitment to Wellbeing Statement in 2022.[65] This arguably went further than the SRA guidance as it included equality and inclusion issues for chambers to deal with too, and established a whole new website where barristers can access wellbeing support.[66]

While these initiatives from both arms of the profession in the UK requiring employers to provide adequate support systems and supervision of their staff to enhance wellbeing are welcome, they will require proper investments of time and money to work, and it may be harder to change systemic attitudes in the profession.

Further afield, the IBA published its own, global report in 2021 on wellbeing in the profession, which identified a 'global crisis'.[67] It recommended that all

---

62 Solicitors Regulation Authority, 'Your Health, Your Career', www.sra.org.uk/solicitors/resources/all-other-topics/your-health-your-career

63 Solicitors Regulation Authority (n 11).

64 LawCare, 'Life in the Law 2025', https://lawcare.org.uk/wp-content/uploads/2025/09/Life-in-the-Law-2025.pdf

65 Bar Standards Board (n 11).

66 'Wellbeing at the Bar', www.wellbeingatthebar.org.uk

67 International Bar Association (n 5).

parts of the legal profession, including law schools, implement at least the key principles from its report, to promote positive wellbeing. These included acknowledging that wellbeing matters and is not a weakness; a commitment to make and review policy changes; keeping an open dialogue; and to share good practice so individuals can learn from others. More recently, in December 2023 the IBA issued guidelines for wellbeing in legal education, which will be examined in more detail later on.[68]

On the face of it, the future for wellbeing consideration in the profession seems positive as the profession has accepted the mantle of change, but there are suggestions that some organizations are only paying 'lip service' to the required actions. More optimistically, a recent review on wellbeing at the UK Bar suggests there have been improvements, highlighting the working group that was set up by the BSB, the training and assistance requirements for barristers, and the easily identified, separate website established to house resources.[69] Unfortunately, these positives only highlight the lack of real action taken by the SRA for solicitors. 'Wellbeing must be seen as an integral aspect of what it is to be a lawyer, rather than merely some stress management strategies added on for good measure.'[70]

A university law clinic case study

Responsibility now rests firmly with law schools to protect the wellbeing of their students undertaking clinical and real-world experiences. The pro bono law clinic at the University of Hertfordshire opened in 2019 and operates like many other university law clinics, with pairs of trained student advisors either shadowing a lawyer giving verbal advice to a client and drafting an attendance note or interviewing the client on their own (to gather detailed facts of the case only) and then drafting a letter of advice.

Family law is the busiest clinic, but there is also an immigration clinic concentrating on asylum issues for young people, and a project assisting litigants in person facing eviction from their home. All of these would be considered potentially stressful situations for the clients, and sometimes this can be passed on to the students too – the secondary trauma explained earlier and recognized by Figley.[71]

---

[68] Emma Jones, Caroline Strevens, Rachel Field and Colin Jones, *International Guidelines for Wellbeing in Legal Education* (December 2023), www.ibanet.org/document?id=International-Guidelines-for-Wellbeing-in-Legal-Education

[69] Nina Caplin, 'Wellbeing at the Bar: Progress and Reasons for Optimism' (2024) *The European Advocate*.

[70] Anna Copeland, 'Ethics, Clinics and the Unbearable Hierarchy of Law' in Marychurch et al (n 2).

[71] Figley (n 26).

When the clinic first opened, it was recognized that students may be at risk of burnout through taking on work in addition to their studies, and secondary trauma through talking to clients experiencing difficult situations. Within six months of opening, COVID-19 shut down the campus, so in March 2020, everything had to move online, with all client meetings taking place on Zoom. Arguably, having the protection of a screen between the students and their client would assist in keeping students removed from the emotions of the client and case, and thus help protect their wellbeing. However, they would also find it harder to build a rapport with the client and show an appropriate level of empathy. Further, the students had less access to their peers and supervisors for support; the only communications were via planned video calls or emails. It was hoped the steps already in place to support students would continue to work well. These included:

- working in pairs, so they had someone to talk to about the case without any concerns of client confidentiality;
- compulsory domestic abuse awareness training, which was expanded to cover trauma awareness for advisors, and taking steps to protect their own wellbeing. This was initially provided by a local domestic abuse support charity, which, while very supportive of the law students providing free advice, recognized the need to protect their vulnerable clients. They wanted the students to have the tools to recognize abuse and appreciate what their client may have gone through, and so ensure they acted in a professional yet sensitive manner. Students needed to appreciate how talking to a client about their case can be very emotional, potentially retraumatizing them. This session has been expanded to include guidance on protecting student wellbeing, on the basis that if the students fail to look after their own mental health, they would not be able to provide a quality service for the client.
- having regular, informal drop-in sessions and encouraging students to get in touch with a member of the clinic team if they need a chat;
- ensuring clients never have personal contact details for the student advisors so that all communications are through the clinic administrator to avoid clients 'latching on' to a sympathetic student;
- providing a wellbeing section in the clinic intranet site for students, with useful resources and links to the university's specialist mental health team. More recently, an interactive whiteboard resource was added so that students could anonymously post questions and concerns, as well as sharing their own coping strategies; and
- online wellbeing sessions each semester facilitated by a clinic staff member in order to offer an informal discussion with no agenda, so that it can be student-led. The aim is for ideally all clinic students to attend the session, but from a place where they feel secure and comfortable.

The clinic team report that the online wellbeing sessions are well attended and work well. The focus is to find out from the students themselves what they find challenging in their clinical work and also share good practice on how they deal with those challenges. The team share a 'Top Tips' sheet afterwards if there are good points to highlight, so even those not attending can benefit.

Common practical considerations which put students under pressure include time management or feeling that the work is not shared equally with a student partner. More emotional issues are raised, but these tend to be about the wellbeing of the clients – for example, how to deal with a client who is crying or visibly anxious and stressed. Interestingly, they never raised a concern about dealing with an angry client.

One specific example of the student experience during the period of COVID-19 lockdown restrictions in England highlights the necessity of good training. A pair of student advisors were interviewing a client in a family case using Zoom. The client had her camera on, but refused to speak out loud and insisted on laboriously typing her comments and replies to the students' questions using the chat box facility. The students found this strange and rather wearisome, so pressed the client for a reason. She eventually confided in them that her abusive partner was working from home in the room next door, and she was terrified he would overhear their conversation and realize she was seeking legal advice on how to leave him.

The students completed the interview and ensured they informed their supervisor of the urgent predicament the client was in. They were offered extra support and follow-up discussions afterwards, but both seemed to take the situation in their stride. The clinic team recognized that such a unique situation could never have been predicted, but it could be learnt from. They also decided that it should not dilute the powerfully positive impact of these real-world learning opportunities on the student experience. Arguably it is better for students to face a challenging experience like this for the first time in a carefully supervised and supported environment than while working in their first job with a law firm.

The students also have their own techniques for protecting themselves, as the majority are from a generation where mental health and wellbeing have been spoken about all their lives. Some students share their methods of personal care during the online wellbeing sessions. Many relate to compartmentalizing their clinic work, so physically getting away after a client interview and maybe going to the gym or for a walk, or setting specific times each day or week for clinic work so that they are not thinking about cases and clients all the time. They also know to remain detached from the client and their situation by recognizing and reminding themselves that they did not cause the problem and cannot solve it. Many share how speaking to someone else about the case (taking into account confidentiality issues) 'lessened the load' and ultimately one student even recognized the need to avoid retraumatizing themselves, so if a case is too difficult to deal with, they should ask to be replaced. However, this then creates an administrative burden if that student is working in the clinic for a credit-bearing module in terms of ensuring they have sufficient cases to reflect on for their assessment.

The clinic team worked closely with the School's wellbeing lead, which led to a correlation becoming apparent between the students working in the clinic and the students who access wellbeing support. Did this mean that those students undertaking clinical work already had poor mental health and so were more susceptible to being adversely affected by their experiences (despite any efforts to protect them), or were those students (who may have already experienced trauma of some kind in their own lives) just more likely to volunteer to help others, as they appreciated how valuable free advice could be to vulnerable people?

The clinic team conducted an anonymous survey of students working in the clinic to try and discover the answer, and to help find a way to improve best practice in protecting clinic students.[72] Around 100 students were surveyed, although only 30 responded. The results showed that 20 per cent had wellbeing concerns before they joined the clinic, but 93 per cent confirmed they had no negative impact from their clinic work. Of the couple who were adversely affected, one student explained that 'during my first interview, I understood … the impact I could have on someone's situation. The preparation helped but it didn't prepare me for how real this was. And I had to understand and accept that I couldn't help that person right there and then'.

All who attended the online wellbeing sessions found them useful, but less than half ever read the 'Top Tips' provided afterwards. Almost half accessed the clinic wellbeing resources and one third had used other school or university resources. Only one student suggested they had sought external support for coping with clinic work concerns, and that was to 'offload' to a partner.

Most of the students didn't want any extra resources. One suggestion was for one-to-one wellbeing sessions, while another sought a more sympathetic supervisor.

Outside of the formal survey, informal feedback from clinical modules and the National Student Survey was overwhelmingly positive about clinical opportunities. Furthermore, evidence of strong graduate outcomes is reflected in the progression of clinic students to paralegal and trainee

72 Research study approved by the University of Hertfordshire Social Sciences, Arts and Humanities, Ethics Committee with Delegated Authority (SSAH ECDA) and Ethics Protocol number LAW/SF/UH/05765.

solicitor positions within firms linked to the law clinic as a direct result of their opportunities to work with, impress and network with external lawyers.

A similar case study was undertaken by the Open University in respect of its Criminal Justice Clinic. It reported wanting to protect its students from vicarious trauma and having the additional complication of isolation, as they have no campus. It reports offering a compulsory training session dedicated to helping students recognize the symptoms of vicarious trauma; appreciating it can be a part of legal practice and signposting appropriate resources. The Open University explains that the training focuses on delivering a toolkit for students from which students help themselves, both now and in the future, heading towards legal practice or other employment.[73]

Practical wellbeing strategies for university law clinics

Given the potential for legal clinic work to have a significant negative impact on student wellbeing, it is essential for law schools and legal clinic teams to implement strategies that promote good mental health. This will also prepare those students for entering the legal profession which we have already highlighted earlier comes with its own risks to the wellbeing of its members.

While clinical education is inherently challenging, there are steps that institutions can take to mitigate any negative effects on students' wellbeing – for example, we have the detailed guidance from the IBA for legal educators.[74] However, this is less a practical handbook and more a demand that law schools take mental health issues seriously – both in relation to students and staff. It proposes the implementation of ten guidelines, from understanding and promoting positive wellbeing, to providing appropriate resources, making curriculum and policy changes to prove long-term commitment, and ongoing evaluation.

In the UK, as already mentioned, there is also the QAA 'Subject Benchmark Statement: Law' that since 2023 specifically requires outcomes that include students appreciating the importance of wellbeing and mental health.[75] This links to the positive outcome of experiential learning – that it increases student engagement, encouraging students to become 'active participants in the development of their own lives and careers, and to exercise autonomy and self-direction in their choices'.[76]

[73] Curryer and Mawdsley (n 38).

[74] Jones et al (n 68).

[75] Quality Assurance Agency (n 44).

[76] Alexander Scherr and Susan Brooks, 'Introduction' in Leah Wortham et al (eds), *Learning from Practice: A Text for Experiential Legal Education* (3rd edn, West Academic Publishing 2016).

Another positive is the concept of universities as a 'just anchor',[77] reminding us of how much benefit vulnerable sections of our society receive from law clinic and pro bono projects.[78] Many universities have created 'strategies to achieve local social, economic and epistemic justice goals through collaboration in networks of other anchors and knowledge co-production with citizens'.[79] As a result, students learn how important it is to 'give back' through volunteering.

One of the key elements of the 'just anchor' as recognized by Hambleton is for universities to work collaboratively with communities, playing a positive and dynamic role in working with local stakeholders to co-create activities that are of shared value.[80]

The arguments are strong for universities to retain their law clinics, and we should therefore look to the practical steps law schools should be taking to protect their students working in these projects.

Supervision

Providing students with adequate supervision is crucial. Good supervision is summarized by Maclean as being a productive relationship that is focused on education and training, is mandatory and is not just about risk management, but is a chance to consider the supervisee's development and health.[81] It is unrealistic for any law clinic team to provide a '24/7' helpline for students; instead, staff should be trained not only in teaching legal skills but also in recognizing signs of stress, burnout or emotional distress in students. Clinic supervisors and staff should encourage an open and supportive environment where students feel comfortable discussing any challenges and seeking help when needed. This could include regular drop-in sessions for students to monitor their mental health and wellbeing, as well as providing access to relevant signposting – perhaps to counselling services or stress management activities.

Fletcher and Weinstein assert that 'the role of the legal supervisor includes not only providing substantive law training and carefully reviewing legal

[77] Liam O'Farrell, Sara Hassan and Charlotte Hoole, 'The University as a Just Anchor: Universities, Anchor Networks and Participatory Research' (2022) 47(12) *Studies in Higher Education* 2405.

[78] Robin Hambleton, 'British Universities: The Sleeping Giants of Place-Based Leadership?' (2018) 12(1) *People, Place and Policy* 1.

[79] O'Farrell, Hassan and Hoole (n 77).

[80] Hambleton (n 78).

[81] Maclean (n 51), discussing Michael McNamara, 'Towards Effective Supervision For The Legal Profession: A Focus on Supervised Practice' (PhD thesis, Griffith University), https://research-repository.griffith.edu.au/items/2186f60e-8f58-404c-bdb7-c7efa0cb7d1c

work product but also attending to the issues regarding students' emotional experiences engendered by and reactions to their legal work'.[82] This is where law schools need to heed at least some of the IBA guidance in ensuring the wellbeing of their staff is also considered and supported alongside that of their students, since, in suggesting this approach, 'a form of emotional labour is placed upon legal educators who must work to forge such connections, regardless of their own workloads stresses and challenges'.[83]

This supportive environment is also about creating a community for clinic students. Gibson argued that community could prevent trauma and heal the profession, with all the arms of the legal profession needing to 'create a community of wellness'. This must therefore be a focus for law schools, albeit one that Gibson feels will require deliberate and strategic planning, involving all stakeholders.[84]

Peer support

Some clinics already use peer mentoring schemes between students, but they can require a lot of resource to supervise and manage. If the student mentors start taking on board part of the role clinic staff are currently undertaking – for example, keeping in touch with clinic students, checking in on their wellbeing and signposting – those mentors would themselves need training and supervision, and arguably we should then be concerned about any extra pressure and negative impact on them as mentors.

Even informal peer support, like students working in pairs, can be beneficial as it allows the students to use their preferred, informal means of communication (like WhatsApp), as even online methods (like Microsoft Teams and Zoom) are seen as too formal, possibly due to the preference of accessing everything through their mobile telephones. To log in to a student system is seen as an extra effort, as it often requires their laptop. Clearly this type of communication would raise issues if clinic staff were involved – for example, access to student personal mobile numbers, administering and supervising the chat content, and ensuring that any questions or concerns are identified promptly and responded to.

Culture change and training

Being open about the whole issue of wellbeing within legal clinics is vital and probably much easier now that the legal profession has taken steps to remove

82 Fletcher and Weinstein (n 8).

83 Jones (n 2).

84 Gibson (n 3).

the stigma. Law schools can integrate wellbeing practices into clinic training, stressing the importance of self-care and the need to maintain a work-life balance. This could include sessions on time management, resilience training (this will be discussed in more detail later on) and mindfulness practices. Ideally, all students within a law school would receive at least an introduction to similar self-care, given the stressful time research tells us they have in studying law and the challenging profession they aim to enter.

Additionally, it is essential that if wellbeing signposting is used, those resources are actually available, and students who apply are not just put on a waiting list. Ideally, this would include on-campus counselling services, stress management training and opportunities for students to engage in activities that promote relaxation and social connection. The supervisors and staff need to encourage students to take breaks, pursue non-academic activities, make social connections with their peers and maintain a healthy lifestyle, as these can all help buffer against the negative effects of academic and clinical pressures.

The concept of providing students with the means to self-care raises the issue of whether any training can actually enable them to increase their resilience. Ferris suggests that: 'Resilience is not something an individual can learn through hard work and application, but the product of external resources such as money, cultural capital, social networks, health care through time as well as lived life history.'[85] A study by Duncan found:

> Students recognised that resilience came, in part, from 'something within' them and saw the most effective way of helping them to develop resilience being to provide practical guidance and opportunities to develop competence through experience. This is what all professional development programs should be seeking to achieve and live clinical work is an important component of that process.[86]

However, we can't just offer something like meditation alone and think the job is done, even though this could be one tool to build up resilience.[87]

Reflection/debriefing

Many clinics that are used for credit-bearing modules already teach their students self- reflection, as it is a useful means of assessment and review of their work with clients. Regular reflection can allow students to face what

[85] Graham Ferris, 'Law-Students Wellbeing and Vulnerability' (2021) 56(1) *The Law Teacher* 1.

[86] Duncan (n 48).

[87] For more on the use of meditation for students, see Anthony Cullen and Lughaidh Kerin, 'Meditation in Legal Education: The Value Added toward the Well-Being of Law Students' in Strevens and Field (n 41).

may have gone wrong in their clinical practice and plan steps to improve to avoid repeating the same mistakes. A debrief with their supervisor at the end of a case can also be useful in not only reviewing any practical issues to be remedied, but also to check in on any emotional concerns and ensure the student is getting the support they need.

Trauma-informed approach

We have previously commented on the recommendation for the whole legal profession to undergo trauma-informed training.[88] Perhaps at least a simplified form should be provided to all law students. Katz and Haldar identify the hallmarks of trauma-informed practice as when a law student (or practitioner):

> puts the realities of the clients' trauma experiences at the forefront in engaging with clients and adjusts the practice approach informed by the individual client's trauma experience. Trauma-informed practice also encompasses the practitioner employing modes of self-care to counterbalance the effect the client's trauma experience may have on the practitioner.[89]

As mentioned earlier, the Open University believes that vicarious trauma (VT) awareness training is vital for clinical students to protect themselves emotionally and will ultimately make them better practitioners when they qualify. It reported that 'if the lawyer has taken steps to care for themselves by proactively engaging with VT awareness, it then follows that the benefit ultimately is to a better informed and able legal workforce'.[90]

Screening students and/or access

A contentious option for clinics is to screen students and/or case content. Most universities hold data about students with disabilities, usually as a way to ensure teaching staff take pre-agreed steps to ensure the student has an equitable learning experience. If it is recognized that some students need extra support in their learning in order to be successful, should we do something similar in law clinics? One option would be to limit the types of cases (or at least case content) that are dealt with by students who are considered more vulnerable or who have a history of wellbeing issues.

---

[88] Sutherland and Budd (n 52).

[89] Sarah Katz and Deeya Haldar, 'The Pedagogy of Trauma-Informed Lawyering' (2016) 22(2) *Clinical Law Review* 2.

[90] Curryer and Mawdsley (n 38).

To prevent such students from working in a clinic altogether, even if this was intended to protect them, would be seen as discrimination. As Maclean recognized: 'Organisations may consider screening potential employees to assess whether they are at risk of vicarious trauma and burnout, in consultation with the prospective employee.' However, it would need to be utilized cautiously to avoid allegations of discrimination.[91]

Even limiting the case details shared with a student raises concerns – for example, how would the level of protection a student needs be identified? Further, if they are volunteering in a clinic rather than undertaking the work as part of a formal module, would access to a student's personal information be readily available, given data protection and confidentiality issues?

Ultimately, these students have chosen to study law and many have decided to become a lawyer, so they will be faced with challenging situations and cases in their working lives. Surely it is better to let them experience some of those challenges in a supported environment within their law school.

This also relates to the earlier discussion on resilience, and whether we can teach students to be emotionally tougher. In the case study at the University of Hertfordshire described earlier, one student explained they volunteered to work in the clinic as they wanted to push themself out of their comfort zone. Dealing with your fears and concerns can be a positive, as Smith explains: 'The number one thing that keeps anxiety going is avoidance of the thing that you fear. If there is something you want to master but it makes you nervous, do it as much as you possibly can.'

In 2019, Seear[92] considered whether law schools, and in particular law clinics, should be checking the content of teaching materials provided to students to avoid the danger of 'triggering', but she identified an initial hurdle of how academics would assess whether material is potentially triggering or not. She also explored some of the pedagogical and practical implications that would flow from the use of trigger warnings in law clinics. She concluded that we should be cautious in deciding to impose trigger warnings in clinical legal education, because they introduce a series of major philosophical, practical and pedagogical problems.

Even if we wanted to try and limit the content of cases that students were faced with, it could prove impossible. Clients are notorious for not being open about their full issues in their storytelling, so that even if during initial triage clients are asked for case details, we cannot guarantee that will identify whether the case involves a sensitive or challenging topic. Not all victims of domestic abuse admit to this fact during triage. It may only be

---

91 Maclean (n 51).

92 Kate Seear, 'Do Law Clinics Need Trigger Warnings? Philosophical, Pedagogical and Practical Concerns' (2019) 29(1) *Legal Education Review* 1.

once the client spends time chatting to a pair of student advisors that they feel settled enough to provide more details, which could include sensitive (and potentially triggering) subjects like domestic abuse or child abuse.

Even if we could find the means to limit student access to certain cases, there is still the question of whether we should. The students working in law clinics are largely en route to becoming legal professionals and working with clients and cases as their chosen career. To shelter students from upsetting or sensitive case information means they are not gaining a true experience of real life as a lawyer. Surely, one of the main reasons to provide law clinic and pro bono projects at universities is to give students a realistic introduction to their working future.

Conclusion

The law clinic environment can be one of the most challenging yet rewarding aspects of legal education. Students gain invaluable practical skills and experiences, but can also be adversely affected by issues and challenges (whether practical and/or emotional) which impact their wellbeing. As the case of the Bristol University student Natasha Abrahart[93] raised earlier shows, universities owe a duty of care to their students and so must ensure that steps are taken to protect them when we put them in potentially traumatic situations. Fleck and Francis consider that 'the risks to practitioners of inadequate training on how to handle traumatic material are borne out starkly in the research and are a cause of significant concern'.[94]

Avoiding the emotional, ethical and time management demands of client work that the students will be expected to deal with in their chosen career is not an option. Therefore, rather than removing them from dealing with these challenges, the educators and supervisors should be supporting students to recognize the pressures and how they can contribute to mental health issues, as well as providing them with the skills and resources to overcome or at least mitigate them.

This is a generation who are lucky enough to be open about personal mental health and wellbeing, and who are about to enter a profession which has finally recognized and accepted its responsibility to its members. By fostering environments where students feel supported and equipped to manage stress, law clinics can provide not only professional development with their law schools but can also contribute to the long-term wellbeing of future lawyers.

---

[93] *University of Bristol v Abrahart* (n 21).

[94] Fleck and Francis (n 50).

Rose et al suggest that:

> clinical supervision can yield a multitude of benefits, including the reduction of burnout, minimisation of vicarious trauma, and enhancement of the quality of legal practice by fostering emotional and interpersonal skills ... The potential benefits of this approach extend to all members of the profession, from new lawyers to seasoned practitioners, and could lead to improved professionalism, reduced attrition, and enhanced wellbeing within the legal profession.[95]

Cooperation and communication within both the UK and international clinical legal education community is healthy and it would make sense to agree the implementation of standard guidelines to ensure student wellbeing is protected, such as the IBA guidelines mentioned earlier. However, clinic teams tend to be small and with limited resources. Significant changes like those proposed by the IBA would need the backing of the law school and ideally the whole institution to make impactful and long-term improvements.

Making educated predictions on the future of wellbeing in legal education will 'ensure sustainable long-term wellness within law schools for both staff and students. In constructing a future agenda for wellness in this way it is informative to draw upon examples from both the legal profession and education more broadly, to discern possible patters or pitfalls'.[96]

It also needs to be remembered that all the IBA guidelines require wellbeing support to be provided for both students and staff, especially for the latter, from whom legal education already demands considerable emotional labour.[97] This will ultimately require broader strategies from more senior management with law schools (and institutions) to seek the resources needed to make effective and long-term changes. Ideally, there needs to be a new frame of mind and, as Jones put it: 'The shift needs to be from not has wellbeing been considered, but how should it be considered?'[98]

References

Appleby M and Bourke J, 'Promoting Law Student Mental Health Literacy and Wellbeing: A Case Study from the College of Law, Australia' (2014) 20(1) *International Journal of Clinical Legal Education* 494

95 Meribah Rose and Chris Maylea, 'The Case for Implementing Legal Clinical Supervision within Legal Practice, and Recommendations for Best Practice' (2023) 32(3) *Griffith Law Review* 259.

96 Jones (n 2).

97 Mary Heath, Kate Galloway, Natalie Skead, Alex Steel and Mark Israel, 'Learning to Feel Like a Lawyer: Law Teachers, Sessional Teaching and Emotional Labour in Legal Education' (2017) 26(3) *Griffith Law Review* 430.

98 Jones (n 2).

Baard PP, Deci EL and Ryan RM, 'Intrinsic Need Satisfaction: A Motivational Basis of Performance and Well-Being in Two Work Settings' (2004) 34(10) *Journal of Applied Social Psychology* 2045

Ballard A, Bozin D and de Prazer V, 'Improving Law Student Resilience: An Australian Perspective' (2020) 27(2) *International Journal of Clinical Legal Education*, https://journals.northumbria.ac.uk/index.php/ijcle/issue/view/90

Bar Council, 'Barristers' Working Lives Survey' (2021), www.barcouncil.org.uk/static/55b160bc-35c7-48a6-b105-e68526019ca5/8a57305c-4c3e-46c9-af44-4c221354e2b7/Working-Lives-2021-wellbeing-analysis.pdf

Bar Standards Board, 'Commitment to Wellbeing Statement', www.barstandardsboard.org.uk/static/2a1fb3c3-5b5e-47ae-9b26-0f7931146d10/78600755-390f-43f8-b366-bcd96a56087a/BSB-commitment-to-wellbeing.pdf

Cantatore F, 'The Impact of Pro Bono Law Clinics on Employability and Work Readiness in Law Students' (2018) 25(1) *International Journal of Clinical Legal Education*

Caplin N, 'Wellbeing at the Bar: Progress and Reasons for Optimism' (2024) *The European Advocate*, https://bareuropeangroup.org/2024/08/20/wellbeing-at-the-bar-progress-and-reasons-for-optimism/#:~:text=It%20found%20that%20barristers%20were,stress%20at%20work%20indicated%20weakness

Conroy D, Benaton T, Babicova I and Eate E, 'Investigating Secondary Trauma in Student Placements: An Exploratory Study' (2022) 52(7) *British Journal of Social Work* 4280

Curryer E and Mawdsley G, 'Navigating Vicarious Trauma: The Importance of Planning, Teaching, and Delivering Vicarious Trauma Training to Support Law Students and the Legal Profession' (2024) 31(1) *International Journal of Clinical Legal Education* 126

Duffy A et al, 'Mental Health Care for University Students: A Way Forward?' (2019) 6 *The Lancet Psychiatry* 885

Duncan N, 'Resilience, Positive Motivation and Professional Identity: The Experience of Law Clinic Students Working with Real Clients' in C Strevens and R Field (eds), *Educating for Well-Being in Law: Positive Professional Identities and Practice* (Routledge 2019)

Ferris G, 'Law-Students Wellbeing and Vulnerability' (2021) 56(1) *The Law Teacher* 1

Field R, Duffy J and James C (eds), *Promoting Law Student and Lawyer Well-Being in Australia and beyond* (Routledge 2016)

Figley CR, 'Compassion Fatigue: Toward a New Understanding of the Costs of Caring' in BH Stamm (ed), *Secondary Traumatic Stress: Self-Care Issues for Clinicians, Researchers, and Educators* (The Sidran Press 1995)

Fleck J and Francis R, *Vicarious Trauma in the Legal Profession* (Legal Action Group 2021)

Fletch LE and Weinstein HM, 'When Students Lose Perspective: Clinical Supervision and the Management of Empathy' (2002) 9 *Clinical Law Review* 147

Gascon-Cuenca A, Ghitti C and Malzani F, 'Acknowledging the Relevance of Empathy in Clinical Legal Education: Some Proposals from the Experience of the University of Brescia (IT) and Valencia (ESP)' (2018) 25(2) *International Journal of Clinical Legal Education*

Gibbons C, Dempster M and Moutray M, 'Stress and Eustress in Nursing Students' (2008) 61(3) *Journal of Advanced Nursing* 282

Gibby C, 'Clinical Legal Education and the Hidden Curriculum in the Neoliberal University in England and Wales' in R Field, C Strevens and R Field (eds), *Educating for Well-Being in Law: Positive Professional Identities and Practice* (Routledge 2020)

Gibson BD, 'Lawyers, Trauma, and Professional Wellbeing: How the Legal Community Takes Back Its Mental Health' (2014) Wake Forest University Legal Papers No 5026587, https://papers.ssrn.com/sol3/papers.cfm?abstract_id=5026587

Giddings J (ed), *Global Clinical Legal Education* (Taylor & Francis 2025)

Hambleton R, 'British Universities: The Sleeping Giants of Place-Based Leadership?' (2018) 12(1) *People, Place and Policy* 1

Hassed C et al, 'Enhancing the Health of Medical Students: Outcomes of an Integrated Mindfulness and Lifestyle Program' (2009) 14 *Advances in Health Sciences Education: Theory and Practice* 1

Health Education England, *NHS Staff and Learners Mental Wellbeing Commission* (2019), https://tinyurl.com/y4nwxzlv

Heath M, Galloway K, Skead N, Steel A and Israel M, 'Learning to Feel Like a Lawyer: Law Teachers, Sessional Teaching and Emotional Labour in Legal Education' (2017) 26(3) *Griffith Law Review* 430

International Bar Association, *Mental Wellbeing in the Legal Profession: A Global Study* (2021), www.ibanet.org/document?id=IBA-report-Mental-Wellbeing-in-the-Legal-Profession-A-Global-Study

Johnston C, 'Medical Students Talk Openly about Their Mental Health Challenges' (2015) 18 *Canadian Medical Association Journal* 1348

Jones E, 'Navigating the Landscape of Wellness in Legal Education: Obstacles and Opportunities on the Path Ahead' in J Marychurch, K Fischer Doherty and J Weinberg (eds), *Wellness for Law: Reflecting on the Past, Shaping the Future* (LexisNexis Butterworths 2024)

Jones E, Graffin N, Samra R and Lucassen M, *Mental Health and Wellbeing in the Legal Profession* (Bristol University Press 2020)

Jones E and Strevens C, 'Legal Education for Wellbeing: Design, Delivery and Evaluation' (2022) 56(1) *The Law Teacher* 1

Jones E, Strevens C, Field R and Jones C, *International Guidelines for Wellbeing in Legal Education* (December 2023), www.ibanet.org/document?id=International-Guidelines-for-Wellbeing-in-Legal-Education

Katz S and Haldar D, 'The Pedagogy of Trauma-Informed Lawyering' (2016), www.law.nyu.edu/sites/default/files/upload_documents/Katz%20-%20Halder%20Pedagogy%20of%20Trauma-Informed%20Lawyering.pdf

Kelk N, Luscombe G, Medlow S and Hickie I, *Courting the Blues: Attitudes towards Depression in Australian Law Students and Lawyers* (Brain & Mind Research Institute 2009)

Kelk N, Luscombe G, Medlow S and Hickie I, 'Distress and Depression among Australian Law Students: Incidence, Attitudes and the Role of Universities' (2010) 32(1) *Sydney Law Review* 113

Krieger LS, 'Institutional Denial about the Dark Side of Law School, and Fresh Empirical Guidance for Constructively Breaking the Silence' (2002) 52 *Journal of Legal Education* 112

LawCare, 'Life in the Law 2020/21' (2021), www.lawcare.org.uk/life-in-the-law/#:~:text=2020%2F21%20report,Life%20in%20the%20Law%202020%2F21,and%20the%20Isle%20of%20Man

LawCare, 'Life in the Law 2024' (2024), https://heyzine.com/flip-book/78a253a6ee.html#page/1

Law Society of England and Wales – Junior Lawyers Division, 'Resilience and Wellbeing Surveys', https://communities.lawsociety.org.uk/Uploads/g/x/g/jld-resilience-and-wellbeing-survey-report-2017.pdf (2017), https://communities.lawsociety.org.uk/Uploads/p/d/i/jld-resilience-and-wellbeing-survey-report-2018.pdf (2018) and https://communities.lawsociety.org.uk/Uploads/b/y/k/resilience-wellbeing-survey-report-2019.pdf (2019)

Lewis EG and Cardwell JM, 'A Comparative Study of Mental Health and Wellbeing among UK Students on Professional Degree Programmes' (2019) 43 *Journal of Further and Higher Education* 1226

Marychurch J, Fischer Doherty K and Weinberg J (eds), *Wellness for Law: Reflecting on the Past Shaping the Future* (LexisNexis Butterworths 2024)

Maxwell Jr L, 'The Development of Collaborative Law' (2007) 16(3–4) *Alternative Resolutions* 22

Mkwebu T, 'Research on Clinical Legal Education: Unpacking the Evidence' in L Thomas and N Johnson (eds), *The Clinical Legal Education Handbook* (Institute of Advanced Legal Studies, University of London 2020)

O'Farrell L, Hassan S and Hoole C, 'The University as a Just Anchor: Universities, Anchor Networks and Participatory Research' (2022) 47(12) *Studies in Higher Education* 2405

Office for Students, 'Meeting the Mental Health Needs of Students' (9 October 2023), www.officeforstudents.org.uk/publications/meeting-the-mental-health-needs-of-students

Office for Students, 'Equality of Opportunity Register', www.officestudents.org.uk/for-providers/equality-of-opportunity/equality-of-opportunity-risk-register/

Quality Assurance Agency, 'Subject Benchmark Statement: Law' (2023), www.qaa.ac.uk/docs/qaa/sbs/sbs-law-23.pdf?sfvrsn=c271a881_6

Rose M and Maylea C, 'The Case for Implementing Legal Clinical Supervision within Legal Practice, and Recommendations for Best Practice' (2023) 32(3) *Griffith Law Review* 259

Sanders M, *Student Mental Health in 2023: Who Is Struggling and How the Situation Is Changing* (King's College London Policy Institute 2023), www.kcl.ac.uk/policy-institute/assets/student-mental-health-in-2023.pdf

Scherr A and Brooks SL, 'Introduction' in L Wortham, A Scherr, N Maurer and SL Brooks (eds), *Learning from Practice: A Text for Experiential Legal Education* (3rd edn, West Academic Publishing 2016)

Seear K, 'Do Law Clinics Need Trigger Warnings? Philosophical, Pedagogical and Practical Concerns' (2019) 29(1) *Legal Education Review* 1

Shanfield SB and Benjamin GAH, 'Psychiatric Distress in Law Students' (1985) 35 *Journal of Legal Education* 65

Skipper Y and Fay M, 'The Relationship between the Sense of Belonging, Mental Wellbeing and Stress in Students of Law and Psychology in an English University' (2023) 4(1) *European Journal of Legal Education* 5

Smith J, *Why Has Nobody Told Me This Before?* (Penguin/Random House UK 2022)

Solicitors Regulation Authority, 'Workplace Environment Guidance' (7 February 2022, updated 4 May 2023), www.sra.org.uk/solicitors/guidance/workplace-environment/

Strevens C and Field R (eds), *Educating for Well-Being in Law* (Taylor & Francis 2019)

Strevens C and Wilson C, 'Law Student Wellbeing in the UK: A Call for Curriculum Intervention' (2016) 11(1) *Journal of Commonwealth Law and Legal Education* 44

Sutherland N and Budd H, 'Trauma Training Should Be Mandatory' *Law Gazette* (6 November 2024), www.lawgazette.co.uk/practice-points/trauma-training-should-be-mandatory/5121402.article

Thomas L and Johnson N (eds), *The Clinical Legal Education Handbook* (Institute of Advanced Legal Studies 2020)

Townes O'Brien M et al, 'Changing Our Thinking: Empirical Research on Law Student Wellbeing, Thinking Styles and the Law Curriculum' (2011) 21(2) *International Journal of the First Year in Higher Education* 1

Wapples E, 'Promoting Positive Mental Health in International Postgraduate Law Students at a Time of Global Uncertainty: A Case Study from qLegal at Queen Mary, University of London' (2020) 27(4) *International Journal of Clinical Legal Education* 104

Weinstein I, 'Teaching Reflective Lawyering in a Small Case Litigation Clinic: A Love Letter to My Clinic Papers' (2006–2007) 13 *Clinical Law Review* 573

Wellbeing at the Bar, www.wellbeingatthebar.org.uk

Wilson S, 'Identifying and Responding to a "Wellness Imperative" in the UK Legal Education: Exploring the Wellness Potential of Law and History Study, through the Significance Attached to "Lives Lived" in the 21st Century' in J Marychurch, K Fischer Doherty and J Weinberg (eds), *Wellness for Law: Reflecting on the Past Shaping the Future* (LexisNexis Butterworths 2024)

World Health Organization, 'WHO Urges More Investment, Services for Mental Health' (12 August 2010), www.who.int/news/item/12-08-2010-who-urges-more-investments-services-for-mental-health

Young Minds, 'Understanding Trauma and Adversity', www.youngminds.org.uk/professional/resources/understanding-trauma-and-adversity/

11

Arts and Clinical Legal Education in Refugee and Migration Contexts: A Culturally Responsive Approach

Ulrich Stege, Lee-Anne Paula Doyle and Lela Aisha Jones

Introduction

This chapter investigates the interdisciplinary intersections between the arts, refugee narratives and migration law, with a particular emphasis on the integration of artistic methodologies within clinical legal education (CLE). It suggests that while CLE initiatives often purport to advance justice and inclusion, especially in contexts concerning asylum and migration, they may operate within culturally restrictive frameworks that risk perpetuating the marginalization of the very communities they intend to support. Through the examination of historical and contemporary engagements with art as a tool for resistance and transformation – including the anti-apartheid movement in South Africa and the civil rights struggle in the US – this chapter advocates for the incorporation of artistic modalities as a means to challenge entrenched epistemic hierarchies in legal education. In doing so, it lays the groundwork for a critical reflection on the potential of creative practices to contribute to a more inclusive, dialogic and culturally situated pedagogy.

The chapter is structured around four interrelated domains of inquiry. First, it critically sets the scene by examining the systemic cultural disparities embedded in the operational logic of legal clinics working within the fields of migration and asylum law, alongside a critical interrogation of CLE's institutional architecture and its implications for inclusivity.

Second, it turns to historical case studies to illuminate the role of the arts in advancing social justice movements. Third, it offers an in-depth analysis of the International University College of Turin's efforts to incorporate artistic practices into legal education. Finally, it proposes forward-looking strategies for developing culturally responsive clinical approaches that centre artistic collaboration as a mode of knowledge production and community engagement.

Collectively, these explorations underscore the transformative potential of artistic engagement in reimagining the pedagogical and ethical contours of legal practice.

Critical reflection about clinical legal education in the field of migration and asylum in Europe

Systemic cultural disparities within the practice of legal clinics working on migration and asylum law

The foundational objectives of CLE are widely recognized for their nobility: providing students with hands-on legal experience, enhancing access to justice for marginalized groups, and fostering a sense of ethical and social responsibility in future legal professionals.[1] However, while these aims represent important aspirations, their practical realization is frequently constrained by systemic limitations, particularly within the field of migration and asylum law in Europe.

Legal clinics working in these areas tend to retain a Eurocentric orientation, which, despite its commitment to social justice, can result in overly simplistic and paternalistic approaches to client representation. This tendency risks overlooking the complex cultural and sociopolitical realities of the clients they serve. Although these clinics purport to empower vulnerable populations, their methods and frameworks frequently neglect the deeper structural and cultural disparities between clinicians and their clients. In many cases, the clinician – typically operating from a position of Western legal privilege – struggles to adequately recognize or incorporate the epistemologies and experiences of ethnically marginalized individuals.

This cultural disparity is not merely a matter of interpersonal misunderstanding or a deficit in cross-cultural communication. Rather, it is embedded within the broader legal and institutional systems, both nationally and internationally, that continue to reflect and perpetuate neo-imperial hierarchies. Within these structures, the 'Western' lawyer is positioned as the

1 Frank S Bloch (ed), *The Global Clinical Movement: Educating Lawyers for Social Justice* (OUP 2011).

agent of justice and reform, while the racialized and displaced client remains the passive recipient of aid.[2] As a result, even the most well-intentioned clinicians may inadvertently reproduce the very power imbalances they aim to dismantle.

Even though legal clinics seek to challenge dominant legal narratives, they often remain confined by the cultural logic of their own institutions. Many law schools in Europe, for instance, operate within academic traditions that prioritize Western legal thought and methodologies, leaving little room for alternative worldviews. Consequently, the potential for a truly collaborative and emancipatory legal practice – one in which clients are seen as equal partners in the legal process – is significantly constrained.[3]

The relationship between clinician and client remains structured along hierarchical lines, not simply due to personal attitudes or ethical failings, but because of a systemic architecture that neither party fully controls.[4] For genuine transformation to occur, this relationship must evolve into a co-creative space in which the knowledge and agency of both clinician and client are equally valued. However, such a shift requires more than behavioural changes; it demands a reconfiguration of the epistemological and institutional foundations of CLE itself.

To address these challenges, we propose integrating artistic methods and perspectives into the structure and pedagogy of CLE. The arts have long served as a powerful medium for political expression and cultural affirmation among marginalized communities. From the anti-apartheid art of South Africa to the jazz movement that underpinned the civil rights struggle in the US, art has historically enabled marginalized groups to reclaim agency and visibility.

As Martin Luther King Jr once noted, jazz music became a political force in its own right, with musicians actively participating in the civil rights movement: 'The music was not only providing a soundtrack for liberation; the musicians were becoming more visible in the fight, some in ways they'd never planned.'[5] Through such artistic engagement, communities have been

2 Ratna Kapur, 'The Tragedy of Victimization Rhetoric: Resurrecting the "Native" Subject in International/Post-colonial Feminist Legal Politics' (2002) 15 *Harvard Human Rights Journal* 1; Makau Mutua, *Human Rights: A Political and Cultural Critique* (University of Pennsylvania Press 2002).

3 Jeena Shah, 'Community Lawyering in Resistance to Neoliberalism' (2022) 120(6) *Michigan Law Review* 1061.

4 John R. Campbell, 'Experts and the Judiciary' (2022) 11 *NAVEIÑ REET: Nordic Journal of Law and Social Research* 15.

5 Ashawnta Jackson, 'Why MLK Believed Jazz Was the Perfect Soundtrack for Civil Rights', *JSTOR Daily* (16 October 2019), https://daily.jstor.org/why-mlk-believed-jazz-was-the-perfect-soundtrack-for-civil-rights/

able to express complex truths, challenge dominant narratives, and construct alternative imaginaries of justice and resistance.

Clinicians in legal education could draw upon these traditions by engaging with their clients through art, music, storytelling and other culturally grounded forms of expression. Such approaches not only honour the agency of migrants and asylum seekers but also challenge the narrow epistemological boundaries of Western legal practice. Rather than attempting to 'empower' clients, clinicians should recognize that the very act of migration is itself a testament to profound courage, resilience and agency.

Incorporating artistic expression into clinical pedagogy thus represents a step toward a more inclusive, reflexive and culturally responsive practice, one that does not merely serve clients, but learns from them, co-creates with them and respects their ways of knowing.

A critical reflection on the institutional logic of clinical legal education

CLE sometimes reproduces cultural hierarchies and systemic imbalances embedded within broader legal, political and educational institutions. In many European settings, legal clinics tend to frame social justice issues through Western legal paradigms and liberal democratic values. While these frameworks are often intended to be inclusive, they may inadvertently marginalize or overlook alternative epistemologies, lived experiences and legal traditions. In this context, there is a risk that the narratives and identities of migrants and asylum seekers may be utilized primarily to support institutional or political goals, rather than being centred as sources of knowledge and agency in their own right.

This dynamic echoes longstanding critiques, including those raised by Steve Biko, the South African anti-apartheid activist and founder of the 'Black Consciousness' movement. In the 1970s, Biko reflected on how, even within liberatory movements, dominant voices can overshadow those directly affected by injustice. He cautioned that true liberation requires attention to the internalized dimensions of oppression: 'The most potent weapon in the hands of the oppressor is the mind of the oppressed.'[6] In contemporary clinical settings, this insight invites reflection on how Western vocabularies and professional norms can unintentionally limit the visibility and participation of non-Western perspectives.

Institutionally, many legal clinics are still predominantly led by Western academics and practitioners. Migrants and asylum seekers are rarely positioned as leaders, decision makers or authors within clinical structures. While representations of diversity – such as images on promotional materials – signal

[6] Steve Biko, quoted in Donald Woods, *Biko* (Paddington Press 1978) 87.

inclusion, they can risk appearing more symbolic than substantive if not accompanied by meaningful shifts in governance and pedagogical approaches. Elevating migrant voices as sources of knowledge and collaborators in shaping clinic practice is essential to ethical and effective engagement.

For CLE to maintain its integrity and commitment to justice, it must engage in critical introspection regarding its institutional positioning and the broader structures within which it operates. Law clinics should strive to remain independent from shifting political ideologies and instead root their work in the dignity, autonomy and cultural contexts of the communities they serve. As Klein has emphasized, clinical educators must remain mindful of their own cultural assumptions and positionality.[7] These assumptions often shape pedagogical methods and interpersonal dynamics within clinics, influencing whose knowledge is validated and how clients are understood.

Further, as components of law schools, legal clinics are situated within academic institutions whose primary function is often to prepare students for roles within prevailing legal systems. This context can pose challenges for integrating radically critical or culturally diverse approaches to lawyering, which may be tolerated only within limited curricular or research boundaries. Although clients and community partners are increasingly visible in CLE discourse, their participation is often structured by academic norms that can constrain the scope of their contributions.

A particularly persistent blind spot within this framework is the underrepresentation of non-Western legal traditions and epistemologies. The exclusion of diverse worldviews occurs not only in curriculum design but also in evidentiary standards and credibility assessments that shape how stories are interpreted and validated.[8] Scholars such as Barkaskas and Bühler have called for the decolonization of CLE, urging legal educators to engage reflexively with their own traditions and biases.[9] Their work on integrating Indigenous legal principles into Canadian law curricula offers valuable insights into how clinical pedagogy can move beyond symbolic gestures towards more substantive inclusion. While promising, such initiatives remain limited and are often framed as supplementary rather than foundational to legal education.

In sum, the future of CLE depends not only on its pedagogical innovation but also on its willingness to engage in sustained reflection

[7] Catherine F Klein, 'Cultural Competency and the Practice of Law in the Twenty-First Century' (1998) 4(3) *Clinical Law Review* 555.

[8] Jenni Millbank and Anthea Vogl, 'Adjudicating Fear of Witchcraft Claims in Refugee Law' (2018) 45(3) *Journal of Law and Society* 370.

[9] Patricia Barkaskas and Sarah Bühler, 'Beyond Reconciliation: Decolonizing Clinical Legal Education' (2016) 1(1) *Lakehead Law Journal* 1.

about whose voices are heard, whose knowledge is valued, and how justice is defined and pursued. By more fully embracing diverse epistemologies and centring the agency of marginalized communities, legal clinics can strengthen their role as transformative spaces within and beyond the academy.[10]

The arts in social justice: historical lessons for Western migration law clinics

From the onset, it appears that art and law are completely opposite disciplines because one could be based on an individual's expression that could often be limitless, whereas the other confines itself strictly to a complex set of rules for the 'collective'. Professor Oren Ben-Dor asserts that: 'Law and art serve both as instruments of oppression and as means for emancipation.'[11] Through looking at the civil rights movement and the anti-apartheid struggle in South Africa, perhaps migration law clinics could gain insight on how art and the law were used to oppress nonwhites, but eventually became tools of emancipation through many efforts led by the arts and artists. However, before delving into this, it is important to define what the arts are and to briefly look at what art justice entails.

Art definition and etymology

The definition and etymology for the word 'art' have many ancient interpretations, but for the purposes of this chapter, it will refer to the Latin word 'ars', which means art, skill or craft.[12] For centuries, many philosophers have debated its definition, and up to the present, it still lacks a universal definition. Nonetheless, 'art' is often divided into three categories known as art as representation or mimesis, which was first developed by Plato and means 'to copy' in Greek.[13] The first category is the idea of art being a representation or mimesis focused on an artist's ability to replicate something beautiful and meaningful.

The second category is known as 'art as an expression of emotional content', which was prevalent during the Romantic movement around the

---

[10] David McDonald, 'Introduction: Pathways toward a Justice-Oriented Ethnomusicology' (2023), www.academia.edu/123090414/Introduction_Pathways_toward_a_Justice_Oriented_Ethnomusicology

[11] Oren Ben-Dor, *Law and Art: Justice, Ethics and Aesthetics* (Routledge-Cavendish 2013).

[12] Stephen Parcell, 'Architecture as a Mechanical Art' in *Four Historical Definitions of Architecture* (McGill-Queen's University Press 2012) 40.

[13] Edith Watson Schipper, 'Mimesis in the Arts in Plato's Laws' (1963) 22(2) *Journal of Aesthetics and Art Criticism* 199.

end of the 18th century, which spread throughout Europe and the US.[14] This art form stressed the importance of feelings and emotions, which were often overlooked due to the Enlightenment era that predominantly focused on reason and rationality. Therefore, this art form was quite appealing as it highlighted the need for the 'individual's' expression, imagination, and liberty even beyond institutional norms.[15]

Last but not least, there is 'art as a form', which was vocalized by Immanuel Kant during the end of the 18th century.[16] Although Kant has not been renowned for being an artist, he was quite influential in laying the foundations for academic art history and historians such as Heinrich Wölfflin and Erwin Panofsky.[17] Kant theorized that art should not have a fixed concept, but instead should be merited on its formal qualities, such as the lines, contours, shades and shapes, to name but a few. This art definition is considered as the roots of 'abstract art' that still continues to be popular up until now.

After assessing the various definitions for art, this chapter relies predominantly on the meaning of art as an expression, which includes dance, song, poetry, artworks and others. This is because when looking at CLE, especially in migration law, the clients' ability to express their experiences that led to their search for safety is what makes their case when applying for asylum. The individual's ability to voice their own stories and to contend with the legal apparatus to recognize their human rights requires immense details that language in itself cannot express. Of course, the legal memo will be compiled through the national language of the state in which the client is seeking asylum, but the process to get there could use various artistic expressions that the client feels comfortable with. Therefore, this chapter makes the argument that using art as an expression in CLE is one of the most influential and empowering tools for non-Western vulnerable clients as they go through the process of retelling traumatic events.

Art in social justice

It is almost impossible to exit or enter public spaces such as train stations, subways and city halls, to name but a few, without coming across the bold artistic visuals of messages around social justice. For instance, artists such as Banksy have repeatedly used his/her/their art to visually speak out against

---

14 ibid.

15 Robert Mitchell, 'Romanticism and the Experience of Experiment' (2015) 46(3) *The Wordsworth Circle* 132.

16 Clive Cazeaux, 'Judging Contemporary Art with Kant' (2021) 26(4) *Kantian Review* 635.

17 Giovanna Targia, 'Writing Images as an Act of Interpreting: Notes on Erwin Panofsky's Studies on Medieval Subjects and the Problem of Language in and of Art History' (2023) 39(1) *Word & Image* 88.

human rights violations and to raise awareness around discrimination, racism and wars, for example.[18] Banksy is renowned worldwide despite the anonymity around his/her/their identity.

Yet it is impossible to mention Banksy without an immediate correlation between his/her/their artworks and the vivid messages of bringing social justice to the people. In saying this, art in social justice goes beyond mere representation or protest, but instead it can: raise awareness about issues affecting Black or various ethnic communities; challenge stereotypes and promote positive representations of people groups that do not have access to do so themselves; provide emotional outlets and healing spaces for communities experiencing trauma as their visual expressions are illuminated in public when mass commercial media outlets silence them; imagine and visualize alternative futures that are not controlled by dominant public narratives; build solidarity within and between communities with similar struggles and discrimination, and preserve and celebrate cultural heritages within public spaces.[19]

Therefore, learning from art's role in general within social justice, legal clinics in Europe can advocate for minorities such as vulnerable clients to own these institutional spaces in a way that allows them to really express their own agency in a culturally appropriate way through co-artistic Street Law activities. Visually, it is more impacting and empowering for ethnic vulnerable clients to compose songs and dance about their struggles and to perform it in front of courts, municipal buildings and detention centres, among others. This is not to say that these actions would necessarily lead to positive legal outcomes or solutions for vulnerable clients, but vulnerable clients would have the opportunity and space to speak directly to an institution that ultimately makes the live-or-die decisions about their lives. Doing so will mean enormous emancipation for vulnerable clients and the lawyers, as the authorities will not be able to hide behind sophisticated legal arguments and behind closed doors.

Art's role in social justice in the US civil rights movement and during South Africa's apartheid era

It is almost impossible to not recognize the arts' contributions to these two historic moments for people of ethnic backgrounds within South Africa,

[18] Coshandra Dillard, 'The Power of Place: Art as a Tool for Social Justice', *Learning for Justice* (10 May 2023), www.learningforjustice.org/magazine/spring-2023/the-power-of-place-art-as-a-tool-for-social-justice

[19] ibid.

the US and across the globe.[20] In both cases, the state refused to recognize nonwhite people as equals to whites and used every single institutional power to discriminate against their basic human rights, such as the right to free and fair elections, the right to an equitable education and the right to associate with anyone outside of their race, to name but a few of the inhumane human rights violations.

Despite the establishment of the Universal Declaration of Human Rights, which was adopted by the UN General Assembly on 10 December 1948, nonwhites across the globe remained subhuman to white people, and they often had to use the arts as their most powerful and nonlethal weapon to engage politically and legally for their rights.[21] Like today, most migrants still do not have access to their basic human rights across many Western states, and legal clinics are instrumental for fighting against this unfortunate phenomenon. However, legal clinics could perhaps enhance their own agency and the agency of their vulnerable clients by using an artistic lens that fought similar battles before.

South Africa's liberation struggle through the arts

In a tribute letter to Miriam Makeba, former South African President Nelson Mandela said: 'Her music inspired a powerful sense of hope in all of us.'[22] As simplistic as the word 'hope' might seem, it had immense power, as it was the driving force behind a people's agency to fight against a system that had every power imaginable to enslave them for centuries to come. However, Miriam Makeba used her art to first recognize that her dignity did not come from any institution, and instead of her asking the institution to recognize her, she criticized its incompetence of not doing so in the first place.[23] Second, she used what she had, which was an incredible talent to unite all races, genders and nationalities, among others, and spoke directly to power without any intellectual jargon.[24] Last but not least, she was

---

20 US Mission, 'A Retrospective: U.S. Civil Society's Commitment and Contributions to the Anti-apartheid Struggle' (US Embassy & Consulates in South Africa 2020), https://za.usembassy.gov/a-retrospective-u-s-civil-societys-commitment-and-contributions-to-the-anti-apartheid-struggle/

21 William Nash, 'Black Arts Movement', *Oxford Research Encyclopedia of Literature* (26 July 2017), https://oxfordre.com/literature/view/10.1093/acrefore/9780190201098.001.0001/acrefore-9780190201098-e-630

22 'Message from Mr Nelson Mandela on the Passing of Miriam Makeba' (Nelson Mandela Foundation 2008), www.nelsonmandela.org/news/entry/message-from-mr-nelson-mandela-on-the-passing-of-miriam-makeba

23 'Miriam Makeba and Her Art of Activism', *University of Cape Town News* (3 March 2022), www.news.uct.ac.za/article/-2022-03-03-miriam-makeba-and-her-art-of-activism

24 ibid.

willing to accept the consequences because her convictions were true to her, regardless of the risks she would encounter.[25]

Therefore, by reflecting on Miriam Makeba's fight for social justice, migration law clinics could learn that human dignity is extremely personal to the individual and not an institution; lawyers need to balance academic rhetoric with speaking to power directly and to accept that social justice has many risks.

Similarly, after the tragic passing of Johnny Clegg, President Cyril Ramaphosa was quoted as saying: 'Johnny Clegg is more than just one of this country's finest musicians and entertainers. He is a national treasure who has brought together all South Africans and reminded us what makes us great as a country.'[26] This is partly because he proactively used his art to demonstrate what equality could look like for a nation that was one of the most divided countries in the world.[27] He did this by forming a music band called Juluku that went beyond the social borders of race and artistically innovated a whole new music genre called Savuka music, which was an infusion of Zulu traditional songs, rock, jazz and reggae influences.[28] His music spoke to the universal themes of hope and liberation, and his musical success accredited him worldwide as a musical pioneer and a voice for the voiceless.[29]

Likewise, through observing Clegg's contributions to fighting against human rights violations and against institutional power, migration law clinics could learn the following: first, it is OK to be white and to fight for social justice so long as your 'whiteness' does not falsely make you believe you have more agency than nonwhite people. Often, white people assume that because they are beneficiaries of the system, they are the 'system'; however, they are equally mistreated if they don't 'toe the line', as Clegg faced a lot of persecution from the apartheid government, and his 'whiteness' could not save him or exempt him from not obeying the apartheid laws.

[25] 'Miriam Makeba: Singer Banned from Her Native South Africa for Fighting Apartheid' (*The Independent*, 10 November 2008), www.independent.co.uk/news/obituaries/miriam-makeba-singer-banned-from-her-native-south-africa-for-fighting-apartheid-1009604.html

[26] 'President Cyril Ramaphosa Sends Condolences to Nkonyeni and Clegg Families' (17 July 2019), www.gov.za/news/media-statements/president-cyril-ramaphosa-sends-condolences-nkonyeni-and-clegg-families-17

[27] Richard Pithouse, 'Johnny Clegg: Rebel, Intellectual, Musician', *Mail & Guardian* (2019), https://mg.co.za/article/2019-07-18-johnny-clegg-rebel-intellectual-musician/

[28] ibid.

[29] Katherine Power, 'Musical Influence on Apartheid and the Civil Rights Movement', https://cupola.gettysburg.edu/cgi/viewcontent.cgi?params=/context/student_scholarship/article/1306&path_info=Power__Katherine__Musical_Influence_on_Apartheid_and_The_Civil_Rights_Movement.pdf

Second, although aware of his higher positionality within South Africa's racial society, Clegg used that bit of privilege to foster the talents of his Black co-band members and did not engage with them from a paternalistic attitude.[30] Therefore, clinics could similarly find the strengths of their clients and find better legal tactics to operate in a system that is hostile towards ethnic migrants. Last but not least, although undermining and challenging the institutional powers, Clegg gave practical examples of what unity and equality could look like, which is important as burning buildings and smearing individuals are divisive and unappealing. Therefore, legal clinics do not have to remain in their constant identity of being anti-Western and anarchist, but instead they could offer practical examples of what their work in collaboration with vulnerable clients can do to uplift, inspire and unite communities.

From civil rights to the Black Lives Matter movement in the US: artistic interventions in legal education and narrative justice

The struggle for civil and human rights in the US remains ongoing and unresolved. Consequently, the reflections presented here are not posited as definitive solutions to the challenges facing CLE in Europe; rather, they are offered as a contribution to an evolving dialogue – one that seeks to deepen our collective understanding of how the arts may inform and transform narrative orientations within legal contexts.

Significant developments in European legal clinics suggest a growing recognition of the role that artistic practices and cultural expressions play in reshaping the epistemic foundations of CLE. In dialogue with European colleagues, it has become evident that there is an emerging openness to integrating artistry into legal education to foster new cultural orientations and participatory methodologies.

To situate this analysis, it is necessary to contextualize the perspective from which it is written. The author, Dr Lela Aisha Jones, is shaped by a cultural grounding in Black communities in the southern US, specifically Tallahassee, Florida. This identity, which is inextricably and comprehensively intertwined with her existence in US society, is experienced and negotiated daily through the lived realities of navigating racial systemic and structural constructs – realities analogous in certain respects to the daily lived experiences of asylum seekers.[31] Both groups remain entangled in systemic structures of oppression,

[30] 'Johnny Clegg and the Ethics of Cross-Cultural Pop Music' (18 July 2019), https://andypaine.wordpress.com/2019/07/18/johnny-clegg-and-the-ethics-of-cross-cultural-pop-music/

[31] Performing Challenges Extended mit Lela Aisha Jones' (2024), www.mdw.ac.at/ikm/gender-studies/performing-challenges-extended-jones/

which continue to privilege epistemologies and cultural hierarchies steeped in whiteness and white supremacy ideologies.

The insights offered herein are deeply informed by a background in community-based artistic practice, including roles as a movement performance artist, choreographer and organizer. Notably, the author was a founding member and lead organizer of Dancing for Justice Philadelphia, a collective active during the peak years of the Black Lives Matter movement (2014–2016). This work formed the basis for an invitation from Lee-Anne Paula Doyle to engage with a European Network for Clinical Legal Clinics (ENCLE), particularly as Europe remains a key destination for migrants from diverse global backgrounds.

At the 10th ENCLE Conference in Liverpool, during the presentation titled 'Social Justice through the Arts and Vibrancy', five core potentials were proposed to legal clinic communities regarding the transformative integration of dance and embodied narrative: (1) embodiment of culture as a way to foster connection to your humanity and to encourage connection to the humanity of those you are serving; (2) valuing the discomfort that emerges in your own cultural orientations when you settle into another being's cultural orientations to understand their humanity; (3) becoming more culturally attuned to how narratives align with the cultures in which they are rooted; (4) building capacity for the discomfort that occurs when cultures collide through dance (embodied artistry); and (5) manifesting diverse perspectives and nuanced narratives of life in marginalized communities.

These change-making potentials can lead to engaging in, writing and systematically submitting more nuanced stories leading to honest exchange and a dynamic shift in the advocacy structure of asylum seeker documents to include more of what Dr Gloria Ladsen-Billings terms 'culturally relevant' orientations.[32] The process of engaging equitably with people from marginalized communities, which includes asylum seekers, and employing methodologies grounded in arts and social change through embodiment and dance can assist legal clinics in more accurately and comprehensively representing the asylum seeker by delving more deeply into their cultural values through artistry.

Collaborative projects undertaken with Black artists and diasporic communities have underscored the importance of embracing the plurality within 'Black living', challenging monolithic constructions of identity and extending this critical lens to asylum seekers, who similarly resist homogenization despite shared regional origins. The overarching goal is the

[32] Gloria Ladson-Billings, 'Toward a Theory of Culturally Relevant Pedagogy' (1995) 32(3) *American Educational Research Journal* 465.

empowerment of individuals – whether artists, legal advocates or asylum seekers – to express their narratives with authenticity and agency.

These approaches are informed by a longstanding commitment to social justice through the arts.[33] As part of the leadership of Dancing for Justice Philadelphia, collective actions were organized in response to the extrajudicial killings of Black individuals in the US. These actions involved convening artists and community members to engage in public marches and performances that drew attention to systemic violence and racial injustice. The performative and symbolic dimensions of these actions aimed to publicly affirm the value of Black life while condemning institutional inaction and complicity.

Beyond protest, a crucial component of this work involved educational and consciousness-raising sessions rooted in choreographic and embodied methodologies. These practices sought to surface and address internalized biases, white supremacist value systems and their intersections with other forms of marginalization, including those experienced by asylum seekers and individuals marginalized by gender, class and disability. Sessions led by organizations such as the People's Institute for Survival and Beyond provided critical historical and structural analysis to contextualize the contemporary manifestations of systemic oppression.

An unexpected consequence of this public-facing work was an observable backlash. Increased visibility often results in increased scrutiny and repression, echoing the prophetic caution of Gil Scott-Heron's statement 'The revolution will not be televised'. Scott-Heron's assertion that true revolution begins with internal transformation – within the mind, body and being – resonates with the trajectory of this work. The real transformative potential lies in changing how narratives are constructed, interpreted and valued.

Engaging with alternative and nuanced narratives – especially those rooted in the lived values of marginalized communities – requires ongoing negotiation. This involves critical decisions about what to reveal, how to frame it and for what purposes. These decisions are complex and demand ethical attentiveness and cultural humility.

Legal clinics, by integrating artistic strategies into their methodologies, can become powerful agents in the transformation of human and civil rights advocacy across Europe. Such transformation necessitates a shift in collective consciousness, one that transcends efforts to merely include marginalized groups within existing Western frameworks. It requires an active reimagining

[33] 'Review: When "Native Portals", Philadelphia Choreographer Lela Aisha Jones Explores the Impact of Lynching through Dance', Philadelphia Sunday Sun (6 May 2016), https://philasun.com/entertainment/review-native-portals-philadelphia-choreographer-lela-aisha-jones-explores-impact-lynching-dance/

of those frameworks themselves. Experience has shown that expecting the oppressed to resolve the systems that oppress them – whether in the context of homelessness, transphobia or political dysfunction – is both unjust and ineffective.

If legal educators and advocates are serious about progressing equity, they must begin by interrogating their own narratives, acknowledging privilege, and embracing narrative forms that reflect the value of others' existence as defined by those communities themselves. Only through this process can CLE move towards a more inclusive, just, and culturally responsive practice.

Drawing on the International University College of Turin legal clinic's arts experience

The International University College of Turin's legal clinic was one of the first legal clinics in Italy and over the years has engaged with more than 330 students from over 55 countries. This clinic is positioned in a particular setting, as it is part of a university that is based on critical thinking and overly deeply invested in the issues pertaining to Global North and Global South country issues. This means that the clinic has always enjoyed the privilege of experimenting with unconventional methods because it was part of an environment that encouraged this type of innovative thinking and educational approach.

Thus, in 2021, Ulrich Stege and Lee-Anne Paula Doyle jointly established a course called 'The Interconnection between the Arts and Refugee Law'.[34] This course was developed with the aim of expanding the teaching methodology at the clinic, challenging students to go beyond their comfort zones, and incorporating refugees and asylum seekers into its teaching pedagogy.

The International University College of Turin promoted an approach which is called 'Teaching refugee/migration law through the arts'. The necessary discomfort in students can be created by asking them to dance or sit on the floor for the first half of the class, therefore bringing them out of their comfort zone. Furthermore, art is an important tool for introducing students to other cultures and enables them to engage with them in depth which also strengthens their understanding of these cultures.[35]

[34] Lee-Anne Paula Doyle Fraschia and Ulrich Stege, 'The Interconnection between the Arts, Refugee and Migration Law in the Context of Clinical Legal Education as a Discourse' (2024) 13(1) *Rivista di filosofia del diritto* 151.

[35] Hannah Franz, 'What Can Be Learned from International Exchange between Legal Clinics' (2023) 30(2) *International Journal of Clinical Legal Education* 138.

In addition, this course also became a common presentation at legal clinic conferences nationally, internationally and globally as a form of encouraging other legal clinics to adopt some perspectives and to exchange ideas. In part, it was instrumental in motivating other legal clinics to move in this direction as well, while also raising awareness of the need to recognize migrants themselves as integral components of the legal clinic infrastructure. In addition to the philosophies echoed in this chapter, we also aim to share our legal clinic experiences on the use of art in other areas of legal education, which include interview skills, cultural mediating and Street Law initiatives, which advocate for migrants to lead these activities alongside students.

Interview skills

It is important to understand that the legal memo-drafting process is secondary to the interview process as the key component of an asylum application is the 'credible story' of the asylum seeker, and students cannot access it if they do not know how to interview their client. In most cases, the lawyer and the asylum seeker may come from very contrasting cultures, yet the client is unable to feel if the lawyer is being authentic or not, and it is hard to imagine telling a very personal story to someone you trust and even more so to a stranger to whom you just don't feel the trust to express your story.

Therefore, our clinic teaches students various theatre and dance movements to be cognizant of how to use their bodies, even if they face language barriers to build a relationship with their client. Furthermore, through dance and theatre, students are also made aware about their 'energy/presence' and how that may impact the relationship they are trying to build with their client. Specifically, as your presence/energy often precedes you, like in the case of when you enter a room and before you introduce yourself, your presence has spoken for you already. Additionally, through dance and theatre, the clinic teaches students how to be aware of their own deep social biases, discomforts and to be conscious of the 'unspoken things'.

In addition, music and theatre help to teach the importance of how to use one's voice. Therefore, lawyers could benefit by understanding a few music lessons to know how to use their voice when asking questions. This is particularly the case around the areas of authenticity, as using pretentious tones is evidence of the lawyer faking it or trying too hard. What is also most common in an asylum seeker's interview is how to use your breath and sighs to further gain trust and to trust to lead the interview.

Cultural mediating

Non-Western art and art from marginalized communities could also serve as a primary source of information that could be useful for pedagogical learning in legal clinics. Thus, studying the primary sources from the cultures themselves allows the legal clinician to a certain extent to reflect on their possible biases, which are often subconscious and 'invisible'. As Rolf Lidskog reiterated: 'A world characterized by migration, transnational networks and global flows, as well as a reorientation of migration and integration policies, brings new conditions for identity formation, and music will continue to be an important means for immigrants and refugees to negotiate and develop their identity in their new environment.'[36] This reinforces the idea that art continues to be an integral aspect for refugees, even when they are outside of 'their national borders'.

Conclusion

The critical approaches in CLE have played a significant role in encouraging legal education and practice to become more responsive, reflexive and nuanced in the pursuit of justice. As Professor Anne Gordon of Duke Law School aptly notes:

> Too often, we seize upon short-term or one-off ideas like Diversity, Equity, and Inclusion (DEI) trainings or discussion groups without taking the time, effort, and discomfort necessary to evaluate our programs and institutions writ large. Simply bringing in more diverse faculty or incorporating diversity language into official statements will not lead to substantive change; we must make institutional commitments to incorporating strategies for diversity – including culture shifts – throughout our schools.[37]

Artists have long worked to shift collective consciousness, and legal clinics are increasingly being called upon to do the same. Yet, meaningful transformation requires more than public declarations or surface-level gestures. As many liberation movements have demonstrated – often through the arts – revolutionary change frequently begins beneath the surface, in the realm of consciousness and community-rooted practice. When efforts towards justice are exposed prematurely or presented without balance, they become vulnerable to co-optation, dilution or suppression – especially by systems structured to maintain dominance and inequality.

We are currently living in a moment marked by reaction and backlash. Public visibility can inadvertently provide a roadmap for dismantling the very

[36] Rolf Lidskog, 'The Role of Music in Ethnic Identity Formation in Diaspora: A Research Review' (2016) 66(219–20) *International Social Science Journal* 23.

[37] Anne Gordon, 'Cleaning up Our Own Houses: Creating Anti-racist Clinical Programs' (2022) 29 *Clinical Law Review*, https://ssrn.com/abstract=4187924

efforts aimed at advancing equity and justice. In response, it becomes vital to preserve spaces for quiet, strategic and collective transformation – spaces that are not always visible or easily documented. Harriet Tubman, for example, held the routes of the Underground Railroad in memory and artistry; they could not be mapped or written down. Similarly, many historical forms of resistance – from *palenques* and *quilombos* to *maroon* communities – thrived precisely because they operated through embodied, cultural and often artistic knowledge that defied codification.

In this spirit, we must engage in the deeper, less visible work of cultivating revolutionary consciousness – an internal shift that precedes and sustains external change. A key element of this process involves reimagining how we narrate and transmit experience. Storytelling, particularly through culturally rooted and artistic forms, becomes not just a method of expression but also a strategy of liberation. Whether through legal narratives, oral histories or performative acts, stories can reveal the enduring struggles of those rendered marginal, and the creative, often artistic, ways in which they have historically fought for dignity, rights and recognition.

Ultimately, the integration of the arts into CLE invites a rethinking of both pedagogy and power. It urges us to move beyond performative inclusion and towards practices that are relational, culturally grounded and ethically accountable. In doing so, legal clinics can more meaningfully support those they serve – not only through legal intervention, but also through participation in a broader, transformative narrative of justice.[38]

References

Barkaskas P and Bühler S, 'Beyond Reconciliation: Decolonizing Clinical Legal Education' (2016) 1(1) *Lakehead Law Journal* 1

Ben-Dor O, *Law and Art: Justice, Ethics and Aesthetics* (Routledge-Cavendish 2013)

Bloch F (ed), *The Global Clinical Movement: Educating Lawyers for Social Justice* (OUP 2011)

Campbell JR, 'Experts and the Judiciary' (2022) 11 *NAVEIÑ REET: Nordic Journal of Law and Social Research* 15

Cazeaux C, 'Judging Contemporary Art with Kant' (2021) 26(4) *Kantian Review* 635

Dillard C, 'The Power of Place: Art as a Tool for Social Justice', *Learning for Justice* (10 May 2023), www.learningforjustice.org/magazine/spring-2023/the-power-of-place-art-as-a-tool-for-social-justice

[38] Martina Mallocci, '"All Art Is Propaganda": W.E.B. Du Bois's *The Crisis* and the Construction of a Black Public Image' (2018) 1 *USAbroad – Journal of American History and Politics*, https://usabroad.unibo.it/article/view/7177/7504

Doyle Fraschia LAP and Stege U, 'The Interconnection between the Arts, Refugee and Migration Law in the Context of Clinical Legal Education as a Discourse' (2024) 13(1) *Rivista di filosofia del diritto* 151

Franz H, 'What Can Be Learned from International Exchange between Legal Clinics' (2023) 30(2) *International Journal of Clinical Legal Education* 138

Gordon A, 'Cleaning up Our Own Houses: Creating Anti-racist Clinical Programs' (2022) 29 *Clinical Law Review*, https://ssrn.com/abstract=4187924

Jackson A, 'Why MLK Believed Jazz Was the Perfect Soundtrack for Civil Rights', *JSTOR Daily* (16 October 2019), https://daily.jstor.org/why-mlk-believed-jazz-was-the-perfect-soundtrack-for-civil-rights/

Kapur R, 'The Tragedy of Victimization Rhetoric: Resurrecting the "Native" Subject in International/Post-colonial Feminist Legal Politics' (2002) 15 *Harvard Human Rights Journal* 1

Klein CF, 'Cultural Competency and the Practice of Law in the Twenty-First Century' (1998) 4(3) *Clinical Law Review* 555

Ladson-Billings G, 'Toward a Theory of Culturally Relevant Pedagogy' (1995) 32(3) *American Educational Research Journal* 465

Lidskog R, 'The Role of Music in Ethnic Identity Formation in Diaspora: A Research Review' (2016) 66(219–20) *International Social Science Journal* 23

Mallocci M, '"All Art Is Propaganda": W.E.B. Du Bois's *The Crisis* and the Construction of a Black Public Image' (2018) 1 *USAbroad – Journal of American History and Politics*, https://usabroad.unibo.it/article/view/7177/7504

McDonald D, 'Introduction: Pathways toward a Justice-Oriented Ethnomusicology' in B Romero et al (eds), *At the Crossroads of Music and Social Justice* (Indiana University Press 2022)

Millbank J and Vogl A, 'Adjudicating Fear of Witchcraft Claims in Refugee Law' (2018) 45(3) *Journal of Law and Society* 370

Mission US, 'A Retrospective: U.S. Civil Society's Commitment and Contributions to the Anti-apartheid Struggle' (2020), https://za.usembassy.gov/a-retrospective-u-s-civil-societys-commitment-and-contributions-to-the-anti-apartheid-struggle/

Mitchell R, 'Romanticism and the Experience of Experiment' (2015) 46(3) *The Wordsworth Circle* 132

Mutua M, *Human Rights: A Political and Cultural Critique* (University of Pennsylvania Press 2002)

Nash W, 'Black Arts Movement', *Oxford Research Encyclopedia of Literature* (26 July 2017), https://oxfordre.com/literature/view/10.1093/acrefore/9780190201098.001.0001/acrefore-9780190201098-e-630

Parcell S, 'Architecture as a Mechanical Art' in *Four Historical Definitions of Architecture* (McGill-Queen's University Press 2012)

'Performing Challenges Extended mit Lela Aisha Jones' (2024), www.mdw.ac.at/ikm/gender-studies/performing-challenges-extended-jones/

Pithouse R, 'Johnny Clegg: Rebel, Intellectual, Musician', *Mail & Guardian* (2019), https://mg.co.za/article/2019-07-18-johnny-clegg-rebel-intellectual-musician/

Power K, 'Musical Influence on Apartheid and the Civil Rights Movement', https://cupola.gettysburg.edu/cgi/viewcontent.cgi?params=/context/student_scholarship/article/1306&path_info=Power__Katherine__Musical_Influence_on_Apartheid_and_The_Civil_Rights_Movement.pdf

President of South Africa, 'President Cyril Ramaphosa Sends Condolences to Nkonyeni and Clegg Families' (17 July 2019), www.gov.za/news/media-statements/president-cyril-ramaphosa-sends-condolences-nkonyeni-and-clegg-families-17

'Review: When "Native Portals", Philadelphia Choreographer Lela Aisha Jones Explores the Impact of Lynching through Dance', Philadelphia Sunday Sun (6 May 2016), https://philasun.com/entertainment/review-native-portals-philadelphia-choreographer-lela-aisha-jones-explores-impact-lynching-dance/

Sandbach J and Grimes R, *The LawWorks Law School Pro Bono and Clinic Report 2020* (LawWorks and CLEO 2020) www.lawworks.org.uk/solicitors-and-volunteers/resources/lawworks-law-school-pro-bono-and-clinics-report-2020

Schipper EW, 'Mimesis in the Arts in Plato's Laws' (1963) 22(2) *Journal of Aesthetics and Art Criticism* 199

Shah J, 'Community Lawyering in Resistance to Neoliberalism' (2022) 120(6) *Michigan Law Review* 1061

Targia G, 'Writing Images as an Act of Interpreting: Notes on Erwin Panofsky's Studies on Medieval Subjects and the Problem of Language in and of Art History' (2023) 39(1) *Word & Image* 88

Thornton M, 'What Is the Law School for in a Post-pandemic World?' in R Dunn, P Maharg and V Roper (eds), *What Is Legal Education for? Reassessing the Purposes of Early Twenty-First Century Learning and Law Schools* (Routledge 2023)

Woods D, *Biko* (Paddington Press 1978)

12

Artificial Intelligence and the Future of Student Legal Clinics: Navigating Opportunities and Challenges

Olga M Piaskowska and Piotr F Piesiewicz

Introduction

The rapid evolution of artificial intelligence (AI) tools, particularly generative AI (GenAI) and large language models (LLMs), is reshaping the landscape of legal education and practice. This unprecedented pace of development has shifted the primary debate in legal academia from whether law students should be taught to use AI tools to how best to teach them, given the rapidly changing nature of AI knowledge.[1] These tools are being integrated at a speed that outstrips traditional curriculum development, leaving educators struggling to prepare students for a professional environment increasingly

[1] Jonathan H Choi, Amy Monahan and Daniel Schwarcz, 'Lawyering in the Age of Artificial Intelligence' (Social Science Research Network, 7 November 2023), https://papers.ssrn.com/abstract=4626276; Oguz A Acar, 'AI Prompt Engineering Isn't the Future' [2023] *Harvard Business Review*, https://hbr.org/2023/06/ai-prompt-engineering-isnt-the-future; Stephanie Wilkins, 'As AI Advances, Is Prompt Engineering the Next Crucial Legal Skill?', *Legal Tech News*, www.law.com/legaltechnews/2023/04/25/as-ai-advances-is-prompt-engineering-the-next-crucial-legal-skill/; Karen Sloan, 'Some Law Professors Fear ChatGPT's Rise as Others See Opportunity', *Reuters* (11 January 2023), www.reuters.com/legal/legalindustry/some-law-professors-fear-chatgpts-rise-others-see-opportunity-2023-01-10/; Angus Norton, 'What Lessons from Past Technology Hype Cycles Can Be Applied to the Hype around Artificial Intelligence?', *Medium* (1 September 2023), https://medium.com/@angusnorton/what-lessons-from-past-technology-hype-cycles-can-be-applied-to-the-hype-around-artificial-b26db57a11c8

shaped by these technologies. At present, the question of whether students should be taught to use AI tools or have access to them is becoming obsolete,[2] as their widespread availability means students will inevitably use them. The only relevant question that remains is how to teach them effectively, particularly in a context where students are likely to adapt to new tools more swiftly than their academic instructors. However, this is not the only reason why universities, in light of technological advancements, face an unprecedented and far-reaching challenge.

The integration of AI into legal education is more than a mere alignment with technological advancements – it is a strategic response to the evolving demands of the modern job market. As AI reshapes legal practice, adaptability and technological proficiency have become essential competencies for future legal professionals. Incorporating AI tools into the curriculum equips students not only with technical skills but also with the ability to critically assess and effectively apply these tools in diverse legal contexts. However, the ultimate form and capabilities of AI in the future remain uncertain, making it essential for students to develop adaptability and a deep understanding of both the potential and limitations of these technologies.

Law clinics, historically the cornerstone of practical legal education, now stand at the forefront of this technological transition. Legal clinics have always served a dual function: fostering client-centred practice and providing a safe environment in which students can develop essential legal skills under supervision.[3] Moreover, legal clinics have played a crucial role in ensuring access to justice for those in need of support.[4] However, these skills – and the methods by which they are taught – are undergoing significant change. While older generations of legal practitioners may have navigated their careers with minimal reliance on AI, the incoming generation of lawyers will find such tools indispensable. Legal firms are rapidly adopting AI for tasks ranging from research to case management, and graduates who are unprepared to harness these technologies risk being

2 Norton (n 1); Sloan (n 1); Wilkins (n 1).

3 Laura Bugatti, 'Legal Clinics as a Leading Force for Changes in Legal Education', https://romatrepress.uniroma3.it/wp-content/uploads/2023/10/02.-Bugatti-RTLR-1-2023-ebook-2.pdf; Patrick Brayer, 'A Law Clinic Systems Theory and the Pedagogy of Interaction: Creating a Legal Learning System' (Social Science Research Network 2012), https://papers.ssrn.com/abstract=3947923; Eduardo M Penalver, 'The Role of Skills Instruction in Legal Education' (2018) 13 *FIU Law Review* 229; Stephen Wizner, 'The Law School Clinic: Legal Education in the Interests of Justice' (2002) 70 *Fordham Law Review* 1929.

4 Stephen Wizner and Jane Aiken, 'Teaching and Doing: The Role of Law School Clinics in Enhancing Access to Justice' [2004] *Faculty Scholarship Series*, https://openyls.law.yale.edu/handle/20.500.13051/1104

left behind in an evolving job market.[5] How, then, should legal clinics prepare for this transition?

One of the challenges, as mentioned earlier, lies in the fact that in today's reality, it is impossible to overlook AI tools in legal practice – or indeed in any other field. This is largely due to the inability to predict how AI's future capabilities will evolve. At the same time, it seems certain that the number of AI-driven tools available to lawyers will continue to grow. Therefore, it is essential to consider how to integrate these tools into the work of legal clinics in a manner that aligns with their mission, ethics and the public interest.

This chapter advocates for a balanced approach to integrating AI into student legal clinics. While AI can significantly enhance clinical work and create new opportunities for legal education, it is essential not to overlook the critical human elements, such as developing skills in critical thinking, empathy and independent decision making. Understanding both the benefits and limitations of AI, as well as fostering the appropriate competencies, will be crucial in shaping future generations of lawyers in an increasingly technologized legal profession. The authors do not take a futuristic approach or speculate on what may happen in the coming months or years, or on how AI will shape legal practice in the future. While it is almost certain that AI will have an impact, the exact capabilities of these tools remain uncertain. Therefore, in this chapter, we focus on the present. As academic educators, we can adapt to current realities by continuously monitoring changes, but none of us can predict with absolute certainty what the future holds.

Although this section focuses on the specific application of GenAI in civil law systems (where the primary basis is the interpretation of codified norms and doctrinal analysis of statutes), many of the operational mechanisms and limitations of LLMs also appear in common law systems. In precedent-based jurisdictions, AI must process hundreds of judicial decisions rather than solely statutory texts. Consequently, although our analysis concentrates on the logical reasoning process employed in continental law countries, analogous technological and ethical challenges can also be observed in common law legal clinics, where AI supports precedent retrieval and the preparation of legal memoranda.

Clinics as spaces for developing legal skills

Legal clinics have a longstanding tradition and a well-established role in legal education. In many academic institutions, particularly in Poland,

[5] Michael C Dorf, 'Is Resistance to AI in the Law School Classroom Futile?' (19 July 2023), https://verdict.justia.com/2023/07/19/is-resistance-to-ai-in-the-law-school-classroom-futile

they are seen as spaces where, in contrast to traditional academic courses, students develop skills that are highly valuable for their future careers as legal professionals. However, teaching and skill development are not the sole purposes of legal clinics.

Legal clinics serve a dual purpose: they operate as public interest entities dedicated to protecting fundamental human rights and ensuring access to justice for specific segments of the population, while simultaneously functioning as educational spaces designed to prepare students for professional advocacy practice.[6] It is important to emphasize that legal clinics may play a unique role in reducing justice gaps through careful, controlled deployment of AI-powered chatbots, especially for legal information dissemination and intake triage. However, it also warns that without careful design and supervision, these tools may mislead vulnerable clients due to LLM hallucinations, jurisdictional errors and the inability of nonlawyers to verify AI-generated legal guidance.[7] Furthermore, existing survey and pilot research underscores the need for thoughtful and strategic implementation in order to maximize the potential of generative AI and ensure its effective use.[8] These studies also highlight the importance of addressing the gender gap in access and usage of such technologies. It is crucial that these tools are used to narrow existing disparities in access to justice[9] rather than inadvertently exacerbating them.

University clinics adopt a distinct approach to understanding and teaching law, offering an alternative framework for engaging with legal science, fostering learning and promoting the ethical development of future legal professionals by placing students in real-world contexts.[10] This approach enables students to acquire essential legal skills and competencies while cultivating values critical to professional practice. When placed in real-world

6 Víctor E Abramovich, 'La enseñanza del derecho en las clínicas legales de interés público. Materiales para una agenda temática. Cuaderno de Analisis Juridico. Serie Publicaciones Especiales' [1999] *Defensa Juridica del Interes Publico*, www.palermo.edu/derecho/pdf/Bibliografia-clinicas-juridicas/la_ensenanza_del_derecho_en_las_clinicas_legales_de_interes_publico(2).pdf

7 Will Cesta, 'Large Language Models and Community Legal Centres: Could Chatbots Help Reduce Australia's Justice Gap?' (2024) 49 *Alternative Law Journal* 181.

8 Colleen V Chien and Miriam Kim, 'Generative AI and Legal Aid: Results from a Field Study and 100 Use Cases to Bridge the Access to Justice Gap' (Social Science Research Network, 14 March 2024), https://papers.ssrn.com/abstract=4733061

9 Drew Simshaw, 'Access to A.I. Justice: Avoiding an Inequitable Two-Tiered System of Legal Services' (Social Science Research Network, 22 April 2022), https://papers.ssrn.com/abstract=4090984

10 Maria Joao Mimoso, Maria do Rosario Anjos and Carlos Miranda, 'Legal Clinics, a Challenge for the Teaching of Law' (2018) 5 *New Trends and Issues Proceedings on Humanities and Social Sciences* 101.

settings, students learn through hands-on experience, actively engaging in tasks and reflecting on their outcomes.[11] This learning process arises not only from direct involvement in real casework but also from analysing those experiences and critically reflecting on what was done, what occurred (or did not) and why.[12] Students benefit from the dual advantage of 'learning by doing' and enhancing their education through reflective practice. Within clinical courses, students are also often encouraged to reflect both during their actions and retrospectively after completing them.[13]

In clinics, students learn not only through hands-on practice but also observation and close collaboration with their clinical supervisors. It is important to recognize that numerous methods are employed in clinical practice. Regardless of the specific approach adopted by a particular clinic or its mode of operation – some focus on simulating cases, while others provide legal assistance to real clients (the latter model being predominant among Polish legal clinics) – the essence of clinical education lies in its adaptability to diverse educational and practical needs. However, much like law schools as a whole, legal clinics are not yet fully prepared for the transition to integrating AI tools into their operations. Questions also arise as to whether these tools are fully compatible with the core missions and methodologies of clinical education, raising concerns about how such technologies align with its fundamental principles and the concept of client-centred practice.

The literature argues that this transition is not fully compatible with the mission and structure of legal clinics.[14] Furthermore, while GenAI offers certain minimal opportunities to enhance practice readiness, it remains largely misaligned with the goals of justice readiness and client-centred lawyering. This misalignment is particularly evident in clinical programmes focused on public interest missions, where the ethical, social and legal challenges associated with the development and deployment of GenAI present significant obstacles.[15] This position is not without its merits. Karr and Schultz highlight the ethical and social implications of using GenAI in legal contexts, emphasizing the potential for AI systems to reinforce unjust labour practices, economic inequalities and social injustices.[16]

---

[11] Bugatti (n 3).

[12] Richard Hamilton Grimes, 'Faking It and Making It? Using Simulation with Problem-Based Learning' in Caroline Strevens, Richard Grimes and Edward Phillips (eds), *Legal Education* (Ashgate 2014).

[13] Bugatti (n 3).

[14] Jake Karr and Jason Schultz, 'The Legal Imitation Game: Generative AI's Incompatibility with Clinical Legal Education' (2024) 92 *Fordham Law Review* 1867.

[15] ibid.

[16] ibid.

They draw attention to the exploitation of workers in the AI supply chain, such as the underpaid Kenyan 'click' workers hired to clean toxic content from AI systems.[17] They also highlight the broader consequences of GenAI's deployment, particularly in the legal field, noting that these tools are inherently conservative, reinforcing existing power structures and perpetuating systemic injustices.[18] There is no doubt that the teaching and use of GenAI tools in legal practice, if undertaken without critical reflection and caution, may contradict the fundamental goals of justice-centred legal education. This, in our opinion, is of the utmost importance. In today's world, where AI is becoming an integral part of legal practice, the critical focus must be on developing competencies that enable the ethical and responsible use of these tools – an inevitability that cannot be ignored. Since legal clinics are places where students develop crucial skills, they too should play a role in this transition by incorporating AI tools into their training practices. However, the challenge with this approach lies in the widespread availability of AI tools. Even if students were prohibited from using AI tools within the clinic setting, such a measure would not be effective. Students can easily access and use these tools outside the clinic environment, meaning that banning their use during training would fail to reflect the realities of legal practice. Moreover, it could inadvertently hinder students from learning how to responsibly incorporate AI into their work. Therefore, the focus should not be on restricting access, but on ensuring that students understand the ethical implications and best practices when using these technologies. In light of this, it is essential for legal clinics to approach the integration of AI tools into their educational practices with caution. We fully agree with Karr and Schultz that clinics should prioritize critical reflection on AI's impact on justice and ensure that its use does not inadvertently perpetuate harm.[19] Therefore, while GenAI may offer technical efficiencies or learning opportunities, its integration into legal education should be approached with caution, ensuring that the tools used in clinical settings align with the values of justice, fairness and client advocacy. It is thus essential to consider the extent to which currently available AI tools can support the work of legal clinics. Consequently, it is also crucial to determine at which stages of legal practice these tools may be applied, to understand their current limitations and to assess whether – and to what extent – AI can support lawyers in their work, particularly in the context of clinical legal education.

[17] ibid.

[18] ibid.

[19] ibid.

Use of artificial intelligence in law and its current limitations

When considering the significance of AI in clinical practice and, more broadly, in the legal profession, it is important to recognize that there is no consensus in the literature on the extent to which AI tools will ultimately transform legal practice. This debate has been ongoing for years, but has recently intensified due to the widespread availability of LLM models and their capabilities, as well as the increasing number of companies offering AI-based tools to both practitioners and students. Many scholars align with the perspective of the expert Richard Susskind, who emphasizes that AI will not only disrupt the world of practising lawyers but will also fundamentally alter our common perception of the legal process, thus completely reshaping the legal profession.[20] Others argue that while AI-based software is likely to enhance legal research and improve lawyers' efficiency, it is unlikely to replace traditional legal work or fundamentally transform legal practice.[21] In addition, the experience of legal clinics in Australia suggests that while LLM-powered chatbots can theoretically help with tasks such as client intake, research support or legal information provision, significant challenges persist.[22] These include technical limitations, governance issues and ethical risks related to misclassification of legal information as legal advice, as extensively discussed by Cesta.[23] Moreover, many clinics lack the resources to fine-tune models or deploy domain-specific LLMs, which leaves them dependent on generalized, error-prone systems.

At present, it is difficult to determine which perspective is correct. However, there is no doubt that AI is already influencing legal practice and will continue to do so. To what extent? That remains uncertain. It is crucial to recognize that our assessments of the future are based on the knowledge available to us today. For this reason, we must evaluate the potential capabilities of AI as they currently stand, without certainty about what the future may hold. It is therefore reasonable to agree with Harry Surden that, instead of engaging in futuristic narratives about AI and law – often speculating on the development of technologies that do not yet exist and may never materialize – we should focus on real, present-day possibilities.[24] While

---

20 Richard Susskind, *Tomorrow's Lawyers: An Introduction to Your Future* (3rd edn, OUP 2023); Richard Susskind, *Online Courts and the Future of Justice* (OUP 2021).

21 Ryan McCarl, 'The Limits of Law and AI' (2022) 90 *University of Cincinnati Law Review*, https://scholarship.law.uc.edu/uclr/vol90/iss3/5

22 Cesta (n 7).

23 ibid.

24 Harry Surden, 'Artificial Intelligence and Law: An Overview' [2019] *Georgia State University Law Review*, https://scholar.law.colorado.edu/faculty-articles/1234

futuristic discussions have their place, it is important to acknowledge that they are often based on significant, and sometimes unjustified, assumptions about the future of technology.[25]

AI involves creating computer programs that can perform tasks typically requiring human intelligence. Currently, and for the foreseeable future, AI technologies allow computers to replicate or even surpass some human cognitive abilities, but they are not capable of performing all human cognitive functions.[26] The literature correctly points out that although AI has applications across various fields, two of its features are currently most relevant in the context of legal applications. First, machine learning encompasses pattern-recognition algorithms that extract insights from data, where 'experience' denotes systematic processing of annotated training datasets rather than independent knowledge generation.[27] This means that AI can not only perform programmed tasks but can also enhance its capabilities. Second, natural language processing enables computers to understand human speech or text, allowing for analyses that mimic human reasoning.[28] Machine learning involves the application of algorithms and statistical models that enable machines to learn from data and progressively improve their performance. This process involves feeding large datasets to the machine, which it analyses to identify patterns, learn from them and make predictions or decisions based on the acquired knowledge. The results of this learning are stored in the machine's memory, allowing it to make more accurate predictions and decisions in the future.[29]

However, AI systems do not understand context in a holistic manner. Their current limitations primarily concern the lack of causal reasoning and the inability to adapt to unforeseen legal scenarios. This is exemplified by *Mata v Avianca*, in which an AI algorithm generated fictitious precedents, highlighting the risks associated with overreliance on AI-generated legal analysis.[30] At present, the future of AI remains uncertain.

---

25 ibid.

26 'What Is AI (Artificial Intelligence)?', www.mckinsey.com/featured-insights/mckinsey-explainers/what-is-ai#/

27 Gary Marchant, 'Artificial Intelligence and the Future of Legal Practice' (2017) 14 *Scitech Lawyer* 20.

28 ibid.

29 Sara Brown, 'Machine Learning, Explained' (30 January 2025), https://mitsloan.mit.edu/ideas-made-to-matter/machine-learning-explained

30 'Mata v. Avianca, Inc., No. 1:2022cv01461 – Document 55 (S.D.N.Y. 2023)' (*Justia Law*, 4 February 2025), https://law.justia.com/cases/federal/district-courts/new-york/nysdce/1:2022cv01461/575368/55/; Robert Lufrano, 'NY Case Gives Insight to the Limits of AI in Law' (*National Law Review*), https://natlawreview.com/article/chatgpt-and-limits-ai-legal-research; 'Limitations and Risks of Using AI in Legal Practice' (*Legal Practitioners' Liability Committee*), https://lplc.com.au/resources/lplc-article/limitations-risks-ai-in-legal-practice

In research conducted by the British Institute of International and Comparative Law in 2023, which involved interviews with lawyers in the UK and other countries, key areas were identified where AI can support daily legal practice.[31] AI, including virtual assistants based on machine learning and natural language processing, has proven helpful in areas such as legal research (understood as support in information retrieval), document automation, predictive litigation outcomes, legal review, case management and client communication. These applications of AI in legal practice are also acknowledged in the literature.[32] The report by the British Institute of International and Comparative Law also highlighted the growing role of technology in streamlining legal processes, enabling lawyers to manage their time and workload more efficiently, while allowing them to focus on more advanced tasks requiring human expertise.[33] However, despite these advances, AI technology still faces significant limitations. Its application in legal practice also raises numerous legal and ethical challenges.[34] The adoption of AI-driven tools impacts fundamental principles governing the legal profession, as well as the rights of clients and citizens. Key concerns include accuracy and accountability, transparency, trust, communication and the duty of competent representation, as well as issues related to bias and fairness, privacy, data protection, conflicts of interest and professional confidentiality. Moreover, the lack of human interpretation and judgement, alongside the risk of job displacement and the erosion of specialized legal expertise, must also be considered.[35] While AI-powered tools can generate initial drafts of contracts and legal documents, these outputs still require thorough review and validation by lawyers to ensure accuracy and compliance with legal standards. Nevertheless, the overall impact of AI in legal practice may contribute to reducing costs for clients and improving access to justice, particularly for individuals without legal representation. As automation continues to reshape certain legal tasks, lawyers will likely need to shift their focus towards strategic decision making and other high-value work that requires human expertise, ethical reasoning and nuanced legal interpretation.[36] Such applications of AI

[31] Irene Pietropaoli, 'Use of Artificial Intelligence in Legal Practice' (*British Institute of International and Comparative Law*, 17 October 2023), www.biicl.org/publications/use-of-artificial-intelligence-in-legal-practice

[32] John O Oladipo, 'Artificial Intelligence and Law' (Social Science Research Network, 19 June 2023), https://papers.ssrn.com/abstract=4562175

[33] Pietropaoli (n 31).

[34] Rowena Rodrigues, 'Legal and Human Rights Issues of AI: Gaps, Challenges and Vulnerabilities' (2020) 4 *Journal of Responsible Technology* 100005.

[35] Pietropaoli (n 31).

[36] Xavier Rodriguez, 'Artificial Intelligence (AI) and the Practice of Law' (2023) 24 *Sedona Conference Journal* 783.

algorithms are also recognized in countries following the continental legal system, as reflected in the position presented by the Council of Europe – European Commission for the Efficiency of Justice in the 'CEPEJ European Ethical Charter on the Use of Artificial Intelligence (AI) in Judicial Systems and Their Environment'.[37] This document highlights AI's potential use in analysing legal issues and regulations, predicting case outcomes, conducting inference and argumentation, performing text mining, drafting legislation, resolving disputes online, profiling offenders, predicting crime and assisting in arbitration courts. However, it should be emphasized that all these documents indicate only the possibility of such applications, which does not necessarily mean that AI algorithms are currently being used in this way.

Given this distinction between potential and actual implementation at present, it is crucial to move beyond media hype and critically assess the real-world applications of AI tools in legal practice. While reports indicate a certain trend in AI adoption across different countries, they do not provide clear evidence of its scale or actual use by legal professionals. Therefore, understanding the extent to which lawyers actively rely on AI tools remains an open question that requires further empirical research.

While AI has significant potential to support lawyers, there remains a critical need to fully understand when and how to use this technology effectively, as well as the inherent risks associated with its implementation. These risks stem, in part, from the fundamental limitations of AI itself. As Harry Surden rightly emphasizes, current AI technology struggles with abstractions, comprehending meaning, transferring knowledge across different tasks, and handling entirely unstructured or open-ended problems. AI's successes are primarily observed in highly structured domains, where clear right or wrong answers exist and distinct patterns can be detected algorithmically – for instance, in chess, credit card fraud detection and cancer diagnosis[38].

Current limitations of large language models as applied in the civil law system

In assessing the potential applications of AI algorithms in legal clinics, it is essential to begin by examining the process of legal reasoning within the civil

[37] 'CEPEJ European Ethical Charter on the Use of Artificial Intelligence (AI) in Judicial Systems and Their Environment – European Commission for the Efficiency of Justice (CEPEJ)', https://rm.coe.int/ethical-charter-en-for-publication-4-december-2018/16808f699c; Anna Bednarek et al, 'Raport 'Rekomendacje w zakresie zastosowania sztucznej inteligencji w sądownictwie i prokuraturze - przygotowany przez Grupę Roboczą ds. Sztucznej Inteligencji Podgrupa ds. etyki i prawa', www.gov.pl/attachment/5e60dcd0-2491-4f83-863c-4f59890a8295

[38] Surden (n 24).

law system and identifying the current limitations of LLMs. These models, such as the widely available ChatGPT, are AI systems trained on vast amounts of text data to generate human-like responses based on statistical patterns. Their potential for widespread use, including free access, justifies a focused analysis of their capabilities and limitations, particularly in the context of legal education and clinical practice. Furthermore, occasional reports highlight ChatGPT's achievements, such as its recent success in passing the bar exam with a score approaching the 90th percentile.[39] It is therefore the power of these particular algorithms that will be examined.

The process of applying the law consists of four key stages. The first is the initial determination of legal status (validation decision and interpretative decision), the second is the establishment of the factual situation (evidentiary decision), the third is the subsumption of facts under the legal norm and the final stage is the binding determination of legal consequences.[40] Lawyers not only develop these skills during their legal education (through legal skills classes and participation in law clinics), but also refine them in professional practice. For humans, once they have mastered this process, it becomes almost automatic. However, the situation is different in the case of AI algorithms. The key question that remains is whether currently available AI systems, particularly LLMs, have the ability to conduct legal reasoning and apply the law in a manner comparable to the human mind. The fundamental issue here is the need to take into account a range of nonlegal variables and contexts, which also evolve with shifts in the law and society.

When considering the potential use of AI algorithms (LLMs) in the process of applying the law, it is essential to first analyse the stages of this process and identify where AI may encounter difficulties. This is important because it will allow us to determine whether AI can, at this stage of development, support humans in this respect or not. Understanding the current capabilities of AI in the process of applying the law is particularly relevant for clinical

[39] Debra Cassens Weiss, 'Latest Version of ChatGPT Aces Bar Exam with Score Nearing 90th Percentile' (*ABA Journal*), www.abajournal.com/web/article/latest-version-of-chatgpt-aces-the-bar-exam-with-score-in-90th-percentile

[40] Jerzy Wróblewski, 'Zagadnienia Procesowego Modelu Sądowego Stosowania Prawa' [1986] *Studia Prawnicze* 3; Andrzej Korybski and Leszek Leszczyński (eds), *Stanowienie i Stosowanie Prawa: Elementy Teorii* (Wolters Kluwer 2015); Leszek Leszczyński, 'The Legal System: A Theoretical Approach' (2017) 64 *Annales Universitatis Mariae Curie-Skłodowska, sectio G (Ius)* 23; Justyna Trubalska, *Podstawy Prawa. Podręcznik*, vol 8 (Innovatio Press Wydawnictwo Naukowe Wyższej Szkoły Ekonomii i Innowacji 2021), https://wydawnictwo.wsei.eu/sklep/podstawy-prawa-tom-viii-2/; Olgierd Bogucki et al, 'Zintegrowanie polskich koncepcji wykładni prawa' [2009] *Ruch Prawniczy, Ekonomiczny i Socjologiczny* 23; Maciej Wojciechowski, *Pewność prawa* (Wydawnictwo Uniwersytetu Gdańskiego 2014), https://repozytorium.bg.ug.edu.pl/info/book/UOGe5a4650a98b244bbb963e651246887ac/

teaching within the civil law system, as it will help assess the potential impact of algorithms on legal education and the functioning of law clinics in this system. At present, modern AI systems can only serve as a support tool; they will not replace lawyers. Apart from ethical concerns and data security issues, students should be aware of the current limitations of AI in order to be better prepared to incorporate new technologies into their work in an effective and responsible manner.

Preliminary determination of legal status

Preliminary determination of legal status in the process of applying the law serves as the first stage, which involves assessing whether a specific event, action or factual situation falls within the scope of legal regulations and identifying the relevant field of law in which a solution should be sought. This stage establishes the legal framework for further actions and, without its correct implementation, it is impossible to properly apply the subsequent stages of the law application process.

At this stage, AI encounters numerous challenges. One of the key issues is its limited ability to identify and interpret complex or ambiguous legal norms, as well as the factual circumstances themselves. Unlike lawyers, AI lacks the sophisticated understanding necessary to navigate legal principles, which often require contextual analysis, knowledge of legal history, doctrinal interpretation and an awareness of customary law, the rule of law and extralegal contexts. Furthermore, the dynamic nature of legal systems necessitates continuous updating of AI databases. Legal norms evolve due to legislative changes, court decisions and administrative regulations, requiring regular recalibration of AI algorithms to maintain their relevance. Court rulings also change over time, meaning that without timely updates, AI systems may base their analyses on outdated regulations, leading to erroneous conclusions at this stage. Additionally, AI algorithms tasked with this stage rely solely on the data made available to them. In contrast, humans first focus on identifying gaps in the presented situation and consider what questions need to be asked or what information is still missing before beginning the case analysis. Another significant limitation is AI's inability to fully capture the broader context in which legal norms operate. In a civil law system, law is not a static set of rules, but a reflection of social, political and economic processes. AI, being primarily based on data analysis, cannot account for these external factors that influence the interpretation and application of legal norms.

Establishing the factual situation

Establishing the factual situation is a key step in the process of applying the law, as it serves as the foundation upon which legal norms are applied.

Legal norms cannot be applied in isolation; they must be applied to a specific set of facts. Therefore, determining the factual situation is essential as, without it, there is no context for interpreting how the law should be applied. Importantly, a particular legal norm may have different implications depending on the established facts. AI also faces significant difficulties in assessing facts, particularly during the evidence analysis stage. Although AI has demonstrated great efficiency in processing large sets of structured data, legal proceedings often rely on elements such as witness statements, which require careful evaluation. AI's current capabilities in assessing the credibility and probative value of such evidence are limited because it lacks human intuition and contextual reasoning, both of which are crucial for determining the reliability of witnesses. Meanwhile, precise factual determination is essential for the next stage of law application. This limitation is particularly impactful in legal settings, where the strength of evidence can determine case outcomes. Furthermore, AI presents a notable risk of errors in evidence analysis. These errors may manifest as misinterpretations of witness statements or the oversight of crucial facts, potentially undermining the reliability of legal decisions.

Subsuming the facts under the legal norm

Subsuming the facts under the legal norm is a crucial step in the process of applying the law. It involves matching or aligning the facts of a case with the relevant legal rules or norms to determine whether and how they apply to a given situation. This step is essential as it allows legal professionals to translate the specific facts of a case into a legal framework, ensuring that the law is applied correctly and consistently. In essence, this stage involves taking the established facts and determining which legal norm or set of norms is relevant to those facts. It requires interpreting the facts within the context of the law, considering both the letter of the law and its intended purpose. This is also where AI algorithms encounter difficulties. As mentioned earlier, AI systems often exhibit limitations in interpreting the law, particularly when dealing with ambiguous, multilayered or flexible provisions. While judges and lawyers rely on precedents, doctrinal debates and interpretative methods to resolve ambiguities, AI lacks a comparable depth of analytical reasoning, which can lead to the erroneous subsumption of a legal norm. Legal norms are often deeply embedded in the traditions, moral values and ethical frameworks of a given community. AI, on the other hand, tends to approach legal interpretation in a rigid, mechanical manner, ignoring the broader conditions that influence how the law is understood and applied. As a result, its analyses can be overly simplistic and fail to capture subtle relationships and nonlegal contexts, such as ethical principles or established customs, which often play a key role in the legal decision-making process. These challenges highlight the need for careful integration and oversight of AI in legal processes to prevent misinterpretations and ensure that justice is served.

Binding determination of legal consequences

The final and most crucial stage in the process of applying the law is the binding determination of legal consequences. It represents the ultimate and authoritative conclusion of the legal process. At this point, the legal system delivers concrete outcomes based on the previous stages of analysis. The decision-making process requires a holistic approach that integrates legal reasoning, factual analysis and an understanding of the case's context. Importantly, any error made in one of the earlier stages of the application of the law has a direct impact on the binding determination of legal consequences. The absence of a holistic approach in AI-based legal analysis raises serious concerns about the reliability of automated legal decisions. Another significant risk is the potential for unfair or disproportionate judgments. Since AI relies on predetermined algorithms and statistical analyses, it may struggle to recognize exceptional cases that require consideration of principles of equity and social justice.

The current limitations of AI in the legal field emphasize its role as a tool to support rather than replace human professionals. AI faces many challenges, particularly in the early stages of law, such as the initial determination of legal status, factual determination, subsumption of facts under legal norms and binding determination of legal consequences. While AI can efficiently process vast amounts of data, it struggles with complex legal reasoning, understanding contextual nuances, interpreting ambiguous legal norms and assessing the credibility of evidence. At this stage of technological development, AI can assist professionals, but it cannot replace human judgement, contextual understanding or the ethical considerations that human lawyers bring to the practice of law. This also has implications for clinical training, one of the key areas where students develop their skills. The limitations of LLMs are significant, as they highlight the need for students to learn to use these tools responsibly and ethically. Students must develop critical thinking skills not only to properly analyse cases but also to assess and question the conclusions generated by AI. Overreliance on AI, without critical judgement and an understanding of its limitations, may undermine students' ability to actively engage in developing their own skills, potentially weakening their analytical abilities in the long term.

Since AI tools, such as LLMs, can only support students in analysis – and, at present, due to their limited capabilities, they are more of a hindrance than a help – it is worth considering in which areas of law AI can be effectively applied. This is undoubtedly important for shaping the skills of young lawyers, who will inevitably use these tools in the future.

The legal clinic as a place for shaping skills for the responsible use of artificial intelligence tools

As indicated earlier, legal clinics are traditionally regarded as places where students develop their skills. There is no doubt that, depending on the adopted work model, students in law clinics acquire competencies such as client representation, case strategy and legal research through real-world experiences. By engaging in simulated courtrooms and real client cases, students gain vital advocacy skills. They typically handle multiple client cases throughout the academic year, providing them with the opportunity to conduct interviews with real clients and solve actual legal problems. In addition, as rightly emphasized in the literature, law clinics embody the principle of social justice and, in many cases, help fulfil the guarantee of the right to a fair trial. The values that guided their establishment cannot be underestimated. As mentioned earlier, these values appear to be in conflict with the introduction of AI tools into law clinics. Can this conflict of values be resolved? Given that law clinics are not only facing technological developments but also the influence of large corporations driving these innovations, the answer is probably no.

The first solution that comes to mind – avoiding the use of AI tools in clinical work – is unsatisfactory and, above all, disadvantageous for students. It is undeniable that they will increasingly use these tools. So, what can law clinics do now? Given the current limitations of AI tools, particularly LLM models, their use in clinical work remains minimal. The future is uncertain, but we believe that law clinics should focus on what aligns with their mission – human-centred, ethical and responsible skill development.

The foundation of legal work lies in its human element, guided by ethical principles, critical analysis, and the ability to verify and question data while considering relevant nonlegal contexts. Furthermore, as Ryan and Hardie emphasize, clinical legal education must ensure that students critically evaluate AI outputs, recognize jurisdictional errors and understand the ethical limitations of GenAI tools before integrating them into client work.[41] Clinics should also educate students about hallucinations, AI bias and confidentiality risks arising from uploading client-sensitive data into third-party LLM systems.[42] While machines excel at processing large datasets, they currently lack the judgement needed to interpret legal nuances or verify facts accurately. Law clinics must stay up to date with technological advancements, as responsible AI use requires skills that are not yet fully

[41] Francine Ryan and Liz Hardie, 'ChatGPT, I Have a Legal Question? The Impact of Generative AI Tools on Law Clinics and Access to Justice' (2024) 31 *International Journal of Clinical Legal Education* 166.

[42] ibid.

developed. For example, effectively using tools like ChatGPT demands the ability to craft precise prompts – an essential skill for students to harness AI's potential responsibly and ethically. However, this is just one aspect. Equally crucial is the ability to verify whether AI-generated content or analysis is accurate and, if not, to identify its shortcomings. Independence and critical thinking are fundamental – these qualities distinguish human decision making from AI tools.

Furthermore, legal education should emphasize that AI is not a substitute for human judgement, but a tool that requires responsible handling. Students must be trained not only in the technical aspects of AI but also in its ethical implications. A core objective of clinical legal education should be to cultivate a deep understanding of legal ethics, ensuring that future lawyers maintain accountability and transparency when integrating AI into their practice. By actively engaging with emerging technologies, law clinics can prepare students to navigate a profession that increasingly relies on AI while reinforcing the irreplaceable role of human judgement, empathy and ethical responsibility in the legal system. This approach ensures that technological progress enhances rather than undermines the core values of legal education and practice.

AI tools can be a valuable asset to students in their development, not only by helping them with research but also by supporting critical thinking – a skill that, at this stage, sets us apart from AI tools. The very process of verifying the accuracy of AI-generated analyses can become a significant learning experience for students. By critically evaluating AI-generated content, students hone their ability to identify legal nuances, recognize inconsistencies and develop solid legal arguments. This practice not only strengthens their analytical skills but also emphasizes the importance of human oversight in legal decision making – an element that remains central to the legal profession.

To effectively teach students the responsible and ethical use of AI tools in legal practice, we propose the implementation of a method we called *the Retrospective Validation Method (RVM)*. This method is structured around the four fundamental stages of legal application – establishing legal status, determining facts, subsumption and decision making – and is designed to develop students' critical thinking skills by allowing them to compare AI-generated legal analyses with traditional legal reasoning. How does it work?

A fully anonymized case is shared with AI (for example, ChatGPT) asking for its solution. Then through controlled exercises, students identify AI's errors, assess its reliability and understand its limitations. This approach ensures that they do not blindly trust AI-generated outputs, but instead learn to critically assess and integrate them into their legal reasoning. By systematically testing AI's effectiveness and verifying its results, students develop a balanced perspective – neither blindly relying on AI nor dismissing it outright. Instead, they learn to treat AI as a complementary tool while maintaining human oversight, ethical responsibility and critical thinking. RVM provides a structured and practical environment (based on the four stages of legal application) in which students can gain first-hand experience in using AI for legal tasks. This method fosters an active, inquiry-based learning process, where students engage in legal problem solving while also assessing the credibility and accuracy of AI-generated content. Furthermore, by identifying AI's limitations, biases and occasional inconsistencies, students develop the skills necessary to apply AI in real-world legal practice responsibly.

In addition to pedagogical frameworks such as the RVM, law clinics – particularly in civil law jurisdictions – must adopt clear ethical guidelines and good practices for the use of GenAI technologies. As AI tools become increasingly prevalent, it is crucial to ensure their responsible implementation in clinical legal education. This requires not only teaching students how to use AI tools effectively, but also establishing institutional safeguards to protect client rights, maintain data security and preserve the integrity of legal reasoning.

First, transparency and informed client consent are fundamental. Before using GenAI systems for any client-related analysis, both students and supervisors must inform clients about the intended use of AI and obtain explicit consent. Documents shared with AI systems should be anonymized wherever possible, in compliance with data protection regulations such as the GDPR. Moreover, any AI-generated content should be clearly marked in clinic records as produced or supported by AI systems.

Second, data confidentiality and security must be prioritized. Even within an educational context, clinical settings are bound by personal data protection laws. All client-related input should be anonymized before being processed by AI tools. Where feasible, clinics should utilize on-premise AI systems or secure 'sandbox' environments that prevent the transmission of sensitive data to external servers. These practices are aligned with the ethical principles outlined in the European Commission for the Efficiency of Justice (CEPEJ) European Ethical Charter (2018),[43] which emphasize minimizing the risk of data breaches.

Third, and perhaps most importantly, human accountability and oversight must remain central. AI-generated outputs serve merely as preliminary suggestions; the final responsibility for all legal documents, analyses and conclusions lies with the students and their academic supervisors.

[43] Council of Europe, 'European Ethical Charter on the Use of Artifical Intelligence in Judicial Systems and Their Enivronment', www.europarl.europa.eu/cmsdata/196205/COUNCIL%20OF%20EUROPE%20-%20European%20Ethical%20Charter%20on%20the%20use%20of%20AI%20in%20judicial%20systems.pdf

Every document issued by the clinic should be reviewed and approved by a qualified legal supervisor. Introducing internal 'double-check' protocols for 10–20 per cent of AI-assisted outputs may further mitigate the risk of factual or interpretive errors.

Finally, we strongly emphasize the need for broader empirical research on the use of AI in civil law legal clinics. While a significant portion of the existing literature and regulatory guidelines focuses on common law jurisdictions, the distinctive characteristics of civil law systems – such as their reliance on codified statutes and doctrinal interpretation – require a different analytical approach. Empirical studies should examine how AI tools affect case handling, student learning and adherence to ethical standards within clinical practice. Such research should primarily focus on how, and to what extent, students and clinical supervisors actually use AI tools in their work. Much of the current theoretical discourse assumes that students are actively using these tools and that such usage is not always ethically sound. However, without comprehensive empirical data, this remains a claim unsubstantiated by evidence. Only through the analysis of real-world practices can we meaningfully improve both pedagogical strategies and regulatory frameworks – that is, develop informed guidelines and best practices grounded in actual clinical experiences.

In our opinion, there is no doubt that legal clinics – as well as broader legal education curricula – must acknowledge that AI is increasingly shaping the legal profession. Building on both structured pedagogical methods like RVM and a robust framework of ethical guidelines, law clinics are uniquely positioned to train future lawyers who are not only technologically adept but also ethically grounded. Therefore, instead of resisting technological advances, legal education should equip students with the ability to navigate AI's role in legal practice ethically and effectively. The integration of RVM, combined with institutional safeguards and empirical inquiry, ensures that future legal professionals are prepared to uphold ethical standards while leveraging AI as an aid rather than a substitute for human judgement.

Conclusion

Incorporating AI into legal education, particularly within student law clinics, requires striking an appropriate balance between leveraging technological advancements and preserving the fundamental human elements of legal practice. While AI can enhance the efficiency of legal research and analysis, it should not replace critical thinking, ethical reasoning and independent decision-making – skills that remain central to the legal profession. Therefore, the role of law clinics cannot be limited to introducing AI as a tool for process improvement; instead, they must ensure that students develop the competencies necessary to navigate an increasingly technologized legal landscape responsibly. To achieve this, we advocate for a structured and reflective approach to AI integration, using its tools to support the development of independent and critical thinking skills. In this context, we propose the implementation of the RVM. By comparing AI-generated legal analysis with traditional legal reasoning, students gain first-hand experience in evaluating the strengths and limitations of AI tools. This method reinforces the importance of human oversight and cultivates the analytical skills necessary for the responsible use of AI in legal practice. Rather than promoting blind reliance on technology, RVM encourages students to critically assess AI-generated results, verify legal conclusions, and apply the law in a more informed and nuanced manner.

However, beyond pedagogical innovations such as RVM, law clinics – especially those operating in civil law jurisdictions – must establish clear ethical guidelines and good practices for the use of generative AI systems. This includes ensuring transparency, informed client consent, data security and human accountability throughout the clinical process. The development and implementation of such safeguards is particularly pressing, given the sensitivity of legal data and the educational vulnerability of the clinical environment.

Furthermore, we strongly emphasize the need for comprehensive empirical research on how AI is being used in civil law legal clinics. While much of the existing discourse focuses on common law systems, the unique features of civil law – such as codified legal reasoning and doctrinal interpretation – demand context-specific investigation. Recent empirical studies conducted in the common law system demonstrated that LLM-based systems, when applied directly by litigants in person, may produce dangerously misleading outputs even in simple legal queries. Ryan and Hardie found that in over 40 per cent of tested queries, LLMs such as ChatGPT, Bing or Bard provided too generic or jurisdictionally incorrect answers. In certain cases, models defaulted to American law while being queried about legal problems in England and Wales.[44] This inability to reliably distinguish between jurisdictions, combined with users' limited legal literacy, creates the risk of inappropriate legal action based on erroneous AI-generated advice.[45] Even more importantly, current theoretical assumptions often presume that students actively use AI tools in clinical work, and that such use may not always align with ethical standards. Yet without empirical data, such claims remain unsubstantiated. Future research should examine how students and supervisors engage with AI in practice, how it influences learning outcomes and what ethical challenges arise. Only through systematic study of real-world experiences can we refine both pedagogical strategies and regulatory frameworks to support responsible AI adoption.

[44] Ryan and Hardie (n 41).

[45] ibid.

Rather than speculate on the future of AI in legal practice, this chapter focuses on the present, recognizing the need to pragmatically adapt legal education to ongoing technological developments. AI is already shaping the profession, but its long-term impact remains uncertain. Therefore, continuous empirical monitoring, ethical oversight and iterative refinement of educational methods are essential to ensure its ethical and effective use. By adopting a forward-thinking yet grounded approach, legal education can prepare future lawyers not only to effectively use AI, but also to maintain the ethical integrity and critical judgement that define the legal profession. Ultimately, law clinics must position themselves as both laboratories of innovation and guardians of ethical legal practice – ensuring that technological progress serves justice, not just efficiency. Any adoption of GenAI tools in legal clinics must be accompanied by continuous empirical evaluation, rigorous ethical safeguards and explicit client consent protocols. Failure to do so may not only reproduce but may even exacerbate existing inequalities in access to justice, especially when wealthier institutions and jurisdictions gain privileged access to more advanced AI systems.

References

Abramovich VE, 'La enseñanza del derecho en las clínicas legales de interés público. Materiales para una agenda temática. Cuaderno de Analisis Juridico. Serie Publicaciones Especiales' (1999) *Defensa Juridica del Interes Publico*, www.palermo.edu/derecho/pdf/Bibliografia-clinicas-juridicas/la_ensenanza_del_derecho_en_las_clinicas_legales_de_interes_publico(2).pdf

Acar OA, 'AI Prompt Engineering Isn't the Future' (2023) *Harvard Business Review*, https://hbr.org/2023/06/ai-prompt-engineering-isnt-the-future

Bednarek A, Kotalczyk M, Kuźma T, Maciejewska K, Wasik K, Wilg D and Wróblewska M, 'Raport 'Rekomendacje w zakresie zastosowania sztucznej inteligencji w sądownictwie i prokuraturze – przygotowany przez Grupę Roboczą ds. Sztucznej Inteligencji Podgrupa ds. etyki i prawa', www.gov.pl/attachment/5e60dcd0-2491-4f83-863c-4f59890a8295

Bogucki O, Zieliński M, Choduń A, Czepita S, Kanarek B and Municzewski A, 'Zintegrowanie polskich koncepcji wykładni prawa' (2009) *Ruch Prawniczy, Ekonomiczny i Socjologiczny* 23

Brayer P, 'A Law Clinic Systems Theory and the Pedagogy of Interaction: Creating a Legal Learning System' (Social Science Research Network 2012), https://papers.ssrn.com/abstract=3947923

Brown S, 'Machine Learning, Explained' (30 January 2025), https://mitsloan.mit.edu/ideas-made-to-matter/machine-learning-explained

Bugatti L, 'Legal Clinics as a Leading Force for Changes in Legal Education', https://romatrepress.uniroma3.it/wp-content/uploads/2023/10/02.-Bugatti-RTLR-1-2023-ebook-2.pdf

Cassens Weiss D, 'Latest Version of ChatGPT Aces Bar Exam with Score Nearing 90th Percentile' (*ABA Journal*), www.abajournal.com/web/article/latest-version-of-chatgpt-aces-the-bar-exam-with-score-in-90th-percentile

'CEPEJ European Ethical Charter on the Use of Artificial Intelligence (AI) in Judicial Systems and Their Environment – European Commission for the Efficiency of Justice (CEPEJ)', https://rm.coe.int/ethical-charter-en-for-publication-4-december-2018/16808f699c

Cesta W, 'Large Language Models and Community Legal Centres: Could Chatbots Help Reduce Australia's Justice Gap?' (2024) 49 *Alternative Law Journal* 181

Chien CV and Kim M, 'Generative AI and Legal Aid: Results from a Field Study and 100 Use Cases to Bridge the Access to Justice Gap' (Social Science Research Network, 14 March 2024), https://papers.ssrn.com/abstract=4733061

Choi JH, Monahan A and Schwarcz D, 'Lawyering in the Age of Artificial Intelligence' (Social Science Research Network, 7 November 2023), https://papers.ssrn.com/abstract=4626276

Council of Europe, 'European Ethical Charter on the Use of Artificial Intelligence in Judicial Systems and Their Environment', www.europarl.europa.eu/cmsdata/196205/COUNCIL%20OF%20EUROPE%20-%20European%20Ethical%20Charter%20on%20the%20use%20of%20AI%20in%20judicial%20systems.pdf

Dorf MC, 'Is Resistance to AI in the Law School Classroom Futile?' (19 July 2023), https://verdict.justia.com/2023/07/19/is-resistance-to-ai-in-the-law-school-classroom-futile

Grimes RH, 'Faking It and Making It? Using Simulation with Problem-Based Learning' in Caroline Strevens, Richard Grimes and Edward Phillips (eds), *Legal Education* (Ashgate 2014)

Karr J and Schultz J, 'The Legal Imitation Game: Generative AI's Incompatibility with Clinical Legal Education' (2024) 92 *Fordham Law Review* 1867

Korybski A and Leszczyński L (eds), *Stanowienie i Stosowanie Prawa: Elementy Teorii* (Wolters Kluwer 2015)

Leszczyński L, 'The Legal System: A Theoretical Approach' (2017) 64 *Annales Universitatis Mariae Curie-Skłodowska, sectio G (Ius)* 23

'Limitations and Risks of Using AI in Legal Practice' (Legal Practitioners' Liability Committee), https://lplc.com.au/resources/lplc-article/limitations-risks-ai-in-legal-practice

Lufrano R, 'NY Case Gives Insight to the Limits of AI in Law' (*National Law Review*), https://natlawreview.com/article/chatgpt-and-limits-ai-legal-research

Marchant G, 'Artificial Intelligence and the Future of Legal Practice' (2017) 14 *Scitech Lawyer* 20

'Mata v. Avianca, Inc., No. 1:2022cv01461 – Document 55 (S.D.N.Y. 2023)' (*Justia Law*, 4 February 2025), https://law.justia.com/cases/federal/district-courts/new-york/nysdce/1:2022cv01461/575368/55/

McCarl R, 'The Limits of Law and AI' (2022) 90 *University of Cincinnati Law Review*, https://scholarship.law.uc.edu/uclr/vol90/iss3/5

Mimoso MJ, Anjos M do R and Miranda C, 'Legal Clinics, a Challenge for the Teaching of Law' (2018) 5 *New Trends and Issues Proceedings on Humanities and Social Sciences* 101

Norton A, 'What Lessons from Past Technology Hype Cycles Can Be Applied to the Hype around Artificial Intelligence?' (*Medium*, 1 September 2023), https://medium.com/@angusnorton/what-lessons-from-past-technology-hype-cycles-can-be-applied-to-the-hype-around-artificial-b26db57a11c8

Oladipo JO, 'Artificial Intelligence and Law' (Social Science Research Network, 19 June 2023), https://papers.ssrn.com/abstract=4562175

Penalver EM, 'The Role of Skills Instruction in Legal Education' (2018) 13 *FIU Law Review* 229

Pietropaoli I, 'Use of Artificial Intelligence in Legal Practice' (British Institute of International and Comparative Law, 17 October 2023), www.biicl.org/publications/use-of-artificial-intelligence-in-legal-practice

Rodrigues R, 'Legal and Human Rights Issues of AI: Gaps, Challenges and Vulnerabilities' (2020) 4 *Journal of Responsible Technology* 100005

Rodriguez X, 'Artificial Intelligence (AI) and the Practice of Law' (2023) 24 *Sedona Conference Journal* 783

Ryan F and Hardie L, 'ChatGPT, I Have a Legal Question? The Impact of Generative AI Tools on Law Clinics and Access to Justice' (2024) 31 *International Journal of Clinical Legal Education* 166

Simshaw D, 'Access to A.I. Justice: Avoiding an Inequitable Two-Tiered System of Legal Services' (Social Science Research Network, 22 April 2022), https://papers.ssrn.com/abstract=4090984

Sloan K, 'Some Law Professors Fear ChatGPT's Rise as Others See Opportunity', *Reuters* (11 January 2023), www.reuters.com/legal/legalindustry/some-law-professors-fear-chatgpts-rise-others-see-opportunity-2023-01-10/

Surden H, 'Artificial Intelligence and Law: An Overview' (2019) *Georgia State University Law Review*, https://scholar.law.colorado.edu/faculty-articles/1234

Susskind R, *Online Courts and the Future of Justice* (OUP 2021)

Susskind R, *Tomorrow's Lawyers: An Introduction to Your Future* (3rd edn, OUP 2023)

Trubalska J, *Podstawy Prawa. Podręcznik*, vol 8 (Innovatio Press Wydawnictwo Naukowe Wyższej Szkoły Ekonomii i Innowacji 2021), https://wydawnictwo.wsei.eu/sklep/podstawy-prawa-tom-viii-2/

'What Is AI (Artificial Intelligence)?', www.mckinsey.com/featured-insights/mckinsey-explainers/what-is-ai#/

Wilkins S, 'As AI Advances, Is Prompt Engineering the Next Crucial Legal Skill?' (*Legal Tech News*), www.law.com/legaltechnews/2023/04/25/as-ai-advances-is-prompt-engineering-the-next-crucial-legal-skill/

Wizner S, 'The Law School Clinic: Legal Education in the Interests of Justice' (2002) 70 *Fordham Law Review* 1929

Wizner S and Aiken J, 'Teaching and Doing: The Role of Law School Clinics in Enhancing Access to Justice' (2004) *Faculty Scholarship Series*, https://openyls.law.yale.edu/handle/20.500.13051/1104

Wojciechowski M, *Pewność prawa* (Wydawnictwo Uniwersytetu Gdańskiego 2014), https://repozytorium.bg.ug.edu.pl/info/book/UOGe5a4650a98b244bbb963e651246887ac/

Wróblewski J, 'Zagadnienia Procesowego Modelu Sądowego Stosowania Prawa' (1986) *Studia Prawnicze* 3

13

Clinical Legal Education in Ukraine During Armed Conflict Caused by Russian Aggression

Mariia Tsypiashchuk, Liliia Amelicheva, Yuliia Matvieieva and Liudmyla Rudenko

Introduction

The first legal clinics in Ukraine emerged in the late 1990s. They primarily function as structural units within higher education institutions (HEIs), serving as practical training bases for law students, though they do not operate as separate legal entities. The legal framework governing their activities is enshrined in the Law of Ukraine 'On Higher Education' (2014) (Clause 2, Part 7, Article 33)[1] and the Model Regulation on the Legal Clinic of a Higher Educational Institution (2006).[2]

In recent years, there has been a growing trend towards integrating legal clinical courses into academic curricula. Most legal clinics provide free legal assistance to the public, including legal information, consultations and assistance in drafting legal documents, with representation being less common. Specialization remains rare, though some clinics focus on specific areas, such as the legal clinic for military personnel at the Ukrainian Catholic University in Lviv, established in 2019, or the war-related legal clinic at Sumy State University, established with the support of the USAID 'Justice for All' programme in 2023–2024.

[1] The Law of Ukraine 'On Higher Education' (2014), https://zakon.rada.gov.ua/laws/show/1556-18#n530

[2] Model Regulation on the Legal Clinic of a Higher Educational Institution (2006), https://zakon.rada.gov.ua/laws/show/z0956-06#Text

Beyond legal assistance, most clinics engage in legal education, often employing the Street Law method. Since the early 2000s, the Association (initially the Foundation) of Legal Clinics of Ukraine (ALCU) has been active, currently uniting around 60 clinics, with its register[3] updated annually. In 2014, the legal clinic community adopted internal Standards of Operations of Legal Clinics of Ukraine,[4] which are periodically revised. In 2017, the Quality Performance Assessment Tool for Legal Clinics in Ukraine (QPAT)[5] was introduced, providing a framework for monitoring and evaluation.

ALCU facilitates the exchange of best practices among legal clinics, integrates them into project initiatives and supports newly established clinics to enhance legal assistance, particularly for vulnerable populations and those affected by the armed conflict. It also conducts research on the evolving needs of legal clinics and displaced Ukrainians, especially during the ongoing conflict, and develops recommendations aimed at addressing these needs. These recommendations are submitted to relevant authorities and HEIs to improve access to legal support.

Since their establishment in the late 1990s, Ukrainian legal clinics have primarily focused on providing legal assistance in domestic matters. However, from the outset, they also had to address international law issues, integrating them into their educational programmes and legal consultations. This need arose after Ukraine ratified the European Convention on Human Rights on 17 July 1997,[6] prompting clinics to introduce specialized sections in their curricula on applications to the European Court of Human Rights (ECtHR). Over time, the Standards of Operations of Legal Clinics of Ukraine came to include the structure and topics of modules for a model curriculum on clinical legal education. One of the key topics covered in this framework is 'Drafting Applications to the European Court of Human Rights by a Legal Clinic'. The ALCU community acknowledges the importance of these subjects in shaping future lawyers and providing legal assistance to the population.

Ukrainian clinics have actively engaged with ECtHR applications. The Ad Astra clinic at Lesya Ukrainka Eastern European (Volyn) National University

---

3 *Register of Legal Clinics of Ukraine* (2024), https://legalclinics.in.ua/wp-content/uploads/2020/11/Reyestr-AYUKU-2024.pdf

4 'Standards of Operations of Legal Clinics of Ukraine' (2014, with amendments), https://legalclinics.in.ua/en/standards-of-the-legal-clinics-in-ukraine/

5 Quality Performance Assessment Tool for Legal Clinics in Ukraine (2017), https://legalclinics.in.ua/wp-content/uploads/Legal-Clinics_Monitoring-Instrument-Final_Eng.pdf

6 The Law of Ukraine 'Law on the Ratification of the Convention for the Protection of Human Rights and Fundamental Freedoms of 1950, the First Protocol, and Protocols No. 2, 4, 7, and 11 to the Convention' (1997), Verkhovna Rada of Ukraine, https://zakon.rada.gov.ua/laws/show/475/97-%D0%B2%D1%80#Text

(Lutsk) successfully prepared applications, leading to their admissibility and further consideration by the ECtHR. Notably, the clinic contributed to two landmark cases: *Gutka v Ukraine*[7] and *Yeroshkina v Ukraine*.[8] Similarly, the legal clinic at the National University, 'Odesa Law Academy' played a role in the case of *Masneva v Ukraine*.[9]

From the beginning, Ukrainian clinics recognized the necessity of studying international human rights law, a need that became apparent soon after their establishment. Whether operating independently or collaborating with organizations such as the Ukrainian Helsinki Human Rights Union, these clinics strengthened their expertise in international law, acquiring skills in case analysis and legal document preparation for ECtHR applications.

In 2012, Ukraine introduced a state system of free legal assistance, regulated by the Law of Ukraine 'On Free Legal Assistance'.[10] This service is provided through a network of bureaus and centres, staffed by their own employees and contracted attorneys-at-law. However, legal clinics are not part of this network, as their primary goal in Ukraine is educational.

Like most institutions and individuals in Ukraine, legal clinics faced significant challenges following the onset of Russian aggression in 2014. They were forced to adapt to constantly evolving conditions, operating amid ongoing physical risks and uncertainty.

Free legal assistance is available to various societal groups who cannot afford paid legal services or belong to vulnerable populations, such as orphans, refugees, veterans and detained persons. With the onset of war in Ukraine, the number of vulnerable individuals has risen dramatically. Millions have been internally displaced, and the number of veterans, missing persons and those in captivity – not to mention their family members, who are facing complex legal issues and require social support – has grown significantly. Additionally, many have lost their jobs and sources of income, increasing the population of low-income individuals. At the same time, the Ukrainian government has had to redirect resources and funds towards military needs, especially following the full-scale invasion, to protect the country.

---

7 *Gutka v Ukraine* Application No 45846/05 (8 April 2010).

8 *Yeroshkina v Ukraine* Application No 31572/03 (20 December 2011).

9 *Masneva v Ukraine* Application No 5952/07 (18 June 2009). The *Gutka* and *Yeroshkina* rulings addressed violations of Article 6(1) of the European Convention on Human Rights, which guarantees the right to a fair trial. In these cases, the Court found excessive delays in legal proceedings that did not meet the standard of reasonable time. Meanwhile, the *Masneva v. Ukraine* decision identified a breach of the procedural aspect of Article 2 (Right to Life), concluding that the state failed to conduct an effective investigation into the applicant's son's death.

10 The Law of Ukraine 'On Free Legal Assistance' (2012), https://zakon.rada.gov.ua/laws/show/3460-17#Text

In this context, legal clinics, alongside civil society, play a crucial role in providing free legal assistance and information to those affected by the war in Ukraine.

The armed conflict in Ukraine: background and current situation

The armed conflict in Ukraine, triggered by Russian aggression, was officially declared on 13 April 2014 when the President of Ukraine enacted Decree No 405/2014,[11] implementing the National Security and Defence Council's decision on urgent measures to counter the terrorist threat and protect territorial integrity. However, Russian aggression had already begun with the occupation of Crimea in February 2014, followed by the invasion of the Donetsk and Luhansk regions. On 24 February 2022, the Russian Federation started a full-scale invasion of Ukraine.

The conflict has had two prolonged 'hot phases' of intense hostilities. The first took place between 2014 and 2015 in the Donetsk and Luhansk regions, gradually subsiding after the Minsk agreements of 12 February 2015.[12] The second phase began with Russia's full-scale invasion on 24 February 2022, leading to the introduction of martial law under Decree No 2102-IX,[13] and continues to the present. Between these phases, hostilities persisted in eastern Ukraine, though at a lower intensity. Despite there being almost no hostilities in Crimea, the peninsula has been under occupation for over a decade, leading to a massive outflow of internally displaced persons (IDPs), and numerous war crimes and human rights atrocities committed by Russia. These include, among many others, arbitrary detentions, forced disappearances, torture and sexual violence, violations of the rights to life, freedom of speech and conscience, the right to a fair trial and the appropriation of property.[14]

---

[11] Decree of the President of Ukraine, 'On the Decision of the National Security and Defense Council of Ukraine of April 13, 2014 "On Urgent Measures to Overcome the Terrorist Threat and Preserve the Territorial Integrity of Ukraine"', No 405/2014 from 14 April 2014, https://zakon.rada.gov.ua/laws/show/405/2014#Text

[12] United Nations Peacemaker, 'Package of Measures for the Implementation of the Minsk Agreements' (2025), https://peacemaker.un.org/en/node/8827

[13] Decree of the President of Ukraine No 64/2022, 'On the Imposition of Martial Law in Ukraine', No 2102-IX from 24 February 2022, www.president.gov.ua/documents/642022-41397

[14] See, for example: Office of the United Nations, High Commissioner for Human Rights, 'Report on the Situation of Human Rights in the Temporarily Occupied Autonomous Republic of Crimea and the City of Sevastopol, Ukraine 13 September 2017 to 30 June

From the very beginning of the 2014 Russian invasion, Russian invaders committed mass war crimes and crimes against humanity in both the occupied territories and throughout Ukraine. Ukrainian citizens have been subjected to wilful murder, torture or inhuman treatment, including biological experiments, wilful infliction of severe suffering or serious bodily harm, extensive destruction and appropriation of property not justified by military necessity and carried out unlawfully and wantonly, outrages upon personal dignity, including humiliating and degrading treatment, sexual violence, including rape and enslavement, and many others.[15]

The war has led to significant loss of life, with many Ukrainian soldiers and civilians killed, wounded, captured or missing. According to the United Nations High Commissioner for Refugees (UNHCR), between 24 February 2022, and 30 November 2024, over 12,340 civilians were killed and more than 27,836 were injured.[16] Additionally, the Ukrainian Commissioner for Missing Persons reported nearly 63,000 people – both military personnel and civilians – registered as missing under special circumstances by the end of November 2024.[17]

The conflict has also triggered two major waves of internal displacement, as civilians fled occupied and frontline areas to safer regions under Ukrainian control. By 2 March 2025, the Ministry of Social Policy had registered 4,622,761 IDPs, including 2,765,063 women (59.81 per cent), 1,857,698 men (40.19 per cent) and approximately 889,000 children.[18]

During the second wave of displacement, many Ukrainians sought refuge abroad, primarily in EU countries, receiving temporary protection or refugee

2018', www.ohchr.org/sites/default/files/Documents/Countries/UA/CrimeaThematicReport10Sept2018_EN.pdf; Institute for War and Peace Reporting (IWPR), 'War Crimes in Crimea', https://iwpr.net/global-voices/war-crimes-crimea

15 See, for example: Office of the Prosecutor, International Criminal Court, 'Report on Preliminary Examination Activities' (2017) 19–27, www.icc-cpi.int/sites/default/files/itemsDocuments/2017-PE-rep/2017-otp-rep-PE_ENG.pdf; Office of the United Nations High Commissioner for Human Rights (OHCHR), 'Advanced Unedited Version – Human Rights Council Fifty-Eighth Session' (2025), www.ohchr.org/sites/default/files/documents/hrbodies/hrcouncil/sessions-regular/session58/advance-version/A-HRC-58-67-auv.docx

16 'Izumi Nakamitsu (UNODA) on the Threats to International Peace and Security – Security Council, 9827th Meeting', *UN Web TV*, https://webtv.un.org/en/asset/k10/k103tf1mnj

17 'Nearly 63,000 people Are Missing in Ukraine Due to the War', *Ukrainska Pravda* (3 February 2025), www.pravda.com.ua/eng/news/2025/02/3/7496547/

18 State Enterprise Information and Computing Center, 'Dashboard of Internally Displaced Persons (IDPs) in Ukraine', Ministry of Social Policy of Ukraine (2025), www.ioc.gov.ua/analytics/dashboard-vpo

status. The UNHCR estimated that by 16 January 2025, approximately 6,863,400 Ukrainians had fled, with data largely provided by the authorities.[19] Between the two phases of intense conflict, displacement continued, but on a smaller scale.

Adapting Ukrainian legislation to EU requirements: a new Ministry of Justice focus

In the context of the war and emergency situations in Ukraine, the support of international organizations is of paramount importance. While we recognize the challenges international bodies face in ensuring peace and sustainable development, Ukraine's cooperation with key organizations such as the EU and the North Atlantic Treaty Organization (NATO) remains a decisive factor in its continued progress and future victory in the war against Russia.

An irreversible course towards European and Euro-Atlantic integration was taken by Ukraine even before Russia's full-scale invasion. On 7 February 2019, constitutional amendments were adopted to solidify this strategic direction. This commitment stems from the events of 2013, when former President Viktor Yanukovych's refusal to sign the Association Agreement with the EU triggered the *Revolution of Dignity*. Millions of citizens across Ukraine protested against the usurpation of power and in defence of their right to free democratic development, the rule of law and human rights.

Following the full-scale Russian invasion on 24 February 2022, Ukraine's European integration efforts gained even greater urgency. The country now relies on substantial financial, military and economic support from international organizations and individual states in its fight to preserve independence. A landmark moment occurred on 23 June 2022, when Ukraine was granted EU candidate status. This development necessitates extensive reforms in the state's legal, economic, financial and tax systems – a long and complex process.

As part of Ukraine's legal system reform, national legislation must be aligned with the EU *acquis communautaire*, a framework consisting of more than 14,000 legal acts and nearly 9,000 rulings by the Court of Justice of the European Union, covering a vast range of regulatory domains. The granting of candidate status and the European Council's official announcement in December 2023 to begin accession negotiations have placed Ukraine before

[19] UNHCR, 'Ukraine Refugee Situation' (2025), https://data.unhcr.org/en/situations/ukraine

a series of major challenges, with the adaptation of Ukrainian law to EU standards being the most critical task.[20]

These developments present significant opportunities for Ukrainian legal clinics. The clinical legal education system can introduce new courses and expand EU law topics, fostering expertise in European legal frameworks. Additionally, clinics can initiate research and advocacy projects, participate in legislative drafting, and develop proposals to align Ukrainian laws with EU regulations. Meanwhile, the ongoing military-political situation in Ukraine has created new legal challenges for the general population, alongside existing hardships, which have made themselves felt in the matters brought to legal clinics.

Emerging challenges for Ukrainian legal clinics amid armed conflict

Significant legal uncertainties have been created by threats to life and security, loss of documents due to displacement, gaps in legislation on citizens' rights under martial law, mobilization procedures, and social protections for combatants and families in connection with war-related disabilities. This has meant that across all territories under Ukrainian control, the demand for accessible legal assistance, reliable legal information and justice services has grown significantly. Legal clinics continue to support the population, adapting their efforts to meet the evolving challenges of wartime. However, they themselves face considerable hardships due to the ongoing conflict. To ensure they can provide quality legal help and information to vulnerable communities, clinics' own operational needs must be addressed first. Identifying and responding to these needs is essential for rebuilding and strengthening clinical legal education and operations in Ukraine.

The needs of legal clinics during the current conflict can be categorized based on their core functions, as outlined in foundational operational documents such as the Model Regulation on Legal Clinics and the Standards of Operations of Legal Clinics of Ukraine, as well as institutional regulations governing their activities within HEIs.

These groups of ranked needs include the following:

- *Security*: ensuring shelter, protection during chemical or radiation alerts, access to personal protective equipment, first-aid kits and adequate heating in colder months or during blackouts.
- *Organizational and technical issues*: providing appropriate office space for training and client consultations, repairing premises, furnishing clinics

[20] Mykola Kozyubra, 'Challenges Facing Ukraine on the Way to Its Accession to the European Union: Constitutional and Legal Aspects' in *Political and Legal Consequences of Ukraine's Accession to the European Union and NATO* (WSPiA Rzeszowską Szkołę Wyższą 2024) 15–38.

with necessary equipment, and ensuring consistent lighting, internet access and mobile communication.
- *Personnel*: addressing staff shortages and turnover, ensuring managerial leadership, securing legal clinic staff positions and offering training in clinical management.
- *Legal issues*: securing official recognition for specialized legal clinics, ensuring client confidentiality in accordance with legal requirements, clearly defining the roles and responsibilities of clinic employees and student clinicians, and enabling the formalization of partnerships through memorandums that establish the legal clinic as an independent entity.
- *Financial issues*: providing fair remuneration for clinic leadership and supervisors, offering incentives for active clinicians and competition winners, and securing grant funding to sustain operations.
- *Communication with ALCU*: expanding training in clinical management, digital literacy, international humanitarian and criminal law, grant writing, and fostering connections with international legal clinics and organizations. Conducting independent assessments to identify specific clinic needs and overseeing the administration of ALCU-led projects.
- *Social wellbeing*: addressing housing and livelihood concerns, assisting staff with obtaining IDP status where appropriate and offering psychological support.

The extent to which clinics can address these needs depends on their classification, considering the evolving military-political landscape in Ukraine since 2014.

Legal clinics in Ukraine, operating under varying circumstances, can be broadly categorized into five groups based on the varying challenges and operational complexities which they face:

1. *Frontline*: primarily conducting online activities in conflict zones, struggling alongside their affiliated HEIs to avoid shutdown.
2. *Twice-relocated*: displaced first in 2014–2015 and again in 2022–2023, being forced to rebuild their operations in new locations from the ground up for the second (or more) time.
3. *Liberated territory*: located in areas temporarily occupied in 2022–2023 and later reclaimed, now facing the aftermath of looting and infrastructural damage.
4. *Long-term relocated*: relocated from occupied territories in 2014–2015 and gradually re-established over the past decade, but still struggling with material and technical needs.
5. *Sustainable legal clinics in controlled territories*: operating in relatively secure regions with dynamic development, often overwhelmed with caseloads and facing wage-related concerns under martial law.

These proposed classifications help assess the evolving needs of legal clinics, with consideration of the research conducted by ALCU, academics and experts within legal clinical education since 2014. Clinics classifying in higher categories (from 5, the lowest to 1, the highest) tend to have broader access to resources and deeper coverage of these essential needs.

Additionally, it is important to analyse how the needs of legal clinics have changed and/or expanded within each of the two 'hot phases' (2014–2015, 24 February 2022 to present) of the ongoing armed conflict caused by Russian aggression.

During the first phase, legal clinics from relocated HEIs in Crimea and certain areas of Donetsk and Luhansk regions suffered operational disruptions – mostly not due to direct shelling, but rather the forced takeover of university premises, leadership replacements and restrictions on pro-Ukrainian faculty.

For the most part, neither the administration of the HEIs nor the leadership of the legal clinics were able to evacuate paper case archives, equipment, office supplies or furniture, as occupiers prevented them from doing so at checkpoints. As a result, relocated HEIs and legal clinics had to rebuild from scratch – establishing documentation, staffing, funding and operational infrastructure, a process that typically took one to three years. Some clinics ceased to exist after relocating to Ukraine-controlled territory due to a shortage of specialized legal clinical professionals.

Clinics in unoccupied areas of the Donetsk and Luhansk regions, as well as nearby regions (Kharkiv, Dnipropetrovsk and Zaporizhzhia), took on a significant burden, assisting IDPs, supporting Anti-Terrorist Operation (ATO) service personnel, and providing legal guidance on civil, administrative, labour and social security issues. Many displaced civilians sought to visit relatives in occupied territories, facing legal hurdles in crossing borders and demarcation lines.

At that time, the Ministry of Education and Science of Ukraine provided considerable organizational, financial and material aid to relocated institutions and clinics, enabling a relatively swift recovery in many cases.

A few years before the second 'hot' phase of the armed conflict, the COVID-19 pandemic occurred, posing a significant challenge for the operations of the aforementioned clinics as well as all other clinics across the country. Their primary needs remained consistent: acquiring new digital skills and tools to facilitate the transition to remote clinical legal education, while also ensuring adherence to sanitary and epidemiological regulations during in-person interactions between staff, clinicians and clients.

The full-scale invasion has made it difficult for legal clinics in Ukraine to function effectively. Many struggle due to faculty and student losses, reduced funding and damaged infrastructure. As a result, their ability to provide practical training has weakened, affecting their role in legal education.

Under martial law, nearly all clinics face similar challenges, albeit of varying degrees. This makes it crucial to find new ways for legal clinics to operate and encourage innovative practices in law schools.[21]

Despite the difficulties that Ukrainian clinics themselves face, their role in providing legal aid and clear legal information remains vital as demand increases significantly. Ukrainians suffer from severe property destruction and loss, and experience other legal challenges. They need guidance on lawful border crossings under martial law and residency in EU countries under temporary protection status and so on. Thus, legal clinics also ensure that legal educators and students properly utilize online information management and understand key martial law regulations,[22] particularly the provisions of the Law of Ukraine 'On the Legal Regime of Martial Law' (2015 No 389-VIII).[23]

After the first few months following the full-scale invasion, in May–June 2022, ALCU conducted an internal assessment of the challenges and difficulties Ukrainian clinics were facing. The most critical issues identified in the survey included limitations in terms of accepting clients and conducting legal education activities due to security concerns; the outflow of clinical legal faculty and students abroad; and the closure of one third of clinics due to damage caused by shelling, preventing clients from accessing legal services.

Other urgent needs reported by the respondents included training in digital technologies to enable remote legal work and proficiency in databases such as LexisNexis, Hein Online and Liga Zakon. Financial support for clinics was of course an issue, along with specialized training for supporting war-traumatized clients. A corollary of this was a need for psychological resilience programmes for staff and clinicians, and expanded education for clinical legal students and staff in key legal areas, including international law, international humanitarian law, genocide investigations and reparations collection. Collaborative legal counselling for clients with foreign colleagues was also indicated in the list of needs.[24]

---

21 Yuliia Lomzhets, 'Ensuring Access to Justice during Wartime: Legal Clinics Will Assist Displaced Ukrainians', Association of Legal Clinics of Ukraine (2022), https://legalclinics.in.ua/zabezpechennya-dostupu-do-pravosuddya-v-umovah-vijny-yurydychni-kliniky-dopomagatymut-peremishhenym-ukrayintsyam/

22 Iryna Bohatiuk, 'The Activities of Legal Clinics under Martial Law' (2022) 3(64) *Juridical Bulletin* 202.

23 The Law of Ukraine 'On the Legal Regime of Martial Law' (2015), https://zakon.rada.gov.ua/laws/show/389-19#Text

24 Davida Finger, Susan Felstiner, Michelle Greenberg-Kobrin and Mariia Tsypiashchuk, 'Empowering Ukraine's First Legal Responders: Ukrainian-US Collaboration and Clinics' (2024) Loyola University New Orleans College of Law Research Paper No 2024–17, 31 *International Journal of Clinical Legal Education* 147.

Areas of international law that legal clinics have encountered during the war

Earlier in this chapter, we noted the longstanding connection and interaction of Ukrainian legal clinics with international law. Nevertheless, the onset of war brought with it new educational challenges. There is a growing need to enhance student training in international humanitarian law, international criminal law and global human rights protection mechanisms. International humanitarian law plays a crucial role in safeguarding victims of armed conflict and restricting warfare methods. While its provisions may seem abstract in peacetime, during war they become essential tools for ensuring protection, life and health.[25]

Since 2022, the number of seminars and training sessions on international humanitarian law for legal clinics has significantly increased, organized or supported by international organizations such as the United Nations Development Programme (UNDP), the United States Agency for International Development (USAID), the Council of Europe and the Organization for Security and Co-operation in Europe (OSCE). This reflects society's growing need to understand legal protections for war victims, the classification of war crimes, accountability for violations and personal security concerns.

Such training has led some clinics, including the Legal Clinic of the Ukrainian Catholic University (Lviv) and Vasyl Stefanyk Precarpathian National University (Ivano-Frankivsk), to engage actively in documenting war crimes. ALCU and individual clinics in its network have also organized various events addressing wartime legal issues.

In November 2022, the *Street Law Hackathon: Ensuring the Legal Needs of People in Wartime* and the *Third Street Law Festival* took place.[26] On 9 February 2023, the *All-Ukrainian Round Table: Countering the Genocide of the Ukrainian People* was held, co-organized by ALCU, Vasyl Stus Donetsk National University, the Council of Young Scientists under the Ministry of Education and Science of Ukraine, and the Scientist Support Office.[27]

---

25 See, for example, 'International Humanitarian Law: Protection of War Victims and Limitations on Warfare', *Prometheus* (2024), https://prometheus.org.ua/prometheus-free/international-humanitarian-law/

26 Association of Legal Clinics of Ukraine, 'Street Law Hackathon Guide: Meeting the Legal Needs of People in Wartime' (2023), https://legalclinics.in.ua/en/street-law-hackathon-guide-meeting-the-legal-needs-of-people-in-wartime/

27 Donetsk National University, 'All-Ukrainian Roundtable: Countering the Genocide of the Ukrainian People' (2023), https://news.donnu.edu.ua/2023/02/10/vseukrayinskyj-kruglyj-stil-protydiya-genoczydu-ukrayinskogo-narodu/

In the spring of 2024, an online school was launched for legal clinic students working as part of a specialized legal clinic at the Educational and Scientific Institute of Law of Sumy State University. Designed to enhance the professional training of clinic legal consultants and law students assisting war-affected individuals, this programme was implemented under the *Development of the Network of Legal Clinics of Ukraine through Strengthening National and International Cooperation* project, supported by the USAID 'Justice for All' programme.[28]

On 14 April 2022, the Verkhovna Rada (Parliament) of Ukraine adopted the resolution 'On the Commission of Genocide in Ukraine by the Russian Federation', recognizing the actions carried out by the Armed Forces of the Russian Federation and its political and military leadership during the latest phase of its armed aggression against Ukraine – beginning on 24 February 2022 – as genocide against the Ukrainian people. The Verkhovna Rada appealed to the UN, the European Parliament, the Parliamentary Assembly of the Council of Europe, the OSCE Parliamentary Assembly and the NATO Parliamentary Assembly, as well as the governments and parliaments of foreign states, urging them to acknowledge the Russian Federation's genocide of the Ukrainian people, along with its crimes against humanity and war crimes committed in Ukraine.[29]

As a result, the study of international humanitarian law, war crimes and genocide has become a national priority, prompting clinics to actively engage with these issues. Since 2005/2006 (with a hiatus between 2011 and 2014), Ukraine has hosted the National Client Consultation Competition (NCCC), an annual competition among clinic teams aimed at deepening law students' knowledge and interest in preventive law and the consultative aspects of legal practice. The winners of the national round go on to represent Ukraine in the Brown-Mosten International Client Consultation Competition (BM ICCC).[30]

The increasing urgency to expand expertise in international humanitarian law was reflected in the 2024 editions of both the NCCC and the BM ICCC, jointly hosted by Poland and Ukraine, emphasizing these vital legal issues.

---

[28] Association of Legal Clinics of Ukraine, 'Training for Consultants of the Specialized Legal Clinic on War-Related Issues' (2024), https://legalclinics.in.ua/start-navchannya-dlya-konsultantiv-spetsializovanoyi-yurydychnoyi-kliniky-z-pytan-pov-yazanyh-z-vijnoyu/

[29] Verkhovna Rada of Ukraine, 'Resolution of the Verkhovna Rada of Ukraine on the Statement of the Verkhovna Rada of Ukraine "On the Commission of Genocide in Ukraine by the Russian Federation"' (2020), https://zakon.rada.gov.ua/laws/show/2188-20#Text

[30] Brown-Mosten International Client Consultation Competition, '2024 Competition – International Client Consultation Competition' (2024), www.brownmosten.com/2024-competition.html

The Ukrainian team undertook intensive preparation for the competition, supported by coaches Liliia Amelicheva and Tetiana Mykhailina, along with a broad team of practising Ukrainian lawyers, past competition participants and trainers. Their dedication yielded impressive results: during the qualifying rounds, the Ukrainian team ranked among the top contenders – Kateryna and Vladyslava earned the highest scores among 22 participating teams, joining the US and Australia as leaders advancing to the semifinals. Ultimately, the Ukrainian team secured a place among the world's top nine teams, with Scotland emerging as the competition's overall winner.[31] During these competitions, students tackled complex cases involving civilians whose rights have been violated due to the actions of the occupiers, encountering instances of war crimes and breaches of the laws and customs of war.

As of May 2024, more than 10,000 Ukrainian servicemen were held captive by the Russian Federation – these being the most optimistic estimates.[32] The Ukrainian Commissioner for Human Rights reported that as of November 2024, Ukraine had successfully returned 3,767 captives, of whom 168 were civilians, while the remainder were prisoners of war (PoWs).[33] By December 2024, over 16,000 Ukrainian civilians remained in captivity, with only 168 individuals released.[34]

Daniel Bell, head of the UN Human Rights Monitoring Mission in Ukraine, confirmed widespread torture of Ukrainian PoWs by Russian occupiers, beginning with their initial interrogations.[35] This testimony aligns with previous reports from the UN Monitoring Mission and corroborates longstanding assessments by the Institute for the Study of War regarding

---

31 Association of Legal Clinics of Ukraine, 'Ukrainian Experience at the International Client Counseling Competition 2024' (2024), https://legalclinics.in.ua/ukrayinskyj-dosvid-na-mizhnarodnyh-zmagannyah-z-konsultuvannya-kliyentiv-2024-roku/

32 'MIPL: Over 10,000 Ukrainian Military Personnel Held Captive by Russia', *Deutsche Welle* (2024), www.dw.com/uk/mipl-u-poloni-rf-perebuvaut-ponad-10-tisac-ukrainskih-vijskovih/a-69009006

33 'Ukraine Has Returned over 3,500 Ukrainians from Russian Captivity – Lubinets', *Suspilne News* (2024), https://suspilne.media/884537-z-rosijskogo-polonu-ukraina-povernula-ponad-35-tisaci-ukrainciv-lubinec/

34 'How Many Ukrainian Civilians Are in Russian Captivity? Lubinets Revealed the Number', *Pravda Life* (2024), https://life.pravda.com.ua/society/skilki-civilnih-ukrajinciv-perebuvayut-u-rosiyskomu-poloni-lubinec-nazvav-cifru-305399/

35 'Tonight on TV: Torture of Ukrainian Soldiers, Olympic Athlete Controversy, Venezuela Unrest', *NOS Nieuwsuur* (2024), https://nos.nl/nieuwsuur/artikel/2531435-vanavond-op-tv-martelingen-oekraiense-militairen-ophef-olympische-sporter-onrust-venezuela. Mr Daniel Bell reported: 'They are tortured during the first interrogation. They are beaten with metal rods and sticks and subjected to severe electric shocks. They are stripped naked. It is horrible. It is the worst I have seen in my 20-year career, visiting prisoners on behalf of the UN. Torture is widespread and systematic. 95% of Ukrainian prisoners of war have been tortured, and this constitutes a war crime.'

Russia's systematic violations of international human rights and humanitarian law in occupied Ukraine and against Ukrainian PoWs.

These circumstances collectively mean that legal clinics find themselves having to address an extremely wide (and important) range of issues which bring together considerations of international humanitarian law, international criminal law and free legal aid.

Complex legal issues

Mobilization and military service

Since 2014, and particularly following the full-scale invasion in 2022, legal clinics have faced an urgent need to provide legal assistance to military personnel, veterans and the families of fallen defenders of Ukraine. The declaration of martial law in 2022 and general mobilization in Ukraine required the enlistment of all conscripted men aged 25–60 for service in the Armed Forces. The legislation sets out the procedures for mobilization, exemptions and the updating of military registration data. In response to the challenges brought about by martial law, amendments have been introduced to mobilization regulations, specifically regarding liability under law for failing to update registration data, delays in doing so, and failure or delays in undergoing military medical commissions.

Between 2014 and 2022, legal clinics primarily dealt with issues such as combatant status granting procedure, terminating or extending service contracts, and providing legal assistance in obtaining free land for agriculture, building a house and so on for veterans of the anti-terrorist operation. The introduction of the anti-terrorist operation regime in parts of Donetsk and Luhansk regions on 14 April 2014,[36] later replaced by the Joint Forces Operation on 30 April 2018, and martial law after 24 February 2022, established a framework of benefits and social guarantees for servicemen involved in military operations.

Given that military law was not a standard component of classical law school curricula, dedicated research and analysis became necessary. The complexity of applying legal norms required a thorough examination of judicial practice, which was often ambiguous. Clinical faculty members and students also had to study local regulations issued by the Ministry of Defence of Ukraine. In response, military law emerged as a specialized academic discipline, and legal clinics adapted accordingly. Notably, the Legal Clinic

[36] Decree of the President of Ukraine, 'On the Decision of the National Security and Defense Council of Ukraine of February 28, 2018 "On the Implementation of Measures to Ensure National Security and Defense of Ukraine"', No 116/2018 from 28 February 2018, https://zakon.rada.gov.ua/laws/show/116/2018#Text

of the Ukrainian Catholic University (Lviv) has developed expertise in providing legal assistance to servicemen, veterans and victims of the armed conflict in Ukraine.

Following the full-scale invasion, clinics expanded their scope of work to include appeals against administrative penalties for violations of mobilization legislation, as well as refusals to grant deferments. A substantial number of cases now involve legal assistance for military personnel, including support in preparing reports, challenging the inaction of military units regarding soldiers' petitions and disputing decisions made by military medical commissions.

Legal assistance for families of prisoners of war, missing persons and fallen soldiers

One of the most complicated areas for legal clinics is assisting family members of PoWs. In Ukraine, several institutions hold authority in this domain, including the National Information Bureau, the Coordination Headquarters for the Treatment of Prisoners of War, the Commissioner for Missing Persons in Special Circumstances, the Joint Centre for the Search and Release of Captives under the Security Service of Ukraine, the Central Tracing Agency of the International Committee of the Red Cross, the National Police of Ukraine, and the Commissioner for Human Rights of the Verkhovna Rada of Ukraine. Given Ukraine's lack of prior experience with PoW exchanges on this scale, only a limited number of legal specialists fully understand the procedures involved in working with both national bodies and international institutions.

When a relative of a PoW seeks legal assistance, clinics typically first determine which institutions the individual has already contacted, then provide guidance on further steps, including recommendations on the relevant international bodies they can still approach. Clinics frequently handle cases related to establishing the fact of deprivation of liberty due to armed aggression, securing financial support for the families of captives, and clarifying the rights and guarantees available to PoWs and their relatives.

It is important to emphasize that the Russian Federation unlawfully detains civilians and systematically violates international humanitarian law in its treatment of PoWs. Additionally, due to ongoing high-intensity hostilities and the use of heavy weaponry, retrieving the remains of many fallen soldiers from combat zones is often impossible, leaving their fate unknown. These individuals are classified as missing, requiring legal procedures to establish their presumed death in court to facilitate their relatives' access to payments and inheritance rights. This process involves preparing legal documentation, gathering evidence and filing court petitions – tasks that can be overwhelming without professional legal assistance.

For such cases, referrals to public organizations and free legal services are particularly important, as some cases are highly complex and require specialized legal expertise. Clinics play a vital role in providing accurate information and ensuring proper referrals. Some clinics collaborate with government institutions and nonprofit organizations, developing referral roadmaps to enhance their ability to support affected families effectively.

Compensation for property damage or destruction and housing certificate acquisition

Continuous shelling by Russia across Ukraine has resulted in widespread destruction of residential properties. Between February 2022 and January 2024, the most significant portion of total direct damage was inflicted on residential buildings, accounting for 37.5 per cent ($58.9 billion) of losses, followed by infrastructure damage, amounting to 23.4 per cent ($36.8 billion). Russia's military tactics, including extensive missile and artillery strikes, have led to severe devastation in urban areas, particularly those near the frontlines. By early 2024, more than 50 per cent of the housing stock in numerous cities and towns had suffered damage or destruction, with preliminary estimates from regional military administrations indicating that around 250,000 buildings had been affected as of the end of 2023.[37] The full assessment of destruction will only be possible once hostilities cease.

Ukraine has enacted several legal measures to support property restoration, including the *E-recovery* programme and a system for obtaining housing certificates for destroyed residences. Since the process of obtaining reparations from the Russian Federation requires a functioning international mechanism, Ukraine has established a compensation programme for citizens whose homes have been destroyed. However, this mechanism remains flawed and faces implementation challenges.

Legal clinics play a critical role in guiding citizens through the legal processes associated with property compensation. They assist in submitting reports on damaged or destroyed property, restoring title documents and navigating legal procedures necessary for compensation claims. In many cases, the application of Ukraine's special law on compensation for war-related property damage necessitates court appeals and official requests to state authorities. Clinics actively support affected individuals through these processes. Notably, the Specialized Legal Clinic on War-Related Issues at

[37] Kyiv School of Economics, 'Report on Direct Infrastructure Damages from the Destruction Caused by Russia's Military Aggression against Ukraine' (2024), https://kse.ua/wp-content/uploads/2024/04/01.01.24_Damages_Report.pdf

Sumy State University, initiated and supported by ALCU, has taken a leading role in providing legal aid in this domain.

Socioethical dilemmas

The period of martial law in Ukraine – both de facto from 2014 to 2022 and officially declared after 24 February 2022 – has given rise to numerous socioethical (moral) and legal dilemmas, which legal professionals, including legal clinics, must navigate.

These dilemmas stem from several key factors. The war deeply polarizes society while significantly increasing the number of individuals suffering trauma due to ongoing security threats and various personal losses. The need to strengthen national security and defence requires mobilization efforts, placing additional pressure on families and leading some to seek ways to avoid enlistment, occasionally by circumventing legal requirements. Additionally, civilians living in frontline or occupied territories endure especially difficult conditions, complicating their legal status and access to resources.

Despite these adversities, social cohesion in Ukraine remains strong and stable. A UNDP study using the *reSCORE Index* measured Ukrainians' national belonging at 8.7 out of 10, with Ukrainian identity scored at 7.3, remaining consistent throughout the full-scale invasion. The study also recorded a civic duty score of 6.2 in 2024, compared to 5.2 in 2021 and 6.6 in 2023, and a community cooperation level of 5.2, reflecting steady engagement.[38]

Another study conducted by the Kyiv International Institute of Sociology (KIIS) in September–October 2024 examined Ukrainians' attitudes towards displaced individuals, refugees and residents of temporarily occupied territories. It found that 47 per cent of respondents were entirely tolerant of Ukrainian refugees, with 40 per cent agreeing they should return to Ukraine – a total of 87 per cent expressing support. However, 13 per cent preferred not to see refugees return.[39]

In relation to IDPs, the social distance index stood at 3.20, significantly lower than the ethnic group average. A total of 58 per cent of respondents welcomed IDPs into their environment, while 35 per cent agreed they should remain in Ukraine, totalling 93 per cent in support. The perception of Ukrainians remaining in temporarily occupied territories (TOTs) was

---

38 United Nations Development Programme, *Social Cohesion in Ukraine: Key Trends Based on reSCORE 2024* (UNDP Ukraine 2024), www.undp.org/ukraine/publications/social-cohesion-ukraine-key-trends-based-rescore-2024

39 Kyiv International Institute of Sociology, 'Attitudes towards Refugees, Internally Displaced Persons, Russian-Speaking Citizens, and Other Population Categories in Ukraine' (2024), www.kiis.com.ua/?lang=eng&cat=reports&id=1469&page=1

somewhat lower, with a social distance index of 3.97. While 40.7 per cent were willing to integrate them into their surroundings, an additional 44.6 per cent believed they should stay in Ukraine, making 85 per cent generally accepting, while 15 per cent held xenophobic attitudes towards IDPs.

Tolerance for Russian-speaking Ukrainians stood at 83 per cent, with 17 per cent expressing xenophobic views. However, Russia's continued aggression has intensified negative attitudes towards the Russian state and its citizens. The KIIS study conducted in May 2024 shows that '60% of Ukrainians believed that Russia seeks either to destroy the Ukrainian nation (26%) or commit physical genocide (34%). Another 6% thought Russia aimed to annex Ukraine's territory while granting limited cultural autonomy'.[40] These figures correlate with a previous KIIS study, which found that social distance towards Ukrainians of Russian nationality was 4.32, with 39 per cent open to interacting with them, 29 per cent accepting their presence in Ukraine and 32 per cent holding xenophobic attitudes.[41]

Another KIIS report tracks Ukrainians' evolving attitudes towards Russia and Russian citizens. As of the study's publication, only 8 per cent of Ukrainians expressed positive views towards Russian nationals, while 84 per cent held negative perceptions.[42]

Much more complicated is the issue of the attitude of Ukrainians towards mobilization and those who try to evade it. While most people acknowledge the necessity of mobilization for national defence, it is deeply intertwined with the fear of death, the disruption of family life and the loss of personal stability. In March 2024, the Institute of Social and Political Psychology of the National Academy of Sciences of Ukraine, in collaboration with the Association of Political Psychologists of Ukraine, conducted a survey on public perceptions of mobilization avoidance. The study, based on face-to-face interviews with 2,000 adults across Ukraine, found that 53.9 per cent of respondents expressed understanding towards those avoiding mobilization, reasoning that 'no one wants to die'.[43]

These findings highlight the varied moral-ethical and socioethical dilemmas that legal professionals, including legal clinics, encounter when providing counselling during wartime. Legal clinics may find themselves handling internal conflicts in legal counselling, such as advising individuals

---

40 Kyiv International Institute of Sociology, 'Ukrainians' Perception of Russia's Purpose in the War against Ukraine' (2024), www.kiis.com.ua/?lang=eng&cat=reports&id=1415&page=1

41 Kyiv International Institute of Sociology (n 39).

42 Kyiv International Institute of Sociology (2024) 'Attitude of Ukrainians towards Russia and Russians', www.kiis.com.ua/?lang=eng&cat=reports&id=1446&page=1

43 Interfax-Ukraine, 'Survey: 53.9% of Ukrainians Believe Those Avoiding Mobilization Can Be Understood' (2024), https://interfax.com.ua/news/press-conference/977329.html

with strong pro-Russian views or active ties to Russian authorities or occupation regimes. They sometimes receive requests for advice on circumventing the law, posing ethical challenges for legal practitioners. Legal clinics must balance conflicting priorities, such as security versus economic survival, or national security interests against the complexities of individual family situations. And still other cases lack sufficient information, making it difficult for legal clinics to determine whether legal assistance should be provided at all.

Problems related to mobilization

In Ukraine, all men over the age of 25 are generally subject to military service and mobilization, with evasion carrying criminal liability under Article 336 of the Criminal Code of Ukraine. Additionally, conscripts cannot freely leave the country during the mobilization period.

However, Article 23 of the Law of Ukraine 'On Mobilization Training and Mobilization' outlines specific grounds for deferment or exemption. These include raising a minor child or a child with a disability, having three or more children within a marriage, caring for an incapacitated or seriously ill relative, the severe disability of a spouse, and the temporary disability of the conscript, among others.

In response to these provisions, some conscripts seek manipulative, corrupt or fictitious solutions to avoid mobilization. Examples include forcibly taking a child from the mother to claim exemption, purchasing fraudulent disability certificates or entering into a fictitious marriage with a woman who has a severe disability. Others attempt to legally avoid criminal liability by finding loopholes within the system. Legal clinics occasionally receive requests for advice on such matters, including inquiries about falsifying grounds for travel permits or illegally leaving Ukraine.

It goes without saying that legal clinics refuse to provide advice in such cases, as doing so would violate both ethical standards and the law.

Issues affecting forcibly displaced people

Issues relating to IDPs encompass a wide range of challenges, including access to social benefits and pensions, employment opportunities, family stability, property rights and maintaining social ties with frontline or border areas adjacent to TOTs or the Russian Federation. Many Ukrainians had relatives, property or workplaces in Russia or the TOTs and frequently spent time in these regions before martial law or occupation was imposed.

Following forced displacement, a significant portion of IDPs struggle to access adequate social or financial assistance, secure employment or find stable housing.[44] Additionally, some male IDPs hesitate to officially register as unemployed due to concerns about mobilization.

As a result of insufficient social support and financial security in controlled territory, some IDPs ultimately choose to return to the TOTs, seeking guidance from clinics on the implications.

Another challenge arises from IDPs needing to periodically confirm their actual place of residence to continue receiving state assistance. While some genuinely reside in their designated resettlement areas, others return to permanent residences in combat zones or TOTs, yet request legal help in securing fictitious residence certificates or contesting payment cancellations, even when such cancellations were legally justified.

According to the Ministry of Social Policy of Ukraine, as of December 2024, approximately 9,000 IDPs returned to territories of possible combat operations, while 1,000 returned to temporarily occupied areas.[45]

Challenges in providing legal assistance to citizens of the Russian Federation

The entry of the Ukrainian Armed Forces into the Kursk region of the Russian Federation in August 2024 has led to an increase in Russian asylum seekers arriving in Ukraine, particularly in the Sumy region, which borders Russia and is geographically closest to Kursk. Some of these individuals previously travelled to Ukraine frequently for private business, but now seek protection under Ukraine's asylum system.

Additionally, there are Russian citizens who resided in Ukraine while receiving pensions from Russia. Among them there are individuals with pro-Russian sentiments, as well as those who actively support the Armed Forces of Ukraine and hold supportive views towards Ukraine. Some of these individuals have expired bank cards issued by Russian banks, requiring them to travel back to Russia for reissuance, while others have expired residency permits, placing them at risk of deportation. Notably, cases have emerged

[44] Mariia Kolokolova, 'Legal Needs of Displaced Ukrainians', *Association of Legal Clinics of Ukraine* (2023), https://legalclinics.in.ua/wp-content/uploads/2024/11/Legal-Needs-of-Displaced-Ukrainians.-ENG.-M.-Kolokolova.pdf; European Parliament, 'Displaced Ukrainians: Challenges and Outlook for Integration in the EU', European Parliament Think Tank (2025), www.europarl.europa.eu/thinktank/en/document/EPRS_BRI(2025)769497

[45] 'Officially, about One Thousand Ukrainians Have Returned to Occupied Territories – Ministry of Social Policy', *Radio Svoboda*, www.radiosvoboda.org/a/news-tysjacha-vpo-povernulysja-na-okupovani-terytoriji/33237780.html

where individuals fighting for Ukraine face uncertainty regarding their legal status and potential deportation.[46]

Legal clinics face significant moral and ethical dilemmas when addressing such cases. Advising pro-Russian Russians may lead to internal hesitation among clinicians, while helping Russians who sympathize with Ukraine presents security concerns, as these individuals risk persecution, punishment or imprisonment if forced to return to Russia.

Survey results among Ukrainian legal clinics

While working on this chapter, we asked the legal clinics affiliated with ALCU to share their experiences regarding the emergence of moral and ethical dilemmas in their work due to the ongoing war. A total of 23 legal clinics (38 per cent of those listed in the ALCU register for 2023) provided responses. Although the sample is not fully representative, it may reflect certain trends in the nature of issues that clinics find themselves facing during martial law.

According to the findings, 52.2 per cent of respondents stated that since the beginning of Russian aggression in 2014, clinics have encountered legal issues intertwined with social and ethical dilemmas. Additionally, about 50 per cent of clinics reported that the frequency of such cases increased significantly after Russia's full-scale invasion in 2022. One of the surveyed clinics was established in 2021, meaning it could not compare cases from 2014 to post-2022 trends.

We also asked respondents whether their clients bring potentially controversial questions to their clinics. Respondents could choose from the following answer options: never, occasionally or frequently. The distribution of responses is shown in Table 13.1.

Additionally, seven clinics (30 per cent of respondents) indicated that they receive other controversial inquiries, with four reporting occasional cases and three receiving them frequently. These inquiries cover issues such as the sale or inheritance of real estate in uncontrolled territories, returning to TOTs due to insufficient financial and social support for IDPs, travel abroad (for conscripts, whose right to leave the country during the martial time is limited), tax reduction and other legal concerns.

One respondent highlighted the complexity of moral dilemmas encountered in legal clinics:

> Under martial law in Ukraine, the number of appeals from military personnel and their families regarding violations of their rights by

[46] 'Fought for Ukraine, Now Homeless in Volyn: Russian Volunteer Soldier Faces Deportation', *VSN News* (2024), https://vsn.ua/news/voyuvav-za-ukrayinu-a-teper-bomzhuje-na-volini-rosiyaninu-dobrovoltsyu-zsu-zagrozhuje-deportatsiya-40589

state institutions has increased significantly. The central dilemma lies in balancing respect for human rights with national security. On one hand, soldiers and their families face interventions into their social, labour, and other rights, leading to a loss of trust in state institutions. On the other hand, the state – operating under wartime conditions – is often forced to make decisions that may restrict citizens' rights, to protect national sovereignty. In addressing these cases, legal consultants often serve as both psychologists and lawyers, and at times, people blame them for contributing to such issues themselves.

Beyond identifying dilemmas, respondents were asked how they recognize and address socioethical challenges in their work. Legal clinics reported that in 62 per cent of cases, contradictions within an issue are immediately apparent. Around 60 per cent discuss cases with clinical students, 33 per cent consult fellow clinicians and 19 per cent rely on personal judgement when navigating complex ethical concerns.

To manage such issues, clinics employ various approaches, ranging from advanced training and specialized education to ensure legal advice remains strictly within the framework of the law, to outright refusal to provide counsel when ethical violations may arise.

These findings lead to several conclusions. First, even during wartime, clinics do not frequently receive inquiries involving morally and ethically controversial issues. However, when such cases do occur, they are primarily

Table 13.1: Controversial questions to clinics

Potential question	Frequency	Percentage
How to circumvent the law to avoid mobilization	Occasionally or frequently	43.5 per cent (30 per cent and 13.5 per cent respectively)
How to circumvent the law to be exempted from military service	Occasionally or frequently	43.5 per cent (34.5 per cent to 9 per cent respectively)
How to exploit legal loopholes to receive double social or pension payments for IDPs	Occasionally or frequently	34.5 per cent (30 per cent and 4.5 per cent respectively)
Potential violations related to a child living with one parent	Occasionally	18 per cent
Collaboration cases (where the applicant may be a potential collaborator)	None	-

related to military service. This can be attributed to both the extensive human and population losses caused by the war, which has lasted for more than a decade, and the state's ongoing efforts to balance national security with human rights protection.

Additionally, there is no universal approach among clinics for determining whether a request contains a morally or ethically contentious element. Instead, clinics often identify these complexities through case analysis and discussion. Regardless of the circumstances, all surveyed clinics ensure their decisions comply with legal and ethical standards, preventing any breaches of law or professional conduct in the provision of legal assistance.

Conclusion

The ongoing war has presented immense challenges for both the Ukrainian people and the nation. Yet, despite these difficulties, universities and clinics remain steadfast in their mission – educating students through legal assistance, conducting legal awareness initiatives and providing additional support services, including mediation, psychological aid and social assistance.

Legal clinics have demonstrated exceptional adaptability in response to evolving circumstances. They have conducted student classes and client consultations in hybrid formats, transitioned legal education efforts online by preparing and disseminating materials via social networks, and mitigated security risks by securing premises with storage facilities where possible, enabling activities to continue even during air raids. Additionally, they have rapidly mastered new areas of clinical legal education, including international humanitarian law, international criminal law, war-related damage compensation, the legal rights of military personnel and their families, mobilization laws, and the impact of artificial intelligence on clinical legal education. Throughout these challenges, clinics have navigated complex professional and ethical dilemmas while upholding the fundamental principles of free legal help and public legal education.

With the help of ALCU, Ukrainian clinics have continued their network development even under wartime conditions. They convene regularly at forums, ALCU congresses and various professional events, including competitions, roundtables and training sessions. In 2024, the ALCU Activity Standards and Monitoring Tool underwent updates, and a new online Assessment Tool was introduced. Similar frameworks are found in only a few countries, highlighting Ukraine's efforts in advancing legal clinic development and best practices.

ALCU will continue to study the impact of war on clinical legal education and the experiences of clinicians – both students and staff – working under these difficult conditions. Additionally, it will support the development and adaptation of effective approaches and techniques to navigate these challenges.

We believe that such efforts exemplify resilience in the face of war and uncertainty, reaffirming the commitment to preparing a new generation of Ukrainian lawyers able to properly address controversial legal and social issues. These future professionals will play a crucial role in rebuilding the country, representing Ukraine in international institutions and advocating for accountability – ensuring justice for all crimes committed against Ukraine and its citizens since the onset of the war in 2014.

References

Association of Legal Clinics of Ukraine, 'Street Law Hackathon Guide: Meeting the Legal Needs of People in Wartime' (2023), https://legalclinics.in.ua/en/street-law-hackathon-guide-meeting-the-legal-needs-of-people-in-wartime/

Association of Legal Clinics of Ukraine, 'Training for Consultants of the Specialized Legal Clinic on War-Related Issues' (2024), https://legalclinics.in.ua/start-navchannya-dlya-konsultantiv-spetsializovanoyi-yurydychnoyi-kliniky-z-pytan-pov-yazanyh-z-vijnoyu/

Association of Legal Clinics of Ukraine, 'Ukrainian Experience at the International Client Counseling Competition 2024' (2024), https://legalclinics.in.ua/ukrayinskyj-dosvid-na-mizhnarodnyh-zmagannyah-z-konsultuvannya-kliyentiv-2024-roku/

Bohatiuk I, 'The Activities of Legal Clinics under Martial Law' (2022) 3(64) *Juridical Bulletin* 202

Brown-Mosten International Client Consultation Competition, '2024 Competition – International Client Consultation Competition' (2024), www.brownmosten.com/2024-competition.html

Decree of the President of Ukraine 'On the Decision of the National Security and Defense Council of Ukraine of April 13, 2014 "On Urgent Measures to Overcome the Terrorist Threat and Preserve the Territorial Integrity of Ukraine"' No 405/2014 (14 April 2014), https://zakon.rada.gov.ua/laws/show/405/2014#Text

Decree of the President of Ukraine 'On the Decision of the National Security and Defense Council of Ukraine of February 28, 2018 "On the Implementation of Measures to Ensure National Security and Defense of Ukraine"' No 116/2018 (28 February 2018), https://zakon.rada.gov.ua/laws/show/116/2018#Text

Decree of the President of Ukraine 'On the Imposition of Martial Law in Ukraine' No 64/2022, No 2102-IX (24 February 2022), www.president.gov.ua/documents/642022-41397

Donetsk National University, 'All-Ukrainian Roundtable: Countering the Genocide of the Ukrainian People' (2023), https://news.donnu.edu.ua/2023/02/10/vseukrayinskyj-kruglyj-stil-protydiya-genoczydu-ukrayinskogo-narodu/

European Parliament, 'Displaced Ukrainians: Challenges and Outlook for Integration in the EU' (European Parliament Think Tank, 2025), www.europarl.europa.eu/thinktank/en/document/EPRS_BRI(2025)769497

Finger D, Felstiner S, Greenberg-Kobrin M and Tsypiashchuk M, 'Empowering Ukraine's First Legal Responders: Ukrainian-US Collaboration and Clinics' (2024) Loyola University New Orleans College of Law Research Paper No 2024–17, 31 *International Journal of Clinical Legal Education* 147, https://ssrn.com/abstract=5049252

'Fought for Ukraine, Now Homeless in Volyn: Russian Volunteer Soldier Faces Deportation' (*VSN News*, 2024), https://vsn.ua/news/voyuvav-za-ukrayinu-a-teper-bomzhuje-na-volini-rosiyaninu-dobrovoltsyu-zsu-zagrozhuje-deportatsiya-40589

'How Many Ukrainian Civilians Are in Russian Captivity? Lubinets Revealed the Number' (*Pravda Life*, 2024), https://life.pravda.com.ua/society/skilki-civilnih-ukrajinciv-perebuvayut-u-rosiyskomu-poloni-lubinec-nazvav-cifru-305399/

Institute for War and Peace Reporting (IWPR), 'War Crimes in Crimea', https://iwpr.net/global-voices/war-crimes-crimea

Interfax-Ukraine, 'Survey: 53.9% of Ukrainians Believe Those Avoiding Mobilization Can Be Understood' (2024), https://interfax.com.ua/news/press-conference/977329.html

'Izumi Nakamitsu (UNODA) on the Threats to International Peace and Security – Security Council, 9827th Meeting' (*UN Web TV*, 2025), https://webtv.un.org/en/asset/k10/k103tf1mnj

Kolokolova M, 'Legal Needs of Displaced Ukrainians' (*Association of Legal Clinics of Ukraine*, 2023), https://legalclinics.in.ua/wp-content/uploads/2024/11/Legal-Needs-of-Displaced-Ukrainians.-ENG.-M.-Kolokolova.pdf

Kozyubra MI, 'Challenges Facing Ukraine on the Way to Its Accession to the European Union: Constitutional and Legal Aspects' in *Political and Legal Consequences of Ukraine's Accession to the European Union and NATO* (WSPiA Rzeszowską Szkołę Wyższą 2024) 15–38

Kyiv International Institute of Sociology, 'Attitude of Ukrainians towards Russia and Russians' (2024), www.kiis.com.ua/?lang=eng&cat=reports&id=1446&page=1

Kyiv International Institute of Sociology, 'Attitudes towards Refugees, Internally Displaced Persons, Russian-Speaking Citizens, and Other Population Categories in Ukraine' (2024), www.kiis.com.ua/?lang=eng&cat=reports&id=1469&page=1

Kyiv School of Economics, 'Report on Direct Infrastructure Damages from the Destruction Caused by Russia's Military Aggression against Ukraine' (2024), https://kse.ua/wp-content/uploads/2024/04/01.01.24_Damages_Report.pdf

Law of Ukraine 'On the Ratification of the Convention for the Protection of Human Rights and Fundamental Freedoms of 1950, the First Protocol, and Protocols No 2, 4, 7, and 11 to the Convention' (1997), https://zakon.rada.gov.ua/laws/show/475/97-%D0%B2%D1%80#Text

Law of Ukraine 'On Free Legal Assistance' (2012), https://zakon.rada.gov.ua/laws/show/3460-17#Text

Law of Ukraine 'On Higher Education' (2014), https://zakon.rada.gov.ua/laws/show/1556-18#n530

Law of Ukraine 'On the Legal Regime of Martial Law' (2015), https://zakon.rada.gov.ua/laws/show/389-19#Text

'MIPL: Over 10,000 Ukrainian Military Personnel Held Captive by Russia' (*Deutsche Welle*, 2024), www.dw.com/uk/mipl-u-poloni-rf-perebuvaut-ponad-10-tisac-ukrainskih-vijskovih/a-69009006

Office of the United Nations High Commissioner for Human Rights, 'Report on the Situation of Human Rights in the Temporarily Occupied Autonomous Republic of Crimea and the City of Sevastopol, Ukraine 13 September 2017 to 30 June 2018', www.ohchr.org/sites/default/files/Documents/Countries/UA/CrimeaThematicReport10Sept2018_EN.pdf

'Officially, about One Thousand Ukrainians Have Returned to Occupied Territories – Ministry of Social Policy' (*Radio Svoboda*, 2024), www.radiosvoboda.org/a/news-tysjacha-vpo-povernulysja-na-okupovani-terytoriji/33237780.html

Register of Legal Clinics of Ukraine (2024), https://legalclinics.in.ua/wp-content/uploads/2020/11/Reyestr-AYUKU-2024.pdf

'Standards of Operations of Legal Clinics of Ukraine' (2014, with amendments) https://legalclinics.in.ua/en/standards-of-the-legal-clinics-in-ukraine/

State Enterprise, Information and Computing Center, 'Dashboard of Internally Displaced Persons (IDPs) in Ukraine' (Ministry of Social Policy of Ukraine, 2025), www.ioc.gov.ua/analytics/dashboard-vpo

'Tonight on TV: Torture of Ukrainian Soldiers, Olympic Athlete Controversy, Venezuela Unrest' (*NOS Nieuwsuur*, 2024), https://nos.nl/nieuwsuur/artikel/2531435-vanavond-op-tv-martelingen-oekraiense-militairen-ophef-olympische-sporter-onrust-venezuela

'Ukraine Has Returned over 3,500 Ukrainians from Russian Captivity – Lubinets' (*Suspilne News*, 2024), https://suspilne.media/884537-z-rosijskogo-polonu-ukraina-povernula-ponad-35-tisaci-ukrainciv-lubinec/

United Nations Development Programme, *Social Cohesion in Ukraine: Key Trends Based on reSCORE 2024* (UNDP Ukraine 2024), www.undp.org/ukraine/publications/social-cohesion-ukraine-key-trends-based-rescore-2024

United Nations High Commissioner for Refugees (UNHCR), 'Ukraine Refugee Situation' (2025), https://data.unhcr.org/en/situations/ukraine

United Nations Peacemaker, 'Package of Measures for the Implementation of the Minsk Agreements' (2025), https://peacemaker.un.org/en/node/8827

Verkhovna Rada of Ukraine, 'Resolution of the Verkhovna Rada of Ukraine on the Statement of the Verkhovna Rada of Ukraine "On the Commission of Genocide in Ukraine by the Russian Federation"' (2020), https://zakon.rada.gov.ua/laws/show/2188-20#Text

PART IV

The Global Picture

14

From Holdout to Forefront: The Contributions of European Clinics to Globalized Clinical Legal Education

Jeff Giddings

Introduction

This chapter reflects on the contributions of European clinics to globalized clinical legal education (CLE). Including the UK in Europe (as the European Network on Clinical Legal Education [ENCLE] does and I have in this chapter) makes that contribution all the more significant. I refer to developments across Europe, seeking to understand the development of clinics in different parts of this vast continent.

Much has changed since Rick Wilson's 2009 description of Western Europe as the last holdout to worldwide acceptance of CLE. Recent books and other writings show the energy and diversity of CLE across Europe.[1]

[1] C Bartoli, *Legal Clinics in Europe: For a Commitment of Higher Education in Social Justice* (Diritto & Questioni Pubbliche 2016); M Lodzhuk, *Legal Clinics in Ukraine: From Legal Education to Legal Practice* (Odesa Feniks 2016); A Alemanno and L Khadar (eds), *Reinventing Legal Education: How Clinical Education Is Reforming the Teaching and Practice of Law in Europe* (CUP 2018); C Blengino and A Gascón-Cuenca (eds), *Epistemic Communities at the Boundaries of Law: Clinics as a Paradigm in the Revolution of Legal Education in the European Mediterranean Context* (Ledizioni LediPublishing 2019); H McFaul et al, 'Taking Clinical Legal Education Online: Songs of Innocence and Experience' (2020) 27(4) *International Journal of Clinical Legal Education* 6. Frank Bloch's 2011 edited collection includes Europe-focused chapters – one on Central and Eastern Europe (M Berbec-Rostas, A Gutnikov and B Namyslovska-Gabrysiak, 'Clinical Legal Education in Central and Eastern Europe' in F Bloch (ed), *The Global Clinical Movement* (OUP 2011) 53–68) and another on Spain

In 2016, Ulrich Stege observed: 'The new quality of the European CLE movement lies in the fact that CLE programmes can now be found in almost all European regions.'[2] Nonetheless, clinics across Europe face a range of challenges. Alemanno and Khadar referred to European CLE 'burgeoning' rather 'blossoming', with relatively few clinics 'genuinely embracing clinical education methods' and qualifying 'such as legal clinics. Often, the self-proclaimed clinics are often mere seminars that host legal practitioners'.[3]

For this chapter, I have drawn on interviews with European clinicians as well as a review of global CLE for the edited collection *Global Clinical Legal Education.*[4] Clinicians have shown great creativity and innovation in their efforts to respond constructively to uncertain and unfavourable conditions. It is clear that the development of local and regional networks can be important in supporting the sustainability of CLE. The development of European CLE has also benefited from the engagement of energetic and insightful individuals.[5] European clinics are forging their own identities, drawing on practices that suit the local context. Many are drawing first and foremost on local insights and models. International exemplars from further afield tend to be most useful in showing clinicians and their supporters what might be possible rather than showing them what must be done – as an inspiration rather than a template.

Globalization

In their 2018 edited collection, Alemanno and Khadar and their contributors called for CLE to be supported in contributing to the reform of legal education across Europe. A key theme is internationalization and globalization, with clinics seen as a vehicle for making legal education more global and practical in orientation. 'By confronting their law students with the reality of contemporary European legal practice in all its complexity, European clinicians are placing CLE at the forefront of a progressive internationalization of legal education.'[6] They also focused on how CLE is being 'Europeanized', showing the flexibility and adaptability of clinical methods.

(D Blázquez-Martín, 'The Bologna Process and the Future of Clinical Education in Europe: A View from Spain' in FS Bloch (ed), *The Global Clinical Movement: Educating Lawyers for Social Justice* (OUP 2011) 121).

2 U Stege, 'How Clinical Legal Education Is Crossing Borders' in Blengino and Gascón-Cuenca (n 1).

3 Alemanno and Khadar (n 1) 42.

4 J Giddings, 'Common Threads and Strength in Diversity' in J Giddings (ed), *Global Clinical Legal Education* (Routledge 2025).

5 ibid chs 5 and 16.

6 Alemanno and Khadar (n 1) 325.

Globalization has impacted European CLE by prompting local and regional competition. Stege states:

> For the first time ever, Europe is facing private competition in higher (and legal) education, which was until recently exclusively in public hands in most of Europe. In addition, through the development of excellence clusters (which determine in part the level of public funding), public universities themselves need to be more competitive. As a consequence, more and more attention is paid to the needs of students and communities – which makes the case for a more practical approach to legal education.[7]

At the same time, globalization and technological developments also offer greater opportunities for clinics to engage in transnational collaboration. Aided by technology, our more globalized world enables greater cross-fertilization. Within countries and across regions, formal CLE networks and informal connections support the work of clinicians and CLE programmes. Networks also enable connections to other civil society groups. Greater awareness of the diversity of clinic models and contexts means there are plenty of examples to learn from when developing new clinics.

Hugh McFaul and his Open University colleagues have written about the Open Justice Centre's active experimentation with online technologies.[8] They note that taking CLE online involves significant challenges, particularly around fostering student collaboration, quality assurance for both clients and students, as well as facilitating the right level of complexity and challenge in the work assigned to students.

Technology has enabled a range of collaborations. In the academic years 2020–2021, the Qatar University College of Law Clinic studied the legal implications of COVID-19, in partnership with 30 legal clinics in 20 countries including England and Spain, and with the participation of about 500 students.[9]

Tides and currents

The CLE literature contains many references characterizing CLE development as coming in waves.[10] I have recently suggested elsewhere that waves tell only

7 Stege (n 2) 10.

8 McFaul et al (n 1).

9 MY Mattar and D AlMalki, 'Providing Legal Aid to Migrant Workers: International Standards, Comparative Models and the Qatari Law Clinic Experience' in Giddings (ed) (n 4) 232.

10 MM Barry, JC Dubin and P Joy, 'Clinical Education for This Millennium: The Third Wave' (2000) 7(1) *Clinical Law Review* 1, 4; D Nicolson, J Newman and R Grimes, *How to Set up and Run a Legal Clinic: Principles and Practice* (Edward Elgar 2023).

part of the story, their size, power and impact being in large part determined by the tide. It takes time to discern the tide and to understand its impacts. Currents, be they ocean or tidal, are also highly influential.[11]

Across Western Europe in particular, the CLE tide remains very much on the way in, supporting the development of new clinics. In the UK, there are now more than 80 law schools running clinical programmes, representing over 75 per cent of the total number of educational institutions teaching law at the degree level. Twenty years ago, the areas for development of clinics were Central and Eastern Europe and Asia. When the incoming tide across Western Europe turns and recedes, clinics may well be less likely to develop and be sustained. Clinical programmes will find it particularly difficult to swim against the tide.[12] CLE in Central and Eastern Europe benefited from an unprecedented incoming tide following the collapse of the Soviet Union (between the mid-1990s and the early 2000s). This boom was largely triggered by substantial funding from U.S. donors (for example, the Ford Foundation, the American Bar Association's Central and East European Law Initiative and the Open Society Foundations) and international organizations (for example, the United Nations High Commissioner for Refugees [UNHCR]).[13] However, many of the early clinics proved unsustainable when external funding ended in the early 2000s. During this time, however, a foundation was laid for the future development of CLE in Europe.[14] Wilson identifies three key factors leading to the widespread adoption of clinical and other experiential methodologies in European law schools: first, the establishment of national clinical networks in a striking number of countries; second, the Bologna reform process creating new space for curricular reforms such as clinics; and, third, new clinics in the East pushing 'the staid and traditional methodologies of Western Europe' towards reform.[15]

Following the signing of the Bologna Declaration in 1999, processes to harmonize the requirements for university courses and diplomas were the first step in moves to develop a 'European space for higher education', enhancing the competitiveness of universities and increasing the mobility and employability of students and scholars.[16] Alemanno and Khadar identify that Genty draws compelling links between Bologna and the growth of CLE during the second wave (that is, the resurgence of CLE from the mid-2000s).

---

[11] G Pretor-Pinney, *The Wavewatcher's Companion* (Bloomsbury 2011).

[12] Giddings (ed) (n 4) 323–324.

[13] M Lodzhuk, *Legal Clinics in Ukraine: From Legal Education to Legal Practice* (Odesa Feniks 2016).

[14] P Genty, 'Reflections on US Involvement in the Promotion of Clinical Legal Education in Europe' in Alemanno and Khadar (n 1) 29.

[15] R Wilson, *The Global Evolution of Clinical Legal Education* (CUP 2018) 191–192.

[16] Bartoli (n 1) 76.

However, they found that apart from Spain, 'there was little evidence of causality between Bologna and the emergence of CLE'. They noted that the Bologna Process 'led all Spanish Faculties of Law to adopt a more skill-oriented and student-centred approach to learning' with CLE as part of the response 'to the call of the Bologna declaration for a greater emphasis on employability through the development of skills and competencies'.[17]

Networks

European clinical networks, most notably ENCLE and the *International Journal of Clinical Legal Education* (*IJCLE*), continue to connect clinical colleagues within Europe and across the globe, including the Global South. The *IJCLE* started running conferences at the turn of the century and Jonny Hall observes that by 2010, participants came from more than 30 countries.[18] Both Maxim Tomoszek and Ulrich Stege identify the significant influence of the *IJCLE* conferences. Tomoszek recalls these conferences as especially important before ENCLE developed in 2012.[19] As the *IJCLE* broadened its focus from the UK to include other English-speaking, common law countries and places where clinics were flourishing, its conferences became focal points for networking and clinical pedagogical development.

Nigel Duncan refers to the value of the *IJCLE* in spreading the word about clinic and establishing and developing networks. Setting up the *IJCLE* was a significant part of the strategy of Northumbria University to make CLE a point of distinction:

> The journal became readily available to international audiences once the initial paywall was dropped and, together with the active linking of regular conferences, has made *IJCLE* a really significant player in developing networks within the UK but especially internationally. So it's an interesting example of how what was originally conceived (I believe) with fairly parochial and competitive objectives can be developed by good people into a valuable resource for a much wider community.[20]

Having been the long-time editor of the English academic journal *The Law Teacher*, Duncan continues to be a key driver of the online *European Journal of*

[17] Alemanno and Khadar (n 1) 335.

[18] Interview with Jonny Hall, 19 December 2024, notes on file.

[19] Interview with Maxim Tomoszek, 15 January 2025, notes on file; interview with Ulrich Stege, 3 December 2024, notes on file.

[20] Email from Nigel Duncan, 19 December 2024, copy on file.

Legal Education (*EJLE*). The *EJLE* has strong clinic expertise on its Editorial Board through Isabela Kraśnicka, Ulrich Stege and Duncan.[21]

Beyond Europe, *IJCLE* conferences have been held in South Africa (2007 and 2022), Canada (2016) and Australia (2009, 2013, 2018 and 2025), sometimes in collaboration with ENCLE and the Global Alliance for Justice Education (GAJE). The *IJCLE* has tended to alternate between European conferences and conferences held elsewhere. They have been particularly important for their encouragement of clinical scholarship beyond storytelling about individual clinics and with a focus on various forms of empirical and sociolegal research. While it is hardly surprising given its title, the *IJCLE* has welcomed contributions from beyond the UK.[22] Technology has also enabled greater availability of international clinical scholarship with Europe and the *IJCLE* being prominent in this.

Since 2012, ENCLE has played an important role in enabling the growth of CLE across Europe. Wilson refers to ENCLE's creation coinciding with the growth and dissemination of CLE: 'ENCLE has provided a locus and a shared space within which clinical programs and participants can generate information and, at least thus far, their passionate devotion to the clinical projects of their home universities.'[23] Blengino and Gascon-Cuenca identify the meetings of the GAJE and the ENCLE networks as crucial opportunities for constantly learning about clinical methodology and exchanging experiences.[24]

ENCLE introduced Quality Standards for Legal Clinics in 2022 which complement those introduced in various countries. The ENCLE website details many of the CLE networks currently operating and provides access to a current and comprehensive collection of useful resources. ENCLE has been important in fostering the development of CLE in the Balkans region (Albania, Macedonia and Croatia) as well as in North Africa (Morocco and Algeria), where clinics work on refugee issues – an area of natural focus and connection.[25] In Algeria, ENCLE members, most notably Ulrich Stege, contributed to a series of EU-supported conferences on the teaching of refugee law. Prior to the convening of the first conference in 2015, Northern African universities did not teach refugee law. These conferences were designed to encourage national authorities to recognize and support this teaching as well as to build the knowledge of lawyers of relevant laws. The lack of lawyer knowledge was overcome through the development of

21 Interview with Nigel Duncan, 19 December 2024, notes on file.

22 L Wortham, 'Strengthening the International Clinical Scholarly Community: Opportunities for the Clinical Law Review and Beyond' (2019) 26 *Clinical Law Review* 393.

23 Wilson (n 15) 315.

24 Blengino and Gascón-Cuenca (n 1) 15.

25 Stege (n 2) 142.

networks of lawyers with relevant knowledge. The conferences also prompted academic interest in areas including CLE. Once external funding finished, it became challenging to maintain those networks.[26] In 2015, ENCLE worked with the University of Rabat in Morocco and the University of Bordeaux in France on a clinical option available to students undertaking a joint two-year (one year in each country) master's programme. A live-client clinic operated off-campus in partnership with a nongovernmental organization (NGO) and over time became focused on migration and human trafficking. The COVID-19 pandemic saw a move to online consultations and a shift towards more strategic work with NGOs. Supported by EU project funding, similar initiatives supporting the teaching of migration law were developed in 2016–2017 at other Moroccan universities and in Tunisia.[27] The Rosa Parks Legal Clinic for Human Rights at Belgium's Catholic University of Leuven coordinates the *Mercator* network of legal clinics working on migration issues. The participating clinics are located on a migratory trajectory from the Democratic Republic of Congo to Canada via West Africa (Senegal), North Africa (Tunisia and Morocco) and Europe (Italy and Belgium). The network brings together students and teachers each year to meet in person for a seminar hosted by one of the network members.[28]

Alan Uzelac, the founder of the University of Zagreb Law Clinic, credits the longstanding student-managed *Juss-Buss* clinic at the University of Oslo as an inspiration for development of the Zagreb clinic. While the practices of the Zagreb Law Clinic were in many ways different from the *Juss-Buss* role model, the influence of the Norwegian model remains strong, with Uzelac and his clinic colleagues recognizing the benefits of students enjoying broad autonomy and participating in all strategic and organizational decisions and being independent in their work as much as possible.[29] Unfortunately, the Zagreb Law Clinic has been seen by some academics as 'more of a systemic irritant than a milestone for future transformation', being perceived by some 'as too democratic, too autonomous and too critical'.[30]

The Polish Law Clinics Foundation (FUPP in its Polish acronym) has been highly successful in supporting the development of law clinics, both in Poland and the surrounding countries.[31] Wilson describes Poland as 'a model

[26] Interview with Ulrich Stege, 13 May 2025, notes on file.

[27] ibid.

[28] https://mercator-uclouvain.com/des-nouvelles-des-cliniques/

[29] A Uzelac, 'Croatia – the Peculiar Case of Zagreb Law Clinic' in Giddings (ed) (n 4) 157–159.

[30] ibid 164–165.

[31] F Czernicki, 'The History and Distinctiveness of the Polish Legal Clinics Program' in Giddings (ed) (n 4) 172–178.

in national integration of clinics, through the Legal Clinics Foundation'.[32] FUPP has sought to develop 'a formula to inscribe legal clinics into the Polish legal system'[33] and strengthen the potential of CLE for the future through 'supporting cooperation between clinics and building a sense of unity … supporting international cooperation in the field of practical legal education, organizing training, conferences, presentations, publishing activity … and propagating the idea of free-of-charge legal assistance'.[34] Maxim Tomoszek highlights the value of the FUPP clinic manual and other resources in developing the clinic at Palacký University.[35] The clinic made use of the Polish model and adapted it.[36] Polish clinicians also assisted the development of clinics in Russia, Belarus and Turkey. Wilson also notes FUPP's contribution to the establishment of thriving national networks in Moldova and Ukraine.[37] Tomoszek refers to the support that ENCLE and European clinicians have provided for clinics in Russia, Belarus and Turkey.[38]

The UK's Clinical Legal Education Organisation (CLEO) is recognized as having 'played a major role' in the growth of CLE in the UK 'through the holding of regular conferences and workshops. The open and informal model used in its formative years brought considerable benefits as no individual or institution was seen as empire-building and a spirit of cooperation and sharing was generated, for example through a bank of resource materials'.[39] CLEO later formalized its identity and is now a registered charity with corporate status based at the University of Liverpool. One of the founders of CLEO, Nigel Duncan, sees CLEO as having blossomed in recent years.[40] Another CLEO founder, Richard Grimes, says it has thus far been focused on Britain and had limited influence outside the UK.[41]

These connections have been strengthened by the various use of technology to overcome the 'tyranny of distance'. A powerful recent example involved a collaboration between Baze University in Nigeria and Italy's International University College of Turin's Against Human Trafficking Law

32 Wilson (n 15) 191.

33 Czernicki (n 31) 172.

34 ibid 174.

35 Interview with Maxim Tomoszek, 15 January 2025, notes on file.

36 M Tomoszek and V Tomoszkova, 'Clinical Legal Education from the Czechoslovakian Perspective' in Giddings (ed) (n 4) 168.

37 Wilson (n 15) 191.

38 Interview with Maxim Tomoszek, 15 January 2025, notes on file.

39 R Grimes et al, 'Legal Clinics in the UK and Ireland: Past, Present and Future' in Giddings (ed) (n 4) 309.

40 Interview with Nigel Duncan, 19 December 2024, notes on file.

41 Interview with Richard Grimes, 27 January 2025, notes on file.

Clinic.[42] Baze students interviewed a victim of trafficking who was living in Italy and running an NGO to help trafficked victims. A collaboration was formed between the two clinics. The victim was impressed by the students and indicated she was ready to form a partnership with the clinic and her NGO. Stege has emphasized 'the potential transformative power' of CLE in the context of Mediterranean Northern Africa and Europe, crossing borders 'for the benefit of those supported by them, but also for the benefit of the clinical students and the legal (and legal education) systems in place around them'.[43]

Distinctive models

From east to west, Europe accounts for an interesting array of clinical models and contexts. It is clear that there is real value in being able to learn from local and regional exemplars. Alemanno and Khadar note that:

> all it seems to take is two or three clinics in a given country to spark a broader clinical movement. This appears to have been the case in Spain, Italy, the Netherlands, Belgium, Germany, and France. And these follow-up clinics (which we might call the 'third wave') seem to take inspiration primarily from their national forerunners (rather than from contact with US legal education).[44]

As an example, the Human Rights and Migration Law Clinic in Turin drew on inspiration from the Polish and Czech clinical movements, and in turn (alongside the Clinic at Brescia Law School) contributed to development of a vibrant clinical movement right across Italy.

Many of the clinics reviewed in Alemanno and Khadar's book emphasize public interest social justice concerns, with their clinics engaged with supranational courts and fora.[45] The 'first common feature shared by these clinics is that 'they place themselves at the service of preexisting organisations (NGOs) whose institutional ecosystem requires the intervention of supporting and often equalizing actors, such as pro bono lawyers, clinical students, or other forms of skill-sharing capacity builders'.[46] Catherine Klein identifies that these university-based clinics expose law students and lawyers to the devastating injustices – both large and small – that exist in

[42] D McQuoid-Mason, E Ojukwu and GM Wachira, 'Clinical Legal Education in Africa: Legal Education and Community Service' in Bloch (n 1) 24.

[43] Stege (n 2).

[44] Alemanno and Khadar (n 1) 339.

[45] ibid 326.

[46] ibid 327.

their communities. Students learn important lessons that most of them will never forget and that they will carry forward with them into practice.[47] Zvonimir Jelinić and Adrian Koch emphasize that law clinics 'should not be confused with other types of practice-related instructional programmes that use the "clinical" prefix but never engage in provision of actual service to actual people'.[48]

It is clear that many European clinicians and their programmes share the strong social justice focus that has driven CLE across the globe. From Spain to Italy to Germany and Norway, there are powerful examples of engaging with communities facing severe disadvantage – migrants, asylum seekers, community groups, prisoners, people with disabilities, victims of trafficking or labour exploitation and homeless people. Tomoszek notes: 'Legal clinics bring the engaging and troubling social justice issues right to the doorsteps of legal academics and law students.'[49] Nonetheless, he notes that in countries with Germanic and Austro-Hungarian histories, there has been less expectation for the state to support social justice causes and vulnerable groups. It has been easier to promote clinics to law schools on the basis of educational outcomes – student profile, skills and capabilities.

This can be contrasted with the stronger focus on student learning in many UK clinics. Grimes et al note that focusing on the education component enabled many clinics to overcome the sustainability problems that some early law clinic initiatives faced: 'The obvious route to a sustainable future lay in providing a clinical experience for law students through the absorption of hands-on and reflective learning into law school offerings – as credit-bearing, stand-alone courses, part of existing curricula provision and/or in faculty-approved extracurricular activity.'[50] It may also be that declining legal aid coverage in England and Wales in particular has contributed to the increasing prominence of CLE in the UK.

English clinics have also been leaders in their engaging with Problem-Based Learning (PBL) in law studies. PBL has been developed at both Northumbria University[51] and the University of York.[52] Northumbria has

---

47 C Klein, 'Preface' in Blengino and Gascón-Cuenca (n 1).

48 Z Jelinić and A Koch, 'Elucidation of the Concept of a Law Clinic as a Prerequisite for Developing the Standards for Law Clinics in Europe' (2020) 7(2) *Asian Journal of Legal Education* 127, 138.

49 Bartoli (n 1) 71.

50 Grimes et al (n 39) 307.

51 C Sylvester, J Hall and E Hall, 'Problem-Based Learning and Clinical Legal Education: What Can Clinical Educators Learn from PBL?' (2004) 4 *International Journal of Clinical Legal Education* 39; J Hall and J Giddings, 'Experiential Education across Disciplines' in Giddings (ed) (n 4) 47–48.

52 R Grimes, 'Delivering Legal Education through an Integrated Problem-Based Learning Model: The Nuts and Bolts' (2014) 21(2) *International Journal of Clinical Legal Education* 228;

also developed as an international leader of the integration of clinic in the broader law curriculum.

A broad range of countries have clinics operating separately from law schools and with student management. While there are examples from beyond Europe,[53] European examples are prominent and powerful in terms of size and impact.[54] These include Germany[55], Norway,[56] Croatia[57] and the UK.[58] Bian Sukrow identifies that about 50 per cent of the German clinics are registered student societies/NGOs rather than part of the university.[59] Often, these clinics have been voluntary programmes rather than part of the curriculum.

European clinics, networks and clinicians are clearly contributing to global developments. Of course, this has not been confined to clinicians from any particular continent with leading contributions from Africa (David McQuoid-Mason), the UK (Richard Grimes) and the US (Leah Wortham and others). Clinicians from Spain and the US have also been prominent in supporting and collaborating with CLE programmes in Latin America.

Clinics fulfilling a civic mission

European clinics are global leaders in demonstrating how CLE can play a key role in universities contributing to their communities. Alemanno and Khadar refer to the emergence within European higher education institutions of an ethic of corporate social responsibility, service learning and community engagement.[60] In Belgium, the rebranding of Ghent University with a focus on 'social commitment' both served as inspiration for the founding of its clinic and provided an institutional lens through which the clinic could be understood and supported.[61]

K Gromek-Broc and R Hedlund, 'Problem-Based Learning at York Law School: Using Medical Law Module and the Integrated Approach' in MM Qafisheh and SA Rosenbaum (eds), *Experimental Legal Education in a Globalized World: The Middle East and Beyond* (Cambridge Scholars Publishing 2016).

53 For example, Kenya: A Kotonyah, 'The Distinctive Aspects of Clinical Legal Education in Kenya' in Giddings (ed) (n 4) 91–93.

54 Giddings (ed) (n 4) 330.

55 B Sukrow, 'Clinical Legal Education in Germany: A Brand New Old Story' in Giddings (ed) (n 4) 190–195.

56 Starting with Juss-Buss, established in 1971: M Langford, D Uehara and T Wærstad, 'Clinical Legal Education in Norway' in Giddings (ed) (n 4) 203–209.

57 Uzelac (n 29).

58 Aberdeen and Strathclyde: Grimes et al (n 39) 312–313.

59 Sukrow (n 55) 192.

60 Alemanno and Khadar (n 1) 323.

61 ibid 334.

Alemanno and Khadar further posit that:

> certain academics may be strategically making use of such narratives to win support for CLE at their respective institutions. While this hypothesis was not universally confirmed, our contributors nonetheless shed light on the ways in which the European CLE movement has managed, in certain instances, to cruise in the tailwind of institutional objectives related to the third mission of higher education institutions. In some cases, clinics have even served as inspiration for mainstreaming community engagement activities beyond the law faculty and across the university.[62]

Tomoszek notes the greater and growing recognition of the civic mission of clinics. CLE can showcase the many different ways in which law schools can meet these social responsibilities. These can include Street Law programmes (where law students work with school students, prisoners, minorities and other vulnerable groups about law and their rights), public lectures and other activities.[63]

While this civic engagement is often local in orientation, it also enables regional and global collaborations. Bartoli refers to the statement of the 2007 London Conference of Union Ministers for Education, which puts it this way: 'Higher education should play a decisive role in cultivating social cohesion, reducing inequalities and raising the level of knowledge, skills and competences in society. The legal clinical education is a perfect example of this social accountability of universities.'[64]

The ties of empire

The strength of CLE in Europe has an influence on clinics elsewhere partly because of the range of links that have endured since colonial times. While the influence of the US on global CLE is greater, we see strong connections across the Network of Francophone Legal Clinics, the involvement of Spanish clinicians in Latin American networks as well as between the UK and various former British Commonwealth countries.

Sathnam Sanghera provides a detailed account of the importance and enduring nature of the influence of the British legal system in a wide range of countries not confined to the British Commonwealth. He notes that the

62 ibid 333.

63 Bartoli (n 1) 72.

64 ibid 16.

'British empire's shaping of law around the world, although profound, was also untidy'.[65] Sanghera offers the view that:

> decolonization, which is growing in popularity as an idea across India, across the former British empire and in Britain itself, can only ever be tokenistic. Having spent years tracing the legacies of British imperialism in Britain, and having now spent several more years tracing the legacies of imperialism across the globe, I realise that the British empire's influence upon the quarter of the planet it occupied, and its gravitational influence upon the world outside it, has been profound.[66]

Richard Grimes has worked in and for clinical programmes and law schools in various parts of the world, from Afghanistan to the University of the South Pacific to the Nigerian Law School as well as universities in Eastern Europe, Central Asia and Africa. His experience has been that locals (including clinicians, academics and lawyers) tend to be receptive to ideas from elsewhere and respectful of clinicians seeking to share what they know. He has found that in such situations, 'speaking a common language really helps'.[67] He sees the key as being to find out what the locals want and develop local experts who can deliver that themselves: 'Building capacity is a self-fulfilling prophesy.'[68]

Tomoszek similarly identifies factors like language, the personal connections that develop around colonials studying abroad, funding schemes to support joint initiatives and the presence of longstanding networks are all important in reinforcing links between countries and their former colonizers.[69]

Founded in 1971, the Commonwealth Legal Education Association (CLEA) is a Commonwealth-wide body with regional Chapters and Committees in Asia, Southern Africa, West Africa, the Caribbean and Europe. CLEA is an important example of an organization with English origins that achieved significant outcomes through collaborations with and leadership from across the British Commonwealth. With early financial support from the UK, CLEA engaged with British Commonwealth countries, particularly in Africa, Asia and Oceania. CLEA continues to work closely with the Commonwealth Lawyers' Association. Its contribution to clinical legal education was catalysed by the leadership first of the leading Indian jurist and legal educator N.R. Madhava Menon, who became President of CLEA in 1994. In 1996, the

---

65 S Sanghera, *Empireworld* (Viking 2024) 155.

66 ibid 7.

67 Interview with Richard Grimes, 27 January 2025, notes on file.

68 Interview with Richard Grimes, 8 May 2025, notes on file.

69 Interview with Maxim Tomoszek, 15 January 2025, notes on file.

South African clinical legal education pioneer David McQuoid-Mason became CLEA President, holding that post until 2023. CLEA contributed to the development of the *African Law Clinicians Manual* in 2013 and also obtained funding from the Commonwealth Humans Rights Development Initiative for a major project to promote CLE (both live-client clinics and street law) across 60 Commonwealth countries.[70]

The Network of Francophone Legal Clinics was created unofficially in December 2014 during a symposium on law clinics organized by Xavier Aurey at the University of Caen Normandy. It became an NGO in 2016 and involves 60 clinics from seven countries (Belgium, Canada, Chad, France, Morocco, Switzerland and Togo). The Board of the NGO currently includes people from Canada, Chad, Switzerland and Togo as well as France.[71] It has produced French-language materials and delivered training as well as working to normalize CLE in the academic and legal landscape.[72]

The main impact of the Francophone Clinic Network has been in some parts of Francophone Africa. A symposium was held in 2015 at Université de Lomé in Togo which was seen as enhancing the academic credibility of clinical methods. Inspired by student interest, a junior instructor-researcher at the Université de Lomé created the Clinique d'Expertise Juridique et Sociale (CEJUS) 'in order to demystify the law and inform the local population about legal and social matters'.[73] Subsequently, with support from the French Ministry of Foreign Affairs, Training of Trainers programmes were conducted in Lomé, Côte d'Ivoire and Morocco.[74] A Massive Open Online Course (MOOC) was also developed and delivered in 2019 as part of a project of the Francophone Network in the Ivory Coast, funded by the French Ministry of Foreign Affairs. Because of COVID-19, some on-site training workshops were cancelled and it was thus decided to do it online and create a MOOC for that.[75]

Aurey considers that collaborations between law schools across the colonial divide work much better when they involve strong interest from local academic and students.[76] He contrasts the Togo experience with a project in Northern Kosovo, which was driven by external funders and was not successful. Aurey also notes that the strong feeling against France

[70] Interview with David McQuoid-Mason, 26 May 2025, notes on file.

[71] Interview with Xavier Aurey, 8 May 2025, notes on file.

[72] O Lagi et al, 'Advancing Clinical Legal Education through Networks' in Giddings (ed) (n 4) 70.

[73] SA Rosenbaum and D Kossi, 'La Clinique Juridique Makes Its Debut in Francophone Africa' in Giddings (ed) (n 4) 87.

[74] Interview with Xavier Aurey, 8 May 2025, notes on file.

[75] Email from Xavier Aurey, 26 May 2025, copy on file.

[76] Interview with Xavier Aurey, 8 May 2025, notes on file.

in some former colonies such as Mali and Burkina Faso has made it difficult for members of the network to engage with law schools and academics in those countries.[77]

The Legal Advice Clinic at London South Bank University (LSBU) has featured prominently in university collaborations with law schools in Egypt and Brazil. When LSBU partnered with the British University in Egypt (BUE) to develop the BUE law degree, the Working in the Law clinical module was based on the LSBU clinic model. In 2016, LSBU's Alan Russell visited MacKenzie Presbyterian University (MPU) in São Paulo, Brazil and subsequently taught a clinic-related unit at MPU designed for postgraduate students and lawyers interested in developing clinics.[78] Since 2018, MPU's Clinica Mackenzie de Orientação Jurídica operates in a shelter and hostel for homeless people in São Paulo linked to the LSBU clinic.[79]

In his PhD thesis, Tribe Mkwebu notes:

> Creating a clinical programme in a target country cannot be the mission of a sole individual. It requires collaboration; collaboration with locals; collaboration with the local legal profession and collaboration with the host government. International based clinicians have travelled the length and breadth of the world's continents sharing clinical programmes experience and expertise.

While rightly calling for sensitivity in relationships between powerful international institutions and/or funders and less powerful local institutions, Mkwebu does not refer to colonialism and does not focus on the adverse aspects of imperialism.[80]

It appears that there has not been an anti-colonial push or response to the endeavours of international clinicians to share experiences and insights, whether from Europe, the US or elsewhere. One important way in which European clinicians and CLE programmes could advance the interests of former colonies and influence CLE elsewhere would be to support initiatives seeking reparations from former colonial powers (including the UK, Spain, France and the Netherlands) such as the Caribbean Community (CARICOM) Reparations Commission involving 20 Caribbean countries.[81]

---

[77] ibid.

[78] Interview with Andy Unger and Alan Russell, 12 May 2025, notes on file.

[79] A Pagani de Souza, 'Clinical Legal Education in Brazil' in Giddings (ed) (n 4) 263.

[80] T Mkwebu, 'Clinical Pedagogy: A Systematic Review of Factors Influential in the Establishment and Sustainability of Clinical Programmes and a Grounded Theory Explication of a Clinical Legal Education Case Study in Zimbabwe' (PhD thesis, Northumbria University 2016) 72.

[81] Sanghera (n 65) 34–35.

Conclusion

There are both challenges and opportunities for European CLE to flourish and to influence trends and developments in CLE across the globe. Alemanno and Khadar observe that while clinics are growing in Europe, they may not be 'blossoming'.[82] The establishment and rapid diffusion of CLE in Europe has not been prompted or accompanied by institutionalization.[83] Further, some see clinics as responding to a deeper and more uniquely European challenge: the crisis of Europe. Julian Lonbay has observed that 'unless the clinics deal with European law (ECHR & EU) they will not have a great impact on promoting a common European legal culture'.[84] Alemmano and Khadar identify that the vast majority of clinics examined in their book 'suggest a deep awareness of and often involvement with, International and/or EU law'.[85]

There is significant scope for European CLE programmes to lead and contribute to international university collaborations involving global universities. The ability to collaborate and the developing mindset that regional and global collaborations are important is set to increase the influence of European clinics on global CLE. The global understanding of how CLE developed now recognizes the contributions of clinicians and CLE programmes from countries including South Africa, the Russian Federation, France, Denmark and Japan, alongside the leading role of the US.[86] There is now scope for international collaborations that involve co-created models with European clinicians playing important roles.

Building local, national and regional networks is important to developing the capacity to influence international directions. The moves of the Trump administration to withdraw US Aid funding are likely to curtail the prominent contributions that US clinicians have made to building and sustaining international clinical collaborations. This may provide another opportunity for European clinics (and those from elsewhere) to step into the vacuum, completing their transformation from 'the last holdout' to being at the forefront of developments in globalized CLE.

References

Alemanno A and Khadar L (eds), *Reinventing Legal Education: How Clinical Education is Reforming the Teaching and Practice of Law in Europe* (CUP 2018)

82 Alemanno and Khadar (n 1) 341–344.

83 ibid 342.

84 Bartoli (n 1) 70.

85 Alemanno and Khadar (n 1) 324.

86 Giddings (ed) (n 4) 4.

Barry MM, Dubin JC and Joy P, 'Clinical Education for This Millennium: The Third Wave' (2000) 7(1) *Clinical Law Review* 1

Bartoli C, *Legal Clinics in Europe: For a Commitment of Higher Education in Social Justice* (Diritto & Questioni Pubbliche 2016)

Berbec-Rostas M, Gutnikov A and Namyslovska-Gabrysiak B, 'Clinical Legal Education in Central and Eastern Europe' in FS Bloch (ed), *The Global Clinical Movement* (OUP 2011)

Blázquez-Martín D, 'The Bologna Process and the Future of Clinical Education in Europe: A View from Spain' in FS Bloch (ed), *The Global Clinical Movement: Educating Lawyers for Social Justice* (OUP 2011)

Blengino C and Gascón-Cuenca A (eds), *Epistemic Communities at the Boundaries of Law: Clinics as a Paradigm in the Revolution of Legal Education in the European Mediterranean Context* (Ledizioni LediPublishing 2019)

Czernicki F, 'The History and Distinctiveness of the Polish Legal Clinics Program' in J Giddings (ed), *Global Clinical Legal Education* (Routledge 2025)

Genty P, 'Reflections on US Involvement in the Promotion of Clinical Legal Education in Europe' in A Alemanno and L Khadar (eds), *Reinventing Legal Education: How Clinical Education Is Reforming the Teaching and Practice of Law in Europe* (CUP 2018)

Giddings J, 'Common Threads and Strength in Diversity' in J Giddings (ed), *Global Clinical Legal Education* (Routledge 2025)

Giddings J (ed), *Global Clinical Legal Education* (Routledge 2025)

Grimes R, 'Delivering Legal Education through an Integrated Problem-Based Learning Model: The Nuts and Bolts' (2014) 21(2) *International Journal of Clinical Legal Education* 228

Grimes R, Dunn R, Samaras R, Price J and Donnelly L, 'Legal Clinics in the UK and Ireland: Past, Present and Future' in J Giddings (ed), *Global Clinical Legal Education* (Routledge 2025)

Gromek-Broc K and Hedlund R, 'Problem-Based Learning at York Law School: Using Medical Law Module and the Integrated Approach' in MM Qafisheh and SA Rosenbaum (eds), *Experimental Legal Education in a Globalized World: The Middle East and Beyond* (Cambridge Scholars Publishing 2016)

Hall J and Giddings J, 'Experiential Education across Disciplines' in J Giddings (ed), *Global Clinical Legal Education* (Routledge 2025)

Jelinić Z and Koch A, 'Elucidation of the Concept of a Law Clinic as a Prerequisite for Developing the Standards for Law Clinics in Europe' (2020) 7(2) *Asian Journal of Legal Education* 127

Klein C, 'Preface' in Cecilia Blengino and Andrés Gascón-Cuenca (eds), *Epistemic Communities at the Boundaries of Law: Clinics as a Paradigm in the Revolution of Legal Education in the European Mediterranean Context* (Ledizioni LediPublishing 2019)

Kotonyah A, 'The Distinctive Aspects of Clinical Legal Education in Kenya' in J Giddings (ed), *Global Clinical Legal Education* (Routledge 2025)
Lagi O, McQuoid-Mason D, Bliss L, Grant C and Lasky B, 'Advancing Clinical Legal Education through Networks' in J Giddings (ed), Global Clinical Legal Education (Routledge 2025)
Langford M, Uehara D and Wærstad T, 'Clinical Legal Education in Norway' in J Giddings (ed), *Global Clinical Legal Education* (Routledge 2025)
Lodzhuk M, *Legal Clinics in Ukraine: From Legal Education to Legal Practice* (Odesa Feniks 2016)
Madhloom O and McFaul H (eds), *Thinking about Clinical Legal Education: Philosophical and Theoretical Perspectives* (Routledge 2021)
Mattar MY and AlMalki D, 'Providing Legal Aid to Migrant Workers: International Standards, Comparative Models and the Qatari Law Clinic Experience' in J Giddings (ed), *Global Clinical Legal Education* (Routledge 2025)
McFaul H, Hardie L, Ryan F, Lloyd Bright K and Graffin N, 'Taking Clinical Legal Education Online: Songs of Innocence and Experience' (2020) 27(4) *International Journal of Clinical Legal Education* 6
Mkwebu T, 'Clinical Pedagogy: A Systematic Review of Factors Influential in the Establishment and Sustainability of Clinical Programmes and a Grounded Theory Explication of a Clinical Legal Education Case Study in Zimbabwe' (PhD thesis, Northumbria University 2016)
Nicolson D, Newman J and Grimes R, *How to Set up and Run a Legal Clinic: Principles and Practice* (Edward Elgar 2023)
Pagani de Souza A, 'Clinical Legal Education in Brazil' in J Giddings (ed), *Global Clinical Legal Education* (Routledge 2025)
Pretor-Pinney G, *The Wavewatcher's Companion* (Bloomsbury 2011)
Sanghera S, *Empireworld* (Viking 2024)
Stege U, 'How Clinical Legal Education Is Crossing Borders' in Cecilia Blengino and Andrés Gascón-Cuenca (eds), *Epistemic Communities at the Boundaries of Law: Clinics as a Paradigm in the Revolution of Legal Education in the European Mediterranean Context* (Ledizioni LediPublishing 2019)
Stege U, 'Introduction' in C Bartoli, *Legal Clinics in Europe: For a Commitment of Higher Education in Social Justice* (Diritto & Questioni Pubbliche 2016)
Sukrow B, 'Clinical Legal Education in Germany – A Brand New Old Story' in J Giddings (ed), *Global Clinical Legal Education* (Routledge 2025)
Sylvester C, Hall J and Hall E, 'Problem-Based Learning and Clinical Legal Education: What Can Clinical Educators Learn from PBL?' (2004) 4 *International Journal of Clinical Legal Education* 39
Tomoszek M and Tomoszkova V, 'Clinical Legal Education from the Czechoslovakian Perspective' in J Giddings (ed), *Global Clinical Legal Education* (Routledge 2025)

Uzelac A, 'Croatia – The Peculiar Case of Zagreb Law Clinic' in J Giddings (ed), *Global Clinical Legal Education* (Routledge 2025)
Wilson R, *The Global Evolution of Clinical Legal Education* (CUP 2018)
Wortham L, 'Strengthening the International Clinical Scholarly Community: Opportunities for the Clinical Law Review and Beyond' (2019) 26 *Clinical Law Review* 393

15

Concluding Thoughts on the Collection

Paul McKeown, Rachel Stalker and Laura Bugatti

The purpose of this edited collection was to explore initiatives in clinical legal education across Europe and analyse the role they play in enhancing social justice. The contributors to the collection have articulated a myriad of goals, methods and values within their contributions, and therefore this concluding chapter will draw together the schools of thought and consider their role in supporting, or indeed undermining, the social justice mission.

This chapter proceeds in sections: the skills/social justice dialectic; sustainability and resilience; contemporary challenges; and the global picture. This analysis draws on the 4M framework articulated by McKeown in Chapter 2 to understand and analyse the development of clinical legal education in Europe.

The skills/social justice dialectic

Across the collection, a fundamental paradox emerges: clinical legal education is simultaneously being pulled towards market-driven skills training (as seen in Hungary and the early development of clinical legal education in the UK) and towards radical social transformation (as articulated in Spain and Italy). This tension reflects simultaneously operating mega-level pressures: university marketization demanding graduate employability on the one hand, and political and economic crises requiring transformative legal education on the other hand. This paradox is not merely theoretical – it manifests in curriculum battles, funding decisions and the daily work choices clinics make about which cases to accept and how to frame their missions.

Havelková and Tóth et al provide interesting comparative perspectives on the development of clinical legal education within Central and Eastern

Europe, considering issues from the Slovakian and Hungarian perspectives. What emerges from these contributions is agreement that the overarching focus of clinical legal education is first and foremost centred upon the student (micro) with both contributions critical of the theoretical dominance within their respective systems of legal education. However, their contributions diverge in that Havelková adopts a social-orientated perspective, while Tóth et al adopt predominantly a skills-orientated perspective.

Havelková focuses on the ability of clinical programmes to foster altruism within students. However, she argues these programmes occur too late in the academic journey, after competitive classroom culture has already eroded altruistic motivation, to effectively inculcate a sense of social responsibility. This observation is influential in terms of curriculum design with the 'competitive and outcome-driven culture in classrooms' cited as a factor in waning interest in altruistic work. Law departments (meso) in developing their curriculum should introduce teaching earlier and, indeed, throughout the programme, familiarizing students to notions of social responsibility.

Tóth et al highlight the influence of the legal profession (mega) in the inclusion of skills development within the law school curriculum as they seek law students better prepared for practice. As we have seen elsewhere in this collection, this has been a significant driver of clinical legal education throughout Europe. Indeed, Blengino and Gascón-Cuenca directly challenge this skills-first approach, arguing that marketization marginalizes subjects such as human rights and the philosophy of law, which are essential for the training of lawyers with a critical vision and a commitment to social justice. Tóth et al suggest that the needs of students and employers are not aligned with the theoretical dominance in the curriculum.

In Western Europe, Blengino and Gascón-Cuenca cite political, economic and educational crises experienced in Italy and Spain as a reason to reclaim clinical legal education as a tool for social transformation. These mega-level factors influence universities (macro) and law departments (meso) due to the so-called 'Third Mission' of universities – that is, to engage in activities of scientific and cultural transfer and productive transformation of knowledge with the aim of promoting economic and social growth (mega).

Brozović provides a resolution to this paradox through the development of a social-orientated clinical programme. As a consequence of the Croatian legislative framework (mega) making legal clinics part of the legal aid system, social justice and equality are at the core of the students' clinical experience. Brozović suggests that this means students understand their social role rather than merely focusing on their future careers. We see the mega-level factor of the legislative framework dictating the type of work the law department incorporates within its clinical activities with a consequential impact on the students' learning outcomes.

The contributions from the UK illustrate how the divide between the competing missions can be bridged through innovative models of clinical legal education. These contributions move beyond the traditional live-client model of clinical legal education and instead advance the case for public legal education and policy clinics. Morse and Ridout make the case for the expansion of public legal education, while McConnell et al advocate for policy clinics.

Public legal education and policy clinics are fundamentally mega level in terms of their outputs with public legal education engaging in activity to educate and empower the wider community, while policy clinics engage in research to influence law reform and policy change. Both these contributions acknowledge the influences across the 4M framework. At the micro level, despite not being live-client clinical work, the contributors acknowledge the development of graduate skills which will assist students in the labour market, while also providing employers, at the mega level, with skilled graduates. Morse and Ridout also acknowledge the marketization of higher education, with public legal education providing an attractive proposition in terms of curriculum development with more modest resource requirements than its live-client counterpart. Similarly, policy clinics do not require the same level of resource as live-client models of clinical legal education. McConnell et al also refer to the fact that policy clinics are inherently research-based projects, thus bridging a gap by facilitating opportunities for more traditional academics to engage in this type of clinical work.

These diverse national responses, from Hungary's employer-driven competency focus to Spain's crisis-driven transformation to Croatia's legislatively mandated integration, reveal a pattern: the dialectic manifests differently depending on local mega-level pressures, yet the underlying tension remains constant.

The 4M framework reveals why this paradox persists and how it can be navigated. At the mega level, marketization and the drive for skilled graduates have created opportunities for clinical programmes. At the micro level, the evidence indicates the acquisition of legal skills motivates student participation. These mega-micro influences permeate the macro-meso levels, encouraging universities and law departments to incorporate clinical programmes. Programmes succeed when they structure this incorporation to respond to both pressures, as Brozović demonstrates, selecting work types that expose students to social issues while developing professional competencies.

The contributions also demonstrate how innovation within clinical methodology can address the skills/justice dialectic while navigating resource constraints. Public legal education and policy clinics advance the social justice mission at the mega level while equipping students with transferable skills at the micro level, achieving both aims with fewer resources than traditional live-client models. This makes them attractive propositions even for institutions primarily motivated by marketization, as Morse and Ridout, and McConnell et al demonstrate.

The paradox within European clinical legal education's mission is not a problem requiring resolution, but a productive dialectic requiring navigation. The most innovative and sustainable programmes, whether through Croatia's legislative mandate or the UK's alternative models, demonstrate that both missions can be pursued simultaneously when institutional structures are designed to support rather than suppress this tension. Yet this navigation remains precarious. The risk is not that programmes choose one mission over the other, but that one colonizes the other, skills training becoming the substance while social justice rhetoric provides merely the veneer, or, conversely, social mission becoming performative when unsupported by institutional resources and student outcomes. Maintaining this balance and resisting the colonization of either mission by the other must be central to the development of future clinical legal education programmes across Europe.

Sustainability and resilience

A significant challenge within the European clinical legal education movement is the sustainability and resilience of clinical programmes. Across the collection, the contributors highlight the range of threats from funding withdrawal (Georgia) to armed conflict (Ukraine) to gradual institutional neglect, challenges that expose clinics' vulnerability when operating without multilevel structural support. Understanding what enables clinics to endure, or causes them to fail, is essential for sustaining and strengthening the European clinical legal education movement.

The Georgian Street Law case study, while demonstrating public legal education's pedagogical and social justice benefits, more importantly reveals the sustainability challenges facing clinical expansion. Reliance on external US funding left the Street Law Academy Project in a precarious position. Combined with an increasingly restrictive political climate, this dependency resulted in a 'hiatus'. Georgia's experience echoes a broader pattern familiar across Central and Eastern Europe. When substantial US funding was withdrawn in the early 2000s, many clinics established in the 1990s collapsed. Georgia's Street Law hiatus represents the latest iteration of this recurring vulnerability.

The Georgian experience demonstrates that even successful programmes that have an impact remain vulnerable when they are dependent on a single external funder. The Street Law Academy Project had achieved significant reach and positive outcomes, yet structural precarity, the absence of institutional integration or diversified funding meant that external political and funding shifts could halt operations entirely.

In stark contrast to the experience in Georgia, Poland offers insight into how legal clinics can be made sustainable at the mega level. The establishment of the Polish Legal Clinics Foundation (FUPP) in 2001 created national coordination and a transition strategy. When external funding ended, FUPP facilitated clinics operating 'in a very modest and efficient way', with law schools themselves financing operations. Today, all state law faculties in Poland have clinics, a sustainability model that Georgia, despite multiple attempts, has not achieved.

Croatia demonstrates a different sustainability pathway: legislative mandate. By embedding legal clinics within the national legal aid system through law, Croatia created mega-level structural support that transcends individual champions or funding cycles. Students and supervisors may change, political winds may shift, but the legislative framework endures, ensuring clinics remain integral to both legal education and access to justice infrastructure. This represents institutional permanence that voluntary programmes struggle to achieve.

Tsypiashchuk et al emphasize the evolution, resilience and transformation of the Ukrainian clinical legal education movement following the invasion of Ukraine by Russia. The impact of war has resulted in significant disruption to law clinics within Ukraine, including displacement, infrastructure damage and safety concerns, with clinics moving their operations online, relocating and rebuilding. Law clinics have also been required to handle a range of complex and ethically challenging matters related to military law and mobilization, prisoners of war and their families, and property destruction. This contribution illustrates the strength of strong networks, both nationally and internationally to support clinical legal education, even through times of significant adversity. Law clinics in Ukraine also plan to continue to innovate and adapt such as addressing accession to the EU. Ukrainian clinics' survival under extreme duress reveals that mega-level networks, when combined with national coordination (the Association of Legal Clinics of Ukraine) and mission clarity, can sustain operations even through armed conflict.

The experiences of Georgia, Poland, Croatia and Ukraine highlight three critical sustainability factors: multilevel support, institutional embedding and independence from individual supporters. Georgia, as well as earlier experiences across Central and Eastern Europe, illustrate that mega-level funding or networks are insufficient without meso-level institutional integration and macro-level university commitment. Further, the long-term success of clinics cannot be reliant upon an individual at the micro level. Mega-level factors such as legislative mandates (Croatia), curriculum requirements (Ukraine) or coordinated national networks (Poland) create institutional permanence beyond the tenure of the clinical programme's founder. Yet even structural embedding proves insufficient unless clinics address recognized needs. Clinical programmes which address institutional and societal problems prove to be more sustainable than those established on educational idealism alone. Examples include the development of legal skills (Poland and the UK), legal aid shortages (Croatia and Norway), or the war-related needs in Ukraine. Clinics addressing recognized problems secure ongoing support, while those pursuing missions peripheral to the institutional priorities will struggle to obtain the necessary resources.

Notably, sustainability appears largely independent of the skills/justice dialectic explored earlier. Poland's skills-focused clinics, Croatia's justice-mandated programmes and the UK's bridging models all demonstrate resilience, suggesting that local alignment with mega-level pressures matters more than which mission is emphasized. However, clinics justified through multiple rationales (skills and justice, employability and community service) may prove most robust when institutional priorities shift.

These findings carry practical implications for clinic development. Sustainable programmes must be designed, not hoped for, requiring deliberate multilevel architecture from inception. Those establishing clinical programmes should prioritize institutional embedding and diversified support over launching quickly with a single-source funding. Most critically, clinics must solve problems that their institutions recognize, whether these are skills gaps, legal aid shortages or community engagement mandates, ensuring their mission aligns with rather than contradicts institutional priorities.

Contemporary challenges

Beyond the skills/justice dialectic and sustainability challenges, European clinical legal education must also navigate challenges of practice in the modern world, challenges that fundamentally reshape pedagogical practice. Examples explored in this collection include decolonizing Eurocentric frameworks, integrating artificial intelligence (AI) and protecting student wellbeing. Each of these challenges requires reconceptualization at the micro level, expanding from student learning outcomes to include client agency, technological literacy and psychological safety.

Decolonizing Eurocentric frameworks

Stege et al arts-based approach, incorporating dance, music and storytelling, fundamentally challenges the epistemological foundations of European clinical legal education. By centring refugee and asylum seeker voices as co-creators rather than service recipients, they expose how ostensibly neutral clinical methodologies may perpetuate Western knowledge hierarchies. This represents a radical reconceptualization of the micro level: the client shifts from passive subject of legal intervention to active knowledge-producer whose cultural expressions shape both case strategy and pedagogical design.

The Turin case study demonstrates how this transformation operates across levels. At the micro level, students experience discomfort as their assumptions about expertise and authority are challenged. This discomfort permeates upward to meso-level curriculum design, requiring new pedagogical methods that accommodate non-Western epistemologies. The result is not merely cultural competency training, but a fundamental questioning of whose knowledge counts in clinical legal education, a challenge that is particularly urgent given Europe's refugee crisis and colonial legacies.

Artificial intelligence

AI presents an unavoidable disruption to clinical pedagogy, simultaneously threatening and enhancing core competencies. As Piaskowska and Piesiewicz demonstrate, AI tools operating at the mega level (which are increasingly adopted in legal practice) demand fundamental curriculum adaptation at the meso level. The challenge is not whether to integrate AI, but how to do so without atrophying the critical thinking skills clinics exist to develop.

Piaskowska and Piesiewicz's Retrospective Validation Method exemplifies the required reconceptualization: rather than treating AI as either forbidden tool or unquestioned resource, students learn to critically evaluate AI-generated legal analysis, identifying errors, biases and limitations. This transforms technological literacy from technical competency to analytical sophistication; students must develop judgement about when AI supports and when it undermines sound legal reasoning.

Notably, AI integration intersects with both earlier themes. It may exacerbate the skills/justice dialectic if used primarily for efficiency (favouring marketization) while potentially undermining client-centred practice essential to social justice. It also affects sustainability: clinics dependent on commercial AI tools face new vulnerabilities, while those teaching critical AI literacy develop enduring competencies.

Wellbeing

Student wellbeing emerges not as a peripheral concern, but as a structural imperative reshaping clinical design. Thurston and Kirsch reveal how clinical work's dual pressures create unique psychological risks: a competitive academic culture (often intensified by skills-focused marketization) combines with exposure to client trauma (inherent to social justice work). The skills/justice dialectic thus manifests in wellbeing terms – each mission carries distinct psychological costs that curriculum design must address.

This transforms wellbeing from an individual student issue to a meso-level design requirement. Universities face legal obligations and professional body guidance (mega) to protect student mental health; this requires pedagogical adaptations that balance experiential learning's benefits against psychological risks (micro). Thurston and Kirsch's frameworks demonstrate that wellbeing protection and social justice commitment need not conflict; properly designed clinical pedagogy can safeguard students while maintaining service to vulnerable clients.

Critically, wellbeing concerns affect sustainability: clinics that burn out students or supervisors prove unsustainable regardless of funding or institutional support.

These three challenges – decolonizing practice, integrating AI and protecting wellbeing – collectively signal a paradigm shift in European clinical legal education. Traditional clinic pedagogy focused on student skill acquisition almost exclusively, with clients as learning vehicles, technology as a neutral tool, and wellbeing as individual responsibility. Contemporary imperatives demand expansion: clients become co-creators whose agency shapes pedagogy; technology becomes the object of critical analysis requiring new literacies; student psychological safety becomes a curricular design prerequisite rather than an individual responsibility.

This expansion complicates both earlier themes. The skills/justice dialectic deepens: whose skills (Western analytical methods or culturally plural approaches), whose justice (for clients or with clients) and at what psychological cost to students? Sustainability calculations shift: clinics must now resource not only legal service delivery but also cultural responsiveness training, AI literacy development and wellbeing support systems. The micro level, once the framework's simplest component, becomes its most complex and contested terrain.

The global picture

European clinical legal education has transformed from Wilson's 2009 characterization of Western Europe as the 'last holdout' to active global contributor. As Giddings demonstrates, this shift operates primarily through mega-level networks, the European Network on Clinical Legal Education (ENCLE), the *International Journal of Clinical Legal Education* (*IJCLE*) and national organizations like FUPP, which enable cross-pollination with clinics across the Global South. Technology has strengthened these connections, overcoming geographical distance to facilitate collaborations between, for example, Turin and Nigeria, or the Francophone network spanning Europe and West Africa.

This global role complicates the decolonization imperative discussed earlier. European clinics engaging with former colonies must navigate the legacy of imperialism, neither imposing Western models nor withdrawing expertise that Global South colleagues actively seek. The most successful partnerships, as Giddings shows, involve co-creation and mutual learning rather than unidirectional knowledge transfer, mirroring the client co-creation model that Stege et al advocate. Europe's path from holdout to forefront thus depends on its willingness to lead through collaboration rather than exportation.

Final thoughts

The 4M framework has revealed European clinical legal education as a complex adaptive system shaped by forces from individual passion (micro) to international crises (mega). Three central insights emerge from this collection.

First, the skills/justice paradox proves productive rather than problematic, driving innovation through tension that different regions navigate in locally responsive ways. Second, sustainability requires deliberate multilevel architecture; clinics embedded through legislation, curriculum requirements or coordinated networks prove resilient where those built on individual enthusiasm and external funding remain fragile. Third, contemporary practice demands fundamental expansion of the micro level to encompass client co-creation, critical technological literacy and psychological safety as design prerequisites.

What emerges is both challenging and promising. European clinical legal education faces unprecedented pressures, such as marketization, funding precarity, technological disruption and cultural reckoning, yet demonstrates remarkable capacity for resilient innovation. From Croatia's legislative integration to Poland's national coordination, from Turin's arts-based decolonization to the UK's methodological pluralism, from Ukraine's wartime adaptation to Europe's emerging global partnerships, this collection documents programmes that navigate complexity with sophistication.

The future remains unwritten. Success depends on whether European clinics can resist simplistic solutions: neither abandoning social justice for marketization nor pursuing justice without institutional sustainability; neither rejecting AI nor embracing it uncritically; neither sheltering students nor exposing them without support; neither imposing European models globally nor withdrawing from collaborative engagement. The contributors to this collection suggest that such navigation is not only possible but already underway, as evidenced by clinicians, students and institutions willing to embrace productive tension rather than seek false resolution. In this willingness to navigate complexity lies European clinical legal education's greatest strength and most promising future.

Index

References to figures appear in *italic* type; those in **bold** type refer to tables. References to endnotes show both the page number and the note number (159n13).

Printed and bound by CPI Group (UK) Ltd, Croydon, CR0 4YY

15/09/2026

14962386-0007